FERENC POZSONY

THE HUNGARIAN CSÁNGÓ
OF MOLDOVA

Corvinus Publishing

Buffalo -Toronto

2006

Translated by

Peter Csermely

ISBN: 1-882785-18-5 CB
1-882785-19-3 NB

Library of Congress Catalog Card Number:
2006924042

Printed in the United States of America.

Table of Contents

INTRODUCTION

In this book of analysis, we will examine the Hungarians living in Moldova,[1] their origins, history, social structure, culture, identity, their 20th century fate and the efforts made at protecting their rights. The Moldovan principality, East of the Kingdom of Hungary, came into existence in the middle of the 14th century, which, by the Middle Ages, consisted of the territory between the Eastern Carpathians and the Dniester River. Moldova united in 1859 with the other Romanian principality, Walachia or Muntenia (Havasalföld in Hungarian), which lay between the Southern Carpathians and the Danube. The territory of the country thus formed became free of Turkish domination only in 1878 at the Berlin Congress, which ended the Russo-Turkish War. The great powers, at the same time, handed southern Bessarabia, formerly a part of the principality, to Russia.[2] Romania's territory was enlarged with that of Dobrudja, lying on the Black Sea, which was freed from the Turkish yoke during the war of independence. The united Romanian principality became a kingdom in 1881. As the Kingdom of Romania fought from 1916 against the Austro-Hungarian Empire on the side of the Western Allies, at the 1920 Treaty of Trianon, ending the first world war, it acquired additional provinces, namely the multi-ethnic territories of Transylvania and Bukovina. According to the terms of the 1939 Ribbentrop-Molotov pact, in June, 1940 the Soviet Union annexed the eastern half of the country's Moldova province between the Prut and Dniester Rivers, meaning Bessarabia. As Romania committed significant military forces on the German side against the anti-Soviet 1941-1944 military campaign, it soon reclaimed Bessarabia, Northern Bukovina, as well as occupying Trans-Dniester along the left bank of the Dniester River to Odessa. The 1947 Paris Peace Accord, ending the second world war, awarded Northern Bukovina to the Ukraine, while the region between the Prut and Dniester, along with the territory of Trans-Dniester was directed by Stalin to form the basis of the Moldova Soviet Socialist Republic. Subsequent to the 1991 break-up of the Soviet Union, the 'independent' Republic of Moldova was born in the shadow of Moscow. The majority of its population speaks Romanian; its capital is Chisinau. In the predominantly Russian-majority areas beside the Dniester

---

1 The name of the area (Moldva, Moldova, Moldavia, Moldau) is of Slavic origin, meaning pine forest. The Moldova River springs in the Eastern Carpathians and flows into the Szeret River, in the vicinity of Románvásár, in the very heart of the territory. (Hajdú-Moharos, József: Moldva - Csángóföld - csángó sors [Moldova - Csángóland - Csángó fate]. Vörösberény, 1995, p. 11.)

2 Bessarabia is that part of Moldova lying between the Prut and Dniester Rivers.

4

and on the lands of the South Bessarabian Gagauz[3] people, a string of autonomous 'republics' soon came into existence.

As the political borders of Moldova changed over the centuries, in our work Moldova refers to that 93,000 km^2 area situated from the foothills of the Eastern Carpathians to the Dniester, South to the lower Danube and to the Black Sea.[4] According to the 1992 census, the territory belonging to Romania (46,070 km^2) had a population of 4.8 million where, beside the majority Romanians, significant numbers of Hungarians, Ukrainians, Germans, Poles, Jews, Armenians and Gypsy communities also live.[5]

The Kingdom of Hungary was born, partly of the former Roman province of Pannonia in the Carpathian basin, in 1001 with the coronation of Saint Stephen. As successive nomad peoples, arriving from the East, threatened the newly established Magyar state, the Hungarian kings, by degrees, established an advanced protective zone to the East of the Carpathians. The migration and settlement of Magyar communities out of the Carpathian basin towards the East was continuous through the feudal period. It was especially so from the Seklerland (lying on the eastern perimeter of Transylvania) from where large masses of Hungarians fled to Moldova during the second half of the 18th century, in the decades following the aftermath of the unsuccessful 1764 rebellion of Mádéfalva. Over the centuries, smaller Magyar groups reached the lands between the Prut and Dniester Rivers, but the significant communities settled on the territory between the Easter Carpathians and the Szeret River. In our opinion, in the Moldovan villages and towns belonging to Romania, even today there are close to 100,000 people who understand and speak Hungarian.[6]

---

3 According to 1990 data, 153,000 Pravoslav religion Gagauz lived in the southern portion of Bessarabia. Beside their Altaic Turkic-Oguz mother tongue, they speak Bulgarian, Romanian and Russian, as well. According to Slav linguists and historians, they are Turkicized Bulgarians. In 1995, they gained their autonomy within the borders of the Republic of Moldova. (Hajdú-Moharos: Moldova ... op. cit. p. 14.)

4 Benda, Kálmán: Moldvai Csángó-Magyar Okmánytár (1467-1706), I-II [Csángó-Hungarian Archives of Moldova (1467-1706), vol. I-II]. Budapest, 1989, p. 9.

5 Hajdú-Moharos: Moldova ... op. cit. pp. 13-15; Stan, Valentin - Weber, Renate: The moldvaian csango. Budapest, 1998, pp. 7-8.

6 According to Vilmos Tánczos, who conducted systematic Moldovan field trips in the mid-1990's, he estimated that there were 62,225 Hungarian-speaking Csángós living in the villages. His data does not include those living in the Moldovan towns. (Tánczos, Vilmos: Hányan vannak a moldvai csángók? [How many are the Moldovan Csángós?] Magyar Kisebbség, III. évf., 1997, pp. 377-380.)

The name: *Csángó*

In everyday Hungarian usage, the term *Csángó* refers to the Magyars living in Moldova, the Gyimes mountains and the Barcaság.[7] The same ethnic title is applied to the Seklers who fled from Seklerland to Bukovina in the 18th century and were later repatriated inside the Carpathian basin (to Déva in 1892, to Trans-Danubia in 1945).[8] Many have studied the origin, etymology and meaning of this ethnic name. According to the most prevalent view, the word *csángó* derives from the verb *csang/csáng,* meaning "to roam, wander, rove." Hence, it applies to an ethnic group of Hungarian-speaking settlers who have separated from the main Magyar block, moved away and separated, yet retained a unique Hungarian culture.[9] In our work, we will examine the history, society and traditional culture of only the Moldovan Magyar communities.

The *csángó* name first surfaces in 15th and 16th century documents, primarily as a family name,[10] then, in written sources from the 18th century, becomes more frequent as an ethnic identifier (ethnonym).[11] The ethnonimic was first employed by pastor Péter (Peter) Zöld in his letter dated 1772, addressed to Colonel Caratto, commander of the 1st Sekler Border Guard Battalion.[12] Domokos Teleki recounted in 1796, based on his travel experiences, that the people of Csík called the inhabitants of Gyimes as

---

7 Kolumbán, Samu: A hétfalusi csángók a múltban és a jelenben [The Csángó from the 'seven villages', in the past and present]. Brassó, 1903.

8 Zsók, Béla: A "csángó" elnevezés és identitástudat alakulása a Hunyad megyébe telepedett bukovinai székelyeknél [The label "Csángó" and the formation of identity consciousness among the Seklers of Bukovina who settled in Hunyad County]. Néprajzi Látóhatár, VII. évf., 1998, pp. 87-89.

9 Benko, Loránd: A csángók eredete és települése a nyelvtudomány szemszögéból [The origin and settlement of the Csángó from a linguistic-science perspective]. A Magyar Nyelvtudományi Társaság Kiadványai 188. sz., Budapest, 1990, p. 6; Szabó, T. Attila: Csángó, In: Erdélyi Magyar Szótörténet Tár II, Bukarest, 1978, p. 23; Tánczos: Hányan vannak ... op. cit. p. 370.

10 1400? "Georgium Chango," Magyar Nyelv Történeti Etimológiai Szótára I. Budapest 1967, p. 477; 1556? "andreas chango ... et Michael chango"; 1560? " Maxán ... az kin lakik Csángó András". (Szabó: Csángó, op. cit. p. 23.)

11 1782? "Csángó Magyaroknak hivattatnak"; 1796? "A Gyémes-lunkai Lakosokat a Tsíkiak Tsángoknak nevezik? lehet, hogy ez a Nevezet onnan jön, mivel ok vándorló Emberek és Lakhelyeket gyakran el hagyták? az a szó Tsángó pedig ollyan értelemben vétetik, mint kóborló, vándorló." (Szabó: Csángó, op. cit. pp. 22-23.)

12 "Hungaris in Lonka residentibus, et Csángó dictis." Szocs, János: Pater Zöld. Csíkszereda, 2002, p. 39.

Csángó.[13] Written sources indicate that the Csángó ethnic designation existed in the 18th century as primarily an external identifier. It is an interesting cultural-historical fact that the poet Mihály (Michael) Csokonai Vitéz used the expression *Tsángó Magyar* in his poem *Marosvásárhelyi gondolatok* [Musings from Marosvásárhely], written in 1798.[14] In 1841, János (John) Ince Petrás identified two groups of Hungarians in Moldova, each with a uniquely individual dialect and culture: Csángó and Seklers.[15]

The Romanians and gypsies of Moldova clearly and consistently use the term *csángó* as a derogatory term for the Hungarians of Moldova. The term is also used today in Sekler Hungarian circles in a patronizing, pejorative manner. In our time, the Hungarians of Moldova rarely employ it to denote themselves. If one were to question them about it, they would most often attribute it to some remote Moldovan Catholic settlement or group of villages.[16]

The Hungarians of Moldova were never a homogeneous group from a historical and cultural perspective. The language and culture of the Hungarians who settled here in the Middle Ages was fundamentally different from the Seklers who fled in large numbers to Moldova in the 18th century. Some researchers tend to use the terms *Magyars of Moldova* and *Seklers of Moldova*,[17] while others prefer the *Csángó-magyar* and *Sekler-magyar* terminology to differentiate the two Hungarian mother-tongued groups of Moldova, each with its own distinct dialects, cultural and identity differences.[18]

The term *csángó* is today a generally accepted term in ethnic, linguistic and historical works. At the end of the 20th century, even those

---

13 Teleki, Domokos: Egy néhány hazai utazások leírása [Descriptions of a few local trips]. Bécs, 1796, p. 83.

14 Csokonai Vitéz, Mihály: Költemények (1797-1799) [Poems (1797-1799)]. Szilágyi, Ferenc /ed./. Budapest, 1994, p. 102.

15 Domokos, Pál Péter: Édes hazámnak akartam szolgálni [I wished to serve my beloved country]. Budapest, 1979, pp. 1328-1329.

16 Pávai, István: Etnonimek a moldvai magyar anyanyelvu katolikusok megnevezésére [Ethnonyms to apply to the Hungarian mother-tongued Catholics of Moldova], In: Pozsony, Ferenc /ed./: Csángósors. Moldvai csángók a változó idokben [Csángó fate. Moldovan Csángós in changing times.] Budapest, 1999, p. 79.

17 Lüko, Gábor: Moldva alapításának mondáihoz [Myths to the foundation of Moldova]. Ethnographia, XLVII. évf., 1. sz., 1936, pp. 10-11; Mikecs, László: A csángók. Budapest, 1941, pp. 95-97.

18 Benko: A csángók eredete ... op. cit. p. 5; Szabó, T. Attila: Kik és hol élnek a csángók? [Csángós: who are they and where do they live?] In: Nyelv és múlt. Válogatott tanulmányok, cikkek III. Bukarest, 1972, pp. 122-131.

Hungarians who came from the Seklerland accept it – and refer to themselves by it – when earlier they held it to be a pejorative, derisive and contemptuous term.[19] Currently, the ethnological concept of *csángó* denotes a group somewhat distanced from Hungarians on language, culture and social planes, while not yet fully embedded or integrated into the Romanians. The late 20th century Hungarian intellectuals of Transylvania refer to the process of *csángóization* as the process during which an earlier Hungarian-languaged, - cultured and -identitied group gradually becomes a part of – and assimilates into – the Romanian national group.[20]

At the May 23, 2000 meeting in Istanbul, the Cultural, Scientific and Educational Committee of the EU Parliament recognized, in resolution 9078, this ethnic, linguistic, cultural and religious minority under the label of *Csángó*, and unequivocally stated that the regional language of the Csángó's is Hungarian.[21]

Their origins

Much work has been done in the last century and a half on the origin of the Csángó of Moldova.[22] Of the various results and theories, three main streams can be distinguished:

1. A small number of researchers identify the original group of Moldovan Csángó as a part of the 9th century Magyars who remained outside the Carpathians, in Moldova, at the time of the conquest.[23] This theory is usually supported by the archaic language form of the Moldovan Hungarians and 9th century archeological evidence from the time of the conquest.

Most recently, István (Stephen) Fodor analyzed the Hungarian-related archeological evidence turned up in the region. The scant number of relics shows that the Hungarian tribes traversing Moldova in the 9th century, and

19 Tánczos: Hányan vannak ... op. cit. pp. 370-371.

20 Pávai, István: A moldvai magyarok megnevezései [Names for the Magyars of Moldova]. Regio, VI. évf. 4. sz., 1995, pp. 149-164; Tánczos: Hányan vannak ... op. cit. p. 370.

21 Moldvai Magyarság – Gazeta ceangailor din Moldova XI. évf., 6 and 9 sz., 2001; Krónika, III. évf., 2001, p. 120.

22 Baker, Robin: On the origin of the Moldavian Csángos. The Slavonic and the East European Review 75, 1997, pp. 658-680.

23 Rubinyi, Mózes: A moldvai csángók múltja és jelene [The past and present of the Csángó of Moldova]. Ethnographia, XII. évf., 1901, pp. 115-124, 166-175; Domokos, Pál Péter: A moldvai magyarság [The Hungarians of Moldova]. Csíksomlyó, 1931; Gunda, Béla: A moldvai magyarok eredete [The origin of the Hungarians of Moldova]. Magyar Nyelv, 84. évf., 1. sz., 1988, pp. 12-24; Zsupos, Zoltán: A moldvai magyarok eredete [The origin of the Hungarians of Moldova]. Néprajzi Látóhatár, III. évf., 1-4. sz., 1994, pp. 53-60.

the 10th century frontier guard communities, left physical evidence. They do not, however, prove conclusively that those who remained in this area lived through the stormy period of the Cuman and Pecheneg migration. "As seductive as it might be to suppose that a connection exists between these early Hungarian finds and the later, Middle Age Moldovan Csángó settlements, our evidence to date simply does not make that possible. Our archeological finds thus do not support the recurring supposition that the Moldovan Hungarians are, at least in part, the descendants of the pre-conquest Hungarians, or perhaps the 10th century frontier guards."[24]

This supposition is also not supported by the place names, as the Hungarians immediately after the conquest typically named their settlements in the Carpathian basin using personal names /of tribal chiefs/ (e.g.- Ajtony, Keszi, Solt, Tass) or their diminutives (Álmosd, Szepesd). In villages with the most archaic dialect, we meet a completely different naming convention (i.e., Szabó*falva*, Jász*vásár,* Román*vásár, etc.),* which corresponds to the much later Hungarian naming convention in the whole of the Carpathian basin of the 13th - 14th centuries, whereby the suffix of -*falva*, -*vására* (-ville, -market) is appended to a name.[25]

2. According to another hypothesis, the Csángó of Moldova are the descendants of the Cumans or some other Turkic-speaking tribes.[26] This supposition also appears in the works of Romanian historians. For example, Bratianu holds it quite possible that this group was born from the intermingling of the Cumans and Pechenegs with the Hungarians.[27] Nicolae Iorga also theorized on the Pechened or Cuman origins of the Moldovan Csángó. In his opinion, it is the only explanation to the difference between the Sekler and Csángó dialects.[28] Similar theories occasionally surface in late

24 Fodor, István: Magyar jellegu régészeti leletek Moldvában [Hungarian style archeological finds in Moldova], In: Halász, Péter /ed./: „Megfog vala apóm szokcor kezemtül…" Tanulmányok Domokos Pál Péter emlékére. Budapest, 1993, pp. 17-38.

25 Benko: A csángók eredete … op. cit.; Benda: Moldvai Csángó-Magyar … op. cit. pp. 10-11; Halász, Péter: A moldvai csángómagyar falvak helyneveinek néhány településtörténeti tanulsága [Some settlement historical conclusions from village names of Moldovan Csángó-Hungarians]. Kazinczy Ferenc Társaság 10. Évkönyve. Széphalom, 1999, pp. 365-372.

26 Jerney, János: Keleti utazás a Magyarok oshelyeinek kinyomozása végett 1844-1845. I-II [Travels in the East to discover the ancient Magyar places, 1844-1845, vol. I-II]. Pest, 1851; Munkácsi, Bernát: A moldvai csángók eredete [The origin of the Csángó of Moldova]. Ethnographia, XIII. évf.,, 1902, pp. 433-440; Veress, Endre: A moldvai csángók származása és neve [The origin and name of the Moldovan Csángó]. Erdélyi Múzeum, XXXIX. évf., 1934, pp. 29-64.

27 Bratianu, G. I.: Origines et formation de l' unite roumaine. Bucharest, 1943.

28 Iorga, Nicolae: Istoria românilor III. Bucuresti, 1993, pp. 27-28.

20th century studies. Sándor (Alexander) N. Szilágyi and Katalin Olosz primarily explain the *csángó* name as reflecting a Magyar-Turkic (Kazar) connection. Géza Ferenczi also stressed this group's Turkish connection, in light of the archeological evidence.[29]

3. Of the various historical, archeological, linguistic and ethnographic research, the generally accepted view has emerged that the original group of Csángó arrived in Moldova from the Kingdom of Hungary in the medieval period as part of a systematic settlement from the Carpathian basin.[30] These earliest transplanted Hungarian communities created a network of settlements along the Szeret/Siret River at the end of the 13th and beginning of the 14th centuries, whose chief task was to provide defense for the eastern boundary of the Hungarian kingdom. Later Hungarian kings also established advanced frontier posts along the Dniester River, well to the East of this contiguous line of defensive border posts. Among these Hungarian controlled border fortifications were Orhei (Orhely/Várhely),[31] Braila, Cetatea Alba (Dnyeszterfehérvár) and Kilia. [Hereafter, Hungarian place names will be shown, as this work was originally written in Hungarian. The list of present day Romanian names is provided in an appendix-*Ed*.]. These original transplanted groups were further supplemented in the 15th century by Hussites fleeing from the Inquisition and later by Hungarians continuously emigrating from Seklerland. The most significant groups of Seklers fled from the 1764 Austrian retribution[32] and settled in Moldova in the area between the Eastern Carpathians and the Szeret River. Written sources, place and

---

29 Szilágyi, N. Sándor: Amit még nem mondtunk el a csángó népnévrol [What we have not yet told of the Csángó name]. A Hét, X. évf., 24. sz., 1979, p. 10; Ferenczi, Géza: Újabb adalékok a moldvai csángók kérdéséhez [Recent addenda to the Csángó question]. Korunk, III. évf., 1990, pp. 628-637; Olosz, Katalin: XVIII-XIX. századi adatok a moldvai magyarok szokásairól és nevéról [18th-19th century data about the customs and name of the Moldovan Hungarians], In: Pozsony, Ferenc /ed./: Dolgozatok a moldvai csángók népi kultúrájáról [Essays on the folk culture of the Csángó of Moldova]. Kriza János Néprajzi Társaság 5. Évkönyve, Kolozsvár, 1997, pp. 27-35.

30 Benda: Moldvai Csángó-Magyar ... op. cit.; Benko: A csángók eredete ... op. cit.

31 László Murádin professes to trace today's Orhei to the medieval Hungarian Várhely. Verbal communication.

32 The Seklers were the defenders the eastern boundary of the Kingdom of Hungary, hence enjoyed collective autonomy and special freedoms in the medieval era. The Austrians wished to strip the Sekler community in 1764 of its ancient rights. The rebellion of Seklers protesting the forcible militarization /recruitment and long service-ed./ was ruthlessly put down by cannon fire in Mádéfalva. (Imreh, István: Látom az életem nem igen gyönyöru. A madéfalvi veszedelem tanúkihallgatási jegyzokönyve [I see my life is not too wonderful. The record of the witness testimony from the Mádéfalva uprising]. Bukarest, 1994, pp. 15-27.)

family names, as well as various ethnographic research, conclusively support this fact.[33]

The works of the most significant Romanian historians also support the previous Hungarian results. According to them, the Hungarian settlers were already living in Moldova in the era before the founding of the principality. The oldest Romanian chroniclers, e.g.- Grigore Ureche, Simion Dascalaul and Miron Costin stress that the old capital of Moldova, Suceava, stems from the Hungarian *szucs* (furrier), its founding attributed to Hungarian craftsmen.[34] In his chronicle written at the end of the 17th century, voivod Georghe Brancovici noted that, in the populating of Moldova, significant numbers of Seklers from Csík, fleeing from Transylvania, took part.[35] Dimitrie Cantemir (1673-1723) in chapter 16 of his historical work *Descriptio Moldaviae* noted that few other countries exist such as Moldova where so many different-tongued people live. Apart from the Romanians transplanted from Marmatiei (Máramaros), Greeks, Albanians, Serbs, Bulgarians, Poles, Cossacks, Russians, *Hungarians*, Germans, Armenians, Jews and Gypsies were living together in the principality.[36] In the opinion of the learned prince, no true Moldovan Romanian farmers can be found in his

33 Benda: Moldvai Csángó-Magyar ... op. cit.; Benko: A csángók eredete ... op. cit.; Domokos, Pál Péter: A moldvai magyarság [The Hungarians of Moldova]. Budapest, 1987. (Fifth revised edition); Horváth, Antal: Stramosii catolicilor din Moldova. Documente istorice 1227-1702. Sfântu Gheorghe, 1994; Kós, Károly - Szentimrei, Judit - Nagy, Jeno: Moldvai csángó népmuvészet [The folk art of the Csángó of Moldova]. Kriterion Könyvkiadó, Bukarest, 1981; Mikecs, László: A Kárpátokon túli magyarság [Trans-Carpathian Hungarians], In: Deér, József - Gáldi, László /ed./: Magyarok és románok I [Hungarians and Romanians, I]. Budapest, 1943, pp. 441-507; Lüko, Gábor: A moldvai csángók I. A csángók kapcsolatai az erdélyi magyarsággal. [The Csángó of Moldova, I. The relations of the Csángó with the Hungarians of Transylvania.] Budapest, 1936; Rosetti, Radu: Despre ungurii si episcopiile catolice din Moldova. Analele Academiei Române. Seria II. Tom. XXVII. Memoriile Sectiunii Istorice nr. 10., Bucuresti, pp. 247-322; Veress: A moldvai ... op. cit.

34 Costin, Miron: Opere. Editat de P. P. Panaitescu, Bucuresti, 1958, p. 215; Binder, Pál: Közös múltunk. Románok, magyarok, németek és délszlávok feudalizmus-kori falusi és városi együttélésérol [Our mutual past. Romanian, Hungarian, German and South Slav co-existence in feudal era villages and towns]. Bukarest, 1982, p. 106; Gabor, Iosif: Dictionarul comunitatilor catolice din Moldova. Bacau, 1996, p. 255.

35 Brancovici, Gheorghe: Cronica Româneasca. Editat de Damaschin Mioc si Marieta Adam-Chiper, Bucuresti, 1987.

36 Cantemir, Dimitrie: Descrierea Moldovei. Bucuresti, 1909, p.214; Cantemir, Dimitrie: Descrierea Moldovei. Editura Minerva, Bucuresti, 1973, p.173.

realm, as they are all either Russians or Transylvanian Hungarians.[37] Regarding their religious life, he notes, "The Hungarians steadfastly retain their Papist faith and although their communities fervently maintain the language of their ancestors, they all understand the Moldovan language, too."[38] In his next statement, the writer sheds light on the interfaith relations of the Moldova of the day: "Although a large number of Hungarians belong to the western Catholic Church, and they have a bishop in Bacau (Bákó), for the Moldavians, no religion is more repulsive than the Papist."[39]

In his memoirs, written in 1787, prince Hauterive, the voivod's French secretary, summarized that the Hungarian community was settled by Stefan cel Mare and that they, although adopting the country's customs and language, succeeded in retaining their their own as well, along with their religion. Their communities, living in 15 villages, are led by foreign born priests who continually urge them to obediance, endurance and work. As they are far more industrious, wealthy and settled, their taverns are never full. Primarily, only at the fairs do they enjoy themselves, dancing with joy.[40]

Nicolae Sutu, son of voivod Alexandru Sutu, published the first statistical summary of Moldova in 1852 at Iasi (Jászvásár). In his book, he stressed that in the region, apart from Romanians, other ancient, indigenous people also live (i.e., Greeks, Bulgarians, Armenians, Jews, gypsies, Hungarians and Germans). Quoting Cantemir, he emphasizes that the western portion of Moldova was a part of Transylvania up to the reign of Stefan cel Mare and that, on the eastern slopes of the Carpathians, Seklers and other Hungarian settlers owned the lands and forests. Later, the followers of Jan Hus settled in large numbers in Moldova, where the established, for example, the town of Hus. The various regulations and forcible militarization imposed on the Seklers also contributed to the Hungarians leaving their former homeland on a continuing basis and settling in Moldova.[41]

At the end of the 19th century, the geographic survey of the counties of the Kingdom of Romania was finally published. Based on it, Lahovari,

---

37 "Taranii nici nu sunt drepti Moldoveni, ci aceia cari se afla tarani, se trag sau din Rusi, sau din Ardeleni, carora le zic Moldovenii Ungureni..." Cantemir: Descrierea ... op.cit (1909) p. 217.

38 Cantemir: Descrierea ... op.cit (1909) p. 218; Cantemir: Descrierea ... op.cit (1973) p. 176.

39 "Nici o religie nu este urâta moldovenilor ca acea papistaseasca, macar de si tin de biserica apusului multime de locuitori Unguri cari au episcop la Bacau." Cantemir: Descrierea ... op.cit (1909) p. 247.

40 King Karl I of Romania, in a speech to the Romanian Academy on March 13, 1900, based on the 18th century memoirs of prince Hauterive.(Hegyeli, Attila: Din Arini la Sabaoani. [From Magyarfalu to Szabófalva]. Roman, 2004, p. 46.)

41 Sutu, Nicolae: Notiuni statistice asupra Moldovei. Iasi, 1852. According to his data, at the time, there were 1,356,908 Orthodox, 55,280 Jews, 44,317 Roman Catholics and 5,600 Armenians living in Moldova. (Hegyeli: Din ... op. cit. p. 32.)

Bratianu and Tocilescu compiled the Great Geographic Encyclopedia of Romania in 1898, which more closely reflects the period ethnographic, demographic picture of the settlements of the day. The authors note regarding Bákó County that, apart from the majority Romanians, there exist a population of Hungarian descent, especially among the village farmers, who have managed to retain their Hungarian mother tongue and Roman Catholic religion up to the very present day. The total population of the county was 172,496 in 1890. Of the 19,200 city dwellers of the day, 9,665 were Romanians, 7,369 Jewish, 1,199 Hungarians, 629 Germans, 530 Armenians, 55 Italians, 45 Greeks, 36 Bulgarians, 20 Russians, 18 French, 12 Swiss, 5 Serbs and 2 Turks. At the same time, the rural population of Bákó County was comprised of 152,296 people, made up of 123,132 Romanians, 24,715 Hungarians, 5,197 Jewish, 111 Germans, 5 Russians, 58 Italians, 47 Greeks, 35 Bulgarians, 5 French and 1 English. According to their figures, Lujzikalagor was inhabited by a total of 1,862 Roman Catholic Hungarians and 76 Romanian nationals, while the populations of Gajcsa and Ploszkucény were completely Hungarian.[42]

The editors of the geographic encyclopedia distinguished between two main groups of Hungarian settlers. The first, *Czango Magyar,* were, in their opinion, living in Moldova from ancient times, possibly before the organization of Moldova itself. They lived in villages on the right bank of the Szeret River, from Lészped down to Rekecseny. The Transylvanian Saxons and Seklers left their homeland in large numbers, with permission from king Sigismund, in 1420. These settlers were received by Alexandru cel Bun, voivod of Moldova, with advantageous rights and exemptions. They later organized Roman Catholic parishes in Forrófalva, Lujzikalagor, Bákó, Barát, Gorzafalva, Tatrosvásárhely and Aknavásárhely, which belonged to the Roman Catholic bishop's see of Bákó. The Romanian authors noted the distinguishing Hungarian dialectical differences of this medieval settler group from those arriving in later centuries, in which some ancient forms were no longer extant. The authors of the encyclopedia list in the second settler group those who fled from Seklerland during the 17th-18th centuries, mainly settling on lands close to Transylvania, especially along the Tatros River.[43]

---

42 According to the author's opinion, the local Romanian population is primarily made up of the

indigenous Moldovans and the mokány (Romanians) recently arrived from Transylvania.

"Populatiunea româna se compune din Moldoveni, bastinasi ai locului, si din Mocani, veniti mai de

curând din Ardeal." (Lahovari, Ioan George: Marele Dictionar Geografic al României. Bucuresti,

1898, p. 173.)

43 Ibid. p. 173.

According to archival research conducted by Radu Rosetti, the ancestors of the Csángó were made up of the groups settled along the Szeret River by the medieval kings of Hungary for the protection of their eastern borders. In his opinion, at the creation of the voivodine of Moldova, and even before, significant numbers of Hungarian settlers lived along not only the Szeret but also the Ojtoz and Tatros Rivers. The noted Romanian historian supported his finding on the fact that the most significant village communities were all located in central Moldova, from Egyedhalma all the way to Románvásár, in the fertile Szeret valley. They were sited to provide protection for the important commercial and military routes from foreign armies arriving from the East heading towards Transylvania in the valleys of the Ojtoz, Tatros, Aranyos-Beszterce Rivers, as well as the narrow passages through the Carpathians at Ojtoz, Gyimes and Békás. Rosetti also coupled his archival research with a systematic examination of Moldovan geographical place names. His conclusion from his study of written documents and topographic names was that the overwhelming majority of names in Bákó County are of Hungarian origin, while the border mountains and other place names in Suceava, Neamt and Vrancea Counties are mostly Romanian. Those Hungarian groups, who were settled along the Szeret before the 15th century for defensive purposes, found a mostly uninhabited territory. They were the first to name the area's significant peaks, waters and settlements, e.g.- Áldomás / Aldamas, Apahavas / Apahaos, Halas / Halos, Kászon / Casin, Kerek-Bükk / Cherebic, Mikes / Mikes, Nagy-Sándor / Sandru-Mare, Nemere / Nemira, Tatros (Tatáros) / Trotus, Tarhavas / Tarhaos, Tázló / Tazlau, etc.[44]

In his 1924 monograph on the Catholics living in Roman County, I. N. Ciocan wrote that the Csángó settled by Stefan cel Mare live in the most productive area of the Szeret River, who work their fields, pastures, lakes and rivers with the greatest expertise and willingness, profiting by their labors, almost every village having a well-to-do farmer. For centuries, they enjoyed special privileges and unique care, defining themselves as *Magyar* (Unguri), a name to which they cling very strongly. According to Ciocan, many are not certain in what country they live. At the beginning of the 20th century, the author found many villages where the small children knew not one word of Romanian and the teacher of the first grade had to rely on older students to

---

44 The author also notes that countless medieval Hungarian place names in Moldova later disappeared in the events of history or were exchanged for Romanian. He supports his statement with a document from 1410 in which Alexandru cel Bun, voivod of Moldova, grants six villages to his faithful servants (Master of the Table Domokos, and his brothers Balázs and Jakab, as well as Miklós Gelebi and his sons), among them the now-disappeared László / Laslovovti. (Rosetti: Despre ... op. cit.; Cihodaru, C. - Caprosu, I. - Simanschi, L.: Documenta Romaniae Historica, A. I. 40. nr. 26. Bucuresti, 1975.)

translate to be able to teach. As a uniqueness of dialect, the pupils consistently pronounced the *s* sound (sh in English) in newly learned Romanian words as *sz* [s in horse, close to a lisping effect-*Ed.*]. For example, instead of *camesa* (shirt) they pronounced *chimesa*. In the opinion of the teacher, these children speak faulty Hungarian among themselves in the school yard and are unable to complete the 4-5 grade of elementary school. Although the local minister holds special religious classes for them in school, the seeds of the Romanian national sentiment promoted by him are difficult to discern in the souls of these youngsters.[45]

Ciocan remarked on the language use of the early 20th century Csángó, whereby the village children only speak Hungarian and the adults, both men and women, speak a very broken Romanian. The author also noted that a significant portion of the women speak no Romanian at all, hence could not teach the country's language to their children.[46] As a result of his fieldwork done in 1903, Ciocan accurately lists that Hungarian was used in the following villages in Roman County: Butea, Miklósfalva, Acélfalva, Szabófalva, Halasfalva, Barticsest, Jugán, Tamásfalva, Dzsidafalva, Domafalva, Kelgyest and Bírófalva. In his opinion, in the listed villages, the most proper Hungarian used was in Kelgyest. In Szágna, Balusest and Kalugarén, almost proper Romanian was widely used.[47] When the Finnish linguist, Yrjö Wichmann, visited the northern Csángó villages in 1907, his findings turned up that Hungarian was still spoken in Bargován, Balusest, Gyerofalva, Jugán, Kelgyest, Kickófalva and Szabófalva.[48]

Nicolae Iorga, the most notable Romanian historian of the inter-war period, also devoted time to study the Hungarian Roman Catholic communities of Moldova. In several of his articles, he unequivocally stated that the Roman Catholics of Moldova are Hungarian originally from Transylvania, who settled in the 13th century in what was then designated as the Cuman bishopric. His conclusions were based not only on archival research but also on field exploration, as he personally visited the significant regions and settlements of the area. In his work covering Romanian history to 1918, he clearly stated that, in the early 13th century, the majority of the territory past the Szeret River was considered to be Hungarian territory. In Iorga's opinion, the vicinity of Románvásár did not belong to the Hungarian crown, explaining the appearance of villages in this area as the northerly

---

45 Ciocan, I. N.: Monografia crestinilor catolici din judetul Roman. Dupa datele culese în 1903. Roman,

    1924, pp. 18-19.

46 Ibid, p. 19.

47 Ibid, p. 21.

48 Wichmann, Júlia: Moldvai csángó mennyegzo Szabófalván [Moldovan Csángó wedding in

    Szabófalva], In: Ethnographia, XLVII. évf., 1936, pp. 57-65.

growth of southern Moldovan Hungarians. According to him, the Hungarian settlers reached the Szeret River valley, primarily along the river valleys that originated in the Carpathians (Tatros, Ojtoz), which, at the time, were considered to be a part of Transylvania. From there, they gradually migrated to its confluence with the Moldova River. In their travels, the Hungarian settlers came into contact, and mixed, with many other ethnic groups, especially Slavs and Romanians. They received their Csángó name as a result. In his travels in Moldova, Nicolae Iorga clearly grasped the dialectical difference the Csángó used [the s / sz (sh / s) as noted earlier-*Ed.*], which fundamentally differentiates them from the Hungarians of Moldova of Transylvanian origin.[49] In his thesis, the Hungarian settlers populated the area around the salt mines in the Szlanik valley by the early 13th century, from where they later drifted down to the region of the Szeret River, the territory of the Cuman bishopric. Although they adopted the costumes and customs of the Moldovan Romanians, to this day, they preserved their Seklerish Hungarian mother tongue and their traditional organization.[50]

The noted historian remarked regarding the village of Egyedhalma that its history also goes back to the early 13th century, when Hungarians settled between the Carpathians and the Szeret River, on the territory of that Cuman bishopric, which was adjacent to the Mongol lands, the Roman Catholic Church's easternmost bastion. He considered the names of Egyedhalma and Szászkút to be undeniably of Hungarian origin.[51] In Vizánta, in Vrancea County, he found handsome children being raised by peaceable-looking Hungarian farmers.[52] Reaching Ploszkucény, he wrote that the Catholic Hungarians who live there arduously retained their mother tongue – in fact, many of their children speak no Romanian. Their women only bother to learn a bit of Romanian to make them understood at the markets held in the neighboring villages. The giggling village girls told Iorga that they would under no circumstances marry Romanian lads, whom they called Vlachs. They were of the opinion that within their own settlement they were living on Hungarian soil (Tara Ungureasca) and that Wallachia (Tara Româneasca) only began at its outskirts.[53] He found terribly poor Hungarians, and Romanians who fled from other parts,[54] living in simple hovels in Mircset, on the property of Vasile Alecsandri (Romanian poet). He noted that the

49 Iorga, Nicolae: România mama a unitatii noastre nationale cum era pîna la 1918. Bucuresti, 1972, pp.

181-182.

50 Ibid, p. 236.

51 Ibid, p. 266.

52 Ibid, p. 275.

53 Ibid, pp. 218-219.

54 Ibid, p. 183.

Hungarians Catholics living in Husz only spoke Romanian but retained, to the beginning of the 20th century, the memory of their origins.[55]

Gh. I. Nastase, professor of history at the university of Iasi, concentrated his research into the Hungarian communities living in Moldova based on the extant account of bishop Bandinus' 1646 visit. In his work, he pointed out that, while rural Hungarians were able to retain their mother tongue and religion for a long time, Hungarian groups living in Moldovan towns assimilated relatively quicker in the areas of language and denomination.[56]

In an encyclopedia published in 1937, Octav George Lecca summed up the Romanian scientific thinking and achievements of the day. According to the author, Seklers were settled in lower Moldova, although widely dispersed, since the 13th century, especially in the Tatros valley. From a religious perspective, they belonged initially to the Roman Catholic bishopric of Milkó, later to the one of Bákó. Sekler founded villages sprang up in the valley of the Szeret River, in the vicinity of Bákó, Román and Jászvásár. These Seklers living in Moldova are called Csángó. The medieval Hungarian (Sekler) settler village communities are still in existence to this day.[57]

In his book published in 1969, P. P. Panaitescu analyzed in great detail the settlement of Hungarians outside the Carpathians. In his work, he specifically noted that the Seklers who settled in Muntenia (Havasalföld), in Secueni County, lying east the crescent of the Carpathians, assimilated relatively quickly into the Romanians, while the Csángó of Moldova living in Bákó, Roman and Putna Counties retained to this day their mother tongue and Roman Catholic religion.[58]

C. Constantin Giurescu turned his attention in one of his books, published in 1967, to the role played by the Transylvanian Saxons and Hungarians in the life of the Moldovan cities. He made special reference to the fact that the Saxons, as well as the Hungarians, were instrumental in the creation of the Moldovan urban network, as evidenced by the Hungarian-originated names of several market towns. According to his research, Tatros was one of the earliest Hungarian colonies in Moldova. He deemed it quite probable that the market place, close to the salt mines known far and wide, existed since the first half of the 13th century In his book, he treated in considerable detail the significant role played by Hungarians in the life of

55 Ibid, p. 200.

56 Nastase, Gheorghe: Die Ungarn in der Moldau im Jahre 1646. Nach dem „Codex Bandinus". Iasi, 1936.

57 Lecca, Octav George: Dictionar istoric, arheologic si geografic al României. Bucuresti, 1937; Hegyeli: Din ... op. cit. p.9.

58 Panaitescu, P.P.: Patrunderea ungureasca dincolo de Carpati. Bucuresti, 1969, pp. 258-263.

Bákó, Szászkút, Egyedhalma, Tekucs, Husz, Szucsáva, Kotnár, Herló and Románvásár. He specifically noted that the Romanian words *oras*, *bâlci*, *birau*, *salgau* derive from the Hungarian words *város* (town), *búcsú* (fair), *biró* (judge), *sóvágó* (salt cutter/miner).[59]

The intolerant, anti-minority and artificially fuelled nationalistic atmosphere of the Ceausescu era (1965-1989) did not favor objective studies into the history of Romania's ethnic minorities. A long time had to pass before Romanian historical research yielded results concerning the ethnic minorities of Moldova that was objective and free of politics. Mihai-Razvan Ungureanu published several such studies in the 1990's.[60] From among the young historians of Iasi, Liviu Pilat recently published an in-depth anthropological paper, based on written records, about the everyday life Kickófalva in the Middle Ages. In his study, stated beyond the shadow of a doubt that the villagers of Kickófalva, belonging to the northern group /of settlers/ were probably living in what is their current homeland well before the founding of the principality of Moldova. The author does not hold the villagers either 'Csángó' or 'Seklerized Romanians,' as the village was not replenished in the 18th century with refugees from Seklerland. Hence, the village population are descendants of medieval Hungarians who gradually lost their mother tongue, a process clearly documented by written sources beginning in the 17th century "The question of origin should not upset anyone, as the aim of history is to uncover origin and not erase it. At the same time, nobody should be ashamed with their origins; the fact is, our ancestors did not consciously implant this sense of origin, hence, socially and intellectually they viewed themselves similar to the other Moldavians. Only their religion played a differentiating role, which became deeper after the reorganization of the Moldovan Roman Catholic Church."[61]

In recent years, Romanian historian Marius Diaconescu of Bucharest, himself with Transylvanian roots, conducted systematic archival research. His studies and lectures, based on his findings, reveal undeniable proof that the majority of the Moldovan Csángó are descendants of Transylvanian Hungarians, who have, over time, become assimilated into the Romanian language and culture. Foreign missionaries in Moldova and the Roman

59 Giurescu, C. C.: Târguri sau orase si cetati moldovene din secolul al X-lea pâna la mijlocul secolului al

XVI-lea. Biblioteca Historica Romaniae 2, Bucuresti, 1967, pp. 81-88, 172.

60 Ungureanu, Razvan-Mihai: Câteva aspecte ale regimului asimilarii confesionale în Moldova.

Genealogii de „botezati". Arhiva Genealogica, I (VI.) nr. 1-2, Iasi, 1994; Ungureanu, Razvan-Mihai:

O harta a comunitatilor catolice din Moldova. Anuarul Institutului de Istorie „A. D. Xenopol." Tom

XXXIII, Iasi, 1996, pp. 345-352.

61 Pilat, Liviu: Aspecte din viata cotidiana a unui sat din Moldova medievala. Optiuni Istoriografice.

Buletinul Asociatiei Tinerilor Istorici Ieseni I/2, Iasi, 2000, pp. 92.

Catholic Church had a significant role in the absorption of this group of people. During WWII, when certain radical Romanian Fascist groups were proposing the deportation of the Moldovan Hungarians (similar to the Jews and gypsies), the local leaders of the Roman Catholic church, in order to protect its followers, proposed the theory that the Csángó were not really Hungarians but Romanians transplanted from Transylvania.[62]

Interestingly, Romanian linguists have never conducted scientific research in the Moldovan villages populated by the Csángó. Despite that, until the 1965 coming to power of Ceausescu, the dialect spoken by the Csángó was held to be a unique local variant of the Hungarian language. Emil Petrovice, for example, makes note of the fact that the Moldovan Hungarians of today still retain the bilabial pronunciation of the letter *v*, typical of old Hungarian.[63] In a 1956 paper, Romulus Todoran points out that the language of the Moldovan Csángó is one regional variant of the Hungarian language, which developed along unique lines due to its centuries of isolation. As the Csángó, living in a minority situation are under strong linguistic pressure, after a transitional period of mixed language use, this Hungarian dialect will eventually disappear.[64] In *Introduction to Linguistics*, Alexandru Graur's Romanian language piece also comments on the phenomena that linguistically, the Csángó of Moldova are slowly melting into the Romanian masses, and that this process is being examined by the Hungarian linguists of the University of Cluj-Napoca, employing scientific methods.[65] In a study published in 1960, Vladimir Drimba warned that the Csángó dialect received substantially more Romanian influence than previously reported by the Finn, Wichmann.[66]

The change in Romanian linguistics after 1965 is tellingly documented by the entries for the Csángó in general linguistic dictionaries. The *Romanian Literary Dictionary* (1955) defines a *csángó* as a Hungarian who found a new home in the vicinity of Bákó.[67] The *Dictionary of Contemporary Romanian* (1958) enumerates those persons into this group whose Hungarian

---

62 Diaconescu, Marius: Péter Zöld si „descoperirea" ceangailor din Moldova în a doua jumatate a

secolului XVIII. Anuarul Institutului de Istorie „A. D. Xenopol" XXXIX-XL. (2002-2003), Iasi,

2003, pp. 247-292.

63 Petrovici, Emil: Egy magyar hangtani sajátosság tükrözodése a román nyelv magyar kölcsönszavaiban.

Magyar Nyelv, LII. évf., 1952, p. 8.

64 Todoran, Romulus: Cu privire la o problema de lingvistica: limba si dialect. Cercetari de lingvistica I,

1956, p. 98.

65 Graur, Alexandru: Întroducere în lingvistica. Bucuresti, 1958, pp. 248-249.

66 Drimba, Vladimir: Materiale pentru stadiul raporturilor lingvistice româno-maghiare. Cercetari de

Lingvistica, Cluj XIV, 1960, pp. 377-390.

67 Dictionarul limbii române literare contemporane. Ed. Academiei R.P.R. Bucuresti, 1955, p. 379.

ancestors settled around Bákó in the 18th century According to the authors, the group's name is undeniably of Hungarian origin.[68] A 1962 dictionary hold the Csángó to be a branch of the Seklers who settled in Moldova, some time around the 15th century, along the Tatros, Beszterce and Szeret Rivers.[69] An encyclopedic Romanian dictionary, published in 1972, also calls the Csángó a branch of the Seklers who settled the Tatros, Beszterce and Szeret Rivers, and in the vicinity of the town of Román in the North, around the 15th century.[70] A later one, compiled by Vasile Breban in 1980, essentially repeats this: the ancestors of the Csángó were Seklers who settled in Moldova in the 15th century.[71] The Romanian explicatory dictionary (1996) defines it in a more complex manner. According to its entry, the *Csángó* ethnonym serves to define a Romanian and Hungarian language, Roman Catholic ethnic group, which, over time, emigrated from South Transylvania to Moldova (settling mainly in Bákó County).[72] Georgeta Smeu's historical dictionary (1997) holds the *Csángó* ethnonym as unquestionably of Hungarian origin, which can be applied to that group of Hungarian (Sekler) descent whose ancestors settled in Moldova, adjacent to the Hungarian kingdom, primarily in the vicinity of the towns of Bákó and Román from the 13th century onwards. In the Tatros valley (Aknavásárhely), their main occupation was salt mining and to the present day have retained their language, Catholic religion, customs and village communities.[73]

According to another, completely unfounded, theory, the ancestors of the Moldovan Csángó were Transylvanian Romanians who were partially Hungarianized by the Roman Catholic Church while in the Carpathian basin and who fled to Moldova in the 17th and 18th centuries from the increasing assimilation.[74] As the assimilation of the Romanians living in Transylvania

---

68 Dictionar al limbii române moderne. Bucuresti, 1958. Hegyeli: Din ... op. cit. p. 2.

69 Dictionar enciclopedic român. Ed. Politica. Bucuresti, 1962, p. 562.

70 Canarache, Ana - Breban, Vasile: Mic dictionar enciclopedic. Bucuresti, 1972, p. 165. The encyclopedia was published in 1947 as Mic dictionar al limbii române. Editura stiintifica, Bucuresti and the Dictionarul explicativ al limbii române, published in 1975. Bucharest again repeats the theory that the Csángó are, in reality, people of Sekler origins who moved out of Seklerland in the 15th century and settled in Moldova.

71 Breban, Vasile: Dictionar al limbii române contemporane. Bucuresti, 1980, p. 87.

72 DEX: Dictionarul explicativ al limbii române. Ed. Univers Enciclopedic. Bucuresti, 1996, p. 157.

73 Smeu, Georgeta: Dictionar de istoria românilor. Editura Trei. Bucuresti, 1997; Hegyeli: Din ... op. cit. p. 3.

74 This theory is contradicted by the fact that these refugees, fleeing to Moldova from Transylvania from Magyarization and Catholic conversion, i.e., into an Orthodox Romanian majority, retained their Roman Catholic religion and Hungarian language into the 20th century, while the overwhelming

20

was only partially successful, their language and culture in their new homeland also remains heterogeneous and mixed, retaining many linguistic characteristics of the Transylvanian Romanian.[75]

Constantin Lozinca first presented his theory regarding the origins of the Moldovan Csángó in a 1935 letter addressed to Nicolae Iorga. The author presented in detail the Romanian style clothing, customs and names of the Catholics of Moldova, while bringing to the attention of the well-known historian that he is in disagreement with those of his writings in which he (Iorga) attributes Hungarian roots to the Catholics of Moldova.[76] His plan met with success as in his 1939 publication, Iorga now attributed a mixed Romanian-Sekler origin to the Moldovan Csángó.[77]

Finally, Iosif Petru Pal, head of the Franciscan order's Moldovan province, laid the 'scientific' basis for the Romanian origins of the Moldovan Catholics.[78] In his work, the Franciscan attempted to prove by historic, ethnic, ethnographic, geographic, ethnologic and linguistic arguments that the Moldovan Catholics were of Romanian origins. In the following year, his work appeared with major modifications where he attempted to show the crucial role the Franciscans had in the creation of a Romanian identity among the Catholics of Moldova.[79] It was shortly followed by two shorter newspaper articles, once again demonstrating the Romanian origins of the

---

majority of Romanians living in Seklerland live in the Orthodox faith to this day. This theory also contains another logical pitfall: why would the Transylvanian Hungarians expel en masse groups who were beginning to converge with them, both in language and religion? (Bárdi, Nándor – Hermann, Gusztáv Mihály: A többség kisebbsége [The majority as minority]. Tanulmányok a székelyföldi románság történetéről. Csíkszereda, 1999; Benko: A csángók ... op. cit. p. 209.) At the same time, every sensible researcher will admit that, for various economic, social, legal and family reasons, many Romanian and Hungarian people moved to Moldova to try and begin a new life. (Metes, Stefan: Emigrari românesti din Transilvania in secolele XIII-XX. Bucuresti, 1971, pp. 71-147.)

75 "The fact that the Csángó have spoken Romanian for centuries - and in their dialect the Transylvanian Romanian linguistic characteristics can be noted - proves that they are descended from Transylvanian Romanians. The phonetical duality of their dialect precisely proves this point, hence, it has a historical message: before they came into contact with the dialects of the Moldovans, they spoke the Transylvanian variety." (Martinas, Dumitru: Originea ceangailor din Moldova. Bucuresti, 1985, p. 73.)

76 Lozinca, Constantin: Scrisoare catre Nicolae Iorga. Revista Istorica XXI. nr. 10-12, 1935, pp. 402-403.

77 Neamul Romanesc, February, 1939.

78 Pal, M. Iosif Petru: Originea Catolicilor din Moldova. Tipografia Serafica, Sabaoani-Roman, 1941.

79 Pal, M. Iosif Petru: Franciscanii minori conventuali si limba româna. Almanahul Viata, 1942, pp. 40-46.

Moldovan Csángó and the pivotal role that the Franciscans played in the establishment of Romanian-language religious life.[80] This theory, constructed so amateurishly, already found some supporters during the years of WWII, i.e., it found resonance and support in the time of extremist nationalism organized on racial lines.[81]

After the 1940 second Vienna Arbitral Award, when Romania lost northern Transylvania, intolerance and mistrust grew against not only the Hungarians of southern Transylvania but also the Catholics living in Moldova. In this atmosphere filled with hate, the Moldovan leaders of the Roman Catholic Church attempted, as a defense, to prove the impossible. They stressed the Romanian origins of the Catholic Csángó. The Romanian authorities were not particularly convinced by these intellectual attempts, hence, the government's appointment of Dr. Petre Râmnentu to prove, through the then-popular blood testing, that the Moldovan Catholics belong to the Romanian *race*.[82] Earlier, Râmneantu was a university professor and researcher in Cluj-Napoca (Kolozsvár) but fled with his institution to Sibiu (Nagyszeben) after 1940. On a commission from the Romanian government, he conducted Fascist-style physical anthropology and biological research in the Catholic Moldovan villages. He presented his findings in a Romanian and a German language study in which he attempted to show that the Moldovan Catholics were undeniably members of the Romanian race, based on his racist influenced blood tests.[83]

The central conclusions of Iosif Petru Pal's book and writings were soon embraced by Ioan Martinas, a Roman Catholic parish priest of Moldova, whose writings, full of imposing rhetorical arguments, exerted great influence on the views of his brother, Dumitru Martinas.[84]

The book *Moldovan Csángó folk art,* published by Kriterion Press in 1981, an ethnographic monograph by Károly Kós, Judit Szentimrei and Jeno Nagy, enraged a number of representatives of the overtly nationalistic Communist authorities of Romania.[85] At the direct command of Ceausescu, Romania's nationalistic and intolerant dictator, the Bucharest propaganda machinery of the Communist party quickly teamed up with the secret service

80 Ibid; Pal: Originea ... op. cit.

81 Pal: Originea ... op. cit.; Râmneantu, Petru: Die Abstammung der Taschangos. Sibiu, 1944;
   Gârniteanu, M.: Catolici din Moldova sunt Daci. Lumina Crestinului, XXX. 2, 1944, pp. 4-5.

82 Bucur, Maria: Eugenics and Modernization in Interwar Romania. University of Pittsburgh Press, 2002,
   pp. 36-37, 136-137, 143-146.

83 Pal: Franciscanii ... op. cit.; Râmneantu, Petru: Grupele de sânge la Ciangaii din Moldova. Buletin
   eugenic si biopolitic XIV. nr. 1-2, 1943, pp. 51-65; Râmneantu: Die Abstammung ... op. cit.

84 Martinas, Ioan: Cine sunt catolicii moldoveni? Iasi, 1942.

85 Kós-Szentimrei-Nagy: Moldvai ... op. cit.

in the interest of proving, by any means possible, the Romanian origins of the Moldovan Csángó. At the same time, the ethnonym *Csángó* was a forbidden term in the Hungarian-language press of Romania.[86]

The Transylvanian-Romanian origins of the Moldovan Csángó is today primarily linked to the name of Dumitru Martinas. He was born in Butea, in the vicinity of Románvásár, into a Romanian-speaking Roman Catholic family, a circumstance which presented him with an identity crisis to the end of his life. He went to school in Jászvásár (Iasi), then taught Romanian language and literature in the mostly Hungarian populated city of Marosvásárhely (Tirgu Mures) between 1925 and 1962 as a 'missionary' teacher. Martinas searched for decades for the facts with which he wanted to prove the Transylvanian-Romanian origins of the Moldovan Csángó in his planned monograph. As his opus was not only dilettantish, but also hasty, extreme and nationalistic in manner, no publisher was willing to accept its publication in the decades after WWII. Finally, in the early 1980's, during the harshest years of the Ceausescu dictatorship, was the book published. Under the direction of the infamous Romanian secret police (Securitate), as part of the action code named 'Tatros,' an extremist anti-Hungarian group within the Propaganda Directorate of the Romanian Communist Party fundamentally 'rewrote' the Martinas manuscript. It was published with picture of the Pope and richly illustrated with photographs of Moldovan churches.[87] The author admits in his book that in the 14th century, Hungarian kings settled significant populations on the eastern side of the Carpathians for the protection of their eastern borders. In his view, the majority of these communities disappeared during the 17th century as a result of the Turkish and Mongol attacks and the rest fled back to Transylvania. To this depopulated Moldovan territory, new settlers arrived from Transylvania in the 17th-18th centuries who were, at least in part, Seklerized Romanians. The Transylvanian population of Romanian origin settled in Moldova at the first chance, with its Orthodox majority, where it soon forgot its Sekler-Hungarian language. In his work, Martinas admits that in many villages of Bákó County (e.g.- Gajdár, Klézse, Lészped, Lujzikalagor, Pusztina, Trunk, etc.) Hungarian was still spoken within the family well into the 20th century. These Hungarian-languaged communities (in his view) should not be seen as of the

---

86 Cuceu, Ion: Recenzie? Dumitru, Martinas ? Originea ceangailor din Moldova, In: Anuarul de folclor V-VII. Cluj-Napoca, 1987, pp. 493-494.

87 According to the opinion of Gabriel Andreescu, Romanian human rights activist, Martinas' theory regarding the Transylvanian-Romanian origins of the Csángós was concocted by agents of the Securitate, the infamous political police, in the 1980's as part of the then active state policy of assimilation. (Hegyeli: Din ... op. cit. p. 13.)

Hungarian *race*, but rather as Romanians who were exposed to more intensive Hungarian cultural influences in Transylvania.[88]

Dumitru Martinas mainly resorted to using ethnographic and linguistic examples in an effort to prove his thesis. In his opinion, the unique Csángó costumes and Romanian language can only be explained by Transylvanian-Romanian parallels.[89] The idea seemed not to have occured to the author that the fundamental differences in the Romanian language used by the Moldovan Catholic and Orthodox communities, those found among the Csángó can be traced back to the ancient Transylvanian-Hungarian linguistic sub-strata.[90]

Martinas was neither a trained linguist, nor a historian of local or European repute with outstanding achievements. And yet, we must devote ourselves to two of his fundamental examples, which he uses in an attempt to prove his theory in his amateurishly assembled book. In the years following the 1989 regime change, the Romanian state authorities were still referring to his unscientific hypotheses when denying the Csángó their basic request to be able to pray in their churches in Hungarian, to have their children use the language of their ancestors in the public schools.

According to a basic premise of the author's theory, the Latin-origin word *lér,* found in the Csángó-Hungarian language, could only have been transplanted from Transylvanian-Romanian. In his opinion, this word, meaning *brother-in-law,* comes from the Latin *levir,* which the Moldovan Csángó retained from the Transylvanian-Romanian linguistic substratum, from where it later disappeared. In his work, Martinas attempts to prove that this Latin word could only have entered the Hungarian language from Romanian. The author seems not to have even considered why this Romanian word, of Latin origin, only surfaced in the Moldovan Hungarian-Csángó community. Why researchers have found no trace of it in other Romanian dialects or historical sources?[91]

A historical linguistic examination proves precisely the opposite of his hypothesis: that Hungarians in the Carpathian basin adopted the word

---

88 Martinas: Originea ... op. cit. pp. 29-31.

89 Ibid, pp. 32-33.

90 When the author attempts to show unique Transylvanian-Romanian examples in Moldovan Csángó usage, in most cases he marshals western Transylvanian or Banate parallels, from areas which were in close contact with the Hungarian language-usage area, or its very centre. Thus, Martinas omits the fact that the Hungarian language had great influence on these Romanian dialects. Hence, if a linguistic example surfaces in the both Moldovan Csángó and western Transylvanian dialects, it does not automatically follow that the Csángós are of Transylvanian-Romanian origin. It more likely speaks of the influence of the Hungarian language in both areas. (Martinas: Originea ... op. cit. pp. 33-34.)

91 Martinas: Originea ... op. cit. pp. 90-92.

directly from medieval Latin and it remained a part of the isolated Csángó-Hungarian language into the 20th century.[92]

While Martinas is unable to document the existence of the word in Romanian dialects, it crops up in widespread use in Hungarian dialects in the Carpathian basin and frequently in medieval written sources. As an example, the Hungarian Wordlist of Beszterce of 1395 (Besztercei Magyar Szójegyzék) contains its first written mention. Furthermore, the Word List of Schlägl (1405), Hungarian Language Master of 1418 (Magyar Nyelvmester) by Johann of Rothenburg, and the 1570 last will and testament of Ferenc Horvát, captain of the fortress of Eger, all attest to the early Hungarian occurences.[93] The word occurs even today in the *rér*[94] form (still meaning *brother-in-law*) in Hungarian dialects not only in Moldova but also among the Slavonian Hungarians (in today's Croatia).[95]

Our statement that *lér/rér* did not enter the Hungarian language from Romanian is supported by other linguistic (e.g.- interpretive) factors. It is a specific uniqueness of Hungarian familial terminology that the names reflect the age of the relative, which is not present in the Romanian system.[96] In Hungarian *bátya* refers to an older male sibling, while *öcs* denotes younger;

---

92 In János Sylvester's Grammatica, dated 1539, this Latin word appears as leuir. (Pais, Dezso: Rér, In: Szó- és szólásmagyarázatok. Magyar Nyelv, XXXIX. évf., 4. sz., 1943, pp. 319-323.) In the opinion of Pais, a role was played in the spread of the word by those churchmen, fluent and excellent Latin speakers, who continued to oppose in-law marriage, or leviratus. The medieval Hungarian Catholic church strenuously opposed the practice whereby a widow was usually married to a younger brother of the deceased husband. (Ibid, p. 323; Tagányi, Károly: A hazai élo jogszokások gyujtésérol. I. rész. A családi és öröklési jogszokások [Family and ingeritance legal customs]. Budapest, 1919, pp. 31-32.)

93 Berrár, Jolán - Károly, Sándor: Régi magyar glosszárium [Old Hungarian glossary]. Budapest, 1984, p. 592; Pais: Rér ... op. cit. p. 319; Szarvas, Gábor - Simonyi, Zsigmond: Magyar Nyelvtörténeti Szótár II. Budapest, 1891, p. 1417.

94 The rér form appears in the 1405, 1418, 1572, and 1590 documents. (A rér szó az intervocalis v kiesésével és az egymás mellé került magánhangzók diftonguson keresztül monoftongussá alakulásával keletkezett. A szókezdo r voltaképpen az l-r : r-r hasonulással magyarázható. A szókezdo l a moldvai csángóban vagy megorzött régiség vagy hasonulással újabban jött létre.)

95 Balassa, József: A slovéniai nyelvjárás [Slovenian dialect], In: Magyar Nyelvor, XXIII. évf., 1894, pp. 307-308; Szarvas, Gábor: A szlavóniai tájszótár {Slavonian regional dictionary]. Magyar Nyelvor, V. évf., 1876, p. 12; Penavin, Olga: Szlavóniai (kórógyi) szótár [Slavonian (Kórógy) dictionary]. Újvidék, 1978, p. 27; Lorinczi, Réka: A magyar rokonsági elnevezések rendszerének változásai [Variations in the naming of Hungarian relationaships]. Bukarest, 1980, pp. 77, 80, 88-89.

96 As an example, in Romanian, frate is simply brother, while sora means sister, without age differentiation.

similarly, *néne* refers to an older female sibling and *húg* to a younger. As part of the same terminology, *lér/rér* does not simply denote *brother-in-law* but rather, specifically refers to the husband of an older sister. In the ancient language, *süv* was used to denote the husband of a younger sister.[97] The specific meaning of *lér/rér* and its unique place in Hungarian familial terminology, as well as the written records of the period, all cast doubt on the view that this expression entered the Hungarian language through borrowing from Romanian.

In his second example, Dumitru Martinas holds the *s/sz* (sh/s equivalent in English) pronunciation such a linguistic anomaly which, according to him, proves beyond the shadow of a doubt that the Moldovan Csángó descended from Transylvanian Romanians.[98] The author again cites Romanian examples of this pronunciation from the Banate, meaning from the westernmost fringe territory of the Ramanian language distribution.[99]

Systematic linguistic research shows that *sz* pronunciation of the *s* phonic is completely absent from the Moldovan and Transylvanian Romanian dialects but does occur, sparsely in places, in Oltenia and its neighbour, the Banate.[100] These two Romanian regions were, for centuries, part of the medieval Kingdom of Hungary, forming an administrative, political and territorial unit with it. Hence, the appearance of this peculiar pronunciation proves a centuries old relationship with the aid of linguistic elements.[101] Interestingly enough, Mircea Borcila unreservedly considered this phenomenon in the Oltenian and Banate dialects as the result of regional, internal development. At the same time, the philologer from Cluj stated in his writing that no linguistic relationship can be established between the Hungarians around Román who speak with an *sz* and the Oltenian/Banate Romanians who speak with a 'hiss' – not through migration patterns, nor historical written records.[102]

While Romanian linguistic researchers have been able to find examples of *sz* pronunciation only in areas contiguous with the main block of Hungarian language distribution (e.g.- the Banate), its widespread existence in the Carpathian basin in the Old Hungarian period (896-1526) is easily

---

97 Szilágyi, N. Sándor: Despre dialectele ceangaiesti din Moldova. Altera, VIII. évf., 17-18. sz., 2002, pp.

81-89.

98 Martinas: Originea ... op. cit. pp. 71-87.

99 Ibid, pp. 74-75.

100 Borcila, Mircea: Un fenomen fonetic dialectal: rostirea lui s ca s si j ca z în graiurile dacoromâne.

Vechimea si originea fenomenului, In: Studia Universitatis Babes-Bolyai. Series Philologia.

Fasciculus, 2. Anul X, 1965, p. 109.

101 Ibid, p. 115.

102 Ibid, pp. 116-117.

documented. According to research carried out by Lóránd Benko in medieval Transylvanian documents, they contain in number the *s/sz* phonetic variation: from 1570: *eszett* for 'esett,' 1573: *adoszágért* for 'adósságért,' 1611: *igaszágban* for 'igazságban,' etc.[103] According to language historians, two dialects were found in the Carpathian basin in the Middle Ages (one who pronounced *s*, the other *sz,* or one who lisped, the other did not-*Ed.*), whose existence is documented by a number of related word pairs, such as *szovény-sövény*. The ancestors of the lisping Csángó, when they resettled in Moldova from the Carpathian basin, belonged to that linguistic dialect branch. Dialecticians have found this unique pronunciation not only among the Moldovan Csángó but also along the western and southern perimeter where a more archaic form of Hungarian is spoken (e.g.- in Slavonian villages such as Kórógy and the Hungarian communities of the Orség (today the Burgenland of eastern Austria)). In other aspects of phonics, pronunciation examples similar to the Csángó were also observed. The fact is that this lisping occured in medieval Hungarian language remnants, and could still be found in the 20th century in western, southern and eastern peripheral areas. The same can not be documented unequivocally in the Romanian language, which provides strong evidence of the Hungarian origins of the Moldovan Csángó.[104] Several language scientists have noted a phenomena where the interchange between *c/cs,* consistent in the Csángó dialect, can only be found in the vicinity of Hungarian villages in Moldova, or in such settlements where the original medieval settlers have completely melted into the Romanians but still managed to retain an earlier phonetic characteristic.[105]

In the second half of the 20th century, Romanian nationalistic groups attempted to bolster the Transylvanian-Romanian origins of the Moldovan Csángó with such interpretable and uncertain linguistic evidence. It is a sad fact that the both church and lay elites cite this unscientific 'myth of origin' to legitimize – at the beginning of the 21st century – the forcible linguistic, cultural and ethnic assimilation of the Csángó. Or, as they term it, the "re-Romanization" of the Moldovan Hungarians.[106]

---

103 Benko: A csángók ... op. cit. p. 35.

104 Ibid, pp. 34-35; Kiss, Jeno /ed./: Magyar dialektológia [Study of Hungarian dialects]. Budapest, 2001,

    p. 310.

105 Ibid (Benko), p. 35.

106 Martinas: Originea ... op. cit. pp. 110-115.

I. HUNGARIANS IN THE HISTORY OF MOLDOVA

In the second half of the first millennia, the rolling mountainous region East of the Carpathians became the temporary stopping place of nomad tribes arriving from the East. The Huns were followed by the Avars and various Bulgar-Turkic tribes, while the 9th century saw the rapid passage of the Magyars, Pechenegs and Oguz. While the Magyar's soon established a country in the Carpathian basin, the Pechenegs and Oguz were pulverized in various military actions and were assimilated. As the forces of the Hungarian king successfully repelled the 11th century attack of the latest arrivals, the Cumans, they temporarily settled - between 1100 and 1241 - in Moldova and Muntenia. To teach them Christianity and convert them, the king of Hungary established a Roman Catholic bishopric in Milkó, which far preceded the organization of the Orthodox Church in this region.[107] The Mongols dispersed most of their settlements during their incursions in the 1240's; smaller groups of them asked for refuge from the king of Hungary, who directed them, with the Jász (descendants of the Alans), to the Hungarian plains between the Danube and Tisza Rivers. Thus, they were settled in the central portion of the kingdom,[108] where they were assimilated linguistically relatively rapidly into the Hungarians.[109]

As the Vlachs migrated in ever-larger numbers from the Balkans to lands North of the Danube, by the 15th century, Romanian-speaking people made up the majority of the population of Moldova.[110] The Byzantine historian, Niketas Khoniates, writing in 1164, recorded that the emperor's nephew, while fleeing, fell into *vlach* captivity before reaching the border of Volhinia.[111] Another early 13th century document mentions the Romanians. In

---

107 Auner, Carol: Episcopia Milkoviei, In: Revista Catolica. Bucuresti, 1912, pp. 533-551; Makkai,

László: A milkói (kun) püspökség és népei [The (Cuman) bishopric of Milkó and its people].

Debrecen, 1936.

108 The Cumans were a nomad people of Turkic origin. They migrated to Eastern Europe to escape the

Mongol pressure. (Kósa, László - Filep, Antal: A magyar nép táji-történeti tagolódása [The regional

& historical of separation the Hungarian people]. Budapest, 1983, pp. 134-137.) The Jász (a tribe

descended from the Alans) are a norther Iranian nomadic people. They settled in Hungary in the 12th

century, along with the Cumans. Their one-time presence is today shown mainly in settlement names

(e.g.- Jászvásár, Jászberény, etc.). (Ibid, pp. 121-122.)

109 Györffy, György: A magyarországi kun társadalom a XIII-XIV. Században [Cuman society in 13th-

14th century Hungary], In: Székely, György /ed./: Tanulmányok a parasztság történetéhez

Magyarországon a 14. században. Budapest, 1953, pp. 248-275.

110 Benda: Moldvai ... op. cit. p. 11.

111 Xenopol, A.D.: Istoria Romanilor din Dacia Traiana. Madrid, 1953; Benda: Moldvai ... op. cit. p. 10.

1234, Pope Gregory IX wrote a letter to King Béla IV, in which he informed the Hungarian king that, in the diocese of Milkó, '*a people called vlach*' could be found, as well as a large number of Hungarian and German settlers who came from lands in the Carpathian basin. As the latter groups are living among the Orthodox, many of them are converting to the Greek Orthodox faith and are being assimilated into the Vlachs.[112] After the destruction in the Carpathian region, caused by the Mongol raids of the 13th century, the 14th century saw the beginning of a more peaceful period, during which King Louis the Great (Nagy Lajos, 1342-1382) significantly strengthened the country's eastern periphery and extended the borders of the kingdom. The armies of the tenacious king, led by the Sekler Constable, András Lackfi, in 1345 forced the Mongols back to lands East of the Dniester River. With the approval of the Hungarian king, Louis, voivod Dragos (1347-1354) relocated from Máramaros (Marmatiei) to lands along the Szeret River, where he established the Principality of Moldova. His son, Sas, who ruled between 1354 and 1363, was, as his father, a vassal of the Hungarian crown, whose primary task was to protect the kingdom's eastern borders from the Mongol armies. Beginning in 1364, ambitions for independence of a Moldovan state were accelerated by voivod Bogdan. The Voivod of Moldova and his court soon set up their seat in Bánya (Civitas Moldaviae). This farming town on the left bank of the Moldova River was founded before the establishment of the principality.[113] The first Moldovan coinage from the 1370's still shows the Anjou family crest on one side, which primarily symbolizes the close relationship between the principality and the Hungarian kingdom, as well as acknowledging its dependency on the Hungarian state of the day.[114] Later, Bogdan and his successors enlarged the boundaries of the principality, until it extended in the East to the line of the Dniester River, in the South to the lower Danube River and to the Eastern Carpathians in the West.

Voivod Laczkó (Latcu, 1369-1377), Bogdan's successor, opened direct communication with Rome and, with the approval of Pope Urban V., established a Roman Catholic bishop's see in the centre of his court, in Szeretvásárhely (Siret).[115] This fact alone definitely proves that by the middle

---

112 Benda: Moldvai ... op. cit. p. 11; Horváth: Stramosii ... op. cit. p. 13.

113 Papacostea, Serban: De la geneza statelor românesti la natiunea româna, In: Barbulescu, Mihai - Deletant, Dennis - Hitchins, Keith - Papacostea, Serban - Teodor, Pompiliu: Istoria României. Bucuresti, 1998, p. 158.

114 Benda: Moldvai ... op. cit. pp. 9-10.

115 Moldova's 1370 integration into western Catholicism was also aided by the 1369 agreement between the Pope and the Patriarch of Constantinople. (Simon, Alexandru: Moldova intre Vilnius si Moscova. Anii trecerii de la Roma la Constantinopol (1386-1388). Studia Universitatii Babes-Bolyai. Historia XLVIII. nr. 1-2, 2003, p. 18.)

of the 14th century, Moldova had a significant Roman Catholic population.[116] The establishment of the bishop's see in Siret lent, at the same time, protection and legitimacy to the principality accepting the influence of western Christianity and its Roman Catholic voivod.[117]

After the death of the Hungarian king, Louis the Great, the influence of Poland gradually grew from 1382 in this region East of the Carpathians. Sigismund of Luxemburg shortly managed to ascend the Hungarian throne but was unable to retain a portion of the territories conquered by Louis. The armies of the Polish king quickly occupied Volhinia, situated between Poland and Moldova. In this new political situation, Peter I. (1377-1392), Laczkó's successor, now oriented Moldova more towards Poland and in 1387 in Lemberg (Lvov) accepted the over-lordship of Vladislav Jagello, crowned the previous year. This political move was bolstered by the fact that the important commercial route linking the Black and Baltic Seas, the *Via Walachiensis,* traversed the territory of the Moldovan principality. The voivod, in a move to forcefully distance him from the Hungarian kingdom, shortly established an Orthodox bishopric in his capital at Suceava.[118] Thus, beginning in 1378, Moldova gradually drifted away from Rome until, by 1412, it was independent of the Holy See.[119] In reaction to the Eastern European and Moldovan events, in 1388 the pope relocated András, Roman Catholic bishop of Szeretvásár, to Vilnius where the prelate played a decisive part in having Lithuania indisputably orient itself, both in religion and culture, to the West. The Eastern European political proceedings of the period led to the result that, while Lithuania became Catholic, Moldova was transformed into an Orthodox entity.[120] As the Eastern Church lost the strategically important Lithuania on the Baltic, it tried all the more to solidify its power in Moldova. As a result, Constantinople lent its support to the Dragos family over the heirs of voivod Bogdan. Interestingly, the Hungarian Sigismund also gave preference to the Dragos family in his plans for Moldova, while building cordial relations with Byzantium.[121]

The independent Principality of Moldova had its heyday in the 15th century when its former subservient role to the Hungarian kingdom was

---

116 Papacostea: De la geneza ... op. cit. p. 159.

117 To counterbalance the power and influence of King Louis the Great, the papal guarantee was far more valuable for voivod Laczkó than the legitimacy offered by the neighbouring orthodoxy. (Simon: Moldova ... op. cit. p. 45.)

118 Papacostea: De la geneza ... op. cit. p. 159.

119 Voivod Peter openly sided with the Orthodox Church in the summer of 1387. (Simon: Moldova ... op. cit. p. 46.)

120 Ibid, p. 16.

121 Ibid, pp. 19-20.

gradually changed and redefined. The voivods of the little country created a large degree of independence and relative autonomy by wisely exploiting the shifting relations between the two significantly larger regional powers, Poland and Hungary. When the Poles set out their demands regarding Moldova, King Mathias Hunyadi resolutely replied: *"Our right to yon land is the oldest ...from time, attested by the royal Hungarian seal, worn not seldom but uninterrupted by our forebears... We know from our ancestors that, since time immemorial, the voivods of Moldova always served the kings of Hungary and that no one could become the head of the principality without their blessing, and that my sire, although merely a governor, consistently and without opposition elevated the voivods into what they were."*[122]

Voivod Alexandru cel Bun (Alexander the Good, 1400-1432), for example, solidified his power by several times aiding the armies of the Polish king in his battles against the Teutonic knights.[123] During his rule, he placed great care on the economic and cultural development of his country. As its security and borders were threatened by the Ottoman-Turkish threat, he began construction of significant defensive structures. At the same time, King Sigismund assured greater latitude and independence to the prince, needing Moldova's unwavering support in the upcoming showdown with the Turks. In the decades following the rule of Alexandru cel Bun (1432-1457), a bitter succession battle ensued, during which time both the Polish and Hungarian kings tried to help their own protégé onto the throne.

In the reign of King Mathias (Mátyás), during the second half of the 15th century, relative power equilibrium was created between Poland, Hungary and the Turkish Empire. This was primarily the result of the Hungarian king, whose strong military forces managed to frustrate the advances of the Ottoman armies. The military victories of János Hunyadi, and his son King Mathias, resulted in a peaceful era for Moldova, too, providing a long-term opportunity for the economic, social and cultural flowering of the principality.

The most famous voivod of Moldova, Stefan cel Mare (Stefan the Great), ruled between 1457 and 1504. He also had to continually reckon with the potential power of the Polish and Hungarian kingdoms, his own interests in the region, all the while the Ottoman-Turkish forces continued to significantly imperil the peace of Central and Eastern Europe. With clever political moves, the voivod of Moldova sought protection at the Hungarian court one day, at the Polish court the next day. In 1459, he tended toward Poland and accepted King Kazimir's over-lordship over Moldova. In 1465, the conquered the fortress of Kilia, the advance bastion of the Hungarian

---

122 Domokos: A moldvai ... op. cit. p. 56.

123 Papacostea: De la geneza ... op. cit. p. 178.

kingdom, thus seriously damaging its commercial and military interests. King Mathias mounted a campaign against Moldova at the end of 1467 but suffered a serious defeat close to the then-seat of the Roman Catholic bishops (Moldvabánya) and withdrew with his forces. However, the military action was not followed by a treaty that significantly altered the earlier relationship of the two countries. In fact, well known Moldovan historians (e.g.- Miron Costin or Ion Neculce) do not even mention this battle among the string of notable victories of voivod Stefan.[124]

As the advancing Ottoman armies were halted temporarily at the borders of the Hungarian kingdom, Constantinople began ruthless campaigns in the second half of the 15th century against the two smaller – and more vulnerable – principalities of Muntenia and Moldova. Sensing the increasing danger, voivod István Nagy offered a new peace treaty to King Mathias in 1475, and acknowledged his vassal relationship with the Hungarian king in an official document written in Iasi (Jászvásár). At the same time, he began a wide diplomatic effort through his envoys, trying to mobilize aid in Christian Europe.[125] The following year, the Sultan attacked Moldova with a vast army consisting of 100,000 men, causing great destruction in lives and property. Later, in 1484, the armies of Bajazid II captured Kilia and Cetatea Alba (Dnyeszterfehérvár) after a short siege. In 1485, the voivod made a pledge of fealty to the Polish king, in order to secure his assistance against the Turks. The next year, he sued for peace with the Ottoman Empire, in return for which Moldova paid a well-defined annual levy into the Sultan's treasury. At the approaching Turkish peril, the Polish king attempted in 1497 to place his brother Sigismund on the - to Poland - militarily and commercially important Moldovan throne. At the end of his unsuccessful attempt, the armies of the Moldovan voivod attacked, in the rear, his retreating forces and inflicted a major defeat while still on the territory of Bukovina. The voivod of Moldova sent a punitive expedition against Poland the following year but quickly sued for peace at the rapid intervention of the Hungarian king.[126]

During the 14th-15th centuries, the Hungarians and Saxons of Transylvania played a significant role in the materialization and growth of the Moldovan town network, handicrafts and commerce.[127] It is an evident fact that the Romanian word for town (oras) was borrowed from Hungarian

124 Kiss, András: Mi sérti az önérzetet? Stefan cel Mare oklevele Mátyás királlyal való hubéri

viszonyáról [What offends one's self-esteem? The document of Stefan cel Mare detailing his vassal

relationship with King Mathias]. In: Kiss, András: Más források – más értelmezések.

Marosvásárhely, 2003, p. 221.

125 Ibid, pp. 224-227; Bogdan, Ioan: Documentele lui Stefan cel Mare II. Bucuresti, 1913, pp. 330-334.

126 Papacostea: De la geneza ... op. cit. pp. 190-193.

127 Giurescu: Târguri ... op. cit.

(*város*). The Moldovan towns were under the jurisdiction of a judge (*biro*. His authority was that of a mayor. Also called by the older title of *soltész- Ed.*), similar to the Hungarian practice in the Carpathian basin; documents of the 15th and 16th centuries were certified by affixing sealed stamps. A significant portion of the commerce of the day in Iasi (the later capital) was concentrated in the hands of the Saxons and Hungarians.[128] The towns in the North of the principality (e.g.- Moldvabánya, Szucsáva, Kutnár, Szeretvásár, Románvásár and Neamco) were mainly dominated by the Saxons, while the market towns found further South (Tatros, Bákó, Barlád and Husz) were mainly Hungarian populated. The majority of the 20 districts (tinut) that comprised late-16th century Moldova had their administrative centers in essentially Saxon- or Hungarian-populated market towns.

Of Hungarian origin is the name of the town of Suceava, which was variously referred to as *Setsch, Schotze, Soczavia, Czaczcze, Szocsva* in ancient written accounts. The Moldovan chronicler, Grigore Ureche, originated the settlement's name from the Hungarian word *szucs* (tailor). When voivod Petru I (1375-1391), grandson of voivod Latcu and son of princess Margit, moved his capital here from Szeretvásár, in a relatively short period the settlement grew into an important commercial, defensive and military center. Later, voivod Stefan the Great improved the castle to the West of the market place into an imposing fortification, while beautifying the princely court in the renaissance manner. During the 16th century, on several occasions a Saxon chief judge stood at the administrative head of the capital, which also had a significant Hungarian population (e.g.- in 1549, the city was represented by Albert Lázár). In 1599, Bernardino Quirini found 30 Roman Catholic families, in all 153 persons. At the same time, he noted that, in the service of the voivod, there were approximately 2,000 Hungarian and Polish soldiers stationed in the city. In the 17th century, the city council still exchanged letters in Hungarian with the judge of the Transylvanian city of Beszterce. The well-to-do Hungarian and Saxon families maintained two Catholic churches and priests in 1623. Later, the city's Catholic population declined when the capital of the principality moved to Iasi. Also, the population was considerably decimated during the 17th century due to the ongoing Polish-Turkish clashes. Close to the end of the 18th century, in 1775, Austria absorbed northern Moldova. As a result, significant numbers of German-speaking Catholics moved to the city and its vicinity.[129]

Románvásár (Roman) was founded around 1390, close to an older, Hungarian built fortress-church named after Saint Demeter. The first mention of this earthwork fort on the left bank of the Moldova River is in a 1392 letter by voivod Roman I. During his reign, the court functioned here

---

128 Benda: Moldvai ... op. cit. p. 36.

129 Binder: Közös ... op. cit. pp. 106-109; Gabor: Dictionarul ... op. cit. pp. 254-257.

for extended periods of time, contributing to the establishment nearby of a civic settlement, fortified by earthworks and a palisade. The settlement appears between 1388 and 1394 among the most significant market town of Moldova.[130] Románvásár had a significant number of well-off Hungarian and Saxon citizens during the 15th and 16th centuries. As an example, the University of Krakow mentions among the matriculants (graduates) of 1464 one student, Andreas Nicolaus, from the city. The taxation rolls of Brassó (Brasov) between 1520 and 1540, records the names of Hungarian citizens of Románvásár (e.g.- János, Kovács, Tamás, László, etc). Among the civic population of the market town, first the teachings of Jan Hus, later Protestantism, found very fertile soil. In 1589, voivod Péter Sánta returned to the Catholics the Protestant churches in the city and the surrounding Hungarian villages but the people of Románvásár continued to remain Protestants.[131] A document from the end of the 16th century casts a light on the period ethnic situation in the market town. In 1588, Demeter Domokos, the judge of the city wrote a Hungarian language letter of attestation in the inheritance case of a bow-maker craftsman from Máramarossziget (Sighetu-Marmatiei) who settled in Románvásár: *"We of Romanwassar, living in the country of Moldvaj, Magyars,Vlahs and Saxons, express our thanks ... Datum Roman Wassarii, in festo Joannis Baptiste. Anno 1588. ...*[132] *("Mi romanwassariak, az moldwaij országban lakozandók, magyarok, oláhok és szászok, adunk tudtára köszönetünk és szolgálatunk utána minden rendbéli népeknek, bíráknak és polgároknak, kiknek illik, hogy ez jámbor személ, az Igijárto Gergel jöt mi elünkbe és kívánt mütolünk az o öcsével, az Igijarto Istvánval, hogy mi pecsétünk alat adnánk egy levelet ti kegyelmetekhez, mivelhogy az mi várassbéli emberünknek, az Igijarto Istvánnak az o atyjától maradot örökségben része vagyon itten Szigethen, Maramarosban, úgy mit az o két bátyjának? az Thörök Jánosnak és az Igijárto Gergelnek egyaránt ...Aziért mindezek által újonnan adom levelemet az romanwassari pecsét alat erossítvén, hogy valamenni az örökségben nekem részem vagyon, annak mindenneknek minden patvarkodás nélkül és háborúság nélkül ura és bírája legyen az én bátyám Igijárto Gergel. Ennek jelen voltán testes fideles asudstant?Igijarto Mihál, Igijarto Máté, Igijárto demeter, ez romanwassari várossi népek, kik pecséteket it megvetvén, kegyelmednek Istentül minden jókat kívánnak. Datum Roman Wassarii, in festo Joannis Baptiste. Anno 1588. Domochus demeter judex oppidi Roman, caeterique jurati cives possessionis ejusdem.")* In 1599, Bernardino Quirini found 138 Roman

---

130 Slapac, Mariana: Cetati medievale din Moldova (mijlocul secolului al XIV-lea – mijlocul secolului al
    XVI-lea.) Editura Arc., Chisinau, 2004, p. 85.

131 Gabor: Dictionarul ... op. cit. pp. 224-225.

132 Benda: Moldvai ... op. cit. pp. 82-83.

Catholic Hungarians and Saxons in Románvásár. In 1623, Andrea Boguslavich noted 72 Hungarian families. By 1641, only 25 adults and 6 small children were found in the vicinity of the abandoned, ruined church. The military events at the end of the 17th century again caused significant losses to the population of the city and its surrounding area, while many among the survivors fled to Transylvanian relatives or acquaintances.[133]

Bákó (Bacau) is situated at the confluence of the Szeret and Aranyos Rivers, as well as the meeting of important trade routes. Its name, most likely, comes from the Hungarian family name of *Bakó*. Its first mention is from 1408, as a royal tax collection toll, when the merchants of the Polish Lvov had to pay taxes in Moldova only in Suceava and Bákó. In the beginning of the 15th century, a populous Hungarian Hussite group settled here with the permission of voivod Alexandru cel Bun (Alexander the Good). At the end of the 15th century, voivod Alexandru, son of voivod Stefan the Great, installed his court and capital here. In 1545, the Hungarian judge of the town (Franciscus Byro de Bako) went into the service of the Moldovan voivod. The chapterhouse located in the Northwest section of town, initially under the direct control of the Franciscans of Csíksomlyó, had a large role in the repulsion of Hussitism and Protestantism. Voivod Ion voda cel Cumplit (John the Cruel) in 1527 banished the Hungarian friars and had the monastery razed to the ground. In spite of it, it continued to function as a parish church under the stewardship of the Minorite Order. Today, only the local toponym Barát (Baratia, Friar) suggests and reminds of the existence of the one-time Franciscan monastery. Voivod Petru Schiopul (Peter the Lame) gave permission in 1582 to have the monastery rebuilt and the return of the monks. The bishop of Bákó, Bernardino Quirini found such a number of Hungarian Catholics in the city and its surroundings that he ordered, in 1591, that on holy days sermons to be preached in Hungarian, also. In 1623, Boguslavich described in detail the Franciscans' monastery in town and the church consecrated in honor of Saint Francis. He estimated the number of Hungarian families at more than 100. By 1641, Baksic acknowledges a Hungarian Catholic community of 400 adults and 120 children in the city. Archbishop Bandini noted in 1646 that, although the Romanians are fewer in numbers in the city than the Hungarians, they undertake an equal share in governing the market town. Thus, in the 12-man council of Bákó, Hungarians and Romanians were in equal numbers, rotating the official post of *soltész* (head of the council). In 1633, for example, the Hungarian Balázs Kanizsa (Conisa Blaj) stood as soltész as head of the 12-man sworn-in citizen council. The military events at the end of the 17th century saw many Hungarian citizens of Bákó, the city on the bank of the Szeret River and the intersection

---

133 Binder: Közös ... op. cit. p. 114; Gabor: Dictionarul ... op. cit. p. 225.

of important military and trade routes, flee to the substantially more secure Transylvania.[134]

Tatrosvásárhely (Târgu Trotuş) was settled in the 13th century, its Catholic population initially belongs to the diocese of the bishop of Milkó. The settlement became an integral part of the Hungarian defensive frontier situated in Moldova after the serious losses incurred in the 1241 Mongol invasion. In the Middle Ages, it had a substantial Hungarian population employed in the crafts and salt mining. The market town, lying in the valley of the Tatros River, astride the trade route between Transylvania and Moldova, was a significant customs post since the 15th century. The name of a student of the town appears among the matriculants of 1470 of the University of Krakow. First the Hussites who found shelter here, later the Protestant communities played an important role in the life of the market town. The first bible translations by two southern Hungarian priests, Tamás and Bálint, were finished here.[135] During the turn of the 16th-17th centuries, there were several occasions when the town's judge was Hungarian. In this town of mixed ethnicity, the town's judges were elected on a rotating basis, one year a Hungarian, the following year a Romanian. In the medieval tax rolls of Brassó (Braşov), the names of many Hungarian citizens of Tatros appear. An inheritance plaint from 1575 mentions a Bene family of Tatros. In 1599, the parish priest is from this family, János Bene, about whom Quirini notes that, before being ordained, he was married to a virgin from whom he had children. By 1663, only 70 Catholic families inhabit it, while in 1641, Baksic only found a Hungarian Catholic community of 94 adults and 28 children. From the end of the 18th century, the nearby Aknavásárhely makes explosive gains and Tatros lost its earlier commercial and social significance, gradually diminishing.[136]

The South Moldovan Egyedhalma (Adjud) lies at the crossing of important trade routes. The Hungarian population that founded and named it settled in the 13th century. Its name comes from the patron saint of its first church, Saint Egyed, and quite probably, belonged to the 'Cuman' diocese of Milkó. This settlement, lying close to the Moldovan and Muntenian border,

---

134 Binder: Közös ... op. cit. pp. 122-123; Gabor: Dictionarul ... op. cit. pp. 18-23.

135 Tamás Pécsi and Bálint Újlaki, both from Sirmium, studied at the University of Prague between 1399 and 1411, where they came into contact with the teachings of Jan Hus. According to the chronicles of the Franciscan order, we can thank them that a significant portion of the scriptures were translated into Hungarian (preserved in the Vienna, Munich and Apor Codicils). Of those, Imre Hensel's son, György Németi, copied the Munich Code in 1466 in the castle of Tatros. (Benko, Loránd /ed./: A magyar nyelv története [The history of the Hungarian language]. Budapest, 1978, p. 46; Szabó, Dénes: A magyar nyelvemlékek [Hungarian language remnants]. Budapest, 1952, p. 27.)

136 Binder: Közös ... op. cit. pp. 119-121; Gabor: Dictionarul ... op. cit. pp. 273-275.

grew into a significant trade center and customs post during the reign of voivod Alexander the Good. The settlement is first mentioned in a written document from 1433, which states that the goods of Transylvanian Saxon merchants, arriving over the Ojtoz Pass, must be counted *"in oppido nostro Egyedhalma,"* as they only paid customs duty on their return trip. Voivod István Nagy's 1460 letter of transit to the merchants of Lvov (Lemberg) stated that those proceeding along the trade route beside the Szeret must pay 2 zloty duty in Egyedhalom after each wagon of merchandise.[137] During the Middle Ages, the town was governed by a judge and a council of 12 local citizens. In 1547, the Hungarian judge, Antal, wears the *judge* title in Egyedhalom. The rotating Romanian-Hungarian election of the *soltész* continued up to the middle of the 17th century. In the neighboring town of Tekucs (Tecuci), Antal Bakos was the soltész in 1661.[138] Due to the war losses of that period, the settlement's medieval founding population died out. It was only at the end of the 19th century, and the renewed industrialization after 1965, that 600 Catholics moved in from the surrounding villages.

The town of Husz (Husi) obtained its name from the Hussites who fled here from southern Hungary. This settlement, famous for its vineyards and wines, had a significant Hungarian population in the Middle Ages. The town was governed through the 16th century by the rotation of Hungarians and Romanians. Although the Hussite 'heretics' returned to the Roman Catholic faith in 1571, lacking Hungarian priests, most of them continued their religious life according to the precepts of Hus or Protestantism. In his 1599 visitation diary, Quirini mentions 72 families, or a total of 435 Roman Catholic inhabitants. The bedlam caused by the Reformation was best demonstrated by the fact that Quirini could find no priests in the town. János, the towns married parish priest, who earlier became a diocesan priest [not belong to an order-*Ed.*] from a Transylvanian Franciscan monk, quickly disappeared before the bishop's arrival. Nicolae Barsi, who visited Husz between 1633 and 1639, found 100 Catholic families and a Dominican priest. In his notes, he especially stressed the hospitality of the Hungarians.[139] In his visitation diary, Baksic noted that in 1640 Husz there lived a total of 400 Catholic adults and 95 children, all of whom were equally fluent in Hungarian and Romanian but that, lead by the deacon, they sang in Hungarian in church.[140] According to Bartolomeo Bassetti's 1643 report, there were 81 Catholic families in Husz, a total of 411 persons, along with

---

137 Gabor: Dictionarul ... op. cit. pp. 6-7.

138 Binder: Közös ... op. cit. p. 122.

139 Calatori straini despre Tarile Române vol. V. [Red. Maria Holban, Maria Matilda Alexandrescu, Paul Cernovodeanu, Ion Totoiu.] Bucuresti, 1968-1983, pp. 75-76.

140 Ibid, pp. 228-229.

411 Greek Orthodox persons. At the same time, an Orthodox bishop was also active in the town, in very modest circumstances. The visitator merely found one untrained, humble Transylvanian Hungarian priest in charge of the Hungarian Catholics.[141] Marco Bandini's 1646 description noted 124 families, a total of 682 Hungarian persons. At the time of the prelate's visit, Husz was the most populous Hungarian Roman Catholic community; city governance was still by rotation between Hungarians and Romanians. The number of Hungarians living here diminished significantly during the succession battles following the death of Vasile Lupu, and later during the 1682 Moldovan peril. In 1691, Francantonio Renzi noted that more than 50 Husz families fled to the surrounding forests to escape the unmerciful slaughter of the Tatars. Life slowly returned to normal in this town too by the beginning of the 18th century. The missionary priests sent here also looked after the spiritual needs of the Catholics of Csöbörcsök, on the bank of the Dniester, as well as the towns of Barlad and Galac.[142]

To this day, Kutnár (Cotnari/Kottnersberg) is the center of Moldova's most northern wine region. This settlement was founded in the 14th century and by the 15th-16th century was one of the major cities of the principality. The Hungarian and Saxon grape growers, as well as the wine merchants, had a leading role in the origin and development of the town. The names of the grape growing hills outside the town (Laszlo/Naslau, Kevely, Szamar, Hurubas, etc) reveal that they were initially planted and owned by Hungarians. Written records have passed down the name of several 15th century vintners of Kutnár.[143] Although Hungarians, Saxons and Romanians took an equal share in governing Kutnár, it was mainly the wealthy Saxons who dominated the town's council. According to Moldovan custom, the chief judge of Kutnár was also called *soltész,* but beside the council of 12 sworn-in citizens he led, there also appeared the position of *porkoláb,* which represented the voivod. A document from 1680 shows that the rotating leadership method was employed in this multi-lingual town. As the voivods of Moldova had extensive wine-growing properties in the area, many Catholic names appear among their vintners. Several of the Kutnár residents who studied at Polish universities found positions in the chancelleries of the voivods of Moldova and Muntenia, being familiar with the Latin, Hungarian, German and Romanian languages.[144] The princes of Moldova often sent the wealthy and cultured citizens of Kutnár abroad as their ambassadors. One such instance is that of Mihály Kotnári and Salamon the gaoler, who were

---

141 Ibid, pp. 179.

142 Binder: Közös ... op. cit. p. 125; Gabor: Dictionarul ... op. cit. pp. 135-141.

143 Lüko: A moldvai ... op. cit. pp. 14-15.

144 Binder: Közös ... op. cit. p. 119.

sent in 1529 by the voivod to the court of István Báthory, ruling prince of Transylvania. Another is that of Gregorius Rosenberg, gaoler of Kutnár, who was sent to Constantinople in 1540 as the representative of voivod Petru Rares to conduct diplomatic negotiations. Quirin visited the city in 1599, which, at the time, consisted of 3,500 houses, 198 Roman Catholic families making a total of 1,083 people. The city's significance at the time is also shown by the fact that it had three stone-built churches, as well as a timber structure. The largest stone church was commissioned by dowager princess Margit. In the attached school, the Transylvanian-born Lutheran Petrus Elman taught, among other things, Latin to the students. In 1623, Boguslavich counted 260 Roman Catholic and 120 Greek Orthodox families. In 1641, Baksic noted 380 adults and 11 children Roman Catholics of Hungarian and Saxon origin. The Tatar raids of 1684-1685 destroyed Kutnár, as well, forcing the city's parish priest, Johann Battista Berkutcza, to seek refuge in Transylvanian Csíksomlyó with the Franciscan prior, János Kájoni. Many of the vine-growing farmers fled to Jászvásár, Forrófalva or to Transylvania. Its main church was rebuilt and came into the care of the Jesuits at the beginning of the 18th century.[145]

The town of Herló (Hârlau) is located in the Northeast of Moldova. Written records first mention it in 1348. Voivod István Nagy had the local buildings of his court enlarged and beautified.[146] In the 15th century, a significant Hungarian population lived in this agricultural town, whose members were mainly occupied in viniculture. This is supported by a 1470 document, according to which voivod István Nagy acquired a largish vineyard for 540 Tatar Forints from their local Hungarian owners "*Korlát, son of László, István Tóth, Staskó, Sebestyén, Fazekas and Imre.*"[147] A contract, dated 1499, mentions as vineyard owners Lorinc Karvak's wife, Ágota, the son of László Kiss, János Oláh and Gáspár Oláh.[148] When Bassetti visited Herló in 1643, he could only see the ruined walls of its Catholic church and only found 16 Roman Catholics in the town.[149]

A substantial Hungarian community lived in Barlád (Bârlad), alongside the Romanians and Armenians, according to medieval records. At the time of Baksic's 1641 visit, he counted 140 Roman Catholic adults and 20 children. By the time of Bandini's 1648 stopover, the town had 30 families and 150 children but the Roman Catholic parish did not have its own priest. Their religious life was directed by a Hungarian schoolmaster who

---

145 Ibid, pp. 114-119; Domokos: A moldvai ... op. cit. pp. 540-542.

146 Gabor: Dictionarul ... op. cit. pp. 130-131.

147 Binder: Közös ... op. cit. p. 125.

148 Ibid, p. 125.

149 Ibid, p. 125.

39

understood Latin and could read. He rang the bell in the wooden church, led the prayers, acted as cantor, read the daily passages from the Postilla (a book of collected sermons-*Ed.*) in Hungarian and baptized the infants. The Tatars burned the Roman Catholic church in 1759, which the parishioners were finally able to rebuild in the early 20th century.[150]

According to written 15th century sources, Hungarians also lived in the town of Vaszló (Vaslau). A court document informs that the town was represented by citizens Tamás and Barta during the second half of the century. In 1599, after the spread of the Reformation, a Lutheran minister was active in the agricultural town. A 1589 directive of voivod Petre Schiopul orders his Catholic subjects of Jászvásár, Kutnár, Herló, Vaszló and Husz to accept the Jesuits. Quirini's 1599 report names a Transylvanian priest, Benedek, as serving the town. Bassetti found the local Catholic church in a ruinous state. In 1646, Bandini found only 16 Roman Catholics who related to the missionary that in days gone by there used to be 300 Catholics living in the town. They had their own school, manse and a nice church, which was first set on fire by the Poles, then later razed to the ground by the Romanians. During the 17th century, the Black Death decimated the local Catholic population, the Tatars abducted a large number, and others converted to the Orthodox faith.[151]

The Moldovan urban centers maintained close commercial ties with towns in Transylvania (Beszterce, Brassó, Nagyszeben) and Galicia (Lvov/Lemberg), while conducting lively trade with centers in Poland, Germany, the Balkans and Asia Minor. The local craftsmen (potters, tailors, carpenters, locksmiths) organized into guild in the early 15th century, while supplementing their family needs through agriculture and animal husbandry. In the 15th-16th century court of the voivods of Moldova, many of the functionaries, clerks and bodyguards were Hungarian. The close diplomatic relationship with the Hungarian kingdom, and later the Transylvanian principality, is reflected in the fact that the court of the voivods regularly employed clerks whose mother tongue was Hungarian.[152] The Hungarian-language letter of voivod Raduj, dated 1623, also bears this practice out.[153]

The voivods of Moldova received not only the Transylvanian craftsmen and merchants with great kindness but also the Hungarian farmers who arrived with the more advanced agrarian practices. At its peak, the principality between the Eastern Carpathians and Dniester River sought to

---

150 Benda: Moldvai ... op. cit. pp. 343; Gabor: Dictionarul ... op. cit. pp. 42-44.

151 Ibid (Benda), p. 343; Binder: Közös ... op. cit. p. 127; Ibid (Gabor), pp. 288-289.

152 As an example,in 1561, Jakab, a Hungarian clerk from Tatros, was in the service of Alexandru

Lapusneanu, and conducted negotiations in the name of Moldova. (Binder: Közös ... op. cit. p. 121.)

153 Lüko: A moldvai ... op. cit. p. 44.

attract Hungarian settlers with favorable freedoms and rights. It is an obvious fact that the Romanian *razes* 'free farmer' derives from the Hungarian *részes* (meaning share owner/sharecropper-*Ed.*). The free Hungarian town communities fell directly under the voivod's authority: they owed him a predetermined amount of produce annually. Their legal issues were also settled by him. Their judges, councilmen, priest and clerk were elected and paid by them. In their villages on the banks of creeks and rivers, the Hungarians were engaged in agriculture, fruit growing in orchards, viniculture and animal husbandry. In later centuries, the voivods of Moldova granted several Hungarian villages, formerly of free status, to Orthodox monasteries, thus reducing the inhabitants to serfs.[154]

After the death of King Mathias, the economic and military power of the Kingdom of Hungary was weakened in its fundamentals. This was immediately exploited by the Turks who, led by Sultan Suleiman, captured Nándorfehérvár (Belgrade) in 1521 and annihilated the Hungarian forces in 1526 at the battle of Mohács, in which the Hungarian king also lost his life. Finally, the Sultan captured Buda, the capital of the Hungarian kingdom, in 1541 through a deceitful trick. The western and northern parts of the country were acquired by the Austrian Habsburgs, the central part remained under Turkish subjugation, while an independent principality was established in the eastern parts (Partium) and Transylvania, which essentially represented and ensured the continuity of the kingdom and statehood of medieval Hungary. On the territories of this independent principality, Protestantism soon became the generally accepted religion with the exception of the eastern Seklerland where the Sekler population of Csík, Gyergyó, Kászon and Felso-Háromszék continued to remain with their Catholic denomination.

In this divided situation, Csíksomlyó was not the religious center merely of the homogeneous Sekler Catholic region but also played a decisive role in the religious care of the Moldovan Hungarians, especially in the 16th century. The disintegration of the medieval Hungarian state with its significant commercial and military might created a new political situation also in the Moldovan principality, which gradually became a subservient, dependent province to the Turkish state, paying an annual levy. The shift in power relations in Eastern Europe soon brought radical changes in the life of the Hungarian communities living in the towns and villages of Moldova: in economic, political and religious affairs, they could no longer rely on the

---

154 Benda: Moldvai ... op. cit. p. 39. As one example, a substantial portion of the lands around Klézse, inhabited by free Hungarian farmers, became the property of the Orthodox monastery of Solca at the end of the 18th century (Cosa, Anton: Cleja. Monografie etnografica. Editura Semne, Bacau, 2001, p. 20.)

41

Hungarian kingdom, or on help from the Hungarian majority living in the Carpathian basin.

In the second half of the 16th century, the political affairs of Central and Eastern Europe were defined primarily by the offensive of the Ottoman Empire and, secondly, by the eastward expansion of the Habsburg Empire. At the same time, Poland was attempting to create an access to the Black Sea through territorial acquisition, specifically through Moldova. The political situation of the era was further complicated by the fact that, in precisely this same arena, the eastward expansion of both the Austrians and the Vatican acme to compete. Rome's primary objective was to stem the tide of Protestantism in Central-Eastern Europe. Secondly, it grasped every opportunity to gain new converts in the territories of the Eastern Orthodox churches.

When the Ottoman Turkish offensive faltered and came to a halt at the Hungarian-populated lands of the Carpathian basin in the second half of the 16th century, the dependent state of the Romanian principalities grew further. As one example, Akkerman (Cetatea Alba), Kilia and Braila on the bank of the Dniester, reinforced in the 15th century by János Hunyadi with Hungarian troops, were quickly captured by the Turks. They had their annual levy raised, year-by-year, which increased the populace's dissatisfaction in the Moldovan principality, too.[155]

Mihai Viteazul (Michael the Brave), prince of Walachia, voivod of Muntenia (1592-1601) wisely navigated in this newly emerged international situation and in a few years set the course for the fate of Transylvania and Moldova, too. First, he concluded a pact with the ruling prince of Transylvania, Zsigmond Báthory, then, with his considerable military support, began a series of anti-Turkish skirmishes. Soon after, he made peace with the Turks but also engaged in secret negotiations with the Habsburgs. Shortly, András Báthory ascended to the throne of Transylvania, who supported Poland's expansion plans in Moldova and maneuvered to have Mihály removed. With the approval of the Habsburgs, the Muntenian voivod suddenly attacked Transylvania in 1599. In the battle of Sellenberk (Selimbar), he trounced the forces of András Báthory - with the significant help of Seklers dissatisfied with the politics of the Báthorys. In 1600, he occupied Moldova. His decrees were aimed at the advancement of orthodoxy and the Counter-Reformation, while actively curbing Protestantism. The Austrians finally had the voivod assassinated in 1601, having become an uncomfortable burden, clearing the way for the Poles to again put Jeremiás

---

155 Ibid (Benda), p. 20.

Movila (Ieremia Movila) on the throne of Moldova.[156] The cruel campaigns of voivod Mihály and the repeated raids of the Tatars significantly thinned the population of Moldova at the turn of the 16th-17th centuries, almost depopulating it. Many were abducted, especially from the larger settlements, and forced into slavery, herds were driven off, and fields remained untilled, so that the population that remained was faced with starvation and deprivation.

Hungarians continued to settle in Moldova in the second half of the 16th century, even after the establishment of the independent Transylvanian principality. Since János Zsigmond, and later the Báthorys, harshly curtailed the freedoms of the Seklers, the discontent of families and communities thrust into servitude erupted many times into rebellion.[157] Many escaped the mounting feudal obligations and bloody reprisals by fleeing Seklerland for Moldova. István Bocskai's letter to the magistrate of the city of Beszterce, dated January of 1596, implies this when he calls on them to guard more closely the roads and paths over the Carpathians because, according to his information, the Seklers are mobilizing in numbers in readiness to depart for Moldova.[158]

During the existence of the independent Moldovan principality, many Sekler soldiers were in the service of the voivod. This practice was accepted by the Sekler 'national' assembly, convened in Székelyudvarhely in 1555.[159] Later, the early 17th century Transylvanian National Assembly edicts sharply forbade the enlistment of Seklers in Moldova. The 1600 meeting of Lécfalva (in Háromszék) stated it more sternly: *"decided that henceforth no one may enter into the service of the two Vlach states, without leave from Prince and country, without the loss of his title, head and goods. Whosoever goes shall lose his head and chattels."*[160] The continued devastation of wars and increased feudal levies made the lot of the Transylvanian serfs unbearable, who fled, *with animals and wife,* to Moldova. The large-scale emigration of the poorer classes to Moldova increased significantly after Transylvania's great deterioration, i.e., the unsuccessful 1657 Polish

---

156 Teodor, Pompiliu: Monarhia feudala. Secolul luminilor în tarile române, In: Barbulescu, Mihai - Deletant, Dennis - Hitchins, Keith - Papacostea, Serban -Teodor, Pompiliu: Istoria României. Bucuresti, pp. 225-238.

157 Benko, Samu – Demény, Lajos – Vekov, Károly: Székely felkelés 1595-1596. Elozményei, lefolyása, következményei [Sekler uprising, 1595-1596]. Bukarest, 1979.

158 Benda: Moldvai ... op. cit. p. 33.

159 Szabó, Károly /ed./: Székely Oklevéltár II. [Sekler Archives II.] Kolozsvár, 1876, p. 124.

160 Benda: Moldvai ... op. cit. p. 33.

campaign of György (George) Rákóczi II and the subsequent Turkish and Tatar devastation that ensued.[161]

At the beginning of the 17th century, Moldova, Muntenia and Transylvania were principalities subservient to the Turks. While Transylvania enjoyed relatively greater independence, in Moldova and Muntenia Turkish interference and oppression increased. The Porte toiled to weaken the local political elite and only backed the territorial ambitions of the Greeks. In the succession difficulties of the mid-17th century (the voivodship changed hands eight times between 1653 and 1661), various Muntenian, Transylvanian and Cossack armies meddled who, essentially, destroyed the country. Finally, in 1658, Tatar forces on a punitive campaign to Transylvania transited the territory, causing terrible destruction in Moldova, too. The majority of the population of the lowlands fled to the forests of the Eastern Carpathians; many left for Transylvania or Poland in the search for a safer refuge.[162]

The Ottoman Turkish forces fought a decisive, life-or-death battle in western Hungary at the end of the 17th century against the united forces of Christian Europe. Due to the cruel depredations of the Tatar forces headed towards Vienna in 1682, two-thirds of the population of Moldova fled from their homes. The remaining third - who stayed home - perished. Finally, the Ottoman Turks met a decisive defeat. In 1686, the Christian forces re-took Budapest and re-conquered the central and southern territories of the medieval Hungarian kingdom the following year. Austria took possession of Transylvania in 1691 and governed it directly from Vienna as an independent province. Although the Turkish forces were expelled from Central Europe, they carried out a looting, reprisal campaign where they were still able. During the course of the campaign, Moldovan settlements became abandoned, the population, which fled, later only established new hamlets in more protected locations. Elsewhere, infectious diseases decimated the remaining families. Public safety was fundamentally shattered in the disintegrated principality, robbers and thieves were active, and highway robbers preyed on travelers. Missionary Francantonio Renzi reported in 1691 that only a few families remained in the city of Bákó, perhaps thirty

---

161 Ibid, p. 34.

162 During the time of the devastating attacks of the Tatars, a portion of the Moldovan Hungarian Roman Catholics, and their clerics, found refuge on several occasions on the Seklerland property of the Captain Commander of Háromszék, Kelemen Mikes, at Zabola. The chapel found in the garden of the count's castle was often the 'workplace' of refugee priests from Moldova (e.g.- in 1678, Angelini da Norscia, a Franciscan friar, stayed at Zabola.). (Ibid, pp. 779, 790; Csáki, Árpád: Ferences plébánosok és udvari káplánok Háromszéken a 17-18. században [Franciscan parish priests and court chaplains in 17-18. century Háromszék. 1999, p. 84.)

sheltering among the vineyards and forests in the immediate vicinity of the city, in what is today Lujzikalagor. The various Moldovan and Transylvanian refugees also found a safe refuge here in later years. During the late 17th and early 18th century, major internal migratory relocation of people took place within Moldova. The population abandoned the settlements along the trade and military roads crossing the flatlands, instead seeking safety in the forested zones. The newly arrived Seklers settlers from Transylvania, arriving in the second half of the 18th century, also favored the mountainous, forested valleys of the Carpathians.[163]

A more peaceful era for Moldova only began after the 1699 peace pact signed in Karlovac, ending the Turkish wars. During the negotiations, Austria strenuously demanded the freedom of religious practice for all Roman Catholics who remained on Turkish territory. This political agreement created a new power equilibrium in the whole of Eastern Europe. In the zone of conflict between the Habsburg and Ottoman Empires, Muntenia and Moldova oriented themselves, more and more, towards Russia.

Dimitrie Cantemir was the ruler of Moldova in 1710-1711. He saw the continued independence of the country ensured by a union with Muntenia and an alliance with Russia. He was forced to flee to Russia after the failure of his anti-Turkish campaign culminated in the July 1711 disastrous battle beside the Prut River. The Sultan installed a Greek-born voivod, the first of the so-called Fanariot voivods, to the vacant throne. For close to a hundred years, Moldova was ruled by rich Constantinople-born Greek families who usually purchased their appointment, which generally did not last long. However, as functionaries of the Porte, they unquestioningly carried out its directives, serving Turkish interests without hesitation. It was noticeable that, in this period, Greek-born business and political elite made gains in the principality. At the same time, this class planned to introduce such economic, financial, social and political reforms, which would ultimately have increased the stability of the region.[164]

During the 18th century, Moldova found itself in the zone of conflict between the Austrian, Ottoman and Russian Empires. The Russian-Austrian-Turkish conflict that broke out between 1735 and 1739 honed the yearning for freedom of the Balkan people. In 1775, Austria seized the northern portion of Moldova. The new Russian-Austrian-Turkish war that broke out between 1787 and 1792 temporarily turned Moldova into a war zone. The conflict ended with more local territorial acquisitions by the Habsburgs. The Austrians made detailed maps and surveys of their occupied lands, which contained important information of the commercial and social data of the

---

163 The Hungarian communities established in earlier years were supplemented in the second half of the

18th century by significant numbers of Seklerland refugees. (Gabor: Dictionarul ... op. cit. p. 166.)

164 Teodor: Monarhia ... op. cit. pp. 299-305.

former principality. One report analyzes the demographic makeup of the province thusly: "The entire population of Moldova barely reaches 300,000, yet barely half are true Moldovan. The rest are Polish and Ukrainian Russians, who migrated through the provinces of Hotin and Soroka in Bukovina, Hungarians from Transylvania, especially in Bákó and Nemec Counties, Turks, Greeks in the area of Lapusna and Iasi, and finally Armenians and Jews, who live sparsely dispersed throughout the country."[165]

Anti-Austrian uprisings broke out in the Carpathian basin at the turn of the 17th-18th centuries. The Transylvanian Hungarian rebels, fleeing from the numerically overwhelming Habsburg armies, headed across the Carpathians first to Moldova, then perhaps Muntenia. Just one example: the Turkish supported Imre Thököly instigated an armed anti-Austrian uprising in Transylvania. His forces beat the Emperor's forces in the battle outside Zernyest (August 21, 1690), after which he was elected as Transylvania's ruling prince (*fejedelem*) in Kereszténysziget. His reign lasted for a very brief time, as the Austrian army chased his forces across the Bodza Pass on October 25, 1690, permanently into Muntenia. Pál Mikes, father of Kelemen Mikes of Zágon, the author of the *Letters from Turkey*, fought in the prince's forces and found refuge on the far side of the Carpathians.[166]

A few years later, in 1703, under the leadership of Ferenc Rákóczi II, another anti-Austrian struggle for freedom broke out on the Hungarian lands conquered by the Habsburgs. The often-outnumbered Seklerland supporters of the Transylvanian prince most often fled from the Austrian forces to Moldovan towns and villages. In the autumn of 1707, count Mihály Mikes (Captain Commander of Háromszék), fleeing from the forces of general Rabutin, found refuge for four years in Moldova, among the Hungarian villages along the Ojtoz, Tatros and Szeret Rivers. Count Mikes already had cordial relations with the most respectable Moldovan Romanian families and the court at Iasi before the revolution broke out. The voivod continued to support the *kuruc* (Hungarian rebel) side even amidst the rapidly shifting political scene. He ensured their freedom to stay in the country, unfettered passage and tax-free status. It was a significant result that the Transylvanian refugees and their families, nobility and ordinary soldiers, came into close contact with the Hungarians of Moldova from whom they received shelter, food and shared their churches during their temporary stay.

165 Domokos, Pál Péter: A moldvai magyarság történeti számadatai [The historical numerical data of the Hungarians of Moldova]. Honismeret, XIV. évf., 3. sz., 1986, p. 19.

166 Veress, Dániel: A rodostói csillagnézo [The stargazer of Rodosto]. Kalauz Mikes Leveleskönyvéhez. Kismonográfia. Kolozsvár, 1972, pp. 7-13.

The majority of the exiles were unable to return to their homeland until after the 1711 Peace of Szatmár.[167]

In the middle of the 18th century, Empress Maria Theresa deeply violated the class autonomy of the Seklers living in eastern Seklerland by her plan to establish two border battalions in Csíkszék and Háromszék. The representatives of the discontented Seklers met in 1764 in Csíkmádéfalva to protest the militarization of the Seklerland, the location of Austrian units in their midst, and to resist any erosion of their centuries-old collective rights and freedoms. The imperial forces surrounded Mádéfalva during the dawn hours of January 7, 1764 and woke the gathered rebels with cannon fire, after which those attempting to flee were unmercifully shot down. The populations of the Csík and Háromszék villages fled in large numbers to Moldova to escape the reprisals following the mass murder at Mádéfalva and the mandatory conscription to come.[168]

The parish priest of Csíkszentlélek, Péter Zöld, who organized the resistance of the Seklers, was imprisoned by the Austrians in Gyulafehérvár (Alba Julia). He managed to make his escape, along with three companions, and follow his parishioners to Moldova over secret paths. In the late 1760's, he visited the Hungarian settlements in the Moldovan principality, even reaching Csöbörcsök on the bank of the Dniester, under the authority of the Tatars. He wrote a voluminous report on January 11, 1781, addressed to Ignác Batthyányi, the bishop of Transylvania, describing the Moldovan Hungarian settlements and religious life. In the years after the massacre of Mádéfalva, he found nine Hungarian-language Roman Catholic parishes (Jászvásár, Mugyilo, Dumafalva, Szabófalva, Talpa, Kalugerpataka, Bogdánfalva, Forrófalva, Gorzafalva). Beside the listed places, he also visited the Catholics of Husz and Csöbörcsök. During his tour of Moldova, he realized that the missionary priests were all Italians, who neither spoke nor understood the language of their flocks.[169]

In most cases, the groups of refugees fleeing Seklerland remained together in Moldova. They established homogeneous settlements with a Sekler majority in unpopulated or sparsely populated areas at the foot of mountains, usually in the valley of streams or smaller rivers (e.g.- Pusztina, Frumósza, Lészped, Szolohegy, Magyarfalu, Lábnik, Kalugarén).[170] The exiles created their new homes in natural and ecological settings similar to

---

167 Csutak, Vilmos: Bujdosó kurucok Moldvában és Havasalföldön 1707-1711-ben [Exiled kuruc in hiding in Moldova and Muntenia, 1707-1711], In: Csutak, Vilmos /ed./: Emlékkönyv a Székely Nemzeti Múzeum 50 éves jubileumára. Sepsiszentgyörgy, 1929, pp. 633-640.

168 Imreh: Látom az ... op. cit. pp. 25-27.

169 Domokos: Édes hazámnak ... op. cit. pp. 91-93; Domokos: A moldvai ... op. cit. pp. 92-100.

170 Tánczos: Hányan vannak ... op. cit. p. 374.

their former homeland, mainly by clearing the forests. To a lesser degree, they settled in existing older settlements, established in the Middle Ages (e.g.- Gyoszény, Lujzikalagor, Klézse, Forrófalva), thus fundamentally altering the existing culture and dialect of the affected settlement. The new arrivals did not settle in the overpopulated Hungarian villages between the Szeret and Moldova Rivers (the so-called northern villages) and have not, to this day, established marriage links with them. As a result of the described population migration, multi-ethnic and multi-creed settlements were established at the end of the 18th century between the Carpathians and the Szeret. Sekler families may have set out from their Moldovan Hungarian villages to settle among Romanians or perhaps establish with them a new community (e.g.- Gerlény, Lilijecs, Szoloncka, Szerbek, Gyidráska, Jenekest, Turluján, Bogáta, Dormánfalva, Szárazpatak) in the valleys of the Tatros, Tázló, Aranyos-Beszterce or beside the Szeret (e.g.- Ketris, Furnikár, Dózsa/Újfalu). This intermingling of the ethnicity and faiths occurred in areas closer to the main ridge of the Eastern Carpathians, too. This is more than likely how the villages of Csügés, Bruszturósza, Gutinázs, Furészfalva and Vizánta came into existence. It is an interesting settlement pattern phenomenon that the existing Romanian villages in the lower reaches of the valleys had, during this time, Hungarian communities being established higher up in the valleys, usually closer to the headwaters (e.g.- Kukujéc, Ripa, Larguca, Esztrugár, Váliri, Berzunc, Szálka, Szalánc, Cserdák, Kápota, Prálea).[171]

As becomes evident from the previous list of settlements, the late 18th century groups of Sekler refugees were dispersed over a relatively large area between the Carpathians and the Szeret. The mass migration from Seklerland began to drop by the end of the century but continued, much diminished, into the beginning of the 19th century. The Napoleonic Wars were followed by infectious epidemics and a long drawn out drought in the Carpathian basin. In these trying years, smaller local uprisings flared up in Seklerland, whose leaders and participants most often looked for refuge from reprisals in Moldova.[172] The refugees who arrived at the end of the 18th and early 19th centuries from Seklerland mainly settled in the unpopulated,

---

171 Ibid, pp. 374-375.

172 As one example, the serfs and sharecroppers in the village of Zabola in Háromszék, revolted in 1802 against the cruelties the landowner farkas Horváth. The local uprising could only be put down with the use of 300 soldiers. After the harsh reprisals, many took to the road and secretly crossed over the Carpathians to Moldova where they looked for refuge in Hungarian villages. After the 1802 revolt in Zabola, a part of the author's family settled in Klézsa, where they still live. (Albert, Erno: Zabolai és szörcsei jobbágyok és cselédek zendülése 1802-ben [The 1802 uprising of the serfs and sharecroppers of Zabola]. Acta 1997. I. Sepsiszentgyörgy, 1998, p. 252.)

agriculturally unsuited regions where their smaller villages earned a livelihood with animal husbandry, forestry and, occasionally, with viniculture. The homogeneous villages established by the Seklers retained their Hungarian mother tongue to this day. In the multi-ethnic villages, the dispersed smaller Hungarian communities living interspersed with Romanians integrated and assimilated relatively quickly in language and culture.

A new Turko-Russian raged between 1802 and 1812. As part of the 1812 Bucharest peace treaty bringing the bloody conflict to a close, Russia occupied the eastern portion of Moldova, the area between the Prut and Dniester. The Moldovan territory between the Carpathians and the Prut continued to be governed by Turkish dominated Fanariot system, which presently made an attempt to regulate the relationship between landowners and serfs, along with administrative and legal reforms. The reforms begun by the Fanariots also had an impact on the churches. The emerging intellectual trends of the age of enlightenment (e.g.- Jansenism) primarily placed emphasis on moral renewal but, at the same time, placed importance on the protection of Eastern Orthodox values, as well. With the decline and fading of the Ottoman Empire, Moldova also saw the birth ideas and attempts that foreshadowed the civic and national freedom movements.[173]

In 1821, Tudor Vladimirescu in Muntenia and Constantin Ipsilanti on Moldova attempted to free the principality from under the Turkish yoke, in the hopes of Russian assistance. Due to personal jealousies and lacking a popular support base, the movement quickly ended in failure. The terms of the peace treaty signed in Adrianople in 1829, bringing the Russo-Turkish war to a close, further increased the dependence of Moldova and Muntenia on Turkey. At the same time, the influence of Russia grew in both.[174]

In the Fanariot period, the Moldovan principality did not have its own army. General Kisselef, commander of the Russian troops stationed in Moldova, decided in 1831 to create a 1,400 man gendarmerie of locals to provide increased law and order. His decrees were soon followed by conscription and every 80 Moldovan households had to supply a recruit. The farmers soon revolted against the edicts and especially the Hungarian villages populated by the northern Csángó became a hotbed of peasant resistance. The citizens of Szabófalva and Tamásfalva demanded that the recruiters show them the orders from the German Kaiser and the Hungarian king before they would obey. A head of the Moldovan Catholic Mission was sent from village to village in an attempt to calm the mood but the protesters threatened, beat and chased him away. The Russian military sent 300 cavalry

---

173 Teodor: Monarhia ... op. cit. pp. 303-343.

174 Hitchins, Keith: Desavârsirea natiunii române, In: Barbulescu, Mihai - Deletant, Dennis - Hitchins,

Keith - Papacostea, Serban - Teodor, Pompiliu: Istoria României. Bucuresti, 1998, pp. 351-356.

to Szabófalva on April 24, 1831, but the peasants routed them. Finally, 1,000 infantry and 500 mounted soldiers first surrounded the village, then the church standing in the center of the cemetery. In vain did they ask the villagers to surrender; instead, they grimly chose death. Finally, Russian general Bigidoff ordered his troop to attack the Szabófalva inhabitants. In the fighting, 96 died and 72 were seriously wounded. Afterwards, the resistance of the more audacious rebels was broken by pillory and flogging.[175]

The Csángó peasants were once again in the center of Hungarian and Romanian public opinion immediately after the 1844 Moldovan visit of János Jerney. While the Hungarian traveler was conducting various sized excavations in the Hungarian populated areas of the principality, the farmers of Lujzikalagor sought him out and complained to him that the lands they received from the voivods were illegally acquired by a few of the boyars through the courts. To prove their claims to ownership, they handed their deeds to the head of the Catholic mission, Carol Magnin. Jerney printed their plaint in the Budapest papers. At the same time, he posted an appeal to the landowners of Hungary for them to make available lands suitable for agriculture and settlement for those Csángó who would resettle in Hungary on short notice. The article caused great protest among the mission and they arranged to have Jerney expelled from Moldova.[176]

Hungarian public awareness during the Reform period concerning the fate of the Moldovan Csángó-Hungarians, their rapidly escalating assimilation, came primarily from the travel reports of Elek P. Gego in 1836 and János Jerney in 1844, and the answers sent by János (John) Ince Petrás to questions posed by Gábor (Gabriel) Döbrentei.[177] These reports all contributed to the idea first proposed by the Battyány, then the Szemere, governments during the 1848-49 Revolution and War of Freedom to repatriate the Moldovan Hungarians to Hungary. The failure of the revolution put an end to the plan and put it back on the shelf.[178]

---

175 Gabor: Dictionarul ... op. cit. pp. 235-237; Domokos: A moldvai ... op. cit. pp. 109-110.

176 Ibid (Domokos), p. 115.

177 Gego, Elek: A moldvai magyar telepekrol [About the Hungarian settlements of Moldova]. Buda, 1838; Jerney; Keleti utazás ... op. cit.; Petrás, Ince János: Döbrentei Gábor kérdései s Petrás Incze feleletei a moldvai magyarok felol [DG's questions and PI's answers regarding the Hungarians of Moldova]. Tudományi Tár, VII. füzet, 1842, pp. 24-26.

178 Spira, György: A magyar negyvennyolc és a csángók [Hungarian '48 and the Csángós], In: Glatz, Ferenc /ed./: A tudomány szolgálatában. Emlékkönyv Benda Kálmán 80. Születésnapjára. Budapest, 1993, pp. 305-318; Vincze, Gábor: Asszimiláció vagy kivándorlás? Források a moldvai magyar etnikai csoport, a csángók modern kori történelmének tanulmányozásához (1860-1989) [Assimilation or emigration?]. Budapest - Kolozsvár, 2004, p. 23.

By the middle of the 19th century, the Ottoman Empire reached terminal weakness and had begun to decay. The matter of the resolution of the Romanian principalities was added to the agenda of the 1856 Congress of Paris, with the western European powers shortly extending their influence over them. In both provinces, the Temporary National Assembly (responsible for electing the voivods) was convened with the purpose of the radical reorganization of the principalities. On January 14, 1857, the Sultan accepted and authorized the convening of the assembly. Each county was represented by seven high ranking priests, a wealthy, large estate-holder boyar, a lower ranked boyar, a craftsman or merchant, a freeman peasant and a serf. However, the representatives of the peasants and serfs were not enfranchised with a direct vote. Nominating meetings were held in every county in June of 1857. Roman County named as its representative of the peasants to the assembly the Hungarian János Rab, a Roman Catholic of Szabófalva. The county prefect and Orthodox bishop strenuously objected on the grounds that Rab was not an Orthodox, Romanian farmer. According to the regulations in effect, the Organizational Regulations (Regulamentul Organic) of 1832, only Romanians of the Orthodox faith had political rights.[179] The Romanian peasant Ioan Vasile (of Cordun) was nominated alongside János (John) Rab, who insisted on his Hungarian-born partner, and forwarded an indignant note of protest to the international observing committee. Although the matter made it to an international plane, in the end, János Rab could not be Román County's representative due to his religion and ethnicity. On November 12, 1857, Kogâlniceanu tabled a proposal before the assembly, in which he asked for the vesting of political rights on non-Orthodox Christians (i.e., Hungarians and Armenians), citing the case of János Rab. Unfortunately, only Costache Negri supported his democratic and tolerant proposal, while the other Orthodox prelates and Romanian landowners at first violently opposed it, then took his proposals off the agenda. The fundamental significance of the debate was that, at the assembly preparing for the birth of the Romanian nation state, the political rights of the Moldovan Csángó-Hungarians was already on the agenda, if from a faith viewpoint. They did not have any citizen's rights before; they received none now.[180]

---

179 In 1861, the total population of Moldova was 1,463,927 people, of whom 80.96% was Romanian, 8.53% Jewish, 6.12% Slav and 6.12% Hungarian. (Demény, Lajos: A csángó-magyarok kérdése Moldva Ideiglenes Országgyulésén 1857-ben [The question of the Csángó-Hungarians at the Temporary National Assembly of Moldova in 1857], In: Pozsgai, Péter /ed./: Tuzcsiholó. Írások a 90 éves Lüko Gábor tiszteletére. Budapest, 1999, p. 40.

180 Ibid, pp. 44-45. The Catholic Hungarians of Moldova finally received civil and political rights equal to the Romanian principality's Romanian Orthodox majority with the 1866 Constitution. (Cosa: Cleja, op. cit.   pp. 33-34.)

51

On January 24, 1859, Alexandru Cuza was elected in both Romanian countries as the ruling prince, thus uniting in one person both Moldova and Muntenia, a union later endorsed by the European powers. The democratic-inclined prince suggested the introduction of fundamental reforms. He soon freed the serfs, brought about land re-distribution, introduced civil legal system and public education, placed the Church under state supervision, nationalized the estates of the monasteries and freed the gypsies from essentially a slave-like existence. His progressive, liberal edicts also had an impact on the existence of Hungarians in Moldova. Prince Cuza's radical decrees soon culminated in intrigue by his enemies, who managed to force his resignation in 1866. In his place, prince Karl of Hohenzollern-Sigmaringen was invited to take the throne of the united Romania.

The armies of the united Romanian principality took part in the 1877 Russo-Turkish wars. Countless Moldovan Csángó-Hungarian peasant youths met a heroic death for Romanian independence. Finally, on May 9, 1877, the Romanian Parliament proclaimed the county's independence. The Berlin peace congress ending the war endorsed Romania's independence but awarded the southern portion of Bessarabia to Russia. On March 14, 1881, prince Karl of Hohenzollern was crowned king. Rapid civic development began and became evident in the decades at the turn of the century. The railway network grew quickly in the Moldovan region, the cities developed rapidly. The resource production sectors (coal, oil, lumber) grew by leaps.[181]

While Romanian cities grew is a spectacular fashion at the turn of the 19th-20th centuries, the villages of Moldova sank deeper into poverty. In vain did Alexandru Cuza distribute land to the landless peasants; by the early 20th century the wealthier boyars had managed to get hold of most of their arable land. "*Had such a spread (estate), the boyar did, had more land than the whole village. Waaal, the villagers all worked for him. ... No place of his own, had to work for the boyar. No grains, no cheese, no flour, you went to the boyar. Sire, I work for you! They all worked, all worked for him. It was hard!*"[182] In 1907, in North-Easter Romanian, in Moldova, local peasant riots broke out, during which the enraged mobs attacked and burned the manor houses of the boyars bleeding them dry.[183] The Moldovan Csángó did not

---

181 Hitchins: Desavârsirea ... op. cit. pp. 374-414.

182 Gazda, József: Hát én hogyne siratnám. Csángók a sodró idoben. [How could I not mourn. Csángós in an uncertain time.] Budapest, 1993, pp. 34-35.

183 "Van ugye Flamânzi, ahogy a zén tátám nevezte, onnat indult meg a revolucia. Botosántól. A gorniszt (kürtös) a goárnával szedte a világot. Hájtok, hájtok verekedészbe, hogy menjünk, nyerjünk helyet (földet)! Nekifogtak, adtak tüzet a zudvaroknak, a bojárházaknak. Világ kiment, hogy gyújtszák meg a zudvarokot. Kimentek oda, ott vala tuz, ég vala! A bojár elfutott, a ficsorok mind elfutottak." (Ibid, p. 35.)

distance themselves from the Romanian peasants' movement and the riots soon spread to the Catholic villages, too. In the stream of events, the men of Pusztina wanted to seize the local under-judge (kisbíró) who signed the tax increase that incensed the locals. As he hid in the forest, the enraged mob went to Eszkorcén, the district seat, where they seized the judge, incarcerated him (barricading him in a fireplace) and elected another in his place. A company of mounted soldiers arrived shortly after and arrested the leaders of the revolt – and beat them bloody with truncheons.[184] The soldiers tied the rebellious peasants to the tails of horses, which they chased from Lészped to Bákó, where they were given a ruthless beating instead of the requested lands. In Újfalu, established close to Bogdánfalva, the peasants demanding land were threatened with cannons by soldiers called out by the judge.[185] The Hungarian inhabitants of Ploszkucén united with the Romanians of the surrounding villages and together attacked the boyar's manor house – causing great damage. The prefect of Bákó County reported to the Prime Minister on March 22, 1907, that there was great unrest in Bogdánfalva, Klézse, Külsorekecsin and Dormánfalva. The inhabitants of Lujzikalagor unambiguously stated that if their demands are not met in two weeks, i.e., a favorable land distribution is not begun, they themselves would administer justice and take as much land from the landowners as they need. Gendarme units were quickly deployed to the rebellious villages.[186] In the end, almost everywhere, the soldiers ruthlessly put down the rioting peasants who only wanted a small piece of land of their own and a more humane life; their movement quashed.[187]

During the first world war, Romania was initially neutral, then declared war on Austria-Hungary on the side of the Allies and sent its troops into Transylvania in the summer of 1916. There were Moldovan Csángó recruits in the units of the Romanian army attacking the Monarchy who were deployed in the first waves to safeguard the Orthodox.[188] Those who safely returned from the campaign recounted with awe to Péter Pál Domokos the wealth of the settlements on the "Hungarian lands," the beauty of the churches they visited and their Hungarian speaking brethren.[189] Most Hungarian families of Moldova retain personal memories of the event of

---

184 Balázs, Péter: Moldvai csángók vallomása az 1907-es felkelésrol [Confessions of Moldovan Csángós of the 1907 uprising], In: Korunk, XVI. évf., 1-2 sz., 1957, pp. 166-167.

185 Ibid, p. 168.

186 Ibid, p. 169.

187 Gazda, József: Hát én ... op. cit. p. 35.

188 Csoma, Gergely: Elveszett szavak. A moldvai magyarság írott nyelvemlékei [Lost words. Written language fragments of the Moldovan Hungarians]. Budapest, 2004, p. 30.

189 Domokos: A moldvai ... op. cit. pp. 200, 205.

WWI: *"On August 15 – in 1916 – they rang the bells at midnight, tolled every church bell in Romania, and announced the first great battle ...When the bells rang, rang in 16, the whole world picked up, they took the youths from the church, dressed them and took them away. My dear brother, my younger brother went, we didn't see him for four years, he was not old enough but they took him anyway. Took him, yes ma'am, took him..."*[190]

When a portion of the units were ordered home, the German, Austrian and Hungarian forces mounted a counter-offensive, capturing Oltenia by October of 1916 and Bucharest, the kingdom's capital, in November. The front stabilized in Moldova, precisely in the Csángó inhabited area, where the Romanian forces halted the Allied offensive in the spring and summer of 1917. The Csángó population was thus able to experience first-hand the customs and behavior of the various language soldiers as the events unfolded: *"Here in the village they burned all the gardens, they burned most everything. They spent a long winter here. The Russians were on the side of the Romanians, the Romanians with the Russians, the Hungarians with the Germans. Then the front halted there at Marasest. Life was hard for us, the Russians took our cattle, took the horses, drove wagons to the rear. Life was hard, very hard. You could not get salt, nor clothing, people walked in mocs (bocskor). Anybody slaughter a pig, there was no salt for it. It was hard."*[191] The soldiers moving through the Csángó villages robbed the families without restraint, keeping the women and girls in constant terror: *"The poor Romanians, they fought, battled with the Germans. The Russians came in as far as Bákó, the Germans, Bulgarians and Hungarians to Marasest ... Lots of soldiers, many-many, never leave, the Russians drank, they were drunk. Then the French came! ... The Germans were strong, with the Austro-Hungarians they were strong, yes. The Romanians could not handle them. The Russians could not break the*

---

190 Gazda, József: Hát én ... op. cit. p. 42. "„Tizenötödikjén az augusztnak – 1916-ba – éjfélkor húzták a harangokat, meghúzták a harangokat Romániéban minden templomban, s akkor dekretálták meg az elso nagy verekedészt ... Mikor megszólamlott a harang, megszólamlott 16-ba, akkor a zegész világot felemelték, a templomból vették a zifjúszágot, felöltöztették, sz elvitték. A zén édes testvérem, az öcsém elment, sz négy esztendore láttuk meg. Még nem érte vót fel a zesztendeje, nem érte vót fel a katonaszágot, s úgyis elvitték. Vitték, mámókám, vitték ..."

191 Ibid, p. 48. "„Itt a faluban elégették a kerteket, elégettek mindenfélét. Ültek itt hosszú télen. A zorosz a román pártján vót, a román vót a zoroszval, a magyar a nímetvel. Sz ott akkor Marasestnél megállott a front. Mik nehezen éltünk, a zoroszok elvették a merhákot, elvették a lovakot, körucákot (szekereket), húzogattak hátrafelé. Nehéz vót a zélet. Zélet nehéz vót, dorsi (nagyon). Nem kaptál sót, nem kaptál ültözészt, jártak a zemberek bocskorokval, jártak ullian icárokval, sz nem vót. Az ember elvágott egy disznót, sz nem vót mivel megszózza. Nehéz vót!"

German either. Then the French came, then they broke them, beat them back."[192]

During the war, the Romanian king encouraged his peasant soldiers with a generous promise of land grants: *"Ferdinand, the redzse (king) said: if we beat the Hungarian, I will give three-four hectare place. Lets beat back the Hungarian, and German, and you will have land. And they broke them, the armies all ran. The Hungarian did not stop till Budapest."*[193]

At the end of the war, they again mobilized all males. This time, the Romanian soldiers were exhorted to defeat the Communist Hungarian state: *"They mobilized, to drive the Communists from Hungarian soil. These Communists overran the country, Hungarian lands, they took us to drive them (out). Emperors made agreement, Czechoslovakia went there, and we went. Met up in Pest."*[194]

Throughout the war, numerous Transylvanian soldiers fell into Romanian captivity and Moldovan Csángó into Hungarian hands: *"The prisoners were from this village, when they were fighting with the Transylvanians, the one time Austro-Hungary. One of my father's younger brothers was captured. That he could speak the language a bit, he got a little ahead. But before that, the Hungarian soldiers were mad, saying 'Hey Hungarian, why did you join the enemy?' He said, there was no other way. Then he said: Why did you come here? They said: no other way, had to go! No matter which country you were in, had to go!"*[195]

---

192 Ibid, p. 50. "„A románok szegények ok verekedtek, háborúskodtak a németekvel. Az oroszok bé vótak jove Bákóig, Marasestig fel vótak menve a németek s a bulgárok, a magyarok... Sok vót a katonaság, sok-sok, nem es mentek ki, ezek az oroszok ittak, ittasak vótak. Osztán jöttek a fráncézok! ...Német vót erosz, ezekvel a zausztro-ungárokval eroszek vótak, dorsze. Nem bírtak velik a románok. Sz a zoroszok sze bírták, hogy megtörjék a németet. Há! Eljöttek a francézok, sz akkor megtörték oket, visszaverték."

193 Ibid, p. 51. "Ferdinánd, a redzse (király) mondta: ha megverjük a magyart, adok három-négy hektár helliet. Verjük vissza a magyart, sz a nímötöt, sz hely lesz tietek. Sz megtörték, sz akkor a zármátá mind elfutott. Sz nem gyultek meg a magyarok Budapesztáig."

194 Ibid, p. 51. "Csántak mobilizárét, hogy hajtszák ki a kommunisztákot magyar fodrol. Meglepték ezek a kommunisztok a zországot, magyar fodet, minket kivittek oda, hogy hajtsuk. Császárok megegyeztek, elment oda Csehszlovákiá, sz mentek tolünk. Sz Peszten vót esszegyulész."

195 Ibid, p. 53. "Tyár (éppen) innét a faluból vótak a prizonérok, mikor verekedtek a tránszilvánokval, a vót Ausztro-Ungáriával. Sz apámnak egy öccse vuót béfogva oda. Hogy tudott felelni egy kicsit, jobban vitte ott is. Aszongya, de hamarébb máj haragudtak a magyar katonák, hogy na, te magyar, mét állottál ellent nekünk? De mondta, ha nem lehetett mászképpen. Há mondta nekik: Tük mét esztetek ide? Aszongya. Nem lehetett, muszáj kellett menni! Melik országba lettél, kell menj!"

55

The Moldovan Catholic Csángó still considered and felt the Magyars of the Carpathian basin as close 'brethren,' in most families parent saw their children off with the admonition: *"If the country put the weapon in your hand, do your duty, the emperor's, because it is necessary. If you don't, it is said to be a sin. Only don't aim at anybody with the weapon. Do your duty, shoot, only don't kill anyone! I didn't shoot anybody. God willing, nobody shot me either. They shot, passed, didn't touch my skin, made hole in my coat. From those Communists! We advanced for three days, from village to village, can barely remember. I didn't understand the language for a while. I understood these Transylvanians but when I crossed the Tisza, those I didn't. Then they explained and they saw that I didn't understand until I slowly began to. Are you Hungarian? I am Hungarian but our speech doesn't connect. Then we talked."*[196]

The battles in Moldova brought tremendous losses to the Csángó population. In reality, they were in a crossfire, as the Romanian military did not completely trust the Hungarian-speaking local residents, either. A lot of the Moldovan Csángó first saw Transylvania and Hungary as a Romanian private during WWI. There they realized that they could talk with them in their own Hungarian mother tongue and that their co-linguists lived among different, much better, circumstances: *"That was good then, with Magyars! They knew not to exchange, to steal! Had everything, all sorts of things! We are behind them by a hundred years! They are much better off than here. We have too many boyars. There, the world is freer."*[197]

The following anecdote is interesting from many viewpoints: *"The boys they were in Debrecen, there was a seminary, with many books, one went in and the soldier chose one, at random, there was nobody there then, all left. Brought a book about the Virgin. In it, it was written that the* (miraculous statue of the*) Virgin was in Barát in 1520, here in Bákó, and the*

---

196 Ibid, p. 54. "Ha a zország a fegyvert a kezedbe adta, csánd meg a zadószágodot, a császárét, me szükszégesz. Ha meg nem csinálod a császárnak, azt mondja bun. Csak ne nézz meg szenkit a fegyvervel. Csánd meg az adósszágot, lojj, de ne lojj meg szenkit! Nem lottem meg szenkit. Úgy adta a zIszten, hogy engem sze lott meg szenki. Luttek, mentek, de borömhöz nem ért, mántám volt meglyukasztva. Azoktól a kommunisztáktól! Három nap mentünk eléfelé, falutól faluig, észbe nem bírom venni. Egy darabig nem értettem az ottani beszédet. Ezekvel az erdélyiekvel értettem, de mikor a Tiszán átalmentem, azokot nem értettem. Osztán explikálják vala, s látták, hogy nem értem, míg egyszer kezdtem érteni. Há maga magyar? Én magyar vagyok, de nem talál a beszédünk. Osztán jól értekeztem velik."

197 Ibid, p. 55. "Akkor vót jól magyarnál! Nem tudták, mi az, hogy seréld el, lopd el! Zegész vót, mindenféle vót! Magyarországtól nekünk kell vaj száz esztendo! Magyarok szokval jobban vitték, mint itt nálunk. Nálunk túl szok vót a bojér. Ott vót szabadabb világ."

56

priests who were here then, they took the statue on oxen cart to Csíksomlyó."[198]

According to the terms of the Treaty of Trianon, concluding the first world war, Romania's territory grew significantly. Moldova and Muntenia were now joined by Transylvania, Bukovina, Bessarabia and Dobrudja.[199] In the country thus formed, the rapid laying of the foundations of the nation state's system of institutions began shortly after. In this phase of nation building, the 'young' Romanian nation state was intolerant with other linguistic groups, other faiths, as the politicians in Bucharest desperately wished to create an ethnically and culturally homogeneous country.[200] The local parish priests, in their 1930's reports to their superiors, consistently describe how the Catholic population, branded as Hungarians, were taunted and segregated by the Orthodox functionaries of the local administration and the courts. In February 1942, at a funeral service in Gorzafalva, Ferent Iacob, the Roman Catholic parish priest, sharply criticized the unfounded segregation and different treatment of the Catholic population, when the Csángó soldiers fought bravely during the first world war in the army of the King of Romania. Very shortly afterwards, a search was made of the Catholic priest's house, who was then charged on the trumped up charge that, in his sermon, he insulted and slandered the Orthodox Church.[201]

In the intolerant, nationalistic atmosphere that came into existence immediately after WWII, Romanian administration forced the Csángó to change their names, their family and given names were Romanianized, or translated. The bigoted public attitude between the wars is reflected quite clearly by the Romanian-language council directive, which was photographed in 1938 by Pál Péter Domokos in the vicinity of Bákó. [202]

> *Ferdinánd village*
> *Beszterce district*
> *Bákó County*

---

198 Ibid, p. 56. "Debrecenbe jártak a fiúk, ott vót egy szeminár, ahol vót sok kárté (könyv), s mikor a zember bément oda, az a katona, választott o es, mit kapott, met akkor ott nem vót senki, mindenki el vót menve. S hozott egy kártét (könyvet) Szuszmáriáról. S abba írja, hogy 1520-ba Szuzmária Barátba vót, itt Bákóba, s a kalagorok (szerzetesek), mellikek vótak ott, azok elvitték a zökrökvel Szuzmáriát, elvitték Csíksomlyóra."

199 Hitchins: Desavârsirea ... op. cit. pp. 415-421.

200 Livezeanu, Irina: Cultura si nationalism in Románia Mare 1918-1930. Bucuresti, 1998, pp. 17-20.

201 Ferent, Iacob: S-a facut dreptate. Lumina Crestinului, XXX, February, 1943, p. 60.

202 Pál Péter Domokos reprints in his book the photograph made in Ferdinánd (today Nicolae Balcescu), the village judge's Romanian-language decree, and the Hungarian translation. (Domokos: A moldvai ... op. cit. p. 195.)

Proclamation

We, the judge of the village of Ferdinánd in the county of Bákó, on the basis of the order of the prefect of Bákó County, number 7621, dated May 3, 1938, hereby decree to the population of the community that at the city hall or other public places, the use of languages other than Romanian is forbidden Roman Catholic services can only be held in Romanian and Latin.

Priests and cantors are forbidden to sing church hymns in languages other than Romanian and Latin.

The priests and cantors have instructions regarding this matter

We will severely punish everyone who does not obey.

Dated today, May 5, 1938
  Judge   *Secretary*
  P.H. Setur   *Tinca*

   The atrocities against the Csángó-Hungarians were primarily fostered and promoted by the gendarmes of the Orthodox faith. Hungarian-language Catholic publications were confiscated from many families; the ringing of Roman Catholic church bells was banned on the grounds that they signify alarm and impending peril. Csángó-Hungarians youths serving in the Romanian army were forcibly taken to Orthodox churches, to take part in nationalistic Greek Orthodox services. Teachers in their schools demanded that the children take part in Orthodox church services, that they make the sign of the cross with three fingers in the Greek Orthodox manner; Romanian principals strictly forbade that Roman Catholic priests and teachers hold religion classes. Against the wishes of the parents, clerks working in the local administration in the 1930's refused to enter in the birth registry as 'Roman Catholic' the children born to mixed faith couples, i.e., Roman Catholic and Orthodox couples. In this anti-minority mood, the Roman Catholic bishop of Moldova, in 1938, banned the use of Hungarian in the singing of church songs, the use of the mother tongue in prayer.[203]

   In the years between the two wars, the civic development begun in the Kingdom of Romania at the end of the 19th century continued. In this era, the Hungarians of Transylvania and Moldova were part of the same country, not separated by political boundaries. Through military service and economic ties, the possibility of encounter and contact grew. A large number of Seklerland craftsmen and trades people sought work in Moldova, leading to

---

203 Jászvásári Római Katolikus Püspöki Levéltár, Dosar 1/1848, f. 254. (Archives of the Roman Catholic
  bishops of Iasi)

leaps in their numbers, primarily in the cities. Since there was no border between Transylvania and Moldova, these decades saw an increase in the number of Hungarian researcher visiting the Moldovan Hungarian village communities (e.g.- Bálint Csury, Pál Péter Domokos, Gábor Lüko, Sándor Veress, etc).[204]

The intolerance of nationalism grew in the second half of the 1930's in Romania with the emergence of the Iron Guard, an extremist Fascist organization. Between the two wars, 32% of the urban population of Moldova was comprised of Jews. In this period, Jewish merchants living in Csángó villages had their families continually ill-treated nightly by persons encouraged, and given drinks, by the local gendarmes. During WWII, bloody pogroms were organized against the Jewry (e.g.- Iasi) with most of them forcibly taken to internment camps East of the Dniester, where more than 260,000 died of starvation, disease or at the hands of execution squads.[205]

On the eve of the second world war, significant changes happened in Moldova, too. As part of the secret Ribbentrop-Molotov Pact between the Soviet Union and Germany, in 1939 Russia occupied the eastern portion of Bessarabia - the part of Moldova East of the Prut River - and, with German agreement, northern Transylvania was annexed to Hungary under the terms of the Second Vienna Arbitral Award of 1940. These events fostered strong anti-Hungarian sentiments in Romania. Chauvinism, bordering on harsh intolerance, mainly affected the Hungarians of southern Transylvania but also was felt by the Csángó of Moldova. The artificially fomented anti-minority feelings increased in the region during the war years: cantors singing in Hungarian were let go, families with pride in their culture were intimidated, religious publications were confiscated when homes were searched and every means was employed to force their emigration from their homeland.[206]

The local new media of the period reflects that the Orthodox officials of the local Romanian state offices grasped every opportunity to place the Moldovan Roman Catholics, deemed to be aliens, under the same constraints as the Jews, robbing them of every basic citizenship right. In one example, the local mayoral offices refused to give out certificates required by

---

204 Szabó, T. Attila: A moldvai csángó nyelvjárás kutatása [Research into the Moldovan Csángó dialect], In: Nyelv és irodalom.Válogatott tanulmányok, cikkek V. Bukarest, 1981, pp. 498-507.

205 Carp, Matatias: Cartea neagra. Suferintele evreilor din Romania 1940-1944. Bucuresti, 1948; Erdélyi, Lajos: Magyar zsidók Romániában, Erdélyben. Múlt és Jövo. Zsidó Kulturális Folyóirat, XI. évf., 1. sz., 2000,   p. 38; Hitchins: Desavârsirea ... op. cit. pp. 422-451. A moldvai zsidóság sorsát legérzékletesebben Curzio Malaparte Caputt címu vallomásos kötetében örökítette meg.

206 Tánczos, Vilmos: "Deákok" (parasztkántorok) a moldvai magyar falvakban [Peasant cantors in the Hungarian villages of Moldova]. Erdélyi Múzeum, LVII. évf., 3-4. sz., 1955, p. 85.

the Moldovan Roman Catholics as proof of their Romanian citizenship. The prefect of Bákó County issued a circular to the mayoral offices, 374.484/1942, that the Romanian Minister of Justice explicitly informed (dated November 26, 1942, file 164.495) the Interior Minister that the Csángó living in Bákó County cannot be seen to be a part of the Romanian ethnic unit.[207] Shortly afterwards, the Interior Ministry accused Iosif Petru Pal, the head of the Moldovan Franciscan order, that he promoted foreign sentiments contrary to the Romanian national interest.[208]

In 1943, Mihai Robu, bishop of Moldova, addressed a letter to Marshall Ion Antonescu in which he informed the supreme military commander of Romania that an "antagonistic environment was created against the peaceful Catholic population of Moldova, and that it was not only private persons but officials working in the Catholic villages grasped every opportunity to degrade the local population by calling them Magyar, Csángó, *bangyin,* etc. Others hold them to be foreigners, the ancient enemies of the country, and refuse to extend to them the Romanian name. Hence, uncertainty and fear grips my flock because they are refused the Romanian certificate they need to hold public office and they should be allowed to retain those offices they now hold. (…) If they dare to turn to a higher authority with their painful letters of complaint, then low-level officials, against whose excesses their complaints are aimed, most often treat them as if they spread unfounded propaganda and threaten them with the full weight of the law."[209] Bishop Robu's letter was compiled by the Franciscan Iosif Petru Pal, in which he again voiced the Romanian origins of the Moldovan Roman Catholics, revealed the excesses of the local authorities who treat Roman Catholic persons as foreigners, labeling them as 'Magyar,' as if they were the ancient enemies of Romania.[210]

The bishop asked Romania's then-leader to end the smearing of the Moldovan Catholics of Román, Bákó and Iasi Counties, the unfounded accusations and campaign of degradation. In another letter, dated 1943, he warned the Romanian Prime Minister that "the decree, which declared that the Moldovan Csángó are not to be taken for an alien element of the Romanian nation, is having little result (especially in Bákó County), with the result that this populace is continued to be looked at as foreign, and the local administrative officials are only willing to make out certificates attesting to their *Csángó origin* (certificate de origine etnica ceangau).[211] As the local

---

207 Cosa: Cleja, op. cit. p. 35.

208 Ibid, p. 36.

209 Ibid, p. 36.

210 Ibid, pp. 36-37.

211 Ibid, pp. 36-37.

Orthodox officials did not provide the necessary papers for the Catholics to certify their Romanian ethnic origins, these persons, labeled as Magyar or Csángó, were thus unable to request any sort of documents to prove the ownership of any real estate in their possession. Thus, they were effectively prevented from buying or selling any property they may have owned or leased. The situation reached such a point during the that, in 1942, those Roman Catholics labeled as 'Hungarian,' were, in many places, stripped of their electoral rights. The prefect of Bákó County, in his letter to the head of the Moldovan Franciscan order, stated, "Whoever is not Orthodox can not be Romanian, therefore you, Catholics, are not Romanians."[212]

The intimidation grew in the Moldovan schools, also, where one teacher openly and without fear said on March 2, 1941, that "after the war, the Roman Catholics will either all move out to Hungary, or covert to the Orthodox faith, or they will all be shot."[213]

Under the laws in effect at the time, it was forbidden that those of the Roman Catholic faith were prevented from serving in the armed forces of the gendarmerie. Catholics were excluded from local administration in most villages. Thos who aspired to filling responsible posts had to convert to the Orthodox faith. In one example, the Roman Catholic judge of Havasfalva converted to the Orthodox religion, shortly to aggressively attack the local Roman Catholic church and its priest.[214]

Romania and Hungary concluded an agreement in 1941 under which the Seklers living in Bukovina were able to return to their homeland in the Carpathian basin. At the time of their repatriation, 140 Moldovan Csángó families (approx. 1,500 people) from Gajcsána, Lábnik, Lészped, Klézse and Pusztina left their Moldovan homelands. The settlers were first directed to Bácska, later fleeing from the Serbs, finally settling in two Trans-Danubian villages (Egyházaskozár and Szárász).[215] Still in the same timeframe, the war years of 1941-1944, a few families of Pusztina were able to relocate to Hungary.[216]

---

212 Ibid, p. 37.

213 Ibid, p. 37.

214 Jászvásári Római ... op. cit. 1/1866, f. 291.

215 Hungarian authorities first settled the Bukovina Seklers and Moldovan Csángós on lands retaken from the Serbs but they fled from there with the approach of the fighting front in October of 1944. Those who stayed behind, in spite of the evacuation order, fell into the hands of Tito's partisans. Finally, they found a home in such Trans-Danubian villages from which the Schwab population was forcibly repatriated to Germany under the terms of the peace treaty ending the war.

216 Vincze, Gábor: Csángósors a II. világháború után [Csángó fate after WWII], In: Pozsony, Ferenc /ed./: Csángósors. Moldvai csángók a változó idokben. Budapest, 1999, p. 203; Földi, István: Mádéfalvától a Dunántúlig [From Mádéfalva to Trans-Danubia]. Szekszárd, 1987, p. 47.

In the first years of WWII, Hungarian and Romanian soldiers fought side by side against the Russians. When the German, Hungarian and Romanian forces were dealt a serious defeat, and the Eastern Front approached the Romanian border, King Mihai had Marshall Antonescu, the supreme commander of Romanian forces, arrested and the country unexpectedly withdrew from the war waged against the Soviet Union, turning its army against its former allies (Germany and Hungary). Romanian forces soon marched into Northern Transylvania and took part in the expulsion of German troops from Hungary and Slovakia. A large number of Moldovan Hungarians fought in the units of the Romanian army on the territories of Transylvania and Hungary where, due to the events of the war, they came into close contact with the core block of Hungarians.[217]

Even though Romania fought on the side of the Russian army in the closing months of the second world war, the Soviet Union, under Stalin, still treated it as a belligerent and conquered country. The new leaders appointed shortly after were all Communists. The Russian military command, headquartered in Bákó, announced to the local Romanian authorities at the end of 1944 that it was their intention to deport the Catholic population of Moldova to the Soviet Union because they were 'Hungarians'. The head of the Moldovan Franciscan order wrote a letter first to Andrea Cassulo, papal nuncio, on January 18, 1945, then to the Interior Minister, on January 20, reporting that the Russian and Romanian parties held a meeting in the city of Bákó to discuss the deportation of the Moldovan Catholic Hungarians.[218] The Romanian Interior Ministry reply to the Franciscan, dated January 28, no. 1505, tried to settle the nervous tension by stating that they were not planning the deportation of the population. The papal nuncio also tried to bring calm by reasoning, in his letter dated March 17, no. 11769, that the Allied Powers monitoring Romania have no knowledge whatsoever that the Hungarian-origin population of Moldova was threatened by deportation to the Soviet Union. In his letter dated April 10, 1945, Iosif Petru Pal informs the nuncio that he was visited at the end of February by the Bolshevik prefect of Bákó County who reiterated the news that the Russians are, indeed, planning the abduction of the Moldovan Roman Catholic Hungarians to Russia.[219] The mutual plan of the Romanian and Russian authorities to forcibly deport the Moldovan Roman Catholic Hungarian communities to Russia did not, in the end, come to pass. The Moldovan Roman Catholic Church had a significant role in early 1945 in preventing the ethnic cleansing planned by the Soviet Union.

---

217 Hitchins: Desavârsirea ... op. cit. pp. 452-480.

218 Cosa: Cleja, op. cit. pp. 37, 180-186.

219 Ibid, pp. 37-38.

To build its popularity, the Groza government distributed land from the large estates of civil and church (mainly monasteries) properties to the poorer families. Many Csángó families were left out of the land redistribution because of their Hungarian origins and the protesters were threatened with deportation to the Soviet Union, after the Saxons and the Schwabs. The Romanian Communist authority, as soon as its power was secure, nationalized the industrial plants in 1948 and declared war in 1949 on the well-to-do rural farming families. They were labeled, after the Soviet model, as kulaks, stripped of their land, turned out of their homes, then banished to distant, desolate areas for forced labor.

In 1946-1947, Moldova was struck with such a severe drought that the entire crop of grains, vegetables and fruits were lost. The grass and hay fields dried out completely; farmers had to slaughter their animals due to lack of winter-feed. In these impossible circumstances, many starving families left their homeland, seeking refuge in the Banate or Transylvania, which was not struck by as long a drought.

There were families who wanted to emigrate directly to Hungary. Their resolve was strengthened by the Csángó example of 1940-41. A few of them managed to slip back to their old villages after the war's end and related that the Bukovina Seklers and Csángó were given the lands of the rich Schwabs deported from Trans-Danubia. The Hungarian Foreign Ministry received information in 1946 that a segment of the Csángó population would be quite willing to relocate to Hungary. Budapest did not encourage the acceptance of the Moldovans for fear of creating a precedent that the Romanians can later cite and, as part of a 'Hungarian cleansing' action, drive hundreds of thousands of Northern-Transylvanian Hungarians out of their homeland. Thus, many Moldovan Csángó were unable to grasp why the Hungarian consulate in Bucharest firmly refused their requests for emigration, even though they were requesting unification with their families who left in 1940-41. Countless families bribed the Romanian authorities to obtain a visa under family unification. Others chose the (extremely dangerous) option of illegally crossing the Romanian-Hungarian border. The situation was complicated by the contrary stand taken on Csángó emigration by the Romanian authorities involved: often discouraged, other times, the process was encouraged. In 1947, for example, the Romanian Interior Ministry granted unilateral exit permits to several hundred Moldovan families. They, in possession of the document, sold all their belongings, renounced their Romanian citizenship and only at the Romanian-Hungarian border crossing did they come to the realization that they cannot enter Hungary without proper entry papers. At the border crossing of Kürtös, close to Arad, they waited for months – without food, money or shelter – for the opportunity to cross to the other side. A few families managed, somehow, but most returned to their village as dejected paupers.[220]

The majority of the Moldovan Csángó came mainly from Gajcsána, Gyoszén, Klézse, Lábnik, Lészped, Pusztina between 1945-47, places from where many had already left after the Second Vienna Arbitral Award. The Settlement Office, headed by György Bodor, directed the resettlement to four Trans-Danubian settlements (Egyházaskozár, Szárász, Mekényes and Bikal) where a total of 724 Moldovan Csángó found a home. Their integration, however, was not smooth. Too many Moldovan families had to live under the same roof as the Schwab family waiting to be resettled to Germany. The Trans-Danubian villages were not only home (beside the few remaining Schwab families) to the Bukovia Seklers and Moldovan Csángó but also to Hungarian refugees from Bosnia, Transylvania, Slavonia and Slovakia. The arrivals from the disparate regions represented large social and cultural differences, while the 'class war' Communist propaganda created numerous artificial tensions. The greatest hardship for the Moldovan Csángó who finally found homes in Trans-Danubia was the fact that the border between Hungary and Romania was closed to traffic until 1989. Thus, those who managed to leave were unable to see relatives for decades, could not visit for significant family events (births, weddings, funerals).[221]

In the years following WWII, before the signing of the peace treaties, the Romanian Communists, who came to power with the help of the Soviet Union, temporarily shared power with left-wing Hungarian political parties, in an effort to give themselves a democratic impression and reputation. Nándor Czikó, leftist activist of the Hungarian People's Alliance of Romania /HPAR/ (Magyar Népi Szövetség) and counselor of the Minorities Ministry in Bucharest, and Árpád Antal, member of the Móricz Zsigmond Kollégium of Cluj, made a visit in 1946 to the Moldovan Csángó settlements to make an on-the-spot assessment of the situation of the Csángó-Hungarians.[222]

---

220 Vincze: Csángósors ... op. cit. pp. 203-205; Vincze: Asszimiláció ... op. cit. pp. 37-42.

221 Laczkó, Mihály: A Magyarországon megtelepedett csángók [The Csángó settlers in Hungary], In: Pozsony, Ferenc /ed./: Csángósors. Moldvai csángók a változó idokben. Budapest, 1999, pp. 193-202.

222 The Romanian-language version of the report to HPAR of Árpád Antal's Moldovan trip, between August 15-19, 1946, was published recently. It was in the Romanian Secret Service Cluj Archives. It location signals that the state security agencies looked with suspicion at any signs of organization in the Hungarian communities of Moldova, deeming it to be a chauvinistic and irredentist activity. (Nastasa, Lucian /ed./: Minoritati etnoculturale. Marturii documentare. Maghiarii din România (1945-1955). [Volum editat de Andreea Andreescu, Lucian Nastasa, Andrea Varga.] Cluj, 2002, pp. 438-444.)

The Alliance, in reality, made the religious and educational issues of the Csángó a plank in its election campaign and gave the impression of full support for religious activities. Immediately after Czikó's 1946 visit, a hundred Hungarian-language prayer books were sent out to Moldova. "The sending of the prayer books to Bákó County is the beginning of the enlightening work, which the HPAR, in unison with the understanding minority policies of the Groza government, wishes to forward to the forsaken Hungarians of Moldova, to enable a cultural flowering through the mother tongue."[223] Gyárfás Kurkó, national president of HPAR, stated in Csíkszereda "the welfare of the Moldovan Hungarians is a core concern of HPAR."[224] As part of this sham politics, it 'generously' paid the travel expenses of Moldovans going on the pilgrimage to the icon of the Virgin of Csíksomlyó on the Feast of the Pentecost – on the condition that they become HPAR members. The result of this vague situation was that in many villages, the local organizers of the pilgrimage were named as the village presidents of HPAR, now openly leftist and thus anti-Church. This action was doomed to failure from the start, as this left-wing political alliance, with its openly avowed and broadcast anti-clericalism, did nothing to raise the status of the Hungarian language that was banned from church liturgy. At the same time, the Csángó farmers clearly saw that the Alliance was in direct opposition to the Roman Catholic Church.[225]

Nándor Czikó made another tour of Moldova in the summer of 1947. During his visit, the local chapters of HPAR were established in Lészped, Újfalu and Klézse. In many places, people joined with enthusiasm as HPAR, at the time, openly demanded the use of Hungarian in church liturgy and the schools. The Romanian Communist Party /RCP/ initially tolerated the Moldovan agitation of HPAR as its demands for the use of Hungarian in churches served well the Party's hardening stand towards the 'reactionary clergy.' They permitted the use of Hungarian in education only to erase illiteracy in the Csángó community, after which, with more effective Communist methods, they would be able to spread leftist ideological propaganda. As the RCP consolidated its power, the center in Bucharest attacked with increasing vigor, after 1947, the Alliance's welfare protection actions in Moldova.[226]

In the fall of 1947, Nándor Czikó again went to Moldova where he made preparations for the establishment of the network of Hungarian schools. The Romanian Education Ministry sent a Hungarian superintendent

223 Népi Egység, 1946. szeptember 30; Vincze: Csángósors ... op. cit. p. 205.

224 Vincze: Csángósors ... op. cit. p. 205.

225 Tánczos: "Deákok" ... op. cit. p. 98.

226 Vincze: Csángósors ... op. cit. p. 206.

at the beginning of the 1947-48 school year who surveyed the number of school aged Hungarian children in every village and the buildings available. Initially, eight teaching positions were created, staffed by volunteer Transylvanian Hungarian teachers. In September of 1949, Hungarian-language instruction began in 24 elementary schools. In 1951, 35 lower elementary schools (grades 1 to 4), and for full elementary Hungarian schools were operating, as well as Hungarian kindergartens in 10 Csángó villages. By 1952, Hungarian schools were established in 35 villages in Bákó County. By comparison, in the same year, Szabófalva in Román County and Vizantea in Vrancea County had no Hungarian-language educational institutions.

The creation of the Hungarian-language school and education network met with strong opposition in Moldova, primarily from the local Roman Catholic priests, who fanned the attitudes. They preached from pulpits that "Hungarian is the Devil's language" and anyone who uses it will certainly go to Hell. They accused the Hungarian teachers of being in the service of the Communists, of being atheists and undermining the values of the Church. The Romanian teachers were in sharp opposition with the worry that, if all the children switch over to the Hungarian schools, they will be left without job and income. It is a self-evident fact that while 12 students were enrolled in the Hungarian facility of Lujzikalagor, at the same time there were 399 in the Romanian institution. Until the new educational law of 1948, the Hungarian schools of Moldova belonged to the district of Háromszék. Afterwards, a separate Hungarian department was established in the Bákó County educational district for their co-ordination.[227]

The Hungarian schools of Moldova were faced with many difficulties, first and foremost of which was the lack of appropriate infrastructure. The Csángó villages all lacked buildings suitable for educational use. In many settlements (e.g.- Lészped), the community got together and, in a short time, raised a new building to be used by the students. In spite of central permission to proceed, local administrations did everything in their power to prevent effective educational activities from taking place, treating the Hungarian schools shoddily. In winter, for example, they did not provide fuel (firewood) for the schools; in the 'Csángó' boarding school set up in Lujzikalagor, three or four children would share a bed. Apart from the financial difficulties, the greatest problem was staffing. While in the first year teachers were chosen from among volunteers, later 'class enemy' persons, mainly teachers of rich middle class or kulak families, were 'exiled' to Moldova. Those teachers who were exiled did everything they could to return to their homelands as soon as possible, others were deterred by the crushing poverty. They attempted to address the teacher shortage in 1951-52

---

227 Ibid, p. 206-207.

66

by selecting 25 Csángó youths and sending them to Székelyudvarhely for eight months to be trained. A significant portion of the teachers arriving from Transylvania (especially from the homogeneous Hungarian Seklerland) to Moldova were unfamiliar with the Romanian language and hence were unable to effectively communicate with the local officials. Furthermore, some instructors in the Hungarian schools were of poor education, many being unfamiliar with basic grammar rules. The tension between the Hungarian teachers was raised to boiling point by the 'class distinctions' of the period, which poisoned the relations between persons of 'proletarian' and 'wealthy' family background. There were other, internal, reasons against the wide spread blossoming of Hungarian language education. The Romanian national assimilation efforts begun in the middle of the 19th century have, in the meantime, reached their stated goals, came to fruition. In Csángó villages where Hungarian was used exclusively in the home, many parents refrained or avoided the Hungarian language education.

Beginning in the spring of 1953, Hungarians were systematically excluded from the central corridors of the Romanian Communist power sphere. The process escalated and came to its conclusion after the death of Stalin (March 5, 1953) when the anti-minority and intolerance of Romanian ethnic policies came to resemble, more and more, the pre-WWII Fascist system. Following central orders, HPAR decided in March of 1953 to dissolve itself,[228] while by the fall, the Hungarian department of Bákó educational district and all the Moldovan Hungarian schools (with the exception of those in Lészped and Gyimesbükk) were closed. In several Csángó villages, the resistance and will of the locals was only overcome with serious threats. In Klézse, for instance, the Roman Catholic priest went from house to house, accompanied by two armed gendarmes, and had the parents sign a petition that they 'voluntarily' asked for an end to the Hungarian school and education.[229]

The Romanian political elite tried to avoid, head off, open conflicts with its national minorities immediately after the Hungarian Revolution of 1956. To this end, László Bányai was appointed to be the president of the Education Ministry's minority department, who immediately suggested the teaching of Hungarian (as a language) in the Romanian schools of Csángó Moldova (e.g.- Szolohegy, Bohána, Diószén, Liliecs, Pusztina, Magyarfalu, Külso-Rekecsin). At the same time, Hungarian classes were begun in the Lészped elementary school and the Bákó teachers college. These initiatives, however, existed for only a short time as all the Hungarian schools were forcibly closed in the Csángó villages in the 1958-59 school year (the same year that the Hungarian Bolyai University of the Arts and Sciences of Cluj

---

228 Nastasa: Minoritati ... op. cit. p. 870.

229 Vincze: Csángósors ... op. cit. pp. 208-209.

was absorbed into the Romanian higher educational system, on direct orders of Nicolae Ceausescu and Ion Iliescu).[230]

The Hungarian language education begun and organized by HPAR in Moldova, in spite of the noted deficiencies, had positive long-term effects. The elementary school level public education of children in the Hungarian language significantly raised the worth and prestige of the mother tongue in the Csángó villages. The Hungarian educators active in Bákó County, at the same time, also actively contributed to adult literacy. In the decades following WWII, 50% of the adult population of the Csángó villages could neither read, nor write. The Transylvanian teachers started cultural groups in many settlements and those groups performed with great success in the various county and national events and competitions in the fields of Csángó-Hungarian folk song, folk dance and theatre.[231] The older folk still recall with pride the thrill it was for them to freely appear with their Hungarian songs, dressed in their distinctive costumes, at public events in the city of Bákó. Although HPAR was organized along clearly defined ideological and political lines, based on external directives, it was a never-before-seen unique form of local self-organization and association. This openly Hungarian oriented organization, with its aim to protect specific interests, managed to lay the foundation of many village schools and cultural centers. Besides organizing education in the mother tongue, it also contributed significantly to the growth of Hungarian language culture, based on folk poetry.

The leader of the Romanian Communist Party, Gheorghe Gheorghiu Dej, had a separate program developed in the 1950's for the industrialization and urban development of the backward and over-populated Moldovan region. Soon, the hydro-electric station of Békás, the chemical works of Savinest outside Piatra Neamt, the petrochemical plant in Onest and the steam-power generation plant of Borzest became symbols of the era. The new jobs in the huge industrial complexes were taken not only by the youths of the neighboring Csángó villages but also by Orthodox Romanians from further afield. In the apartment blocks built next to the industrial plants, the young Catholic Csángó families were intentionally mingled with the Orthodox Romanian families.

Between 1949 and 1962, the better off farming families of Romania were stripped of their lands, putting them into impossible situations: first forced to deliver impossible quotas of produce, then having their lands nationalized, finally deported to the distant and inhospitable regions of Dobrudja and Baragan, where they were forced into doing inhuman labor. The kulakization process affected primarily the well-to-do population in the

---

230 Ibid, pp. 209-210.

231 Vincze: Asszimiláció ... op. cit. pp. 356-360.

Hungarian villages around Románvásár. Only there were a number of prosperous Csángó families with significant wealth and properties.

The forced collectivization of 1962 also stripped the small and medium landholders of their means of existence, the land that gave meaning to their lives. The population of the Csángó villages was degraded to becoming laborers in the Stalinist collectives and state farms. After the forceful collectivization, only members of the older generation remained in the villages; middle-aged males began to commute daily to the nearby industrial centers. Also, the younger generation was no longer satisfied with the poorly paid agricultural jobs, preferring instead to gravitate to more attractive urban industrial jobs. On finishing their elementary education, they immediately left their villages and enrolled in technical schools in Moldovan or Transylvanian cities. There, on completion of their studies, they found jobs and settled down, starting families and establishing homes.

Nicolae Ceausescu took over the leadership of the RCP after 1965. He announced shortly the accelerated development of cities and the industrialization of backward regions. In the areas settled by the Csángó, historical city centers were ringed by huge swaths of apartment blocks, the outskirts of Catholic villages saw the construction of energy guzzling, environment polluting, vast industrial complexes.

The targets of migration of the younger generation were not only the cities of Moldova and Muntenia. After 1968, many enrolled in technical schools in Transylvania's smaller cities with a Hungarian majority. There, as 'Romanians' from Moldova, they were able to get a residence relatively quickly, and thus start a family. The identity of the young Csángó, settling in Seklerland, was defined by several factors. Since the Ceausescu regime encouraged and supported the settling of young Romanians in the homogeneous Transylvanian Hungarian zones, the interests of the Moldovan Csángó furthered their assimilation into the Transylvanian Romanians. Amid the serious consumer distribution difficulties, their only access to the material goods offered by the state depended on their declaring themselves to be Romanian in official events, or in front of co-workers. Due to this, the young Seklers made use of exclusionary techniques, in schools and factories, against these poverty struck Csángó who spoke, to them, a strange, archaic Hungarian dialect. Those arriving from Moldova did not speak fluently the Hungarian spoken in Transylvania (which they did not really accept as a 'real' dialect) and with their archaic linguistic elements, and Romanian expressions, could not effectively communicate with people, either at work or in private. Their external contacts were accomplished through a more refined medium, everyday Romanian, whose worth they never questioned and with which they were extremely familiar from their homeland. Their identification with the Romanians of Seklerland was aided by the fact that they did not look strangely at these Csángó who spoke fluent Romanian.

Thus, while they moved as strangers amidst the Hungarian culture of Seklerland, which they knew only partly, they slowly became segregated from their immediate Hungarian neighbors. As they had already felt, back in their homeland, the contempt of the Orthodox Romanians, in Transylvania they wanted to avoid becoming part of a minority living an existence of continuous conflict. Rather, they wished to side with the Romanian majority, enjoying material and symbolic advantages.

In addition, the Romanian political police, the Securitate, continually harassed Csángó students in the Seklerland high schools and technical colleges (e.g.- Csíkszereda, Sepsiszentgyörgy and Kézdivásárhely), severely threatening them if they dared to attend Hungarian church services. Those who settled in Seklerland received innumerable pointed hints from the authorities before 1989, and afterward too, to request Romanian language services in the Roman Catholic churches of these smaller towns with Hungarian majorities. For these reasons, at the more important family events (christenings, weddings, funerals) they usually settled on Romanian language church services. The end result of these facts was that the assimilation trend and process, begun in their homeland, was completed in Seklerland - with its Hungarian majority. Their Romanization is, thus, a significant occurrence in Transylvania too, even though the intellectual strata of the Carpathian basin, both civil and religious, would like to safeguard them in their Moldovan homeland or incorporate them into the larger Hungarian ethnic community.[232]

A somewhat different picture emerges in those Seklerland villages with a Hungarian majority. Those young Csángó who settled there through marriage are absorbed relatively quickly, in language and religion, into the village community, their buried Hungarian identity coming to the surface in a relatively short period. At the same time, their differing cultural and ethical value system, and the unique traditions, brought from home, place a daily stress on them, continually weigh them down.[233]

In the aftermath of the Czechoslovak events of 1968, Romanian authority temporarily loosened its intolerant minority practices. In 1971, Kriterion Publishing, established in Bucharest, published Zoltán Kallós's

---

232 Tánczos, Vilmos: "Én román akarok lenni!" Csángók Erdélyben ["I want to be Romanian." The Csángó in Transylvania], In: Tánczos, Vilmos: Keletnek megnyílt kapuja. Néprajzi esszék..Kolozsvár, 1996, pp. 174-189.

233 The 35-40 year old bachelors of the villages of Csík and Gyergyó would 'acquire' 18-25 year old Csángó girls for a wife, with the assistance of the priests and relatives. The age and cultural differences between the partners came to the surface after about two decades. (Balázs, Lajos: "Száz lejes feleség." Az exogámia különös esete Csíkszentdomokoson ["A wife for 100 Leu." The strange case of exogamy in Csíkszentdomokos], In: Pozsony, Ferenc /ed./ Csángósors. Moldvai csángók a változó időkben. Budapest, 1999, pp. 159-162.)

Book of Ballads (Balladák könyve), then, in 1973, his *Beside my new spinning wheel* (Új guzsalyam mellett), his critically acclaimed folklore collection, both at home and in Hungary. Both books illustrated the archaic nature, classical values and rich variations of Moldovan Hungarian folk poetry. Soon, young intellectuals from Hungary and Transylvania were visiting the Csángó settlements, who discovered long lost elements of medieval European and Hungarian culture in the structures of Csángó culture, held to be exotic. The powers interested in the cultural, linguistic and social assimilation of the Moldovan Hungarians soon deemed 'dangerous' the ever more frequent meetings between the Csángó and Carpathian basin Hungarians. Hungarian ethnographers and interested tourists, enjoying the traditional Moldovan welcome offered to visitors, began to be harassed.[234]

On the orders of Ceausescu, the soon-to-be infamous decree 225 of December 6, 1974, took effect, which strictly forbade foreign citizens from staying in private residences in Romania. As the dictator's oppressive policies increased, increased fines and penalties were levied against those Transylvanian and Moldovan families who offered lodging for a night in their homes to Hungarian or German 'foreigners.' At the instructions of the nationalistic dictator, as part of its special programs, the Securitate continuously watched, and knowingly prepared the minorities of Romania, among them the Moldovan Csángó, for assimilation. This institution cooperated closely with several local representatives of the Moldovan Roman Catholic Church, as well as Fascist circles abroad. With their help, it was felt, Hungarians abroad could be 'handled' more effective, should they take bolder steps in safeguarding the interests of Hungarians in Romania, including the Csángó.[235]

---

234 Vincze: Asszimiláció ... op. cit. p. 367; Halász, Péter: Nem lehet nyugtunk. Esszék, gondolatok, útirajzok a moldvai magyarokról. Budapest, 2004, pp. 429-441.

235 Andreescu, Gabriel: Extremismul de dreapta in România. Cluj-Napoca, 2003; Hegyeli: Din Arini ... op. cit. p. 14.

II. RELIGIOUS LIFE IN THE MOLDOVAN HUNGARIAN COMMUNITIES

The Moldovan Hungarians consciously cleaved to their own religion, language and traditions over the centuries. Their link with the Roman Catholic religion, which fundamentally differentiated them from the Orthodox Romanians, was an important facet of their identity, going back to the centuries of the Middle Ages.

The Hungarian monarch established the first Moldovan Catholic bishopric in 1227, in the town of Milkov, for the purpose of converting the pagan Cumans to the Christian faith.[236] Pope Gregory IX (1227-1241) first sent Dominicans into this perilous region who soon achieved, through their dedicated missionary work, that one of the most significant Cuman chieftains converted, along with 15,000 of his people. On this momentous occasion, Prince Béla, heir to the Hungarian throne, was part of the papal delegation, as was Robert, the archbishop of Esztergom, accompanied by the bishops of Veszprém and Transylvania, who anointed the Dominican priest, Theodoric, as the bishop of Milkov. The young Hungarian king, Béla, assumed the task of building a cathedral for the see. We also learn from the pope's letter, dated November 14, 1234, that a significant number of Hungarian and German Catholic settlers also live in the area, apart from the converted Cumans, whose numbers were significantly reduced by the Mongol incursion of 1241. The bishop of Milkov was a member of the synod of Hungarian bishops, taking part on several occasions in its deliberations. The first Roman Catholic bishopric of Moldova ceased to exist in 1375.[237] A list of its prelates was published by Pál Péter (Paul Peter) Domokos.[238]

The second Roman Catholic bishopric was formed in 1370, during the reign of King Louis the Great of Hungary, in Szeretvásár. Initially, it was subordinated directly to Rome but the Hungarian king held a dominant defining role.[239] Its formation was at the personal behest of voivod Latcu (Laczkó, 1367-1375) who, through his Franciscan emissaries to Avignon, requested Pope Urban V to raise Szeret to the rank of a city, its church to a cathedral. The pope soon acquiesced to the voivod's petition and asked the bishop of Krakow to make a visit and analyze the justification for the creation of a new church center. The Franciscan Andreas (confessor to the mother of Louis the Great) was ordained as bishop of Szeret in Krakow on

---

236 Ferent, Ioan: A kunok és püspökségük [The Cumans and their bishopric]. Budapest, 1981, pp. 114-151.

237 Simon: Moldova ... op. cit. p. 30.

238 Domokos: Édes hazámnak ... op. cit. p. 40.

239 Benda: Moldvai ... op. cit. p. 41.

March 9, 1371 - a post he held until 1388.[240] The Vatican provided profound support for the Moldovan see directly under the control of the Holy See, and offered every assistance to voivod Latcu if he continued to remain on the path of western Catholicism. Pál Péter Domokos also listed its bishops. The bishop's see of Szeretvásár was filled after Andreas by the Dominican Johannes until 1394, followed until 1412 by Stephen, also a Dominican. A significant event in the life of the Roman Catholic bishopric was the establishment between 1403 and 1407 of the first Moldovan Orthodox metropolitanate. When the Rome elevated Lvov to archbishop rank in 1412, Szeretvásár was assigned as its dependency. The Vatican hoped that the new Moldovan see will soon become the Roman Catholic Church's center in Moldova and its further eastern spread. The ruler of Moldova, Latcu, his wife, princess Margit, as well as his son, Petru I (1375-1391), extensively supported until 1387 the growth of the Roman Catholic Church in Moldova, and the activities of the Szeretvásár bishops, where later (1393 or 1394) the princess was buried.[241] The Holy See's last appointment to Szeretvásár was the Franciscan Johannes. The written documents of the age make no mention of a single prelate after 1433 with the tag 'Seretensis.' Hence, the bishopric essentially ceased to exist almost seven decades after its establishment.[242]

After the 1382 death of Louis the Great of Hungary, two Roman Catholic bishoprics were active in Moldova. This points to the fact that a significant number of Hungarians inhabited the region. Among the heirs of Louis, only his daughter Hedvig (Jadviga, wife of the Polish king Vladislav) played a significant role in the spiritual care of the Moldovan Hungarians. Between 1417 and 1420 (most probably in 1418), she established the next bishopric in the territory's eminent capital, Moldvabánya (Baia, Moldenmarkt). The church she commissioned in the 1410's, and offered to the Holy Virgin, was one of the most monumental edifices of the territory. It was the burial place of princess Margit, wife of voivod Alexandru cel Bun (Alexander the Good). He also played a defining role in the life of the

---

240 In the interim period, at the request of Pope Gregory XI, he also led the church district of Volhinia from 1372. Although he spent little time in Szeretvásár, he played a significant role in the Roman Catholic affairs of Moldova and Poland until 1388, when Pope Urban VI named him as head of the Lithuanian bishopric in Vilnius. (Damoc, Mihai: Episcopia de Siret. Mesagerul. Revista de spiritualitate a franciscanilor minori conventuali. X. nr. 61, 2003.)

241 According to Romanian historical sources, princess Margit (Musat) had two sons, Petru and Roman. In all probability, Costea was the father of both. (Simon: Moldova ... op. cit. p. 42.) After the death of prince Latcu, the voivod assuming the throne, Petru I, placed his country under the protection of Byzantium after 1387. Later, Roman followed the same path. (Ibid, p. 43.)

242 Domokos: Édes hazámnak ... op. cit. p. 45; Damoc: Episcopia ... op. cit. pp. 26-27; Gabor: Dictionarul ... op. cit. p. 246-248.

Moldovan Catholics. He commissioned, and had built, several imposing gothic churches in his realm and employed a large number of Transylvanian Hungarian functionaries in his court.[243]

According to written records, Transylvanian Saxon (German) and Hungarian settlers established Bánya (Mine), most likely in the years before the 1241 Mongol incursion, who worked the local gold and silver deposits. They build the town's first church, which was later enlarged by a Franciscan monastery. After the establishment of a bishop's see, Dominicans also arrived on the scene who built a new church and monastery for their own use. The medieval seal of the town bears the inscription *SIGILIUM CAPITALIS CIVITATIS MOLDAVIE TERRE MOLDAVIENSIS,* encircling a stag adorned with the cross of Saint Hubertus.[244] The mining town was not only a significant economic and political center but played a defining role in the religious and cultural spheres, too. In the early 15th century, the names of several students from Moldvabánya surface among the matriculants of Prague, Krakow and Vienna universities, and even a few in Rome. After completing their theological studies, they would return and take up posts in Moldovan towns (e.g.- Kotnár, Suceava, etc.). The Catholic bishops of Moldvabánya were greatly troubled first by the Hussites, then the spread of Protestantism. Unfortunately, the church burned down on December 14-15, 1467 during a battle between King Mathias and voivod Stefan. Later, the armies of Sultan Mohamed II again devastated the settlement in 1476 and, due to the serial damaging events, the town's eventual decline slowly began.[245]

Until the 1541 dissolution of the independent medieval kingdom, Hungary continuously supplied priests and friars to the Hungarians living in Moldova. The bishops appointed by the Hungarian kings during the 14th-15th century to Szeretvásár and Bánya in Moldova and Árgyes in Muntenia ensured that there were adequately trained priests to minister to the Hungarian communities living on the far side of the Carpathians. At the same time, the neighboring Transylvanian Franciscans of Csíksomlyó were the spiritual guides and leaders of the Moldovan Hungarians until 1574. A branch of the chapter house of Csík operated in Bákó, from where 8-10 friars from the Carpathian basin tended to the spiritual needs of the Hungarian community of the vicinity. Voivod Alexandru cel Bun had a church built for the Franciscans of Bákó. At the beginning of the 16th century, the priors in

243 Papacostea: De la geneza ... op. cit. p. 200.

244 Horváth, Lajos: A csodaszarvas monda kései hajtása, avagy Moldva bölényfejes címere [A late reference to the tale of the White Stag, or the bison headed crest of Moldova], In: Székelyföld IV. évf., 5 sz., 2000, p. 64.

245 Domokos: Édes hazámnak ... op. cit. p. 48.; Gabor: Dictionarul ... op. cit. p. 26-30.

the Franciscan monastery of Bákó were still Hungarians and thus, they were conversant with the language of the parishioners in their care.[246]

During the 14th-15th century, the growth of the Moldovan Roman Catholic Church was first supported by the Hungarian kingdom, later by Poland. When the political relations of the Moldovan principality soured with either kingdom, the persecution of the Catholic Church began immediately. Voivod Alexandru cel Bun, who ruled between 1400 and 1432, welcomed the Hussites, branded as heretics and persecuted, from the territories of the Hungarian kingdom. Moldovan civil authority did not particularly pose obstacles for their particular religious practices, in their mother tongue, or their public activities. The Hungarian- and German-speaking Hussites were permitted by the voivod to settle in the town of Kotnár in 1420.[247] The Moldovan princes gladly received the more developed, western economically advanced refugees who were allowed to live and prosper in peace. In fact, initially, they were permitted by the voivod to freely spread their tenets. In a letter of 1432, the bishop of Krakow attributed the rapid spread of Hussitism primarily to the weakness and disorganization of the Moldovan Roman Catholic Church, the friendly reception of the Hussites to the anti-Polish posture of the voivod (Alexandru cel Bun).[248]

The settlement of the Hussites is mentioned in the 1446 Bull of Pope Eugene IV, as well as a 1571 report.[249] Their exodus from the Carpathian basin took about 50 years. They first arrived from the southern portion of the Hungarian kingdom, Syrmia (Szerémség), and from southern Transylvania. Later, in 1480's, they came from the country's northwestern perimeter, from the vicinity of Pozsony (Bratislava). It is most likely that Germans and Czechs also settled in the northern parts of Moldova, accompanying the significant sized Hungarian groups. The refugees established several settlements of significant size, as evidenced by the names of Husz (Husi) and Jeromosfalva, named after Jerome of Prague. They also had larger communities in Románvásár, Tatros, Kotnár and Szászkút.[250] They had a role

---

246 1533? Franciscus de Somogyvár; 1535? Joannes de Petherd; 1537? Martinus de Enyedino; 1544? Mathias de Ebretz; 1546? Gasparus de Várallya; 1550? Laurentius de Kolosvár; 1552? Petrus de Sancto Michaele; 1556? Laurentius de Vásárhely; 1570? Mathias de Satmár. (Ibid (Domokos), p. 48.)

247 Papacostea, Serban: Stiri noi cu privire la istoria husitismului in Moldova în timpul lui Alexandru cel Bun. Studii si cercetari stiintifice, In: Istorie nr.2, Iasi, 1962, pp. 253-258; Giurescu, C. C.: Cauzele refugerii husitilor în Moldova si centrele lor în aceasta tara. Studii si articole de istorie VIII, 1966, p. 28.

248 Ibid (Papacostea), pp. 253-254.

249 Binder: Közös ... op. cit. p. 123.

250 Ibid, p. 120.

75

in establishing new rural settlements, as well as strengthening existing Hungarian-speaking communities: as in Csöbörcsök[251], Szentpéter, Szentjános and Szentantal. Franciscan friars turned Hussite priests, Tamás Pécsi and Bálint Újlaki translated the four Gospels into Hungarian in Tatros. A subsequent copyist of the first Hungarian bible translation later notated after the closing passage of the Gospel according to John that the original was finished in 1466 in *'citie of Tatros'* (Tatros varasaban /sic/).[252] This Bible translation, partly in Hungarian, was passed down through the ages in the copy made by György (George) Németi in what is known as the Munich (or variously as the Jókai) Codex.[253]

The Moldovan Hussite congregations continued to expand in peace during the reign of voivod Stefan the Great (1457-1504), in spite of the increasing attacks by the Roman Catholic Church, aided in part by the antagonism that erupted between the Moldovan ruler and the Hungarian Minorite clerics. Voivod Stefan expelled from Moldova the Franciscan missionaries after a Minorite friar re-baptized in 1462, according to the Catholic rites, a woman who had previously been baptized into the Orthodox faith. Doing so, he essentially renounced the validity of baptism according to the Orthodox rite, thus upsetting the established and functioning practice whereby both churches mutually acknowledged the sanctity of baptism.[254] After King Mathis captured Moravia in 1481 and forced the Hussites living there to leave their homelands, primarily Moravian Hussite refugees arrived in Moldova at the end of the 15th century. There, they settled in a relatively

---

251 The last remaining Hungarian residents moved to Husz at the beginning of the 19th century (Halász, Péter: A protestáns vallások szerepe a moldvai magyarok életében [The role of Protestant religions in the life of the Moldovan Hungarians], In: A Ráday Gyujtemény Évkönyve IX., Budapest, 1999, p. 167.)

252 "This booke finisheded by the hand of Németi György son of Hansel Emre in Moldova city of Tatros in the year of our Lord one thousand four hundred and sixty six." ("E könyö megvégeztetett Németi Györgynek Hansel Emre fiának keze miatt Moldovában Tatros városában Úr születetének ezer négyszáz hatvan hatod esztendeiben.") (Szabó, T. Ádám /ed./: Müncheni Kódex (1466) [The Munich Codex (1466)]. Európa Könyvkiadó, Budapest, 1985, p. 343.)

253 Gálos, Rezso: Legrégibb bibliafordításunk [Our oldest Bible translation]. Irodalomtörténeti Füzetek, 9. sz., Budapest, 1928; Sógor, Csaba: „Elszertült" reformátusok Szászkúton [The scattered Reformed believers of Szászkút], In: Felebarát, III. évf., 1-2. sz., 1992, p.14.

254 The anger of the Moldovan voivod was aroused when the Franciscan priests re-baptized into the Catholic faith an Orthodox woman who was possessed by the devil. (Gorovei, Stefan S.: Moldova si lumea catolica. Anuarul Institutului A. D. Xenopol, Iasi, 1992, XXIX., p. 83.)

widely dispersed manner. It is interesting to note that their teachings found no fertile soil or converts among the Orthodox Romanians.[255]

During the 16th century, at the urging of Bartolomeo Brutti, the representative of the Vatican, under the reigns of voivods Bogdan Lapusneanu and Petru Schiopul (Peter the Lame) the crusade against the Hussites was raised to state policy. One of voivod Petru's most important political advisors was the just mentioned Brutti, of Albanian descent, who convinced the prince to request that the pope send Jesuits to fight the Hussites and Protestants. The first Jesuit priests arrived from Poland in 1588. Their most important goal was to fend off the dangerous 'heretical' beliefs spread from Transylvania and the establishment of a permanent college. In many places, they drove out the married parish priests, took over the duties of the village clerics, said masses, administered the sacraments, etc.[256] Their aggressive missionary work was mainly hampered by having had to communicate with the Moldovan Hungarian flock through interpreters. Several written documents, however, recount the success of their missionary activities. As an example, György Vásári (secretary to the Catholic bishop of Kamanyec) proudly related in his 1571 letter to the Papal Nuncio to Poland that Mihály Thabuk, parish priest of Tatros, converted to Catholicism nearly 2,000 Hungarian Hussites in Husz, Románvásár and the surrounding villages. At the same time, he urgently requested parish priests for the care of their souls because, lacking priests, they returned to their former heretical religion. In response to his plea, the Polish bishop anointed 12 priests to help in his conversion efforts. Voivod Bogdan also saw the significance of the conversion work of the Tatros priest, whom he shortly recommended for elevation to a higher church post as reward for his efforts.[257]

The Hussite communities reached a difficult position by the middle of the 16th century, partly due to internal events. Since their priests grew old and died and since replacements no longer came from the Carpathian basin, a part of the leaderless congregations converted to the quickly spreading Reformed Church. A small group, interestingly enough, remained extant into the 20th century in Szászkút, both in their faith and Hungarianness. The settlement of the Hussite congregations presented a temporary dilemma in Moldova but, over time, the majority was gradually absorbed into the Roman Catholic Church. Deodatus, Catholic bishop of Sophia, found few families in Husz in

---

255 Craciun, Maria: Protestantism si ortodoxie in Moldova secolului al XVI-lea. Cluj-Napoca, 1996, pp. 16-17.

256 Ibid, pp. 170-184; Domokos: A moldvai ... op. cit. pp. 60-61.

257 "Ungari, qui erant in oppido Hustwaras, item in alio oppido dicto Romanwaras est in villis vecinis duo millia hominum in circa sunt conversi ad fidem catholicam, qui prius sequebantur haeresim Ioannis Hus ..." (Benda: Moldvai ... op. cit. p. 71. Cites Craciun: Protestantism ... op. cit. p. 185.)

1641 who still followed the precepts of Hus. At the time of Bandinus' visit, well after their conversion, they still sang church hymns in Hungarian. The major significance of the presence of Hungarian Hussites in Moldova was that they added impetus to the practice of religion in the mother tongue. However, since mainly foreign-tongued clerics came to their converted Moldovan communities who were unable to maintain a deeper spiritual communication with their Hungarian speaking flocks, many among them moved on to the Orthodox faith.[258]

During the 16th century, several religious reform influences were competing in the Hungarian communities of Moldova. Beside the tenets of Hus, the Protestant teachings of Luther and Calvin were also popular, mainly among city dwellers. We have reports of clashes in many settlements between the Protestants and the Hussites. In other hamlets, as a result of the Reformation, the priests simply married, started a family but retained their faith and religion. The Moldovan religious panoply was made more complex by the fact that, in many cases, the converted Hussites accepted the Lutheran or Calvinist doctrines after their re-conversion.[259]

Around the middle of the 16th century, a significant portion of the Hungarian population of the Carpathian basin converted to the beliefs of one of the Protestant sects. In Transylvania, only a narrow eastern band remained in the Catholic faith and thus, in the monastery of Csíksomlyó, only a few member of the clergy remained. Seklerland was thus unable to send neither priests, nor Franciscan friars to the Moldovan Hungarians. In the independent Transylvanian principality, the Saxons *en masse* embraced the Lutheran faith, while the Hungarians (with the exception of Csík, Gyergyó, Felso-Háromszék and Felso-Nyárád valleys) primarily followed the new Calvinist and Unitarian teachings. The religious rebirth did not, however, stop at the crest of the Eastern Carpathians but swept through the Hungarian and German communities of Moldova, too. The spread of the ideals of Protestantism in this mainly Orthodox setting was attributable to a great extent to the Hungarians and Saxons of Transylvania.[260] The tenets of Martin Luther took immediate root in those Moldovan cities in which a sizable

---

258 Benda: Moldvai ... op. cit. pp. 31, 41, 71-72.

259 Halász: A protestáns ... op. cit. pp. 168-169.

260 Protestantism did not develop a major base among the Moldovan Romanians. Its influence extended only to that narrow elite strata (e.g.- Luca Stroici and Ieremia Movila) which already had earlier close contacts with the Polish and Hungarian cultural spheres. (Craciun: Protestantism ... op. cit. pp. 194-195.) Some reports indicate that Romanians living in close proximity with sizable Saxon or Hungarian communities were influenced by Protestant beliefs. As an example, a 1577 letter of the minister of Jászvásár recorded that a Romanian youth living among the Saxons converted to the Lutheran faith (probably as a result of mixed marriage). (Ibid, pp. 195-196.)

Saxon or Hungarian population lived and which maintained close trade and family contacts with the Protestant centers of Transylvania. The spread of the Reformation was aided by the priest shortage in Moldova. For that reason, many places extended a warm welcome to the visiting Lutheran ministers who preached to them in their own tongue.[261]

The Transylvanian Protestant intellectuals - interestingly enough - did not pay particular attention to a planned, systematic conversion of the Catholic Hungarians of Moldova. In spite of it, a significant portion of the Catholic populations of Moldovan towns became Protestant in the 1540's. At the same time, the more conservative rural Moldovan Hungarian population retained a stronger grasp on its earlier religious traditions, maintaining its Roman Catholic religion to this day.

The western reformers, on the other hand, followed the spread of Moldovan Protestantism with great interest. They saw a potential ally in an Orthodox Church independent of Rome, which they wished to win to the cause of a global religious reform and the reunification of the European Christian churches. The spread of the Reformation was initially aided by the tolerant religious policies of voivod Petru Rares (1527-1538 and 1541-1546), too. Since the success of his internal policies greatly needed the support of the urban Hungarian and Saxon populace, he granted them the widest religious freedoms. Similar to the Turks, he was tolerant towards the Reformation, hence was able to count on the significant support of the western Protestant world.[262]

Later, under the brief rule of Stefan Rares (1551-1552), a virtual persecution was begun against the non-Orthodox churches, their churches reduced to rubble, books and vestments burned. A letter from 1552 informs that the voivod intended to force the conversion of every Moldovan Hungarian to Orthodoxy but his fury also turned on the Lutheran Saxons, too. He did not go easy on the Roman Catholics, either, ruthlessly destroying the Szeretvásár bishop's cathedral. His angry and merciless behavior can be explained through his need for the unwavering support of the Orthodox clergy to the uncertain Moldovan throne.[263] Next on the throne, Alexandru Lapusneanu (1552-1561) also tried to garner the support of the Orthodox Church. Especially in the early years of his rule, he began a fierce battle against the Protestant movements and communities, branded as 'heretic.'[264] During the reigns of the noted voivods, religious intolerance flared up,

---

261 According to Maria Craciun's view, the mixed (allogen) communities played a significant role in the spread and acceptance of Protestantism in Moldova. (Ibid, p. 43.)

262 Ibid, pp. 45-49.

263 Ibid, pp. 58-61.

264 Ibid, pp. 65-98.

beginning with the stripping, burning and razing of many churches, ending with the forcible conversion, i.e., re-baptism, of the Hungarian faithful to the Orthodox faith.[265] Quirini, the head of the Moldovan Catholic mission, warns in a report to the Vatican that the Greek Orthodox priests usually forcibly re-baptize those Hungarian partners before administering the marriage rites to mixed couples. Due to the shortage of anointed priests in the Moldovan Hungarian communities, many Hungarians resorted to accepting the services of Orthodox priests, which promoted the transposition of countless Greek Orthodox elements.[266]

The spread of Moldovan Protestantism was greatly advanced by the Greek-born[267] Despot- Voda (1561-1563) who introduced religious tolerance in the principality as soon as he took the throne.[268] This educated and traveled voivod was preparing for the fundamental reorganization of his country. Since he had no liking for the Roman Catholic priests and clergy, in 1562 he invited Protestant missionaries from Poland and with their help attempted to convert his own people, also.[269] In the formation of the voivod's religious and political views, a large role was played by the Protestant advisors from Poland, e.g.- the Polish Jan Lusinski (Johannes Lusenius) and the German Johann Sommer. He employed a number of foreigners in his court and founded a royal library in Szucsáva. In the town of Kotnár, he established a school, which soon became the center of new religious thoughts. He himself paid for the costs of the Latin school, which was open to youths of any tongue or denomination. He asked Sommer to direct the

---

265 Papacostea: De la geneza ... op. cit. pp. 221-222.

266 Craciun: Protestantism ... op. cit. p. 196.

267 dictus Basilides seu Basilicus Despota. (Hermán, M. János: A moldvai reformáció lengyelországi támogatása [Polish support for the Moldovan Reformation], In: by the same author: Johannes a Lasco élete és munkássága (1499-1560). Nagyvárad, 2003, p. 160.)

268 Despot-Voda, born in the Greek islands, was an ambitious man who cultivated influential people from his early years. After his studies in Paris, in the early 1550's, he visited Melanchthon in Wittenberg, returning there in the service of Charles V, then on to Denmark and, through Königsberg, to Lithuania. Johannes a Lasco introduced him into the circle of Polish religious reformers at the court of the Lithuanian grand duke. While there, he made the acquaintance of Jan Lusinski, Lasco's talented pupil. In 1557, he met the boyars exiled by voivod Lapusneanu, and immediately cast his eyes on Moldova. Finally, in November of 1561, he defeated the voivod's army and shortly occupied the Moldovan throne. (Ibid, pp. 160-162.)

269 Since the voivod gained the Moldovan throne with foreign help, he felt a great need for external assistance, not only the Polish and German Protestants but also from the Viennese court. (Ibid, p. 160.)

school that was organized along the western style.[270] Jan Lusinski probably arrived in early 1562 and was installed in Kotnár with the title '*episcopus nationis Saxonica et Hungarica.*'[271] He immediately renovated the local church and by the summer of 1562 sermons were given regularly and communion dispensed. In the spring of 1563, at the request of voivod Despot, he requested from Calvin a copy of the printed regulations of the Geneva church. To aid in the printing of the Bible in the local tongue, he invited Wolfgang Schreiber to Moldova. Unfortunately, for his political behavior, the voivod soon handed him over to the Turks.[272] Moldvabánya, with its wealthy Saxon and Hungarian inhabitants, became Protestant by the middle of the 16th century, a fact borne out by the decorations of the grave markers of the period. After Lusinski, the Saxon Jacob Otth filled the bishop's post during the reign of voivod Petre Schiopul. The tolerant stance of voivod Despot-Voda created a deep-seated resentment in his circle, and in the rulers who followed. Immediately after the removal of the Protestant voivod Despot-Voda, his earlier enemies mercilessly hung bishop Lusinski's wife, destroyed the royal library at Szucsáva, and razed to the ground the new Protestant church under construction in Bákó. Although Protestantism in the principality was dealt a serious blow with the death of voivod Despot-Voda (November 9, 1563), the Reformation did not disappear without a trace in Moldova; Luther's teachings were extant among the Saxons a century later, Calvin's among the Hungarians. However, with the ascension of Alexandru Lapusneanu to the throne, Polish influence over Moldovan Protestantism came to an end.[273]

Voivod Petru Schiopu (Peter the Lame), who reigned several times in Moldova (1574-1577, 1578-1579 and 1582-1591), with crafty tactic first removed those people from positions of power who exerted a large influence on the local communities, either through their social, financial or intellectual standing. Secondly, he began to persecute the Protestant preachers, while

---

270 Sommer was the Rector of the Lutheran school of Brassó (today Brasov) until 1567, and died in Kolozsvár (Cluj Napoca) in 1574 as a Unitarian theologian. (Craciun: Protestantism ... op. cit. p. 165.)

271 Moldova's Protestant bishop died in 1563 in the town of Galac, probably from poisoning, while touring the country in the company of voivod Despot-Voda. The bishop was buried in Jászvásár by his wife, who later died during the anti-Despot-Voda revolts. (Bârsanescu, Stefan: Schola Latina de la Cotnari, biblioteca de curte si proiectul de academie al lui Despot-Voda. Bucuresti, 1957; Ibid (Hermán), pp. 162-163.)

272 Ibid (Hermán), p. 164.

273 Ibid, p. 164.

doing his utmost to help rebuild the Roman Catholic clergy.[274] During his reign, he organized a Roman Catholic synod in 1586 in Kotnár, which declared the local tasks of the Counter-Reformation.[275] He expressed his respect to the Vatican by expelling from the country the German and Transylvanian 'heretic' ministers, while gladly receiving Jesuits expelled from Transylvania or arriving from Poland. As a result of his harsh commands, all the Hungarian-speaking Protestant ministers serving in Moldova fled to Transylvania. Voivod Petru sternly warned even his 500-strong Hungarian bodyguards that if they wished to remain in his service, there was no place in his court for any heretics. His intolerant decrees were viewed with great satisfaction by the representatives of the civil authorities, the Orthodox archbishop and the bishops of Románvásár and Szucsáva.[276] In place of the Hungarian Protestant priests driven out by him, foreign Catholic clerics soon arrived who could not at all communicate with their flocks. The voivod clearly realized the communication gap between priests and parishioners, so, in 1587, he requested Hungarian- and German-speaking clerics from the papal nuncio to Poland. The situation was made more complex by the fact that those converts, who seemingly became Catholics under duress, immediately flocked to those Protestant ministers who came to their hamlets after their conversion and preached in their mother tongue.[277] The same was reported in 1641 by Petrus Deodatus, Roman Catholic bishop of Sophia, who noted, in the area around Tatros, that "Due to the proximity of Transylvania, many become heretics."[278]

During the reign of voivod Aron (1591-1595), a fundamental shift in relations was apparent towards the Moldovan Protestant sects. England, through its ambassador in Constantinople, Edward Barton, exerted decisive pressure on the voivod's religious policies. The English, looking to establish relations with the Turks, clearly saw that the Vatican was casting about for allies in the Orthodox world for its Counter-Reformation plans. Consequently, they did everything possible to protect and aid the eastern

---

274 Barbu, Violeta: Contrareforma catolica in Moldova la jumatatea secolului al XVII-lea, In: Barbu,

    Violeta-Tüdos, S. Kinga /ed./: Historia manet. Volum omagial. Demény Lajos emlékkönyv. Editura

    Kriterion, Bucuresti-Cluj, 2000, pp. 332-333.

275 Ibid, p. 339, Benda: Moldvai ... op. cit. vol. 1, pp. 231-237.

276 Ibid (Barbu), pp. 333-334; Craciun: Protestantism ... op. cit. p. 182. Cites Benda: Moldvai ... op. cit.

    p. 85; Calatori ... op. cit. vol. III, p. 278.

277 The Moldovan situation between 1585 and 1587 is astutely described by the Jesuit Giulio Mancinelli?

    " ... essendo condotto in una chiesa latina, lo trovo profana dalli ministri luterani, che spesso

    venivano in quel locco per servitio delli artegiani, che sono quasi tutti Tedeschi overo Ungari

    luterani." (Craciun: Protestantism ... op. cit. p. 185.)

278 Benda: Moldvai ... op. cit. pp. 77, 205.

European Protestants. Since the Jesuit's Counter-Reformation activities strengthened during voivod Petru's rule (1588-1591), thanks to the support of Bartolomeo Brutti, voivod Aron before long had the - now unwelcome - head of the mission killed. The missionaries were expelled from the principality in 1592, thus fulfilling the English request. The following year, Barton offered support to the voivod on his throne only if he returned the Hussite and Protestant churches to them and permitted freedom of religion throughout the principality. The change in the English direction can be attributed to the fact that the Pope had earlier excommunicated Queen Elizabeth I from the Church.[279]

The spread of the tenets of Protestantism presented serious problems in the stronger, cohesive Roman Catholic communities, also. In many places, parish priests broke their vows of celibacy, married and openly raised their children. Bernardo Quirini's 1599 report serves as a good example. In Kotnár, he found a congregation of 1,080 Catholics, headed by the Transylvanian priest, Dániel, who married a widow. Their marriage was performed by another married priest. The bishop sternly rebuked the woman and immediately relocated her to another Moldovan village but, due to the serious shortage of priests, left the errant priest at the head of the congregation. During his tour of visitation, Quirini found the married Laurentius Demuth in Bánya, a 70-year old Saxon parish priest (and family) in Németváros (Tîrgu Neamt) and the also wedded János Bene of Tatros.[280] In view of the priest shortage, the prelate also left the Saxon Lutheran schoolmaster from Transylvania, Petrus Elmon, at the head of the Kotnár congregation. Elmon had established a Hungarian- and Latin-language school in the town and was in the possession of several Hungarian 'heretic' books and banned Bibles, which Quirini immediately burned.[281] In Husz, Quirini recorded regarding the locally active Franciscan priest, János (John), that he was married and had several children.[282] In some places, he noted that unanointed priests led congregations, in others that only the Transylvanian Protestant ministers carried on missionary works.

Cesare Alzati, the 20th century Italian Church historian, sees not so much a Protestant influence in the non-observance of celibacy of the period but rather suspects the Orthodox example. In many places, the congregation asked the priest to marry and start a family before being anointed, similar to

279 Craciun: Protestantism ... op. cit. pp. 160-169.

280 Benda: Moldvai ... op. cit. pp. 123-124.

281 Ibid, pp. 47, 118-119.

282 Ibid, p. 118.

the Greek Orthodox clergy.[283] Quirini attempted to introduce stricter controls in Moldova to counter the decline of Church discipline effected by Protestantism. Many, however, did not agree with the stricter regulations introduced in the spirit of the Council of Trent (such as celibacy) and these malcontents tried to organize an attempt on Quirini's life.[284]

After the dissolution of the Kingdom of Hungary (1541) and the rapid spread of Protestantism in the 16th century, the Vatican declared Muntenia and Moldova as missionary territory, assigning Muntenia to the see of the archbishop of Marcianopol. The first head of that see was Marco Bandini, who later made an inspection tour of Moldova from there. A significant portion of the missionaries came from the Franciscan *provincia* of Bulgaria, whose work was directed by the *Holy Congregation for the Propagation of the Faith* (Sacra Congregatio de Propaganda Fide), established in Rome in 1622. In 1644, another shift followed. Muntenia remained in the sphere of the archbishop of Sophia, while the bishopric responsible for Moldova was assigned to be overseen by the archbishop of Lvov. Between those two dates, Poland's support for the spread of the Polish Roman Catholic Church grew - with an eye to Moldova's conquest -, culminating with the acquisition of the bishopric of Bákó. The prelates appointed there never stayed in Moldova for any length of time, having got accustomed to the luxury at home, directing the collection of the church tithes from Galicia in this impoverished and oft fleeced land. At the same time, there was constant friction between the Polish bishops and the Franciscans - who obeyed only Rome - active in the territory.[285]

The Vatican developed a new strategy at the end of the 16th century to eradicate eastern European Protestantism and to prepare for, and ensure, the planned expansion in those countries with a non-Catholic (Orthodox) majority.[286] Its first priority was the planned forcing back of Protestantism, while the suggested diplomatic and political relations with the Orthodoxy were far more flexible. The special training of missionaries preparing for Moldova was directed by the *Propaganda Fide*. Since the Polish bishops appointed by the *Propaganda Fide* did not reside in Moldova, from 1622 Rome appointed a head of mission, a *visitator*, to the bishopric, as well as sending mostly Minorite clerics to the principality. Between 1622 and 1812,

---

283 Alzati, Cesare: „Riforma" e Riforma cattolica di fronte all ortodossia nel secondo cinquecento

romeno, In: Studia Borromaica 5. Milano, 1982, pp. 263-269. Cites Craciun: Protestantism ... op.

cit. p. 188.

284 Ibid (Craciun), p. 192.

285 Benda: Moldvai ... op. cit. p. 46. See the report of Blasius Koicevic in same, pp. 531-532.

286 Ferro, Teresa: I missionari catolici italiani in Moldavia nei secc. XVII-XVIII. Annuario dell Instituto

Romeno di Cultura e Ricerca Umanistica di Venezia, Venezia, 1999.

a total of 50 *visitators* were active in Moldova, not one of whom spoke Hungarian. The clerics usually came for a short period, did not speak the congregation's language (most never even bothering to try and learn Hungarian) and hence were never able to establish a deeper emotional connection. The heads of mission sent regular report to the Vatican regarding the numbers in their congregation and their church lives. The Rome archives of the *Propaganda Fide* contains a wealth of information about the everyday and religious lives of the Moldovan Hungarian Roman Catholic communities of the 17th-18th century.[287]

Propaganda Fide worked out a new strategy in the 18th century to overcome Protestantism. Between 1622 and 1658, Rome intended to decisively and rapidly reconvert those who earlier strayed to the Protestant faith, while preventing, with all possible means available, the further growth of the Reformation. Thirdly, it intended to conquer new territories in eastern Europe for the Roman Catholic Church. In the second half of the century, especially between 1659 and 1670, it decided on the training of aboriginal and indigenous (autochton) clergy loyal to Rome. It strove for cordial relations with the local political powers and its leaders; deemed it mandatory to maintain peace between the missionary orders in the territory. The diplomats directing the Vatican's foreign policy rightly suspected that, if they approach local (pagan) folk traditions with greater tolerance, then they can be removed later with greater success. They also grasped that the intended cultural accommodation urged by the Roman Catholic Church could best be achieved through the local language liturgy of the target group.[288]

Well after the beginning of the Church's Counter-Reformation offensive, in the early and mid-17th century, missionaries criss-crossing Moldova still met Protestants in many places. In 1623, Andreas Bogoslavich found Lutheran faithful in Husz, Karácsonyko (Piatra Neamt), Szucsáva and Tatros; a Lutheran priest was still active in Kotnár in 1630. Another Franciscan missionary reported to the *Propaganda Fide* in 1632 that, "... *in Tatros, Bogdánfalva and elsewhere some 200 Catholic families can be found, who avail themselves to the sacraments like Calvinists because they have no priest of their nation.*"[289] Simon Appoloni recorded the conversion of a Lutheran couple in Jászvásár in 1643. On his Moldovan visitation tour,

---

287 Alzati: „Riforma" ... op. cit.; Alzati, Cesare: Terra Romena tra Oriente e Occidente, chiese ed etnie nel tardo 1500. Milano, 1991; Ferro, Teresa: Ungherese e romeno nella Moldavia dei secoli XVII-XVIII sulla base dei documenti della „Propaganda Fide", In: Graciotti, Sante /ed./: Italia eRomania. Due popoli e due storie a confronto (secc. XIV-XVIII). Florence, 1998; Domokos: Édes hazámnak ... op. cit. pp. 71-72; Pilat: Aspecte din ... op. cit. pp. 91-103.

288 Barbu: Contrareforma ... op. cit. pp. 330-331.

289 Benda: Moldvai ... op. cit. p. 170.

Bandinus only found a single Calvinist priest in Bákó who, for 15 years, took conscientious care of the Hungarians in the town and its surroundings.[290]

At the beginning of the 17th century, the Vatican urged the coalition of its European believers to counter the pagan Turkish peril and expansion. At the same time, the Catholic Church saw as an important goal the strengthening of its weakened positions in the territories East and South of the Carpathians, the reorganization of the Moldovan and Muntenian bishoprics and finally, effectively repulse Protestantism. Since the Tatars devastated the bishop's see in Mardos (Mardosch), Quirini transferred his seat in 1597 from there to Bacau.[291] In the last decade of the 16th century, Pope Gregory XIV appointed Bernardino Quirini as Bishop of Moldova, with his seat in the Franciscan monastery active in Bacau. This bishoprics remained active from 1607 to 1818. Because of unsettled, warlike conditions, the prelate only reached Moldova after seven years. There, he found a congregation, spread over 15 cities and 16 villages, consisting of 1,591 Catholic families, the majority of them Hungarians, totaling 10,704 souls. Quirini was on good terms with the Franciscans of Csíksomlyó and would have gladly entrusted his flock to their care. The voivod at this time was Ieremia Movila, who assumed the Moldovan throne in 1595, mainly with Polish support. He ruled, with the exception of a few months, until 1606. For the almost two centuries after Quirini, Polish-born bishops filled the Moldovan post. Since they could not establish deeper devoted dialogue with their Hungarian-speaking flock, they neglected the spiritual care of the flock assigned to their custody.[292]

As the shortage of priests worsened, the Moldovan Hungarians often turned directly to Rome and asked for missionaries. Unfortunately, the Vatican only sent Italian, Croatian and Bosnian Franciscans who did not speak the language of the congregation. Most of them, after their arrival, learned the Romanian language, as being closest to the Italian with which they were familiar. A few grasped that the needs of the Moldovan communities would be better served only through knowledge of the Hungarian language. Bartolomeo Basetti wrote the following in 1642 about the educated Hungarian Jesuit, Pál (Paul) Beke: *"If he were a missionary, he would be of the greatest assistance to these poor Hungarians, he could do far more than us, all the other missionaries, since he knows the Hungarian language. In this province, all the Catholics are Hungarians."*[293]

290 Halász: A protestáns ... op. cit. p. 171.

291 Benda: Moldvai ... op. cit. p. 42.

292 Domokos: Édes hazámnak ... op. cit. p. 71.

293 Calatori ... op. cit. vol. VII, p. 53.

Marc Bandinus, missionary bishop visited all the Moldovan Catholic settlements in 1646, accompanied by Pál Beke, and summarized his findings thus: *"The gracious father of the Roman Church should send pastors here who speak the language."* Rafael Petrus Arduini, apostolic vicar of Moldova, called it a folly to attempt to compel the Romanian-language religious instruction by the missionaries to a people who only speak Hungarian.[294]

The missionaries who arrived here were virtually in shock by the backwardness and poverty of the Moldovan settlements. The clerics in the poverty stricken villages lived at the level of their flocks, usually resorting to some farming for sustenance, since they could not hope for any sizable donations from their destitute parishioners. Rome only sent occasional financial support, and that irregularly. We must not ignore the fact that the missionaries who volunteered for this eastern end of Europe were usually not the best kind. This was documented by the visiting prelates or the letters of the local communities, which reflected the sense of demoralization and abandonment of the missionary priests. This is shown in the October, 1671, letter from the residents of Szabófalva addressed directly to the *Propaganda Fide*, in which they complain about the immoral and domineering behavior of the foreign missionaries sent to them.[295] *"To us, our lives are similar to the illiterate beasts who can never praise God but live in ignorance. We humbly beseech Your Excellencies and Graces and the Holy Congregation that the missionary friars sent here by Your Graces and the Holy Congregation, they wish to dwell on us forcibly, not behaving as required by the Rule, rather they are drunkards, chase after womenfolk with whom they banter, carry on a indecent hideous existence, which is abhorrent to all people but especially us Hungarians: we can take from them no sustenance for the salvation of our souls, they only wish to live on us by force."*[296] [Written in the archaic dialect of the period-*Ed.*] At the end of their pleading letter, the writers warned the heads of the *Congregation* that if they did not replace the *soul destroying and immoral* priests, then they will *switch to the schism of the Vlachs* and henceforth heed their bishops.[297] The conflict between the two rival branches of the Franciscans (Observant and Minorite) and personal

---

294 Cites Lestyán, Ferenc: Ki felelos a moldvai római katolikusok sorsáért [Who is responsible for the fate of the Moldovan Roman Catholics]? In: Erdélyi Figyelo VI. évf., 1. sz., 1994, p. 4.

295 Benda: Moldvai ... op. cit. pp. 667-669.

296 Ibid, p. 668.

297 The representatives of Szabófalva personally paid a visit to the Bákó residence of the nuncio, where they lamented to him that if the transgressions of the missionary Giovanni Battista del Monte are not ended, then they will all convert to the Greek Orthodox Church. The letter of protest was signed by Gergely Varga, Bálint Demö, Péter Kati, Lorinc Jano, Janó Kadar, Gergely Dobos, György Thamo, Gergely Deske. (Ibid, pp. 668-669.)

jealousies and recriminations only further complicated and poisoned the relationship between the Catholic Church and the village communities in its care.

The 17th century letters and reports indicate that the Moldovan faithful still definitely required, and continually requested, Hungarian-speaking priests, as their relationship became impossible with the foreign-speaking clergy. Marjanus Kurski, Polish-born bishop appointed to Moldova in 1652, managed to spend the assets of the Franciscan monastery of Bákó in a mere two weeks, after which he had the remainder packed on wagons and sent to Poland. The bitter leaders of Bákó begged in their Hungarian-language letter for the appointment of another bishop and to have the monastery reinstated under the authority of the Hungarian Franciscans of Transylvania. *"We Catholics of the city of Bákó, in the country of Moldova, together with the surrounding Hungarians ... beg of you, deign to hear our cry. It is quite possible, Your Excellencies, that we are threatened with many-many kinds of ills, being in the middle of the Vlach nation, but among them the hardest and worrisome that we are without spiritual shepherds for a long time now. Our old monastery, formerly used to be a part of the Hungarian provincial, called Salvatoris, but since it became a bishop's residence we were continually made sad, then our faith was also shamed by some, seeing that the bishops do not heal, support and strengthen us in the True Faith, rather dishonored us, especially the Polish bishops, of whom the actions of His Excellency Marjanus Kurski struck most heavy, who in the last year, that is to say 1652, came to Bako, not as shepherd but as the wolf, showing no good example, with his servants ate and drank all the food and wine in the cellars collected by the old bishop, may God rest his soul, and gathered by the friars; two weeks later, that which was not squandered was piled on wagons, household furnishings and the effects of the deceased bishop, and left ... Having sent an evil drunkard servant from Poland, he wanted to turn the poor priests out from here ...We beg mercifully of you, Sires, ... return the poor friars to their old monastery, as we will not receive any foreign bishops from now on ... and we fervently ask the Holy Congregatio that this monastery henceforth be a part of the Transylvanian custodia, two days walk from us here.*[298] [Again, in the period dialect-*Ed.*]

In the summer of 1644, the Hungarians of Csöbörcsök, living along the Dniester among the Tatars, pleaded with Pál Beke, the Jesuit missionary visiting them: *"Have mercy on us, at least you, Christian brethren, have mercy and send us a priest to be our savior."*[299]

---

298 The letter was signed by István Gencze(sworn judge), Balázs Koszin, Gergely Bodor, György Zorát, György Kadar, Márton Vincelerd (formerly the town's judge). (Ibid, pp. 497-498.)

299 Ibid, pp. 269-279.

Petrus Parcevic, Moldova's apostolic vicar, clearly saw that the most effective spiritual care of the Hungarian speaking community could only be tended by the Transylvanian Hungarian clergy, only two days travel away. For that reason, he suggested that the monastery of Bákó be given back to its former owners, the Franciscans of Csíksomlyó. In his Latin text, dated 1670, he clearly stated that the majority of Catholics in Moldova can only speak Hungarian and that they resolutely request Hungarian priests. They refuse to go to confession to Romanian speaking ones, nor listen to their sermons. Parcevic made an agreement with the custodian of the Transylvanian Observant Franciscans that he will return their monastery in Bákó where, once again, the priests of the Csíksomlyó monastery may perform services.[300]

The prelate named the prior of Csíksomlyó, István (Stephen) Taploczai, to the head of the missionary base, to repair the war damaged monastery buildings and take in hand the disintegrated community. Higher politics soon brought to an end the commencement of the new agreement and posting. Since Moldova was under the authority of the Polish Catholic Church, the Polish Rudzinski (bishop of Bákó) strenuously objected to the return of the Franciscans. As well, Parcevic's proposition was not supported by bishop Nerli, the papal nuncio of Warsaw, either.[301]

The Jesuits also carried out extensive missionary work in Moldova, along with the Franciscans. At the close of the 16th century, the head of the Polish *provincia* began negotiations with voivod Petru Schiopul, who wished to establish good relations with the Vatican. In the meantime, the National Assembly, convened in 1589 in Medgyes, made a decision to expel the Jesuits from Transylvania, many of whom escaped to nearby Moldova. They settled mostly in Jászvásár, playing an important missionary role in the village communities.[302] By the beginning of the 17th century, Jesuits only occasionally toiled in this province. Newer priests sent in 1660 now came from Poland and operated mainly in Jászvásár and Kotnár. They operated a Latin school in what was the center of the province, Jászvásár, teaching mostly the children of the Moldovan elite families. Pál Beke, who accompanied archbishop Bandinus on his Moldovan visitation circuit, established a school in Jászvásár, within the framework of the Jesuit mission (with the permission and support of the voivod) and they taught in it up to 1651.[303]

Relations between the Jesuits and the Franciscans were not the most harmonious in Moldova, either. The Jesuits' main goal was to win over the

300 Benda: Moldvai ... op. cit. pp. 603-606.

301 Ibid, p. 612.

302 Ibid, p. 45.

303 Ibid, p. 781.

ruling elite class, fearlessly interfering in political matters and decision making. They also looked with scorn and disdain on the Franciscan friars working and living in modest circumstances in the villages. These conflicts substantially undermined the effectiveness of the care to the flock.[304] A letter written by the inhabitants of Tatros, of March 15, 1653, clearly illustrates how every external initiative or change was rejected: *"Our priests, the guardians of our faith and sharers our austere existence, are adequate for our needs and they are satisfied with the meager life. Let the Jesuit priests depart far from us, this land is not for them, even our sons will not make it to the higher schools because it is enough for our children if they learn the basic religious learning and learn the prayers from the cantors, who we ourselves keep to serve our church."*[305]

Half a century on, in 1706, the residents of Csöbörcsök repeated their request even more adamantly to the ambassadors of Prince Ferenc Rákóczi II (ruler of Transylvania) to the Tatar Khan. The diary of Mihály Bay and Gáspár Pápai recorded the wishes of the people of Csöbörcsök thusly: *"This village called Csebercsik, along with others, was settled by King László, as well as other villages, around Akkerman or Neszter-fejérvár, in Besarabia or Bucsák. Most of the other villages are destroyed, this one remained, even if half is a Vlach village. They still speak Hungarian to this day, a serf-village of the Tatar Khan it is, belongs to the Khan's treasury. They still are thirty farmers, with many children and servants, good tough men. They complained that they had no priest for several years, being Catholics. They marry and multiply among themselves without a priest, in fact, there are four-five year old children from those priestless marriages unbaptized, many of the unbaptized children have died. They complained to us with great pain of their soul about the shortage of their priests; wish – they said – a priest would come among us every three, four years who would baptize the children, perform marriages and hear confession. They are faithful to their religion, even though a Vlach priest lives in the village, they are more willing to bury unbaptized children than to have them baptized by the Vlach priest. They begged us to report this to our gracious Lord, His Highness, and ask His Highness to send them a priest, ready they are to pay according to their ability and keep the padre; but the need is for a padre who knows Hungarian because other than the Vlach and Hungarian tongues, they know no other."*[306] [Also in the period dialect-*Ed.*]

When Mihály Bay and Gáspár Pápai returned from the Tatar mission, they reported the request of the Csöbörcsök Roman Catholics to Prince Rákóczi II in Érsekújvár on June 6, 1706. The prince acted immediately and

---

304 Ibid, pp. 45-46, 315.

305 Barbu: Contrareforma ... op. cit. p. 357.

306 Benda: Moldvai ... op. cit. p. 765.

90

István Lippay was already on the scene by August. In his report to the prince, he wrote that the Hungarian flock, living between the Tatars and the Romanians, at first received him with mistrust.[307]

Péter (Peter) Zöld arrived in Csöbörcsök in May of 1767 to the jubilation and tears of welcome of the locals who have not seen a minister for 17 years. For two weeks, he said Hungarian-language Masses, handed out Communion, heard confession, baptized, performed weddings, instructed the young in the Catholic faith and taught the midwives the correct way to perform baptisms. At the end of his missionary stay, the populace of Csöbörcsök followed the departing Péter Zöld for a mile and begged him, through sobs, to send them a priest who could speak Hungarian.[308]

The ongoing shortage of priests made the role of deacons (cantors) more important in the religious life of the Moldovan Hungarian communities. Although they had relatively little education, many of them studied in the eastern Transylvanian Franciscan monasteries (Esztelnek, Kanta, Csíksomlyó, Gyergyószárhegy). As an example, Ince János Petrás, father of the parish priest serving in Klézse, studied in Kézdivásárhely in the first half of the 19th century and fluently spoke, read and wrote Hungarian, Romanian, Latin, as well as Italian.[309] Lacking priests and friars, the Moldovan Hungarian communities hired Transylvanian teachers or deacons, often at great financial sacrifice, turning to midwives to have their children christened. Francesco Maria Spera was amazed, in 1645, that in Moldova the deacons christen the newborn, say the Masses in church, perform the rite of acceptance of the newly married women, bless the dwellings at Pentecost, read the liturgy and bury the dead.[310] The literate deacons, those able to read and write, played a great role in the managing of civil matters with the institutions of authority, over and above the practice and leading of spiritual life.[311] In those villages, where not a single priest might set foot for years on end, they baptized, married, buried, led the prayers and the singing of the common hymns, taught the younger children to pray, read and write. This

---

307 Ibid, pp. 766-767.

308 Domokos: A moldvai ... op. cit. (1931) pp. 56-58.; Domokos: A moldvai ... op. cit. (1987) pp. 95-98.

309 Domokos: Édes hazámnak ... op. cit. pp. 1344-1345.

310 Barbu: Contrareforma ... op. cit. p. 358; Calatori ... op. cit. vol. V, pp. 387-391.

311 Tóth, István György: Diákok (licenciátusok) a moldvai csángómagyar muvelodésben a XVII. században [Deacons (licentiates) in Moldovan Csángó-Hungarian education in the 17th century], In: Zombori, István /ed./: Az értelmiség Magyarországon a XVI-XVII. században. Szeged, 1988, pp. 139-147; Tánczos, Vilmos: Gyöngyökkel gyökereztél. Gyimesi és moldvai archaikus népi imádságok.[Rooted with pearls. Archaic folk prayers from Gyimes and Moldova.] Csíkszereda, 1955.

was the situation the assistant Moldovan apostolic vicar, the Franciscan Blasius Koicevic, captured in his 1661 report: "In the Hungarian villages, if there is no priest, there is usually a teaching master (teacher) or sexton who leads the singing of hymns in church, reads the Gospels and teaches the children."[312]

The majority of Moldovan choir master-teachers were of Transylvanian origin. Well into the 19th century, it was a widespread custom that the Roman Catholic congregation of a Moldovan Hungarian village would invite a deacon from Transylvania. As but one example, Sándor Bertalan, born in 1872 in the upper Háromszék village of Kézdialmás, educated by the Minorites in Kézdivásárhely, to spend his 'apprenticeship' in Moldovan Ploscuteni beside the old cantor, Baka. Later, he served for decades as a Catholic deacon in Onest, earning a living to support his numerous family mainly as a carpenter.[313]

In the early 1860s, József (Joseph) Héja of Háromszék volunteered to work in the largish village of Gorzafa, on the banks of the Ojtoz: "*As in my poor Hungarian land, I tried to bring the children into the teachings of the Christian Catholic faith, I would have wished to teach the children of these timid people without charge but I don't think I will have any to struggle with over the winter...* "[314] The young teacher was shocked by the biblical poverty of the Moldovan families, the people's indifference. With growing homesickness, he petitioned the Head Dean of Háromszék to post him back to his homeland. Kozma Funtak, parish priest of Gorzafalva wrote a letter of November 20, 1862, to the Head Dean of Kézdi-orba, in which he pointed out that the young man, tormented by homesickness, would like to go home: "*He yearns for the bosom of his land, poor soul, he wishes nothing more than to see Your Honor with his own eyes, he says often and even when he does not say it, if he were only closer, he wishes for the removal of restraint, I see that the lad very much admires Your Honor, being from the same place, not to get sick sooner or later, I worry about him and take him with me everywhere but he mentions Your Honor and his parents at every turn, I think the promise would benefit him ... to give him free rein ...*"[315] In my opinion, József Héja did not leave only on account of homesickness because we learn from his own letter that he was unable to establish a really good

312 Benda: Moldvai ... op. cit. p. 47.

313 Domokos: A moldvai ... op. cit. (1987) p. 176.

314 Sávai, János: A székelyföldi katolikus plébániák levéltára I-II-III. Missziós Dokumentumok Magyarországról és a hódoltságról I-III [The archives of the Catholic parishes of Seklerland, vols. I to III. Missionary documents from Hungary and the Turkish occupation]. Szeged, 1997, p. 800, vol. II.

315 Ibid, p. 801, vol. II.

relationship with the cantor of Gorzafalva, who was much respected by the flock. *"As Your Honor also saw, the state of violence these people live in ... these people do not acknowledge me as the teacher of the cantor and I much fear if I move into the cantor's house what will happen – to me, that one night the cantor will come with some others, drunk, and beat me to death, as they came to the reverend's windows, they are sure to come to mine ..."*[316] The letter József Héja sent to Háromszék clearly illustrates that the cantor played a more important role in the 1862 Gorzafalva flock than the parish priest.

Due to the chronic shortage of priests in the Csángó villages for centuries and the lack of deeper contact between them and the foreign missionaries sent to them, numerous archaic, medieval and apocryphal religious practices were preserved in Moldova. At the same time, under the influence of the neighboring Orthodox communities, countless mystical and superstitious practices (charlatan healing and quackery, exorcism) took root.[317] Even archbishop Bandini remarked that in the Church of Saints Kozma and Damian in Tatros, miraculous events took place. The sounds of "heavenly angels" could be heard coming from the building, a torch-like illumination circled the church, which then rapidly disappeared over the mountains. At this miracle of Tatros, a Lutheran Saxon returned to the Catholic fold.[318] The Jesuit Pál Beke recounted his experiences of his 1644 trip in detail to the head of his Austrian district, who in turn summarized the missionary's observations in his annual report to Rome. The detailed report shed light on the fact that the Moldovan Catholics practiced, and kept alive, numerous superstitious habits they acquired from the Greek Orthodox. Similar to the Romanians, they hold festive meetings in the cemetery at Easter, carousing on the graves of their departed, to cheer up the poor souls suffering in Purgatory.[319] Petrus Deodatus noted during his 1641 visit that the parishioners definitely demanded the blessing of grains and fruits at major holidays or feasts, similar to the Orthodox Romanians.[320]

Forcible wife seizure and frequent divorce was common practice in their communities; whoever had enough of their mate simply turned her out.[321] The parish priest petitioned during the 1642 synod of Kotnár to have the power to sanction divorces, up to now vested with the bishops. The Moldovan Catholic flock rather lived out of wedlock, similar to the

316 Ibid, p. 800, vol. II.

317 Pilat: Aspecte ... op. cit. pp. 99-103.

318 Benda: Moldvai ... op. cit. pp. 483-484.

319 Barbu: Contrareforma ... op. cit. p. 351.

320 Ibid, p. 359.

321 Pilat: Aspecte ... op. cit. pp. 94.

Orthodox, than to make the long trip to see the bishop. As there was no Church Curia active in Moldova, they chose to live in illegitimate relationships. Others converted to Orthodoxy.[322]

The Moldovan Hungarians of the day were convinced that the Orthodox ministers were more effective in exorcising the devil from the afflicted, possessed persons. A Greek schoolteacher was so bewitched by his lover that the Romanian *kalugers* (Orthodox clergy) were unable to rid his the devil from his body, even by pummeling him with sticks, until finally it was accomplished by the fervent prayers of the Jesuits. A Catholic, who did not regularly attend Masses, was tormented by wild nightmares and broke into screams in front of the church. A Romanian soothsayer seared the inflicted one with hot pieces of metal to drive the demons out of him. They also performed confessions similar to the Romanians, meaning partially, in that they only confessed one or another of their sins at a time.[323]

Under the leadership of Bartolomeo Bassetti, a Catholic synod was organized in the fall of 1642, which established the methods and means of restoring the slackened Church discipline. During the deliberations, the prelate expounded that a unique feature of Moldovan Catholicism was ethnic diversity. In his opinion, the confusion in the liturgy sprang from the differing ecclesiastical rules observed by the Polish, Hungarian and Italian clergy and missionary monks and the necessarily great role played in religious life by the deacons and Kapellmeister-teachers due to the serious shortage of priests.[324]

In the 18th century, a fundamental shift occurred in the Vatican's eastern policies. In this century, the conversion of the newly discovered parts of the world, especially the primitive tribal people of South America, became the stated goal. Persons who influenced the Pope's foreign policies had earlier come to the realization that it would be impossible to make headway against the Orthodox from the direction of Moldova. Hence, they deemed the extensive missionary work at an end and, with that decision, abandoned the Moldovan Hungarians even further. At the same time, the papal advisors grasped from the ever increasing number of reports that the fathers coming from abroad, and not able to speak Hungarian, are unable to effectively minister to the Hungarian communities there. In 1774, the Pope issued a directive to his missionary orders for them to learn the language of their communities in six months. An examination was to follow, without which

322 Barbu: Contrareforma ... op. cit. pp. 359-360.

323 Benda: Moldvai ... op. cit. pp. 314-315.

324 Barbu: Contrareforma ... op. cit. pp. 352-353.

they could not continue to operate. Alas, the text composed in far off Rome remained on paper only, no one made efforts to implement it locally.[325]

As part of the terms of the Peace of Sistovo (1791), the Vatican placed the Moldovan Catholic missionary territories under the supervision of Austria at the end of the 18th century. It was never in the interest of Vienna to realistically advocate on behalf of the Moldovan Hungarians. It strove with every means available to prevent the work of the Hungarians priests serving in Moldova, or at least extremely difficult. On behalf of the Austrian administration, Franz Joseph Sulzer traveled to Moldova in 1779 and in his report noted the existence of about 6,000 Hungarian families, or about 25-30,000 people.[326]

After the 1764 massacre of Mádéfalva, the rebellious spirited Sekler priest, Péter Zöld, lived and toiled among the Moldovan communities until the learned bishop and library founder, Ignác Batthyány, recalled him to his homeland. The priest, serving in the parish of Csíkdelne, prepared a detailed report for the bishop in Alba Iulia, in which he meticulously recounted his travel experiences and the state of he Moldovan Hungarians. He suggested in his writing that the bishop should attempt to achieve with the *Congregatio* that, instead of Italian missionaries, Hungarian-speaking priest of the sterner Franciscan order be sent to Moldova. *"These priest are so necessary in these parts that, without them, the Catholics can only be called Catholics by name, since the Italian fathers are unable to educate them in the religious details of the faith ... being content with the saying of mass. On top of it all, only God knows how they hear the people's confessions from their written questions, which in my opinion as an accomplished judge, can not be complete since they do not understand the circumstances of the sins of the people, especially those that affected the race; regarding the latter, these unfortunate Hungarians often complained among bitter tears that, due to the previously mentioned unfamiliarity with the language, they did not avail themselves of the sacrament of confession in their entire lifetime."*[327]

Bishop Batthyány gained a reliable update from the minutae of Péter Zöld's report, and came to the shocking realization that no one kept the pope's 1774 instruction. As Austria occupied the North-eastern portion of Moldova in 1775-1776, it acquired significant influence in the region; the Transylvanian Roman Catholic Church tried to garner the support of the Habsburgs for its Moldovan aims. The Observant Franciscan friar from Hunadoara, István (Stephen) Szántó, forwarded an in-depth report to

---

325 Domokos: A moldvai ... op. cit. (1987) p. 100.

326 Ibid, p. 101; Sulzer, Franz Joseph: Geschichte der transalpinischen Daciens, das ist? der Walachey, Moldau und Bessarabiens II. Wien, 1781, p. 85.

327 Domokos: Édes hazámnak ... op. cit. pp. 91-93; Ibid (Domokos, 1987) pp. 92-100.

Emperor Joseph II, in which he asked the Austrian ruler to attach the missionary territory east of the Carpathians into the bailiwick of the Roman Catholic bishop of Transylvania, who will then send Hungarian priest to Moldova who are also able to speak Romanian.[328]

The next step of bishop Batthyány was to send, after appropriate diplomatic groundwork, the Paulist friar András (Andrew) Dudássi to Rome in 1787, to convince the Holy See to permit him to send Hungarian-speaking priests to Moldova instead of the Italian missionaries. In his monumental letter addressed to the pope, he sharply criticizes the work of the Italian friars serving in Moldova. With cunning strategy, he expounded that they operated in such a huge territory – Moldova, Bessarabia, the Crimean peninsula – that they were unable to adequately look after the spiritual care of the large number of Catholic flock by themselves. The prelate stressed that the failure of the missionary work was fundamentally characterized by the fact that the friars did not speak the mother tongue of the flock entrusted to their care. *"Do not believe, Your Holiness, that it does not matter if all the missionaries are unfamiliar with the Hungarian language because we are not talking of a few scattered Hungarians, wandering hither and yon. Many a Hungarian family occupies a district and are equally unfamiliar with the Vlach (tongue) as they are steadfast to their native tongue. ... Unfortunately, when these missionaries hear confession, they bring along a list of sins and, instead of those confessing opening the wounds of their hearts, the missionaries list their sins, much as the confessions of the mute are accomplished; or, more often, the words are varied and twisted in such manner as to be barely comprehensible. The Hungarians so abhor this method of confession that many lat 20 years pass without confession."*[329] The bishop of Transylvania asked in a resolute tone to have the vast territory East of the Carpathians placed under the church district of Alba Iulia and to be able to send such priests and friars there who equally spoke both Hungarian and Romanian – at the expense of the *Propaganda Fide*. András Dudássi also presented, besides the letter of Ignác (Ignatius) Batthyány, a copy of the report of Péter Zöld and a short extract from the 17th century report of Bandinus.[330]

In his letter of January 2, 1788, Pope Pius VI replied to the Transylvanian bishop, in which he argued that, in his opinion, there was no need to modify the status of the Moldovan missionary district but that he authorized the dispatch there of two Hungarian friars.[331] The solution of the

---

328 Diaconescu: Péter Zöld ... op. cit. p. 270.

329 Domokos: A moldvai ... op. cit. (1987) pp. 100-101.

330 Archivum Secretum Vaticanum, Fondo Grampi, vol. 96, G. See Diaconescu: Péter Zöld ... op. cit. pp. 270-271.

331 Ibid, p. 271.

situation he ultimately assigned to the *Propaganda Fide,* whose heads shortly decided to send two Hungarian-speaking Franciscan friars – at the expense of the *Congregatio.* József Batthyány, archbishop of Hungary asked the head of the Minorites on February 7, 1788, to find two volunteers. The solution to the problem was simplified by the political situation as the Austrian forces once again invaded Moldova. Although the military events deterred volunteers, finally Tamás (Thomas) Posonyi, a Franciscan father serving in Beszterce accepted the challenge, arriving in Moldova in early December of 1788. the friar did not live up to the expectations accompanying him, his private life soon led to a scandal. As he was living in Gorzafalva with to women, he was soon expelled from the missionary territory.[332]

During the course of the 18th-19th century, new groups of Hungarian Protestants arrived from Transylvania who dispersed in Moldova, settling in smaller groups, which encouraged their relative quick assimilation into the Roman Catholic communities. In the cemetery of Klézse, the graves of the Protestant families formed distinctive groupings from the majority Catholics into the early 20th century.[333] The Hungarian Protestant artisan's lesser or greater groups also settled in the Moldovan cities - like Jászvásár - beginning from the early years of the 19th century. Sparse data suggests that Protestant families lived in Prála and Bucsumon, in the vicinity of Onyest, in the middle of the 19th century, who were later converted to Catholicism in 1860 by the Gorzafalva parish priest, Kozma Funták.[334]

A significant number of Protestants lived in Vizánta, in Vrancea County, who migrated from Transylvania in 1814, to settle on the eastern slopes of the Carpathians. Initially, a Hungarian minister led the Protestant congregation of Vizánta, who was denounced to the Austrian consul in Moldova by the local Roman Catholic parish priest. As a result of the consul's harsh intervention, the Protestant minister was forced to leave the village. Two years later, a new Protestant came from the adjoining Transylvanian county. In 1817, the presence of the Hungarian-preaching priest so enraged the Roman Catholic bishop of Bákó, who also protested to the Austrian consul and asked the diplomat to ask Vienna to take stern steps and order the recall of the Calvinist priest to Transylvania. However, in 1817 Benjamin Beder still continued to serve his Hungarian flock in Vizánta. Eventually, due to the continued persecution, he left the village for the more populous Protestant community of Szászkút. In 1858, only the large family of

---

332 Ibid, pp. 271-272.

333 Domokos: A moldvai ... op. cit. (1987) p. 543.

334 Ibid, pp. 542-543.

János Nyújtó remained in the Protestant faith; the abandoned Protestant church soon collapsed.[335]

A rural Hungarian Protestant community remained in existence in Moldova to the 20th century only in Szászkút. This large settlement had a substantial Saxon population in the Middle Ages, which kept in close contact with the center of Transylvanian Protestantism, Brassó and the Barcaság (the region around Brasov-*Ed.*), and were openly receptive to the religious reform ideas of the 16th century, including the Hussites. The Reformed congregation of Szászkút continued to grow from the middle of the 18th century to the middle of the 19th with the families fleeing from Transylvania's Háromszék. Theirs priests also were primarily from there. Although they lived in extremely modest circumstances, the Protestants of Szászkút operated a Hungarian-language parochial school.[336] Into the 1870s, their pastor made regular trips to a village South of Egyedhalma, by the name of Domnesti, where he ministered to 39 Hungarian Reformed families, who all converted to Catholicism by 1898. The congregation's last Hungarian Protestant pastor, György (George) Dobai, came from a farming family, completed his theological studies in Debrecen and Sárospatak, taking a wife from Esztelnek in Upper-háromszék. This erudite minister served his Szászkút flock with dogged determination from 1875 until his death in 1925. The settlement's Protestant church and rectory burned to the ground during the first world war. The 1930 Romanian census only recorded 115 Roman Catholics in Szászkút. Of those, 109 declared themselves as Hungarian nationals and 103 as having Hungarian as mother tongue.[337]

In 1807, Hammer, the Austrian consul operating from Jászvásár, reported to his superiors on the existence of 10 Roman Catholic parishes (Forrófalva, Klézse, Gorzafalva, Bogdánfalva, Lujzikalagor, Tamásfalva, Dumafalva, Halasfalva, Szabófalva and Husz). According to his data, these villages represented a total of 4,182 Roman Catholic families, or 21,307 persons.[338] Vienna instructed the Transylvanian authorities to review whether the claim of the Franciscan friars of Csíksomlyó to the monastery of Bákó was justified. The Imperial court's initiative bore no tangible fruit.[339]

---

335 Czelder, Márton: Missziói levelek Ballagi Mórhoz [Missionary letters to Mór Ballagi]. Protestáns Egyházi és Iskolai Lapok. 13 sz., 1861, p. 159.

336 Ibid, pp. 11-13.

337 Gazda, István: Szászkúti múlt és jelen [The past and present in Szászkút], In: Felebarát. Gyülekezeti lap a szórványban élo magyar református családok számára, III. évf., 1-2. sz., 1992; Halász: A protestáns ... op. cit. pp. 174-177; Sógor: „Elszertült" ... op. cit.

338 Auner, Károly: A romániai magyar telepek történeti vázlata [Short history of the Hungarian settlements of Romania]. Temesvár, 1908, p. 65; Domokos: Édes hazámnak ... op. cit. pp. 93-94.

339 Domokos: A moldvai ... op. cit. (1987) p. 108.

The Seklers arriving after the massacre of Mádéfalva possessed a more articulated, robust linguistic consciousness, thus asking more consistently of their religious and civil leaders access to the liturgy in Hungarian and religious practice in general. In their disappointment, they turned on several occasions not to Rome but directly to the Austrian Emperor with their petition for a Hungarian priest. In response to their persistent pleas, Imre (Emery) Dénes of the Pécs archdiocese was sent to Moldova who opened a school in Jászvásár, in which he taught religion in Hungarian. During his 12 year stay, he fruitfully served his Hungarian flock first in Jászvásár, then Prezest and Kaluger. Soon, István Bocskor also arrived in 1803 in Moldova after the relentless appeals, where he attended with great enthusiasm to the spiritual care of the hitherto neglected rural settlements. Unfortunately, by the early 19th century, the heads of the missionary territory took more and more resolute steps against persons demanding the liturgy in Hungarian and those cantors who guided religious services in the local vernacular. Dominicus Brocani, head of the missionary territory, unequivocally ordered in a letter dated June 15, 1804, that the faithful in Lujzikalagor, Bákó, Barát and Prezes may only use Romanian in their prayers and religious instruction. He also did not favor the activities of the mentioned Bocskor and did not agree to move this helpful priest to Szabófalva, in spite of the repeated pleas of that flock. Brocani shortly slandered Bocskor to the Austrian consul and Hammer saw the activities of this parish priest as so harmful and dangerous that he had him arrested in 1807 and thrown in the jail of Temesvár in the Banate.[340]

Paroni, apostolic regent of Moldova, finally had enough of this unfortunate situation and made a trip to Kolozsvár in 1825. There he met with Rudolf Studer, head of the Hungarian Minorite order and came to an agreement, and signed a contract, that the Transylvanian order will annually send six Hungarian priests to Moldova – for 100 Thalers. The Italian missionaries active in Moldova looked with jaundiced eyes at the swelling number of Hungarian preachers and, through denunciations to the authorities, intrigued to force the Transylvanians to leave. As the annual fee was not always remitted on time by the poor Moldovan missionary center, the Transylvanian Franciscan prior notified in writing that, until the outstanding debts were not paid, he would be sending no more Hungarian priests to Moldova.[341]

The contempt and intolerance of the Italian priests towards their flocks was unmistakable after the 1831 uprising of Szabófalva was put down. Carol Magni, the head of the Catholic mission, began Romanian-language public and cantor schools during his Moldovan stay, between 1832 and 1838. An

---

340 Ibid, p. 108.

341 Domokos: Édes hazámnak ... op. cit. p. 1350; Ibid, p. 110.

earlier head of the mission made every effort to break the influence of the Hungarian-sympathizer cantors, including fundamentally changing the church taxes. In many cases, the Moldovan Roman Catholic parishes hired Hungarian speaking and feeling cantors directly from Transylvania, paying from their own church incomes. Under the new regulation, the parishioners were to pay a separate portion to the rectory, so that the priest may choose and pay a cantor according to his own wishes. The discontented of Szabófalva turned directly to the *Propaganda Fide* to prevent the head of the mission from changing their previous way of life. In their letter, they resolutely asked for a Hungarian priest to guide their community. In the same breath, they threatened the leaders of the Catholic Church with mass conversion to the Orthodox faith if their plea fell on deaf ears. The rebellious flock finally barred the unwanted priest (Remigius Silvestri) and also reported their indignation at the princely court. There, they were first offered the option for all to convert to Orthodoxy. Then the ruler of Moldova, Alexandru Ipsilanti, appointed a committee of boyars to examine the state of affairs, who suggested a compromise: two local farmers of Szabófalva were appointed to collect the taxes.[342]

The foreign missionaries took such an active and zealous role in the humiliation of the rebels of Szabófalva that Rafael Petrus Arduini, the newly appointed apostolic vicar of Moldova, was forced to make temporary but highly visible concessions. He was forced to stop the open persecution of the Hungarian language. *"He is foolish who wishes to preach in French to those who only understand German or Slav, as in this given case ... where the missionaries try to turn religion into Romanian language education to a people who only understand Hungarian."*[343]

As a result of the previously related events, the number of Hungarian speaking priests in Moldova plummeted in the first half of the 19th century. This artificial and intentionally created trend prompted Sándor Pap, parish priest in Tatros, to commit the following thoughts to paper: *"Regarding the decline of the Hungarian priests ... it would be extremely harmful to the Hungarian people because it is the love of their own tongue that will keep them in the Catholic faith, not the toils of the missionaries, as proven by the desertion of many cities and villages from The Catholic faith because they have forgotten their mother tongue, and this could also happen to the inhabitants of Husz, too, who do not know the language of their parents. This has happened before, and can happen again."* Sándor Pap felt that the greatest dereliction was that, during confession, the priest was unable to realistically communicate with his adherent, could not influence their emotional or moral development. In his bitterness, he closed his thoughts

---

342 Gabor: Dictionarul ... op. cit. pp. 234-235.

343 Domokos: A moldvai ... op. cit. (1987) p. 110. Cites Auner: A romániai ... op. cit. p. 74.

with: *"He who knows this, could he deny that the Hungarian language is necessary in Moldova? And yet, they propose that the number of Hungarian priests must be diminished. This would be remedied by the Holy Congregation, if it were not badly informed."*[344]

In the summer of 1841, János Ince Petrás, the Moldovan-born Hungarian-speaking parish priest of Pusztina, accompanied Arduini to the spa at Borszék in Transylvania. At the resort, they struck up an acquaintanceship with Gábor Döbrentei, a young Hungarian scientist of Buda. The meeting began with mutual esteem, and grew into a scientific relationship. From the voluminous written answer of Petrás to the questions posed by the Hungarian scholar, we learn that in 1839 Moldova there were 57,300 Catholics and that 8 priests were active in the territory in 1841.[345] In a later letter of 1844, he reports to the Hungarian Scientific Academy that the church and civil authorities paid particularly discriminatory attention to the Romanization of the northern Hungarian Csángó. In his report, he stressed that Hungarian-language liturgy in the vicinity of Románvásár was only to be found in the church of Szabófalva, which was just recently terminated after extended pressures, unpleasantness and scandals. As the first step of the "resolutely planned Vlachization, it was ordered that, every second Sunday, prayers and hymns be in Romanian." Then, under the terms of a new regulation, beginning with the Easter festivities Hungarian could no longer be used in prayers, hymns or sermons. The erudite parish priest rightly suspected that Szabófalva 'buried' its ancient Hungarian tongue on that Good Friday.[346] It is interesting to note that, when the new Church administrator visited Szabófalva and Ploscuteni to the South, he sternly ordered that "only every third Sunday was the cantor permitted to sing and lead prayers in Hungarian, although, in all of this small settlement, he would be hard put to find 10 people who did not speak Hungarian."[347]

The petty and financial discord between the Moldovan Catholic mission and the Transylvanian Franciscans worsened significantly during the 1840s, when János Jerney wrote in the Budapest papers about the civil rights infringements of the Moldovan Hungarians. In the meantime, the Primate of Hungary, József (Joseph) Kopácsi, undertook to regularly pay the expenses of the Hungarian Minorite friars active in Moldova. He asked for a significant increase in their numbers from the Transylvanian order. At the intercession of the Italian missionaries, the Moldovan government decided to expel all the Hungarian priests from the principality. Pál (Paul) Sardi, the

---

344 Domokos: A moldvai ... op. cit. (1987) pp. 110-111.

345 Ibid, pp. 111-113; Domokos: Édes hazámnak ... op. cit. pp. 1317-1351.

346 Ibid (Édes hazámnak ...), pp. 1429-1430.

347 Ibid, p. 1433.

apostolic administrator was only able to partially block the decree from coming into effect. At his request, the *Propaganda Fide* firmly condemned the meddling of Kopácsi and the two last Hungarian friars sent by the Primate were forced to immediately leave Moldova. Since Kopácsi continued not to pay his obligations regarding the missionary expanses of the Minorites, the head of the Transylvanian order, Román Szabó, finally recalled the Hungarian friars on May 4, 1848.[348]

The 1851 Roman Catholic register of Moldovan priests lists 22 parishes and 186 *filia*, a total of 208 settlements. According to the annual census, in 16 parishes (Dsidafalva, Bákó, Bergova, Butea, Kalagor, Klézse, Forrófalva, Foksány, Gorzafalva, Halasfalva, Prezest, Szabófalva, Pusztina, Tatros, Bogdánfalva and Valé) they still spoke, sang and prayed in Hungarian.[349] The register also recorded that in 1851 the Roman Catholic churches of Gajcsána, Szolohegy and Pusztina had, as their patron saint, Saint Stephen, while Vizantea's was Saint László, both kings of Hungary.[350] The Hungarian language still played an important role in the religious education of Moldovan children in the middle of the 19th century. As an example, Elek Gego noted during his 1836 Moldovan travels that the school of Forrófalva, which later operated in Tatros, was established by the Hungarian missionary, Sándor Papp.[351] Also, Kozma Funták played an important role in organizing religious education in Gorzafalva.[352] It is indicative of the importance that Hungarian played in the liturgy that in the middle of the 19th century, the Apostolic Visitator of Moldova published a bilingual catechism (in Romanian and Hungarian) in Jászvásár. Thus, the Church was forced, in 1841, to satisfy the need and close attachment to Hungarian-language religiosity. A fundamental change in this practice occurred when Iosif Salandri (apostolic visitator) appeared in Moldova and, thanks to his 'blessed' actions, the concerted exclusion of Hungarian soon began in parochial school education.[353]

The new state, created in 1859 by the union of Moldova and Muntenia, was ruled from 1881 to 1947 by members of the German Hohenzollern dynasty. The rapidly developing young Romanian state felt it demeaning that

---

348 Chelaru, Rafael: Documente privind activitatea episcopului Paolo Sardi si catolicismul în Moldova

(1843-1848). Arhiva Istorica a României, Serie noua, Vol. I. nr.1., Bucuresti, 2004, pp. 117-118;

Domokos: A moldvai ... op. cit. (1987) pp. 115-116.

349 Domokos: Édes hazámnak ... op. cit. p. 94; Domokos: A moldvai ... op. cit. (1986) p. 19.

350 Domokos: A moldvai ... op. cit. (1986) p. 20.

351 Gego: A moldvai ... op. cit. p. 20.

352 Dobos, Danut: Biserica si scoala. Din istroia operelor sociale catolice în România I. Editura Presa

Buna, Iasi, 2002, pp. 138-139.

353 Domokos: Édes hazámnak ... op. cit. p. 94.

missionaries directed by Rome were active on its territory. In 1881, the prelate Nicola Giuseppe Camilli was appointed Moldova's apostolic vicar who, with support by the Romanian state, organized the missionary territory into a bishopric in 1884. It was confirmed by Pope Leo XIII in his letter of June 27, 1884. As a result of his activities, a bishopric was established in Jászvásár and, from 1886, a theological seminary and novitiate, also.[354] In 1897, a Romanian-language Minorite monastery was located in Halaucesti (Halasfalva), which shortly incorporated a Roman Catholic seminary and cantor training school. When the Romanian superintendent of Orthodox views, Ciocan, visited the institution in 1903-1904, he found that the seminary rectors completely isolated from their families and home contacts those children who were accepted, after having finished their elementary education. They were not permitted to return home even on summer vacations. When anxious and loving parents traveled to the school to see their children, they could only do so in the presence of the priests in charge of their re-education – and only communicate in Romanian.[355]

The bishopric active in Jászvásár went to great extents to serve Romanian national ambitions because that was the stipulation of the new state under which it permitted the extension and operation of Roman Catholic institutions. As an expression of its gratitude, the Roman Catholic Church of Moldova surpassed the ethnic homogenization, now raised to state policy, consciously preparing the linguistic and national assimilation of the Hungarians. Its leaders employed every means to suppress the Hungarian-language religious experience in the villages inhabited by the Csángó. Youth coming from the Moldovan Hungarian communities were turned into the kind of priests in the theological institute of Jászvásár who took the most extreme position against their mother tongue and own people in their parishes. While Camilli led his diocese with a resolute hand, he unambiguously instructed his priests that, in the Roman Catholic churches in Moldova, they were to use only the language of the country, that is to say, Romanian. In his 1889 letter to his diocese, he ordered that the prayers prescribed by the papal encyclical were only permitted to be said in Romanian. In 1893, he directed that the earlier bilingual catechisms were to be replaced by unilingual ones. Before long, his measures had the result that in most of the villages a deeper spiritual bond became impossible between the priests who took a role in the brutal repression of the Hungarian language and the faithful, frightened by their crude methods.[356]

---

354 Almanahul Presa Buna. Iasi, 2000, p. 167.

355 Ciocan: Monografia ... op. cit. p. 59.

356 Actele nr. 9, Iasi, 1913, pp. 78-79, Actele nr. 15, 1914, p. 210, Actele nr. 24, 1914, pp. 256-259,

Actele nr. 26, 1914, pp. 294-299; Domokos: Édes hazámnak ... op. cit. p. 94.

The Hungarians of Moldova were unable to accept the orders of the bishop of Jászvásár and petitioned in countless appeals for Hungarian language masses, sermons, prayers and hymns. In one instance, bishop Camilli rebuffed the plea of the farmers of Lujzikalagor in a manner unbecoming a prelate, whose only wish was to hear the scripture in church in their mother tongue and continue to pray and sing in Hungarian. *"The petitioners should know that in Romania the language of the people is Romanian and it can not be anything else. It would be unjust against their own country and a shame on their own countenance to speak a foreign language in this country, for example Hungarian ... I ask the people of Lujzikalagor who, as they themselves write, live in this country mingled with other nationalities with civil and political rights, were born and grew up in this country, earned their living here, to tell me whether they are Hungarians or Romanians? If they are Hungarians, let them go to Hungary where they speak Hungarian but if they are Romanians, which they certainly are, they should be ashamed for not knowing the language of the country ...*[357]*"*

The unsettling 1860 letter from the farmers of Gorzafalva precisely pointed out how important a role the Hungarian ministers played in the retention, strengthening and passing on of the mother tongue and ethnic identity: *"We 600 farmers from the vicinity of Ojtozhatárszél, having gathered on the Moldovan side, discussing our great grievance, we who so far remained Hungarians and Roman Catholics in the true faith for 500 years, endured everything in the mist of all adversity, suffered, multiplied, grew in the true faith, this we can only thank our poor Hungarian priests but not the Italians ...Oh how the multitudes cry out: Dear God! Give the poor Hungarians Hungarians priests, Vlach priests for the Vlach ...*"[358]

In the years following the 1867 Austrian-Hungarian Compromise, interest among the Hungarian intelligentsia within the Carpathian basin once again developed regarding the fate of the Hungarian communities of Moldova. The Szent László Society formed a separate committee to document the indigenous problems of the Csángó-Hungarians. A member of the fact finding mission sent to Moldova was Mihály (Michael) Kubinszky, canon-prior of Kalocsa, lawyer Károly (Karl) Majer, Károly Veszely, Roman Catholic Dean of Marosvásárhely, Ferenc (Frank) Kovács, religious instructor in Gyulafehérvár, as well as Fülöp (Phillip) Jákó Imets, high-school teacher. In their report, based on their impressions gathered during

---

357 Domokos: Édes hazámnak ... op. cit. pp. 94-95.

358 Veszely, Károly - Imets, Fülöp Jákó - Kovács, Ferenc: Utazás Moldva-Oláhországban [Travel in Moldova-Wallachia]. Marosvásárhely, 1870, p. 77; Domokos: A moldvai ... op. cit. (1987) pp. 180-181.

their 1868 tour, they firstly remarked that Hungarian-language Roman Catholic schools must be established in the villages settled by the Csángó and the children enrolled in them be supplied with catechisms in their mother tongue. Secondly, they encouraged gaining the support of the apostolic vicar of Moldova so that, with his permission, Hungarian priests may be able to visit the Csángó settlements. Thirdly, they planned to draw the Moldovan Hungarians under the authority of the bishop of Transylvania.[359] The Society was mostly able to only send religious pamphlets and devotional objects to Moldova but it did provide support for the building of several churches in the region. The Society tried to secure the support of the apostolic vicar in the early 1880s for the establishment of Hungarian-language educational institutions but its initiative was without success due to strong political pressure.

In 1895, the Vatican sent a Swiss prelate of French extraction to assume the bishop's see of Jászvásár, replacing Camilli. Dominique Jaquet approached his Hungarian faithful, then still in the majority, with substantially more tolerance than his predecessor. Since King Karl I no longer supported the Moldovan Roman Catholic Church to the same degree, the bishop and the diocese found themselves in serious financial trouble. In the summer of 1895, he turned to Hungary for help. The Bánffy government was only willing to assist the operation of the Jászvásár seminary and novitiate if certain subjects were taught in Hungarian, too. Under Camilli, the seminary positions were mainly decided by the Jesuits, however, the new bishop favored the Franciscans. He proposed the establishment of a new seminary in Halasfalva. The Hungarian prime Minister, count Dezso (Desiderius) Bánffy, told the bishop in no uncertain words that he would support this new Franciscan seminary with significant funds but only if he allows and ensures Hungarian-language instruction within its walls. The dialogue, begun in 1897, was soon ended by the foreign minister of Austria-Hungary who did not wish to exacerbate the already tense relations between Romania and Austria-Hungary with the difficult Csángó question. It would not be taken well in foreign political circles that the Hungarian government was preventing the Kingdom of Romania from supporting Romanian schools in Hungary while, at the same time, the Hungarian side devotes significant amounts to the operations of a seminary among the Csángó. Thus, in the last decades of the 19th century, the institutionalized assurance of religious practice in their mother tongue for the Moldovan Csángó-Hungarian failed due to Hungary's internal minority politics, the interests of the Monarchy and the assimilative aspirations of the Romanian authorities.[360]

---

359 Ibid (Veszely - Imets - Kovács).

360 Dobos: Biserica... op.cit. pp. 140-142; Vincze: Asszimiláció ... op. cit. pp. 26-27.

After the Treaty of Trianon, ending the first world war, Romania's territory grew with new lands and denominational communities. In 1920, the Romanian king, Karl Hohenzollern, enacted that in his country the Catholics should enjoy similar rights as the majority Orthodox. In 1927, Romania and the Holy See signed a concordat, which permitted and assured freedom of religion for the Romanian Roman Catholics.[361] At the same time, they created the Saint Joseph Provincia, consisting of 10 major Csángó parishes (Szabófalva, Halasfalva, Dsidafalva, Prezest, Bákó, Lujzikalagor, Forrófalva, Tatros, Galac and Husz) and placed them in the care of the Minorites in perpetuity.[362]

The union of Transylvania and the Kingdom of Romania contributed to the easing of the isolation of the Hungarians of Moldova with the disappearance in 1920 of the political, millennial border along the crest of the eastern Carpathians. Within the boundaries of Greater Romania, the Csángó were free to visit, without a passport, the Franciscan monastic center of Csíksomlyó for the traditional pilgrimage of Pentecost.[363] In the decades between the two world wars, the Transylvanian friars and parish priests (e.g.- Kukla Tarziusz) visited the more significant Csángó settlements during the summer and on the significant Church feasts, where they spread the Gospel in Hungarian and administered the sacraments. Fortunát Boros took part in the 1924 pilgrimage of Szalánc where the Hungarians welcomed him with open arms. Although he could not give a sermon in Hungarian, could not hear confessions, he did bless the local's newly made St. Anna flag at an altar erected in the ruins of the old church, could quickly mumbled the Gloria and, after the Mass, bless their chapel. The gathered faithful sang the popular hymn *Szép liliomszál, szüzek virágának...* [Beautiful lily, flower of virgins ...] in Hungarian, Latin and Romanian. As this tiny Hungarian community did not have its own parish priest, a cantor who happened here in 1923 from Gyergyóditró substituted. He placed great emphasis on having the faithful carry out the services based on the *Erdélyi imádságoskönyv* [Transylvanian missal].[364] According to a newspaper article of the period, Ferenc (Frank) Jénáki visited the northern Gyerofalva and its surroundings in 1924 and wrote that there the young met on the square in front of the church on

---

361 Almanahul ... op. cit. p. 77.

362 Domokos: Édes hazámnak ... op. cit. p. 95.

363 Barna, Gábor: Moldvai magyarok a csíksomlyói búcsún [Moldovan Hungarians at the pilgrimage of Csíksomlyó], In: Halász, Péter /ed./: „Megfog vala apóm szokcor kezemtül..." Tanulmányok Domokos Pál Péter emlékére. (Budapest, 1993) pp. 45-62.

364 Boros, Fortunát: A szalánci búcsú [The pilgrimage of Szalánc], In: Erdélyi Tudósító VII. évf., 29. sz., augusztus 15, 1924.

Sundays, after lunch, where they played games and danced.[365] The intolerant local gendarmes could not tolerate these meetings and, beginning in the '30s, they quickly escorted every Transylvanian or Hungarian priest, friar, researcher, tourist or traveler out of the Csángó-Hungarian villages as suspicious foreigners.[366]

In 1924, Iosif Petru Pal established a theological and philosophical institute in Luzikalagor. Its pupils were already traveling to Italy to further their studies. In the restored and enlarged buildings of the parish,[367] a theological seminary and cantor training school operated, named after St. Bonaventura, from 1932 until the communist educational reform of 1948. When the impatient nationalism grew in the 1930's Romania, the Moldovan priests even forbade that the cantors sing in Hungarian. They threatened with police action those Transylvanian-trained teachers who conducted a portion of religious life in the mother tongue. Those who dared to protest against the forcible Romanization of religious experience were branded in most villages as Bolshevik rebels and agitators.[368]

A Moldovan Csángó man wrote in 1931 to Pál Péter (Paul Peter) Domokos: *"There be a seminary in Iassi and Bucharest but we well know that if our sons learn the priesthood in the Regat, they will forget the ways of our dear language because that is what happened to every Csángó boy who became a priest there. Our bishop in Iassi is a pure Csángó man but knows no Hungarian but very much hates and forbids the speaking or singing of Hungarian in church. (...) Our bishops in Iassi were always Italians and only brought Italians for the poor Csángó peoples who detested and forbade the speaking of our dear Hungarian tongue. The Csángó boy, who studies priest craft in Iassi was forbidden to speak, write or read anything in Hungarian so that the lad, after much taunting, himself came to hate the sound of his own mother tongue. It is so with our present bishop, who loathes his Hungarian tongue."*[369]

The intolerance against the Hungarian language intensified in Moldova in the decade following the first world war. The escalating prejudice hit particularly hard at those preaching in Hungarian but did not spare those who spoke other languages, either. As an example, the German Franciscan priest,

365 Jénáki, Ferenc: Egy vasárnap a moldvai magyarok között [A Sunday among the Hungarians of Moldova]. Erdélyi Tudósító VII. évf., 25. sz., június 22, 1924.

366 Boros, Fortunát: Csíksomlyó, a kegyhely [Csíksomlyó, the the place of pilgrimage]. Kolozsvár, 1943, p. 135; Baumgartner, Sándor: Moldva, a magyarság nagy temetoje [Moldova, the vast cemetery of the Hungarians]. Budapest, 1940, p. 27.

367 Gabor: Dictionarul ... op. cit. pp. 168-169.

368 Vincze: Csángósors ... op. cit. p. 214.

369 Domokos: A moldvai ... op. cit. (1987) pp. 259-260.

Petrus Mathias Neumann, was let go from his Bogdánfalva parish, after 40 years of service, because he fluently learned the language of his parishioners who were thus able to make their confessions in Hungarian to this meek and honest friar. Since Hungarian prayers and hymns were continually heard in his church, the church fathers, infected with Romanian nationalistic notions, quickly stripped him of his parish. This honest and moral elderly priest did not despair and built a wooden house and chapel on a small plot in the outskirts of Bogdánfalva, living a saintly life while supporting himself by tilling the soil. As his former flock continued to visit him in large numbers to have him hear their confessions in Hungarian, his superiors shortly banned him from administering that sacrament. He bitterly remarked to Pál Péter Domokos, who visited him in 1929, that: "*The final wish of the deathly ill was to have me hear their last confession but they forbade me... My heart aches at the sight of the oppression and Romanization of these totally honest, upstanding people. I, a German, say that, as one who has never did and never will meddle in politics, I hold as the most basic and sacred right of the people to speak in their own language, to pray to God in their own language, to sing in their own language. I have seen in my 41 years this insult and trodding underfoot of this most fundamental and sacred right among the Moldovan Csángó.*"[370]

In this intolerant, and increasingly Fascist atmosphere, a petition with a mere 1,396 Csángó-Hungarian signatories from Forrófalva, Nagypatak and Újfalu reached the Pope at the end of the 1920s in which the asked for priests who could say Masses in Hungarian. Lajos (Louis) Shvoy (bishop of Székesfehérvár, head of the St. László Society) reported to the Pope during his 1933 trip to Rome that the Csángó of Moldova live in very sad and abandoned circumstances. He reminded the Holy Father that only recently 374 farmers from Bogdánfalva requested that the Holy See send them a priest who could hear the elderly people's confession in Hungarian, who could administer the last rites to the dying in Hungarian.[371]

Mihai Robu, Roman Catholic bishop of Moldova, delivered a stern decree in 1938 in which he categorically banned any religious expression in Hungarian. In many villages, the priests (e.g.- Bonaventura Romilla in Forrófalva) threatened the Hungarian-speaking faithful from the pulpit with excommunication, banned the communal spinning evenings (making homespun and a natural occasion for Hungarian speech) and threatened the young to withhold the marriage rites if they did not know their catechism in Romanian.[372]

---

370 Ibid, pp. 186-187.

371 Vincze: Asszimiláció ... op. cit. pp. 29-30.

372 Ibid, p. 31.

In the spring of 1938, the bishop of Iassi named József (Joseph) Talmacsel to the parish of Lészped, a Transylvanian-Csángó settlement. In short order, the priest announced that it was strictly forbidden to sing and pray in Hungarian in the church, on the streets or at home. The priest's decrees resulted in sharp protests in the village. The priest, fearing a revolt, asked for police to come to the village, who surrounded the church and immediately arrested Ferenc György Tamás, the village cantor who, in spite of the priest's ban, to fulfill the flock's wishes, continued to sing sacred songs in Hungarian in the Lord's house. The priest addressed a thunder-and-brimstone sermon to the assembled throng who were of a contrary opinion and very dissatisfied, in which he threatened to hand them all over to the police. After the intimidating 'sermon,' the priest went from house to house in the village, accompanied by the gendarmes, and collected all the much-cherished prayer books and hymnals, confiscating the elementary school primers and other literary works, as well. In vain did the flock insist on singing in Hungarian, the priest soon found a proud Romanian cantor to come to the village. The enraged farmers ran him out of the village. The priest immediately wrote a report to the head of the police detachment in Bákó, to inform him that a Bolshevik revolt has broken out in his village and that the malcontents should be punished with cannon fire. In short order, heavily armed soldiers arrived in Lészped to take up the fight with the revolutionaries but were met with relative calm. In the absence of official retribution, the irate priest finally closed the only village church and simply left the settlement for four months. In that time, the locals, of necessity, had to hold baptisms and funerals without the benefit of priest or cantor.[373]

During the second world war, especially between 1940 and 1944, the hatred of strangers and specifically anti-Hungarianism intensified in religious circles. This intolerant behavior manifested itself through the firing of all the cantors who, through their activities, lead the Hungarian singing and prayers. They were ejected from their church provided homes, too. Their actions were forbidden in the private sphere, also, and their persecution began if they organized and lead Hungarian-language prayers or hymns at a funeral or at the pilgrimage of Csíksomlyó. Beside the ecclesiastics, civil authorities also began to hound the Hungarian-hearted cantors. At the behest of the priests, the cantors were cited to the police stations where they were threatened with imprisonment and deportation. With their forceful action, they wanted to root even out of the private sphere, the family circles, the practice of Hungarian-

---

373 Balázs, Péter: Egy csángófalu harca anyanyelvéért a jasi püspökség elfajzott ügynökei ellen [The battle of a Csángó village for its mother tongue against the degenerate agents of the bishopric of Iasi], In: Igazság, IV. évf., február 2, 1948; Balázs, Péter: Vatikáni janicsárok rabságában [Captives of the janissaries of the Vatican], In: Utunk, IV. évf., 5. sz., 1949, p. 15.

language prayer and singing. Those priests who accepted the Romanian assimilative propaganda turned to composing Romanian-language publications espousing Fascist ideology in the years following the Vienna Accord. In them, they tried to prove, based on the masses of blood samples taken in the Csángó villages, that the Moldovan Catholics could only be of Romanian origin as shown even by their blood types.[374]

Immediately after the takeover of communism after the second world war, relations between the Vatican and the new Romanian authorities, openly espousing atheism, worsened. In 1948, the Greek Catholic Church, united with Rome, was forcibly banned, all its churches and other assets confiscated, then given to the Orthodox Church, its priests sentenced to lengthy prison terms, along with the Transylvanian Hungarian Roman Catholics. In 1949, the papal nuncio was declared *persona non grata*. However, in spite of the decree, he did not leave his post in Bucharest. At the same time, the Romanian Communist authorities did not hinder – in fact, extended far-reaching support for - the activities of the Moldovan Roman Catholic bishopric, whose institutional infrastructure, strangely enough, was completed during the Stalinist, then Ceausescu decades, between 1965 and 1989.[375] During the harshest years of the communist dictatorship, forcibly spreading its atheist world-view, university level Roman Catholic theological education was unhindered in Jászvásár and strikingly ultra-modern architecture churches were allowed to be erected in Moldovan villages and towns. In exchange for all this, the Roman Catholic Church of Moldova offered servile support for the linguistic and cultural assimilation and the forcible redefinition of the national identity, raised to the level of state policy, of close to a quarter of a million Moldovan Csángó.

Immediately after the end of the second world war, in 1945-1946, the Hungarian People's Alliance of Romania /HPAR/ began to urge the beginning of not only Hungarian-language education on Moldova but also the introduction of the liturgy in the mother tongue. In several villages, they recruited the local HPAR leaders from among these former peasant cantors and pilgrimage guides because they represented the intelligentsia of the

---

374 Iosif Petru Pal ended his 1942 book, on the origins of the Moldovan Catholics, with a chapter titled

"The message of blood [A vér szava]." In it, he refers to the racist conclusions of the Romanian

physical anthropology, the blood typing analysis done by Petru Râmneantu Petru. (Râmneantu:

Grupele ... op. cit. pp. 51-65.) In his opinion, this investigation also supports his 'scientific'

historical research that: on an ethnic plane, too, the Csángó are of Romanian origin. (Pal: Franciscanii

... op. cit.) It is a clear indication of today's situation in Romania that this work was republished in

1977 in Bákó, with a large press run. (Sylvester, Lajos: A vér szaga. Egy könyv margójára. [The

smell of blood. Marginalia for a book.] Háromszék X. évf., 1998, október 3.).

375 Almanahul ... op. cit. p.77.

Csángó settlements, the only ones able to read and write Hungarian. Documents from the archives of Romanian interior security agencies clearly show that the local repressive institutions continuously observed, even after the end of the second world war, the movements and statements of persons petitioning for Hungarian-language liturgy.[376]

The chief of police in Bákó County reported to his regional superior at Jászvásár in a letter (Nota informativa) dated August 29, 1945 that János (John) Róka, president of the Plow Front in Klézse (Frontul Plugarilor), sent a letter to the local parish priest. In it the president sternly reminds the priest that, with the emergence of the people's democracy, the methods of the 'old times' are a thing of the past. Based on the Groza government's recently announced freedom of religious practice, he asked the priest to spread the Gospel in the local church in Hungarian. Clearly, before accepting the suggestion and a response, the Roman Catholic cleric immediately handed the letter over to the county prefect, then to the mayor of Bákó. When János Róka was giving the keynote speech on August 12, 1945 at the establishment of a collective farm, *Brotherhood*, in Rekecsin, he said that the police continue to side with the rich. He openly encouraged the Csángó not to be afraid of the police, to replace the Hungarian signs at the intersections, to not persecute children in elementary school for not being familiar with the Romanian language.[377] Another police report, this time from 1947, details that Gheorghe Frâncu of Klézse visited the parish priest and asked for his permission to hold the liturgy in the village church in Hungarian.[378]

Amidst the political changes following the second world war, at the intercession of HPAR, a priest who was very familiar with the community's mother tongue was assigned to Lészped. At the installation of the new parish priest, the priest Talmacsel made an appearance, he who was earlier forced to leave by the community. In his passionate speech, the priest clearly told the villagers that they can all use their mother tongue – but only outside the church. Later, he recruited drunk parishioners with the aim of driving out the Hungarian-sympathizer priest. Soon, a letter arrived from the bishop's chancery in which the newly appointed priest was removed from Lészped, citing the wish of the people, and the church was again closed.[379]

Shortly after, the bishop appointed Ferenc Simon as the village's parish priest so that he may break the local's resistance with a strong hand. The bishop's appointee incited and bought drinks in the local tavern for Romanian-sympathizers who then attacked with their staves the faithful,

---

376 Nastasa: Minoritati ... op. cit.

377 Ibid, pp. 166-167.

378 Ibid, pp. 492-493.

379 Balázs: Egy csángófalu ... op. cit.

singing and praying in Hungarian in the church garden. The fleeing and humiliated flock sent a delegation and a letter to bishop Antal (Anthony) Durkovics in Jászvásár, asking the prelate for a religious existence in their mother tongue. In the chancery, administrator Lorenz and chaplain Backmayer, of Schwabian origin, threatened the delegation with having the malcontents' lands confiscated, the violent arrested and forcibly deported to assigned homes. Since the bishop definitely rejected the request of his flock, in Lészped, the drunk followers of the priest planned to attack the Hungarian-praying faithful during Pentecost, resulting in a melee inside the church. In his sermon, Father Simon excommunicated those locals who dared to demand Hungarian-language liturgy and religious experience in Jászvásár. Due to these events, the parish priest was forced to quietly depart from the village but, before he left, he again firmly bolted the church doors.[380]

As a result of these events fomented from higher up, the church council of Lészped asked the dean of the church in Bákó, in the name of the 400 parishioners, to have the Hungarian liturgy reinstated in their village, as the democratic authorities of Romania guarantee the right of minorities living on its territory. The church elder replied to the petitioners, that the issue of the language of the masses is definitively concluded and thus must be celebrated in the Romanian language – and, if they continue to make waves, they will not be assigned a parish priest for another decade. Bishop Durkovics finally visited the Lészped parish and addressed the assembled populace in Hungarian in the village school. When the prelate was leaving the village, a ticklish situation arose in its outskirts, with the assembled throng sending him off with a Hungarian-language rendition of the Internationale.[381]

In light of the events, in 1946, the Hungarian parishioners of Lészped turned directly to the Ministry of Nationalities and Religious Affairs in Bucharest to be allowed to hear Masses in Hungarian in their village. When a written request was demanded, they countered that a plebiscite was held in the village regarding the question and a total of 310 supported the re-introduction of Hungarian-language liturgy. At the same time, the 'reactionary' Roman Catholic priest could only intimidate 92 persons to vote against Hungarian-language sermons.[382]

The Hungarians of Lészped justified their brave and determined demonstration with the reasoning that the prefect of Bákó County, the minority laws and the Constitution permit the free use of minority languages. While this was progressing, relations between the parish priest, Ferenc Simon, and the authorities deteriorated to such an extent that finally the local council banished the priest from the village. In an attempt to settle the

380 Ibid; Balázs: Vatikáni ... op. cit. p. 15.

381 Ibid, (Vatikáni) p. 7.

382 Nastasa: Minoritati ... op. cit. p. 878.

prevailing mood, Padre Gherghina, born in Nagypatak, was posted to Lészped who held masses in Romanian and Hungarian and who blessed and supported the local Hungarian school. After a long, long time, Hungarian songs were finally heard in the village church on Christmas eve of 1947. Ioan Gherghina (born János Györgybíró), the Csángó descended parish priest of Lészped, who forwarded his parishioners' request to the bishop in Jászvásár, in short order received a written instruction from his superior that, in matters pertaining to religion, he is permitted to use only Romanian and Latin. In the same breath, the bishop firmly censured and punished those 16 Csángó who took a brave stance for Hungarian-language liturgy.[383]

The brave stand of the Csángó farmers, and a fear of the HPAR activists, shortly led to a general 'softening' by priests in other villages. As but one example, the priest in Gorzafalva began to preach to his flock in Hungarian, his cantors (János (John) Gál and Mihály (Michael) Valentin) sang in church in Hungarian at the request of the people. According to a written 1951 report, the priests of Gyoszén and Dormánfalva sided with sympathy alongside those petitioning for a liturgy in Hungarian.[384]

A Csángó-Hungarian delegate informed the Hungarian Mission in Bucharest in October of 1946 that the democratic minority policies announced by the Groza government could not be observed in any meaningful way. The Hungarian diplomats accredited to Bucharest protested regarding these events in 1947 to Peter Groza, Romania's new Communist Prime Minister. Although Moldova's Catholic bishop, Anton Durcovici, permitted the use of Hungarian in religious and church matters in his written decree 317 of 1947, it was not carried out in a single village. Pastors serving in the vicinity of Bákó (in Lészped, Klézse, Nagypatak, Ferdinánd, Trunk, Tratosvásár and Pusztina) threatened with excommunication, shunning and public humiliation those of the faithful who dared to sing and pray in Hungarian. In a few villages, they marked the defenders of Hungarian-language liturgy with a black cross, after which they were chased from the church. In these villages, the priests not only continuously stirred the mood against minority language liturgy but also against the Hungarian language schools, as well. The Cluj (Kolozsvár) newspaper, *Világosság*, in its August 11, 1947 issue sharply condemned the behavior of those priests of the Csángó territories, their feudal terror, who, in speeches from the altar, branded Hungarian as the language of Satan. Nándor Czikó, an activist of HPAR, on his 1947 tour of Moldova encouraged the Csángó to fearlessly use their mother tongue in spite their priests' disapproval, while handing out Hungarian-language song books in their midst.[385]

---

383 Ibid, p. 878.

384 Vincze: Csángósors ... op. cit. pp. 220-234.

385 Nastasa: Minoritati ... op. cit. pp. 438-444.

113

In this troubled and complex age, the communist authorities, advocating an atheist ideology, made use, in a perverse way, of the tensions between the local communities pleading for a Hungarian liturgy and the Roman Catholic priests. For example, a farmer of modest means in Rekecsin, who became a communist during his earlier Russian incarceration, began to openly attack the local priest, since he was loath to initiate Hungarian-language liturgy in the church. Mihai Baba, the local judge, tried to have his staunch supporters abduct the 'reactionary' priest of Külsorekecsin, Carol /Karl/ Susan in February of 1949. since the local women prevented the arrest of the priest, the head person of the village quickly called out the political police. The farmers, however, bravely surrounded the automobile that arrived at the scene and forced the armed soldiers inside to beat a hasty retreat. After the events, the men organized an around-the-clock watch, gathering quickly at the tolling of the bell when, in the early hours of May 10, 1949, authorities surrounded the settlement with a substantial armed force. The farmers grabbed scythes, pitchforks and axes to protect their church, families and priest. The sounds of automatic gunfire forced them to flee. The soldiers relentlessly arrested those who defied them, took the prisoners - beaten unconscious - to Bákó where they were jailed. As they were unable to arrest the wanted priest, the soldiers attacked the house of the cantor, the leader of the 'miniature revolution,' and shot to death Antal Beke, a father of nine, in front of his family.[386] The concealed priest, seeing the pressure brought to bear by the authorities soon surrendered and the summary judicial court sentenced him to 10 years in prison. Many fled to the forests to escape retribution but were eventually caught after many months, subjected to brutal beatings, sentenced and carried off to the construction site of the Danube canal. There they were in the company, and suffered along with, the farmers similarly rounded up from Bogdánfalva, Forrófalva, Klézse, Lujzikalagor, Pusztina and Trunk. In a sense, the events in Bákó County were a close reflection of the political turn of events of the day in Romania: through extensive electoral fraud, the Romanian Communist Party won the elections of November of 1946 and immediately undertook a ruthless campaign against its unswerving opposition, the Roman Catholic Church,[387] which it branded as reactionary.

The police account, dated April 5, 1947, reported that one György (George) Tót, a farmer of Gerlén of 'irredentist' views and recently returned from Hungary, along with the parish priest, Ioan Minut, together conspired to

---

386 A son of the murdered cantor, Sylvester by name, decided there and then to become a priest. (Grossu,

Sergiu: Calvarul României crestine. /no place given/, 1992, pp. 74-77.)

387 Ferenczes, István: Ordasok tépte tájon [A land ravaged by wolves]. Riport-novellák. Csíkszereda,

1997, p 79-85.

incite the local Hungarians. They entered the Roman Catholic church of Lészped where they assaulted and drove out the cantor, by the name of Patrascu, on account he refused to sing in Hungarian. As a result of these events, the Roman Catholic dean in Bákó shortly suspended the Hungarian-sympathizer priest who, however, was allowed to remain in the village after the intercession of the Hungarian Workers Alliance /HWA (Magyar Dolgozók Szövetsége /MADOSZ/, one of the legal cover organizations of the pre-election Romanian Communist Part). Later, the county prefect, along with the HWA representative, reviewed the events *in situ,* then made enquiries at the deanery as to why they oppose the introduction of Hungarian-language liturgy. The church official informed them that firstly Hungarian schools should be established, as it would not be normal for small children to be learning in school in Romanian and then to be exposed to the liturgy in Hungarian. The chief of the county police unequivocally summed it up at the end of his letter as to why he was reluctant to permit local introduction of Hungarian-language religious practices: If one community succeeds in introducing Hungarian as the language of the services, then (in his opinion) it would immediately follow that Bákó County, and all the Csángó settlements, would follow its example in avalanche fashion.[388]

In the years following the Second World War, deep antagonism grew between the local Romanian administration and the Csángó farmers resolutely taking a stand for the introduction and enforcement of the Hungarian language. The former intimidated and threatened the latter with: if the Russians leave Romania, the malcontented Hungarian-Csángó villages will be wiped off the face of the Earth with cannon fire.[389] As an indication of how serious the authorities took this possibility, padre Gherghina was accused, after the religious rebellion of Lészped, of being in the service foreign reactionary powers. He was arrested and jailed in 1959 on trumped up charges and sentenced to forced labor, which he spent in the horrific Romanian 'gulag' of Insula Mare a Brailei amidst inhumane circumstances. His gentle humanity and broad European knowledge and culture rapidly impressed his fellow prisoners, who treated him with great respect during his prison years. Finally, he was released after nine years of harsh, inhuman labor, in 1964. After gaining his freedom, this modest and decent priest

---

388 "semnalam aceasta actiune ce se duce pentru introducerea limbii maghiare in biserica în mijlocul populatiei ceangaiesti, întrucât reusita acestei actiuni într-o comuna ar atrage dupa sine introducerea limbii maghiare în toate comunele ceangaiesti din acest judet si din Moldova..." (Nastasa: Minoritati ... op. cit. p. 500.)

389 Vincze: Csángósors ... op. cit. pp. 217-219.

served his flock in Burjánfalva, Kelgyeste and Somoska, who could say their confessions not only in Romanian but also Hungarian.[390]

The Moldovan Roman Catholic priests, with close ties to the Romanian secret services,[391] continued to dominate the rural communities in their regions with medieval methods and means, in spite of the changed power shifts following the Second World War. In spite of the drought of 1946-1947, they demanded such huge amounts of produce, labor and monies, which the modestly-living locals were unable meet. To illustrate, in 1948, the priest of Klézse, Hojdin, demanded 500 Lei for each funeral ceremony, 50 for each baptism and 600 for a marriage. The parish priest also demanded payment-in-kind (usually in the form of a plump hen) for the 'initiation' of the newborn and the young maidens. If any forgot to shoulder their duty in such manner, he refused to consider such an infant as truly baptized, such maidens as later women, and refused to bury their dead relatives.[392] In several settlements, the parish priest crowned, in front of the altar, the heads of unwed mothers with a wreath of thorns, making her parents hold black flags and candles. The priest of Trunk, Gergucz, disgraced the daughter of Márton Vak by locking her in a pigpen as punishment. He publicly excommunicated János (John) Zsitár for organizing a dance in his own yard for the young people, and for joining HPAR.[393]

Nicolae Ceausescu reached the pinnacle of the Romanian Communist Party in 1965 and was forced to loosen, for a few years, his ideological and minority policies in the aftermath of the 1968 events of Prague. As part of this process, dialogue between Romania and the Vatican was restarted, which Ceausescu attempted to use to boost his personal prestige in international affairs. As a result of these discussions, the Pope received Ceausescu in Rome, in 1973, and thus, even the Holy Father lent a certain legitimacy to the double-dealing Romanian communist dictator. The dialogue between Romania and the Holy See continued in 1978, which finally ended with Ioan

390 Sylvester, Lajos: "Voltunk mük es ... " Gyergyina páter halálára ["We also was ..." On the death of pater Gyergyina]. Honismeret XXVII. évf., 2. sz., 1999, pp. 101-102; Hegyeli: Din Arini ... op. cit. p. 70.

391 Dobrincu, Dorin: Informatorii Securitatii în comunitatile religioase din centrul Moldovei (1950). Arhiva Istorica a României, Serie noua. Vol. I, nr. 1., Bucuresti, 2004, pp. 223-224.

392 Balázs, Péter: Papi kíngyóntatás – csendori segédlettel. Nem rossz üzlet háromnegyed millióért Klézsában papnak lenni [Hostile priestly confession – with police assistance. Not a bad business to be a priest in Klézsa for three quarters of a million], In: Igazság IV. évf., február 6, 1948.

393 Balázs, Péter: Egyházi átok, középkori töviskoszorúzás, vesszofuttatás Ferdinándon [Church anathema, medieval wreath of thorns and running the gauntlet in Ferdinand], In: Igazság, IV. évf., február 19, 1948.

Robu ascending to the Roman Catholic bishop's throne of Moldova.[394] During the bleakest years of Ceausescu's dictatorship, the Orthodox patriarch of Romania, Teocist, a most subservient subject of the Conducator, visited Rome in 1989, where he met with Pope John Paul II in the Vatican.[395]

After 1972, Ceausescu introduced an increasingly more brutal dictatorship into Romania, beginning an open war against the Hungarian minority and the non-Orthodox churches. The all-powerful dictator strove, with the assistance of the Roman Catholic Church, to conclude the linguistic and ethnic assimilation of the Hungarians in Moldova. The majority of the Roman Catholic parish priests serving in the Csángó villages were induced to co-operate with the infamous Romanian political police, the Securitate. A significant number of the clergy thus made a devilish compromise, since, to secure permission for to be active in a religious life, they had essentially to serve the intolerant dictator's assimilative policies. They intimidated the faithful through medieval methods (e.g.- excommunication, public humiliation, celebrating a Mass based on black magic, etc.), sharply opposed the use of the mother tongue, even banning Hungarian in private, and very often it was they who sent the secret police after the folklorists who dared enter into the Csángó villages. They persecuted those Csángó who dared to travel to Csíksomlyó, in the Seklerland, and take celebrate the feast of the Pentecost, there to sing, pray and confess in Hungarian. They maintained the same attitude towards parents who sent their children to Hungarian schools in Transylvania.

After the regime change of 1989, in the slowly democratizing Romania, the power and societal prestige of the Church strengthened by leaps and bounds. In a country with an Orthodox majority, the resurgence of the Church was indicated by the fact that the clergy actively interfered in the worldly events of everyday life, being represented at every significant national and political event. With a deft political touch, Romania positioned its diplomatic relations with the Vatican by having archbishopric of Bucharest promoted to a representative Roman Catholic center. Although Transylvania contained close to a million Roman Catholics, while their number barely tipped the scale at 300,000 east of the Carpathians, in 1999, the Pope could only visit Bucharest. The Vatican's point of view with regards to the Csángó of Moldova has not changed in the past decades. Its diplomats see more significance in the retention of a single Romanian-language Roman Catholic community than the slow linguistic, cultural and ethnic assimilation of the Moldovan Hungarian communities. When the Pope visited Hungary for the first time in 1991, a large delegation of Csángó petitioned him for His permission for them the use Hungarian in their

---

394 Bozgan, Ovidiu: Cronica unui esec previzibil. Bucuresti, 2004, pp. 288-390.

395 Almanahul ... op. cit. p.77.

liturgy.[396] During the Pope's second Hungarian visit in September, 1996, the plea was again repeated. Their petition remains unanswered to this day.

After the regime change in Romania, the faithful of Moldova also felt the new opportunities presented by the social and political shift. Many rid themselves of the fears previously pounded into them, so that, in 1990, several Csángó villages (Pusztina, Lészped and Klézse) petitioned the bishop of Jászvásár, in writing, for permission to hold the liturgy in Hungarian. The petitioners were threatened everywhere and publicly denounced by the parish priests; in several villages they were forced to withdraw their petition and signatures. Since Masses can not be held in Hungarian even today, those persons with a strong Hungarian ethnic and linguistic consciousness continue to be forced to practice their religion in their mother tongue within small, trusted circles.

Since 1990, in many Csángó villages (Pusztina, Lészped and Klézse), Hungarian-language masses were organized, with the assistance of Transylvanian priests, in the gardens of private houses but these practices soon provoked the objections of the local Roman Catholic clergy. It became all the more apparent that the ministers do not serve their people, living in biblical poverty, but, exploiting their deep devotion, are actually implementing their feudal-style oppression. They are deaf to any initiative coming from them, take a sharply opposing position to any attempted proposal, any modest 'civil' initiative. As we already noted, a significant majority of the Roman Catholic ministers serving in Moldova were ensnared by the Romanian secret police, the Securitate, well known for its brutal and anti-minority penchant. For this very reason, even after the 1989 change of government, the members of the Moldovan clergy were unable to completely escape the clutches of the secret police since the Church leaders, closely co-operating in the previous era and thus deeply compromised, were readily open to blackmail after 1990. Their intolerant stance is shown by their public condemnation, humiliation and intimidation of those members of their flock who took part in the pilgrimage to the Transylvanian Csíksomlyó to celebrate the feast of the Pentecost. The Csángó of Moldova have a centuries-old custom of taking part, in large numbers, in this Hungarian-language annual religious Transylvanian event. The prohibition for them to attend, thus, would mean a termination of the spiritual connections maintained with the Roman Catholic Hungarians of the Carpathian basin. The parish priest of Onest, as part of his sermon during the 2004 celebrations during the King Saint Stephen feast, accused those of 'other views' with Satanism.

Pope John Paul II visited Romania between May 7 and 9 in 1999. The Orthodox Church refused him permission to visit the Roman Catholic

---

396 Bodnár, Erika /ed./: Szentmise a Szentatyával Budapesten a Hosök terén. 1991. augusztus 20.

Budapest [Mass with the Holy Father in Budapest on Heroes' Square].

118

populated areas of Transylvania and Moldova, allowing only an ecumenical audience in Bucharest. The synod of Romanian Catholic bishops[397] asked the heads of the Orthodox Church on March 8, 1999, not to restrict the time and place of the papal visit, since the majority of his Romanian followers happened to live in Transylvania and Moldova. This fundamental request, that the Pope meet with members of his flock in the Moldovan town of Bákó and Transylvanian Cluj /Kolozsvár/, the Orthodox Church, in its position as the pseudo-state religion, was stymied with wily means.[398] At the open air Mass held on May 9, more than 500,000 Christians took part. It was celebrated in the vast square before the palace built for the megalomaniac Ceausescu at the cost of many innocent lives. A significant number of those present came from the Moldovan Csángó villages. The insulted Roman Catholic leaders of Transylvania did not urge their flocks to travel to Bucharest. Local and international media reported the Pope's Romanian visit as a symbolic rapprochement between the Roman Catholic and Orthodox churches.

---

397 In Romania, the bishop's synod is made up of a total of 16 bishops, 9 Roman Catholic and 7 Greek Catholic. The Roman Catholic bishop's forum was formed shortly after the 1989 regime change, on March 16, 1991 but it only received official sanction on November 25, 1993. (Almanahul ... op. cit. p. 74.)

398 Ibid, p. 74.

III. HISTORICAL AWARENESS OF THE MOLDOVAN HUNGARIANS

A society's historical awareness is closely linked with its sense of identity. In fact, every memory becomes an integral part of building identity. Since there was no functioning Hungarian language school or religious network in the Moldovan rural communities during the civil era, and lacking an intellectual stratum of its own, the elite did not play a significant role in the formation of individual, collective or societal 'memory' until the second half of the 20th century. In their settlements, education is of varying quality to this day, their historical knowledge primarily formed by the Roman Catholic priests. However, the interactions of the rural communities with their priests are extremely ritualized, resisting their best effort to fundamentally change the grasp that the Csángó have on their history, at least in the short term.

In their communities, religious culture in the mother tongue was mainly maintained and spread by peasant-born lay persons and cantors. These simple people lacked proper education, usually leading a farming existence and, under the increasing pressure of Romanian nationalism, were unable to continue to pass on, from generation to generation, even the outstanding events of the history of the Hungarian nation or the deeds of its heroes; they dared not make more conscious use of Hungarian national symbols, such as, the National Anthem or the flag. In fact, up to the 1989 regime change in Romania, we can not document one instance among the Csángó communities of a single physical or intellectual structure or construct relating to Hungarian identity, i.e., there are no special memorials or myths of a cultural nature that in any way cleave to a Hungarian identity. The historical awareness of the Hungarian communities of Moldova is, today, unarticulated and scattered, existing at the personal and biographical oral-history level. Since they fail to receive adequate and accurate information in their schools regarding their own past, their historical knowledge can not come together into a well articulated body. For most young people, their source of information regarding the past is primarily the tales recounted within the family unit, mostly the story of an ancestor's outstanding accomplishment or fate. The collective historical memory of the Moldovan Csángó contains several folklore and popular elements, which have not, however, settled into a strictly chronological order.

According to the inhabitants of Klézse, Hungarians originated in Asia and their most gallant warriors (Csaba, Magyar and Hun) reached their current home during a deer hunt. (What follows is a short quote – in the local dialect – of a version of the Hungarian pre-conquest myth drawing into the same tale the actions of Hunor and Magor /Magyar/ of the Hungarian version and that of prince Csaba, reputedly the leader of the Sekler settlers. The underlying events are centuries apart-*Ed.*)[399] These inhabitants probably brought this conquest myth with them from Transylvania since it is integrally intertwined with the Hungarian myth of Hunor and Magor and the Sekler's myth regarding prince Csaba and his Huns.

In 1844, János (John) Jerney noted that in the vicinity of Galac, the Romanians called a flat stretch where a ford crossed the Danube as *Vadul Ungurului*, or *Hungarian ferry*. István (Stephen) Györffy is of the opinion that this name marks the very spot where, according to the Seklers inhabiting Moldova, Árpád and his people crossed from the Bulgarian populated Dobrudja to reclaim the Carpathian basin, Attila the Hun's one-time realm.[400] In Magyarfalu, the elderly still hold that the Csángó came to Moldova from Transylvania: *"It was told that a man and a woman resettled from Transylvania, and there they just multiplied."*[401] The folks in Pokolpatak stressed that Moldova was first populated by the Hungarians, and that the Romanians arrived later: *"The Hungarians of Moldova were there three hundred years before the Romanians, three hundred years later did the Romanians occupy Moldova."*[402] The folks around Szabófalva feel that Voivod Stefan the Great settled the Hungarians on his territory: *"That's the way I heard it from the old folks, so it may well be so. They said that when*

---

399 „Mikor jöttek Ázsiából a magyarok, mikor jöttek Ázsiából, akkor ugye Csaba, Magyar s Hun. Ezek

megindultak Ázsiából vadászni, jöttek vadászni. Akkor rábukkantak egy szarvasra. Az a szarvas

addig jött, de ok lóháton utána, a szarvas után, és akkor jöttek, s akkor fedezték fel Magyarországot,

itt ezt a területet. Akkor visszamentek. Mikor visszamentek, hát akkor mondták ezek a fiak, mert a

magyar királynak a fiai voltak ugye, s akkor azt mondták, hogy:

Fiaim válasszatok magatoknak embereket!

A Magyar, a Hun s a Csaba, hárman vótak azok a királyfiak. Esszeszedte a csapatjait mindegyik

királyfi, esszeszedte ezerivel a népet, megindultak, harcolunk, elfoglaljuk. S akkor jöttek ide.

Hát Csaba megállott az erdo szélin, azt mondta:

Itt székeljetek, míg én visszajövök.

Mert Csaba visszament, hogy hozza a többi csapatokat ki. Akkor kiabáltak:

Vissza Csaba, vissza, mert ölnek meg az ellenségeink!

Itten még lakók voltak, aztán szemben álltak azokval. Akkor jött Csaba, lovakval, lóháton, úgy jött,

mintha a felhobe jött volna, és kiverte az ellenséget. S akkor itt maradtak a magyarok."

(Bosnyák, Sándor: A moldvai magyarok hitvilága [The belief structure of the Moldovan

Hungarians]. Folklór Archívum 12, Budapest, 1980, p. 54.)

400 Györffy, István: Néphagyomány a Székelyföld délmoldvai határáról (1923) [Folk tradition about the

South Moldovan border of Seklerland (1923)], In: Magyar nép – magyar föld. Budapest, 1942, pp.

470-471.

401 Bosnyák: A moldvai ... op. cit. p. 57.

402 Ibid, p. 54.

121

there were wars, Stefán Cselmáré or Stefan Nogy /sic/ asked for assistance from the Hungarians against the Turks. War came, many Romanians, Vlachs died, and these lands stood empty. He said: They are empty, stay. And now the Romanians are often angry at us, we took the prime places, in the best spots, Moldova, Szeret, these are the best growing places.[403]

It is interesting to note that the southern Csángó also enshrine in memory that the Voivod brought in the Hungarians to raise the agricultural standard of his country: *"We were brought in from Hungary by Alexandru cel Bun, to be farmers, so the Vlachs can learn from us, to be farmers, too."*[404]

In the Sekler populated Csángó villages, many recall that their ancestors fled to Moldova after the bloody retribution after the 1764 rebellion of Mádéfalva, to escape the brutal Austrian reprisals. (Again, a reminiscence in the local patois, recounting the original Sekler villages from where some of the Moldovan Hungarian families came-*Ed*.)[405]

Among the Moldovan Hungarian communities, countless instances remain extant tied to the myths and legends of King Saint Stephen. There are several churches in Moldova dedicated in his honor but primarily it is the folk versions of old religious hymns about him that can be heard at the pilgrimages. Many Csángó even today still refer to Hungary as *the country of King Saint Stephen*.[406] The cult of the first, saintly Hungarian king most likely spread to Moldova with the colonists of the 13th-14th century, to be reinforced and embroidered with late-Baroque elements by the Sekler groups of the 18th century.

Kickófalva, situated in the northern-Csángó block, dedicated its church to his memory back in the Middle Ages, while of the Sekler Csángó village churches established during the 18th century, only the churches of

---

403 Ibid, p. 57.

404 Gazda: Hát én ... op. cit. p. 11.

405 „Madéfalván mikor vót egy nagy verekedés, hogy lepallták (leverték) mind a németek vagy ausztriákok, magyarok melyikek vótak azok, akkor sok világ elfutott bé oda héjzánk, elcsángottak, elfuttak bé oda, keresztül Gyimesen s bé Moldovába, héjzánk, s hol megkapták ezeket a falukot, asztán sokan jöttek. Pusztinába ... Pálok jöttek onnat Madéfalváról, Kispálok, s asztán Sebestén az Kostelekrol, Golombán a Hidegségrol, azok bé vótak csángotva héjzánk, s azér monták csángó." (Pávai: Etnonimek ... op. cit. p. 77.)

406 Gunda, Béla: Mi a magyar? [What is a Hungarian?] (Virrasztók. Vígilia – antológia. Budapest, 1985, p. 583. Cites Magyar, Zoltán: Szent István alakja a moldvai magyar néphagyományban [The figure of Saint Stephen in Moldovan Hungarian folk legend]. Honismeret XXV. évf., 4 sz., 1997, p. 6.

122

Pusztina, Gajcsána and Szolohegy were dedicated to him.[407] Kickófalva is one of the oldest of the northern-Csángó settlements. Its older name (Steckófalva) is of Slavic origin, which retains a familiar form [nickname-*Ed.*] of Stephen's name. Its main altar was decorated with a statue and oil painting of Saint Stephen, which was removed in the 1980's.[408] His feast day was popular for centuries with the surrounding population, which, according to a document from 1679, was celebrated every August 20, until it was moved to September 2 at the beginning of the 20th century.[409] According to Pál Péter (Paul Peter) Domokos, in his compilation made in the 1930's, only the aged cantor, Lajos (Louis) Jancsó, spoke Hungarian in the village. For the parishioners, who no longer understood Hungarian, he translated into Romanian the song *About King Saint Stephen* /Szent István királyról/ found in the third edition of János (John) Kájoni's *Cantionale Catholicum*. In vain did the cantor exchange *Catolicilor* for *Hungarians* in the Saint Stephen song, the local priests, in the end, advised against it.[410]

The text of the Codex Bandinus also recorded that in the 17th century, the pilgrims at the fair of Sztánfalva, on the banks of the Tatros, sang songs about the patroness of Hungary. Zoltán Magyar felt that among these may have been heard some songs of Saint Stephen, popular in Seklerland in those days, brought by the pilgrims from Transylvania to Moldova. We feel quite possible that, beside the pilgrimages, their spread

---

407 According to an 1871 report of the Katholikus Néplap /Catholic People's Paper/, large masses took

part in the festivities organized in honor of Saint Stephen at the end of the 19th century in Szolohegy.

(Magyar, Zoltán: Szent István a néphagyományban. Budapest, 2000, p. 213.)

408 In 1991, Zoltán Magyar came across a memorial at the former site of the church where a retired

economist erected a cave-like structure in which he placed statues of Saints Stephen and Peter, as

well as the Virgin. Since then, a Mass is celebrated there every year in the first week of September.

(Halász, Péter: A moldvai csángó falvak társadalmának néhány sajátossága [A few peculiarities of

the Csángó communities], In: Novák, László (ed.): Az Alföld társadalma. Nagykorös, 1997, pp. 423-

433.)

409 Pope Innocent XI fixed this day to honor King Saint Stephen. However, the Hungarians of the

Carpathian basin continue to observe his feast on August 20.

410 The Romanian version of the first verse read:

Astazi ziua renumita

Si câta-i de vesela

Catolicilor.

Pecând o sarbatorim

Si cu cântari pomenim

Pe Sfântu Stefan.

was aided by the fact that the 1676 first edition of the Kájon hymnal contained two songs about our saintly first king.[411]

The main altar of the Pusztina church still shows King Saint Stephen in the act of offering his country to the protection of the Virgin, proffering the holy crown of Hungary towards her. In the first half of the 20th c., the date of the traditional fair to the memory of our first king was shifted from August 20 to the first Sunday in September. The folk version of the religious hymn from the Middle Ages that starts *O, praise be Saint Stephen* is still popular in the village.

In the Sekler populated Csángó villages the religious song that begins *O, where are you, shining star of the Hungarians* (Ó, hol vagy magyarok tündöklo csillaga[412]) is widely known, which can be found in 18th century hymnals (e.g.- Szent Mihályi and Bozóki) in fundamentally differing variations. This popular hymn was once sung all across the Carpathian basin as a national anthem, several variations are known from Moldova.[413] Its melody is medieval, a folk-adapted version of the song *Mittit as virginem,* with close to a hundred variations known. Zoltán Magyar posits that its popularity spread on Hungarian-speaking territories after the 1771 return of the saint's reliquary, his intact right hand. It is quite possible that enjoyed a great deal of popularity in Seklerland in the middle of the 18th century from where those masses fleeing the aftermath of Mádéfalva brought it with them from their homeland, popularizing it in several corners of Moldova.[414] At the pilgrimage fairs organized in Szolohegy in the 1970's, this hymn to Saint Stephen could still be heard.[415]

The population of Szolohegy grew rapidly in the decades after the Mádéfalva events that in 1791 the inhabitants erected a belfry and a wooden church to the honor of King Saint Stephen. Popular legend has it that the carpenters consumed six sacks of snuff and drank six barrels of wine. Both structures were torn down, the damaged church after the earthquake of the 1980's and the belfry immediately after the 1989 regime change. The parish priest noted on the information poster he hung in 1974 by the church door that the 50 kg. bell, cast in 1009, originated from neighboring Tatros, which was buried in the vicinity of a village, Diószeg, during one of the Tatar

---

411 Domokos: Édes hazámnak ... op. cit. pp. 833-834, 835-836.

412 Pozsony, Ferenc: Újesztendohöz kapcsolódó szokások a moldvai csángóknál [Folk customs connected with the new year]. Néprajzi Látóhatár III. 1-2. sz., 1994, pp. 138-139.

413 Pávai: Vallási ... op. cit. p. 12; Seres, András – Szabó, Csaba: Csángómagyar Daloskönyv [Csángó-Hungarian songbook]. Budapest, 1991, pp. 31-32, 525; Pozsony: Újesztendohöz ... op. cit. p. 262.

414 Magyar: Szent István ... op. cit. p. 216.

415 Tánczos, Vilmos: Keletnek megnyílt kapuja. Néprajzi esszék. [The gates of the East opened. Ethnographic essays]. Kolozsvár, 1996, p. 125.

incursions. This unique artifact of cultural history was intentionally destroyed at the end of the 20th century, melted down into one of the bells of the new church. The ancient pictures, processional flags and other church equipment also didn't find a new home in the new church. Also, its patron saint was replaced. The most important village fair is now held on August 22, the day dedicated to *Regina Maria*, Mary, Queen of Heaven.[416]

The Catholic communities of the Carpathian basin usually offer remembrance to Saint Stephen the Martyr on December 26, as part of popular name-day congratulations. In many regions, the figure of our first king, interestingly, crept into the text of the recited salutations. Folklorists have noted and documented this process in Moldova, too. As but one example, in Klézse, the folks circle the village, singing Christmas carols, saluting all the farmers named Stephen with the song *O, where are you, shining star* ...(Ó, hol vagy magyarok ...).[417] Recently, Imre Harangozó recorded a Saint Stephen song in Szitás, between the Tatros and Ojtoz Rivers, which originated from Seklerland,[418] and which was usually only sung during the pilgrim processions of the Sekler Csángó villages. Several historical-based songs survived in some of the villages (Lujzikalagor and Lészped), which immortalize the figure of King Stephen marching to war.[419] Zoltán Kallós came across a historical song in Lészped in the 1950's, which also sang of King Stephen going off to war – against the Ottomans, whom he successfully beat. Even though the source of the song knew no Romanian, he held that the song was actually a voivod of Moldova, Stefan the Great.[420] The linking of the figures of the Hungarian king and the Moldovan voivod promoted the popularity of the colored prints of the heroic deeds of Stefan Nagy that were in circulation at the fairs during the end of the 19th century. Elek Gego remarked on seeing such an image in a Bákó inn.[421]

The Roman Catholic Hungarians of Moldova (as opposed to the Orthodox Romanians) celebrated the end of the carnival with merriment, masquerades and dancing – even to this day. The traditional legends connected to these festivities in many northern and southern Csángó

---

416 Ibid, pp. 126-130.

417 Gelencsér, József: Szent István a csángóknál [Saint Stephen among the Csángó]. Fejér Megyei Hírlap, augusztus 18, 1990, p. 8. Cites Magyar: Szent István ... op. cit. p. 189.

418 In Seklerland, all the Stephens were saluted with this song on the day after Christmas.

419 Kallós, Zoltán: Ismeretlen balladák Moldvából [Unknown ballads from Moldova]. Néprajzi Közlemények III. 1-2, 1958, p. 51; Vargyas, Lajos: A magyar népballada és Európa I-II [The Hungarian folk ballad and Europe, vol. I-II]. Budapest, 1976, pp. 573-574.

420 Ibid (Vargyas), p. 573.

421 Gego: A moldvai ... op. cit. p. 23.

settlements often are linked with King Stephen, in other cases, it harkens to Saint Ladislaus [László, another saintly Hungarian king-*Ed.*].[422]

At the turn of the 19th-20th century, Romanian national intolerance gained strength in Moldova, too, which intensified during the first world war when, in 1916, the Kingdom of Romania suddenly turned on, and attacked, the Austro-Hungarian Empire. As a result of the turn of events, most Csángó villages intentionally took steps to eradicate forever the cult of King Saint Stephen. In the village of Gajcsa, they took down the painting above the altar, showing our first king in his robes, holding a sword and orb, and replaced it with another showing the Martyr Saint Stephen. The old painting, however, they retained until a few decades ago in the sacristy.[423] During his 1932 tour of Moldova, Pál Péter Domokos saw the painting in the choir of the church, Zoltán Magyar saw the image on a no longer used processional banner in 1992.[424] This reality clearly shows that nationalist restrictions of the 20th century reached even this backward village, although the locals could not bear to completely destroy the icons. We have taken part, several times in the past decades, in the festivities organized in Pusztina in honor of Saint Stephen where we can attest that the sermons of the Moldovan clergy merely make mention of his religious and church activities. They consciously omit any mention of the importance of his 'worldly' achievements, of having founded a country.

Saint Emery /var. Emeric/, the son of King Stephen, died very young amid tragic circumstances. He was officially canonized shortly after, in 1083, to become a symbol of Catholic Hungary, along with his father. The figure of the prince, embodiment of hope and meaning to our first great king, was presented during the Hungarian Middle Ages and the subsequent Age of Chivalry, i.e., during the 14th-15th centuries, as the symbol of purity, the 'lily-white' prince living in this world exclusively for the afterlife. His popularity temporarily waned during the Reformation but by the 17th-18th century, baroque interpretation painted him as an ideal for youth, as an example of a patriot. The prince enjoyed a certain popular following in Moldova, too. The 1851 publication, *Schematismus S. Missionis Romano-Catolicae in Principatu Moldaviae,* contained several prayers to the memory of Saint Emery.[425]

Prince Emery's tragic accident was retained in the memory of the Moldovan Hungarians, too: *"He was the son of King Stephen. He went*

422 Magyar: Szent István ... op. cit. p. 186.

423 Halász: Nem lehet ... op. cit. p. 353.

424 Magyar: Szent István alakja ... op. cit. p. 7; Magyar: Szent István ... op. cit. p. 214.

425 Domokos: A moldvai ... op. cit. (1987) p. 116.

hunting. He went hunting on horseback and when he came to the forest, an old woman shouted and told him, she said:

Don't go further, great peril awaits you!

Well, Prince Emery drew his sword and says:

My sword is strong, my sword is sharp, without God's knowledge not a hair will not be harmed on my head.

Weelll, she says, it is so, but goes on, don't go further, turn back because a terrible danger awaits!

He repeated anew, he said:

Without God's knowledge not a hair will not be harmed on my head!

He started. The old woman said again:

Turn back, understand my words, a terrible danger awaits!

He did not heed and went on. A large boar jumped out , a big male, and tore into him. He fell from his horse, got torn , his red blood drained. And this was his peril. That old one was an angel, God sent the angel, not to go on, to turn him back. He did not heed, that was his danger."[426]

Another version of the legend recounts the tragic event thusly: *"Saint Emery went hunting. An old woman stepped out and told him: Ayee, young man, go back! If you go on, a great danger awaits. Then, Saint Emery drew his sword and said: My arm is strong, my sword is sharp, not a hair on my head will be bent without God's knowledge! He turned to go but the old woman said: Turn back and listen to me! Turn back! Cause grave danger awaits! But Saint Emery repeated: My arm is strong, my sword is sharp, not a hair on my head will be bent without God's knowledge! He went and a large boar jumped out, tore him and his red blood flowed. The angel told him but he was loath to listen. He who does not heed God's words go into danger. He did not heed the words of warning and the boar tore into him. This is the story of saint Emery."*[427]

The figure of king Saint László /Ladislaus/ has been retained in the memory of the Hungarian people in varied forms, especially among those living on the eastern periphery of the Hungarian-speaking territory, among the Seklers and the Csángó, where his popularity rivaled that of many biblical figures. We can assume that the reverence toward our knightly king among the Moldovan communities already manifested itself in the Middle Ages.

---

426 The legend was recorded by Sándor Bosnyák in Lujzikalagor. (Magyar, Zoltán: A liliomos herceg.

Szent Imre a magyar kultúrtörténetben [The lily-white prince Emery in Hungarian cultural history].

Budapest, 2000, p. 128.)

427 Harangozó, Imre: „Anyám, anyám, szép Szuz Márjám ..." Régi imádságok a moldvai magyaroktól.

["Mother, mother, my dear Virgin ... " Old prayers from the Hungarians of Moldova.] Lüko Gábor

eloszavával [Foreword by Gábor Lüko]. Újkígyós, 1992, pp. 75-76.

Although the influence of Hungarian lay and religious institutions radically diminished and almost disappeared in the region East of the Carpathians beginning in the second half of the 16th century, about the time of the dissolution of a centralized Hungarian monarchy, the memory of King László is still fresh in the collective memory of the Moldovan Hungarian communities of today. The medieval legacy was strengthened by the Sekler settlers of the 18th century who, for instance, raised their church in Vizánta in honor of Saint László.[428]

The cult of our knight king was formed, to a degree, by the Hungarian religious hymns about him. The Moldovan Csángó still retain to this day fragments of the Saint László hymn popular in the 15th century.[429] The Moldovan Hungarians most probably read the words of the hymn on the exterior wall of the Saint Anthony of Padua chapel in Csík during the annual, and very well visited, Feast of the Pentecost. As an interesting aside, the book of prayers published by the Moldovan bishopric in 1851 contained, among other things, prayers to Saints László and Emery.[430]

The *Annales Hungarica* /Magyar Évkönyv/ most probably was compiled in the Benedictine monastery of Szeretvásár, founded in 1377, which was later used in the 18th century Moldovan chronicle, *Eustratie logofat*. It recounts an interesting legend about a brave deed of King László.[431] Gábor Lüko posits that the source of this Moldovan tale of Saint László is the legend recounted in the Dubniczi Chronicle, in which Endre Laczkfi, Voivod of Transylvania, marched against the Tatars at the head of his army. In the midst of the battle, the Sekler warriors turned to Saint László

---

428 Domokos: A moldvai ... op. cit. (1987) p. 116.

429 Ki iél, megálggyad,

Ki holt, nyugosszad,

Ki messze, meghozzad,

Bunösz lielkünkért,

Jézuszt imággyad,

Idvezlégy kegyelmesz

Szent László királ!

Magyar, Zoltán: Szent László a magyar néphagyományban [Saint László in Hungarian folk tradition]. Budapest, 1998, p. 267.

430 Domokos: A moldvai ... op. cit. (1987) p. 116.

431 In referencing the Hungarian annal (letopisetul unguresc), the Moldovan Romanian chronicle of about 1645 consistently refers to the king as Laslau, instead of the Slav form, Vladislav. (Kogâlniceanu, Mihail: Cronicele României. Bucuresti, 1872, p. 378; Lüko: A moldvai ... op. cit. p. 84; Magyar: Szent László ... op. cit. p. 135.)

for aid and with his intercession and guidance they successfully defeated the Tartar forces – and managed to repel them for a long time.[432]

The author of the *Bandinus Codex* noted in the 17th century of the castle ruins near the town of Barlád that, according to folk tradition, that is where Saint László pursued the Tatars.[433] At the same time, an Italian missionary reported that Saint László had a church built in Dnyeszterfejérvár, which was still in existence in 1779.[434] The Hungarian and Saxon inhabitants of Kotnár, famous for its wines, celebrated with a Mass on Saint László's day, during the medieval centuries, that the Hungarian king freed Moldova from Tatar oppression. Zoltán Magyar senses the echo of a church festival behind it.[435] An interesting fact is that, in the middle of the 17th century, one of the best vineyards close to town was to be found on László's Mount.[436]

A Romanian chronicle of the 17th century recounted the origin of the Szeret River in conjunction with King László: "*They chased them through the snowy mountains, those Tatars, they drove them away, those who lived in Moldova because they pursued them until they crossed the Szeret. There King László, who is called Stanislaus in Polish, stood on the river's bank and shouted in Hungarian: I love it, I love it (szeretem, szeretem)! Or: how lovely (asa mi place). Later, when they founded the country, they named the river Szeret after his words. Szeretem.*"[437] It is an interesting fact that among the Moldovan, a tradition has remained to this day that Saint László, after expelling the Tatars, extended the eastern boundary of his country all the way to the *Száraz Szeret* (Dry Szeret).[438] In this regard, Imre Harangozó recently recorded the following in Bogdánfalva: "*Moldova was a part of Hungary! The border was the bank of the Dry Szeret, towards the interior! This was so in the time of Saint László.*" The Protestant missionary, Márton (Martin) Czelder, printed in his newspaper in 1868 that the Seklers hold the valley of the Dry Szeret, between the towns of Galac and Tekucs, as the eastern boundary of Seklerland. When traveling towards Transylvania, on reaching this sand filled riverbed, they pause and doff their hat.[439]

---

432 Ibid (Lüko), pp. 84-85.

433 Domokos: A moldvai ... op. cit. (1987) p. 359.

434 Mikecs, László: Csángók [The Csángó]. Budapest, 1989, p. 91.

435 Gunda, Béla: A moldvai magyar népi muveltség jellegéhez: néprajzi gyujtoúton a moldvai magyaroknál [Addenda to the characteristics of the Moldovan Hungarian folk civilization: an ethnigraphic gathering tour among the Hungarians of Moldova]. Népi Kultúra–Népi Társadalom XV., Budapest, 1990, pp. 58-59; Magyar: Szent László ... op. cit. p. 262.

436 Domokos: A moldvai ... op. cit. (1987) p. 415.

437 Lüko: A moldvai ... op. cit. p. 50.

438 Magyar: Szent László ... op. cit. p. 138.

439 Györffy: Néphagyomány ... op. cit. pp. 469-471.

The oral traditions of the Moldovan Hungarians only retained the final day of the battle of Saint László against the Tatars, falling on the first day of Lent, as the origin of that feast. As already noted, the Romanian chronicle, making use of Hungarian sources, also contains the following script, translated by Gábor Lüko: "*King László returned with honor and victorious, arriving on the day of fast, asked for the blessing of his bishops, to be allowed to feast for three days with the queen and the lords. They gave their blessing for the court to begin the fast on Tuesday (Shrove Tuesday). In their religion, they still hold to the tradition of abstaining from meat during Lent.*"[440] Since this legend was only found in Moldova and Ghimes, it is probable that it was born during the Middle Ages among the Hungarian communities East of the Carpathians, who retained it during the 16th-17th centuries, from there to spread to the folklore of the Csángó, who gradually populated the valley of the Ghimes during the 18th-19th centuries.[441]

This widely known legend was recounted in Klézse thusly: "*King Saint László, when he was away at war, came late from the war, did not reach home before the day of the fast, he returned late. Where he rode his horse, his sword left a furrow and when he reached home, he said to his Hungarian Catholic people, now we will fast, abstain from meat. That is why the days of fast are different from the Romanians and others.*"[442]

Sándor (Alexander) Bosnyák came across another version in Gyoszén that contained more details: "*Now I will tell a tale as I remember it from my old father when they would meet in the spinning room, one told a store, then another. They told other stories but those I don't well recall, but this one I remember as it was about the fast. They said, as told by my father, and the other aged men, too, that a long time ago, when the Tatars were here, then King László mounted up with his army and his vassals and chased them away. And to keep the Tatars in fear forever, so they will never return, they took a big bell, tied it with rope, tied it to the branch of a tree. That branch, when the wind blows, the branch rings the bell, always rings the bell. The Tatars never, ever returned because they knew that it was a reminder of King Saint László, that they are there, guarding it to this day. When King Saint László returned, it was on the market day, Sunday, late at night they returned. They had no more time to abstain from the fast, not to submit. Then he asked the good Lord, to grant him two days, so they too may make merry. And the Lord granted them two days, Monday and Tuesday, so*

---

440 Lüko: A moldvai ... op. cit. pp. 48-56. Cites Magyar: Szent László ... op. cit. p.135.

441 Ibid (Magyar), p. 136.

442 Bosnyák: A moldvai ... op. cit. p. 54.

that they may feast for two days, which is why I remember because in the years after, there came Shrove Monday and Tuesday[443]

Interestingly, in the villages around Románvásár (in Jugán, for example) Saint Stephen is the chief character in the mythic tale: *"Stefan, the great king, when he was in the fighting, when he drove out the pagans, when he returned, they gave up eating meat on Sunday night."*[444]

In our times, the identity of the Roman Catholic Csángó receives a great emphasis from the denominational differentiation from the Orthodox Romanians. It is worth stressing that the Orthodox Romanian religious calendar lacks the carnival cycle, hence, in their communities, they have merry masked revels tied primarily to celebrate the winter solstice and the new year. Interestingly, the Hungarians of Moldova have retained, to this day, their 'meatless' merry-making traditions, signaling the end of the carnival at winter's end – which originated from the Carpathian basin. In Szabófalva, they end the weeks of the carnival season on Meatless Tuesday, before the start of Lent, with open-air amusements of teasing, amusing and ribald games, provided by masked *matahala*.[445] Since the beginning of Lent among the Orthodox is two days earlier than among the Hungarians, the legends that justify and explain this difference has a great significance in their communities, even today.

Oral tradition still ties a tree in the outskirts of each of the villages of Csík and Klézse to the person of Saint László.[446] Up until the second world war, travelers in Csík would rest under the centuries old tree and, after their meal, would leave some scraps of food by its trunk.[447] On a folklore gathering trip in 1994, Imre Harangozó recorded that the villagers of Bogdánfalva recounted that Saint László planted a tree on the banks of the Dry Szeret (*Asszuszeret*). When the lot of the Hungarians is good, the tree turns green; when their situation becomes worse, the tree dries up: *"When the Hungarians were battling the Turks in Hungary, and the Turks won, the tree dried up. It turned green about twice but now it's dried up. It's here but it's dry."*

According to those living in Gyoszén, *"There is a poplar in Klézse, twelve paces around, an even twelve steps to go around it. From the time of Saint László, his act, it was. Don't know if it's still there or not, but I think it*

---

443 Ibid, pp. 54-55.

444 Lükő: A moldvai ... op. cit. p. 52.

445 Wichmann, Júlia: A moldvai csángók szokásaiból [Traditions of the Moldovan Csángó], In: Ethnographia XVIII., 1907, pp. 288-289.

446 Gunda: A moldvai magyar ... op. cit. p. 58; Bosnyák: A moldvai ... op. cit. pp. 54, 59.

447 Ibid (Gunda), p. 58.

is because they said that it still hangs on."[448] The populace of Klézse recount it thusly: *"That tree was planted by king Saint László. Came to the village, went down to the Szeret and planted that tree. It is his memorial."*[449] *"Well, there is an old tree our way by the Szeret. They say that it was planted by king Saint László hisself. But it is such a tree, planted in memory, when he drove the outsiders from the country. When the Tatars returned, the tree dried up. When they were driven them out, it bloomed. If the Turks came, it again dried. When the Turks were driven out, then it grew leaves. When Rákóczi was beating the Germans, it was nice and green and later, when they defeated Rákóczi's soldiers, it dried out. When Kossuth's soldiers came in 'forty eight, it again blossomed, to dry out again and so it remained to this day. Who knows when it will turn green one day?."*[450]

This ancient tree in Klézse has, in modern days, been associated with the person of the Romanian king and events of the first world war: *"There was a great tree in Klézse beside the rocky road. In the first world war, when it was over, the king, King Karl came there to review the troops. He came with his children and they made a large podium where the queen sat. The queen wove some nice white wool and a woman approached on her knees and asked permission to wear Hungarian costumes because they were forbidden. And the queen gave permission for Hungarian attire."*[451]

Beside the personages of Saints Stephen, Emery and László, the memory of the figure of King Mathias also remained fresh in the collective memory of the Moldovan Hungarian communities. As but one example, the folk ballad, *Ifjú Mátyás király olyan álmot látott* [The young King Mathias saw a dream], in authentic classical Hungarian vernacular has, to date, only surfaced in Moldova. In its text, it paints the great Renaissance king with symbolic devices.[452]

---

448 Ibid, p. 54.

449 Ibid, p. 59.

450 Recorded by Sándor Bosnyák. See Magyar: Szent László … op. cit. p. 186.

451 Bosnyák: A moldvai … op. cit. p. 59.

452 Pozsony: Újesztendohöz … op. cit. pp. 68-69.

    Éfjú Mátyás kérál ulyan álmot látott,

    Évegablaka alatt nagy hosszú almafa,

    Nagy hosszú almának tizenkét szép ága,

    Tizenkét szép ágán hatvanhat virágja,

    Hatvanhat virágja, három szász levele,

    Éfiú Mátyás kérál sírogatni kezde.

    S ez o kicsi lánya, s az o kicsi lánya,

    Azt mondá nekije, s azt mondá nekije.

The wise girl, able to unravel the riddle, is a well-known device in Hungarian storytelling. The girl, able to fulfill the king's impossible demands and successfully answer the mysterious riddles is present in every European culture. In the ballad form, we only meet her in the Moldovan compilations of the 20th century. The ballad (according to Lajos (Louis) Vargyas) might have originated from the Hungarian folk tale, *Mátyás király és az okos lány* [King Mathias and the wise girl]. The attribute *young*, when applied to the monarch, primarily exists in South Slav poetic literature. The text is built mainly upon Medieval symbolism; researchers found more recent variations in English folk poetry. The figure of the girl giving sage answers to the king's difficult questions also appears in English ballads. The symbolic devices of Hungarian folk ballads and tales fundamentally express that the king wishes to marry this wise and clever girl but she, to escape the regal marriage, chooses death. It is interesting to note that a ballad associated with King Mathias should remain in existence among the Moldovan Hungarians.[453]

Moldovan folk poetry has also enshrined the figure of Mathias, walking among the people in disguise. Pál Péter Domokos first visited the Moldovan Csángó villages in 1932, on a wagon rented in Transylvania. The wagon he packed with pottery from Csík and the police paid him no special notice. Mária Balló of Lészped related that many locals thought the Transylvanian researcher to be King Mathias, the king of Hungary in

---

Mét sírsz, mit keseregsz, édes kedves apám,

Mét sírsz, mét keseregsz, édes kedves apám?

Hogyne keseregnék, édes kicsi lyányom,

Nekem azt mondották, hogy fejemet veszik.

Ne sírj, ne keseregj, édes kedves apám,

Ne sírj, ne keseregj, édes kedves apám.

Mert a te álmod majd felfejtem lesz én:

Nagy hosszú almafa, nagy hosszú esztendo.

Nagy hosszú almafa, nagy hosszú esztendo,

Tizenkét szép ága, tizenkét szép hónap.

Háromszáz levele, háromszáz mies nap,

Háromszáz levele, háromszáz mies nap.

Hatvanhat virágja, hatvanhat vasárnap,

Hatvanhat virágja, hatvanhat vasárnap.

Éfiú Mátyás kérál mosolyogni foga,

Az o iédes liánya álmát feltalálta.

453 Kallós, Zoltán: Balladák könyve. Élo népballadák. [Book of Ballads. Living folk-ballads] Bukarest, 1970,   p. 635; Vargyas: A magyar ... op. cit. pp. 528-531.

mufti.[454] The tale, recorded by László (Leslie) Lukács, is also interesting in that it reveals the unique mechanism of a people's historical awareness. The handling of time by the Csángó permits them, even today, to easily link a 20th century event or personage with a 15th century king who visited his oppressed people in disguise and righted the wrongs meted on them by the imperious nobility.

Several legends exist among the Csángó about Moldova's most famous prince, Stefan cel Mare. Many in the southern Csángó villages hold that, during his reign, the Voivod turned to the Hungarian king for assistance when the Turkish armies attacked his small country. The Moldovan ruler later settled those Hungarian warriors, who arrived to help his people and country, on lands depopulated during the drawn out hostilities.[455]

It is quite probable that the historical legends of the Csángó were enriched by the Romanian-language of education. For instance, a late-19th century Romanian public school text recounts the events following a lost battle by the Voivod. After the lost battle, the ruler hurries to the castle of his mother but there they refuse to open the gates to him. The haughty mother announces from atop the wall that she will only allow him entry when he returns victorious. On hearing this, the Voivod turned around and his forces successfully defeated the Turks. Mózes Rubinyi reported seeing a colored picture in the Klézse parish hall which illustrated this scene – Stefan returning to his mother's castle after losing the battle.[456]

Another legend recounts the marriage of the Voivod. The tale, heard among the southern Csángó, tells of a young girl taking water to his father when the Voivod happens by and asks for a drink from maiden. Since the girl happily offers him a drink, the Voivod slips a golden ring into the girl's pail. When the girl grew a little older, the Voivod again visited them and asked the father to show him the ring he gave her. When they brought it out, the Voivod asked for her hand, there and then. Both of the ruling couple did many good deeds for their people but the Hungarian-descended wife of the Voivod founded two more churches than her husband.[457]

A third legend recounts how Voivod Stefan once secretly entered the employ of the Vlach priest of Nagypatak, as a shepherd. When the priest's wife served lunch to the disguised young ruler, he left a note on the table that he was there and had lunch. When the priest returned, he was astounded at who had been a guest of his. With Voivod Stefan, he went to the

---

454 Lukács, László: Domokos Pál Péter, Magyarország királya [Pál Péter Domokos, the king of
    Hungary]. Honismeret XXIV. 3. sz., 1996, pp. 58-60.

455 Bosnyák: A moldvai ... op. cit. p. 57.

456 Rubinyi: A moldvai ... op. cit. p. 170.

457 Ibid, p. 170.

neighboring village where the ruler fell in love with the lovely daughter of János (John) Forró, whom he promptly married. After the wedding, they came to an agreement that the girls will be Hungarian, the boys Vlach. The Voivod's wife asked for eight Hungarian lads for her daughters, to whom the Voivod later allotted land for their faithful service. There, they founded the Forrófalva of today.[458]

In most of the Csángó villages, it is from public education that they know that the Voivod founded a new church after each of his victorious battles. In Klézse, the locals attribute the Romanian ballad of Master Manole, *The Walled-up Woman*, to one of the church foundings of the Voivod.[459]

The knowledge of the Moldovan Csángó with the more recent national historical personages of Hungary (Prince Ferenc Rákóczi II, Lajos Kossuth, etc.) is quite sparse. Usually, it occurs in those families where a cantor-grandfather came from Transylvania. There is some knowledge of the poet Sándor (Alexander) Petofi, whose name is mentioned in post-second world war textbooks in the chapter relating to the 1848 revolution.

Their awareness is far wider of local and Hungarian events of the 20th century (first and second world wars, kulakization, collectivization, etc.), mainly as related by their parents and grandparents. In most of the villages, they talk with nostalgia about the dictatorship of Ceausescu (1965-1989), since at the time, everybody had a secure job, a salary and an apartment. To them, this era does not represent a time of dire need but, rather, a time when their children could get an education, move to the city, and "climb up the ladder." They view the decade following the 1989 Romanian 'revolution' as troubled, confused and unpredictable.

Summary

The Moldovan Csángó left the block of Hungarians living in the Carpathian basin during the 13th-18th centuries. The connection of those living outside the borders of the Hungarian state, with those within, gradually grew sparser, seemingly to disappear later.

The rural Hungarian communities living in Moldova were left out of the significant Hungarian civil national and cultural achievements, e.g.- the results of the linguistic rebirth failed to reach tem, lacking schools and liturgy in the native tongue, they did not come into contact with the elite of Hungarian culture, they had no way of knowing the outstanding pieces of national literature and were unable to participate in the political and cultural movements of the age of Reformation. They did not partake of the community-building spiritual experience of the 1848 revolution and War for

---

458 Ibid, p. 171.

459 Bosnyák: A moldvai ... op. cit. p. 56.

Freedom, as a result of which every Hungarian-speaking group within the Carpathian basin gradually took its place within the Hungarian civil nation. Perhaps the Moldovan Csángó form the sole Hungarian-speaking group, which did not become an integral part of the Hungarian nation during the 19th-20th centuries.[460]

The vast amount of folkloric text and narrative collected in their communities stands as proof that the historic memories of the Moldovan Csángó retained a great deal of medieval elements. Their historical knowledge is primarily of an age when Moldova was under the sovereignty of a strong and centralized medieval Hungarian kingdom and they had closer ties with the homeland that sent them forth.

In our times, the memories of the Moldovan Csángó fundamentally diverge from the historical consciousness of the Hungarians living in the Carpathian basin. This conclusion is valid even for the Sekler-Csángó villages, too. Although they possessed a more developed linguistic version at the time of their escape (i.e., late 18th century) and already possessed the seeds of a civil national consciousness, by the end of the 20th century, the influence of the society which accepted them gradually dimmed the memory of their origins. Today, it is getting to be a rarity to find a person in Moldova who holds himself to be descended from Transylvanian Seklers.

In many Csángó communities, a medieval sense of identity exists, which could be called more ethnic than national. Under this ethnic consciousness, we mean a pre-national identity in which the group's cohesion is primarily based on common rites, linguistic, cultural, religious and moral traditions. Since the fundamental strategy of retaining an ethnic identity is based on traditions, the passing on of customs and a sense of belonging, it is a crucial basis for the creation of a sense of community based on ethnicity. We must stress that, in the value system of the Moldovan rural communities, the national or ethnic affiliation was not of the most paramount importance. Rather, it was health, the ability to work, to continue to exist, that played a more important role. Thus, these are overshadowed by the role and importance of personal and local problems played out in the here and now. We have noticed in our fieldwork that, in the structure of peasant thinking and mentality, history does not play a major part. In fact, over time, forgetfulness further dims, selects and reinterprets the communal memories based on an oral tradition.[461]

---

460 Tánczos, Vilmos: Hungarians in Moldavia. Institute for Central European Studies No. 8, Budapest, 1997, p. 383.

461 Turai, Tünde: Történeti tudat vizsgálata Klézsén [Examination of historical awareness in Klézse], In: Pozsony, Ferenc /ed./: Csángósors. Moldvai csángók a változó idokben [Csángó fate. Moldovan Csángó in changing times]. Budapest, 1999, p. 139.

The official institutional structure of Romanian public schools, church, political and public administration continuously strove, in this civic era, to link the Moldovan Csángó to the Romanian nation. To this end, it strove to fill their collective historical memory with Romanian elements. As a result of the Romanian-language education and national propaganda, their historical consciousness was also gradually encroached with elements of the Romanian national myths. Lacking appropriate information and critical facilities, these new events linked, and interfered, with the earlier traditions of Hungarian origin, such as associating the figure of Saint Stephen (the first Hungarian king) with the activities of Stefan cel Mare, the leader of the 1514 peasant's revolt, György (George) Dózsa, with the communist dictator Gheorghiu Dej, while thinking that Seklerland was Hungarian terrirory but that Transylvania was Romanian.[462] The clerical and laic intellectual strata, of Romanian identity, raised memorials to the anti-Turkish resistance of 1877, the first world war, as well as to local religious leaders, in the decade following the events of 1989. These presented proper backdrops in which to remember the outstanding historical events of Romanian national history.

Hungarian-language folklore, which retained a great number of historical elements, quickly lost its earlier function and popularity, following the cultural turmoil of modernization. Its place was taken by common, Romanian-language pop-culture, without the ability or power to weld a Hungarian community identity. By the second half of the 20th century, the archaic, Hungarian-language, folklore traditions played a scant part in the retention of an identity. At the same time, the disappearance of communal and normative traditions predicts the encroachment of the individual and the breakdown of the group cohesion of the Moldovan Csángó rural communities. This progression is reflected in the mirror of the personal makeup of historical awareness, as can be ascertained in countless individual cases today.

---

462 Ibid, p. 137.

IV. THE SIGNIFICANCE OF HUNGARIAN-LANGUAGE FOLKLORE

The Csángó have lived for centuries outside the boundaries of the Hungarian state, yet, due to the unique historical, societal, cultural, political and ethnic Moldovan circumstances, have managed to retain, to the end of the 20th century, the many archaic aspects and elements of a Hungarian and European culture. The Hungarian intelligentsia of the Carpathian basin discovered relatively early, by the end of the 18th century, the existence of the Csángó-Hungarian communities living in Moldova. The heightened interest in Hungarian communities living outside the borders of the Hungarian state developed in the middle of the 19th century, peaking during the 20th, in spite of strong political and ideological opposition. During the last century and a half, researchers interested in this archaic folk culture have amassed a vast amount of Hungarian-language floric material in the Csángó villages. The area inhabited by the Csángó-Hungarians has become, as a result, one of the most intensively researched regions.

Elek Gego, a priest-teacher of Csíktapolca, first visited the Csángó in 1836, on assignment from the Hungarians Scientific Academy. He introduced the life and culture of the Moldovan Hungarians based on his first-hand experiences during his travels. His book of the settlements he visited, published in Buda, was the first to narrate the Moldovan version of the classic Hungarian ballad, *Szilágyi and Hajmási,* which lyrically recounts the brave deeds of the vastly outnumbered valiant warriors who stood up to the Turkish hordes.[463]

The first dedicated researcher of Moldovan-Hungarian folklore, János (John) Ince Petrás, was born in 1813, in Forrófalva. He was an extremely cultured Roman Catholic parish priest who, at the request of Gábor (Gabriel) Döbrentei (Secretary of the Hungarians Scientific Academy), began in 1841 to systematically collect the Hungarian-language texts and folk traditions in his homeland.[464] He was first to record several of the classic Hungarian authentic folk ballads (*A zsivány felesége, A hagyakozó pásztor, Az elcsábított menyecske, A szívtelen anya, A három árva, A kegyetlen anyós, A párjavesztett gerlice*). It is also due to his collecting that we have the written Moldovan-Hungarian versions of some ballad types (*Guzsalyasban, Tündér Ilona, A húség próbája*) and other ancient prisoner songs.[465] Petrás is undeservedly forgotten and overshadowed by his more

---

463 Gego: A moldvai ... op. cit. pp. 80-81.

464 Faragó, József: Balladák földjén. Válogatott tanulmányok, cikkek [In the land of ballads. Assorted essays, articles]. Bukarest, 1977, pp. 9-28.

465 Ibid, pp. 25-26.

famous contemporaries, János (John) Erdélyi and János (John) Kriza, yet the amount, quality and significance of the folkloric material collected and recorded by him remains invaluable to this day.

The systematic research done in the past 150 years into folk poetry shows that we only know some classical Hungarian ballads only from this Moldova source (*A Lengyelországba eladott menyasszony, A katonák által elrabolt lány, Az esküvöre hazatéro kedves, Magyari császárnak Lázár fia vala, Langos szép Ilona, Tündér Ilona, A rest feleség, A talányfejto lány, A katonalány, Az eladott feleség, A halott testvér*).[466] We feel it to be quite probable that these ballad types originated in Moldova or, if they existed earlier within the Carpathian basin, were already lost from memory by the beginning of the folk-recording movement.[467]

Although the Csángó lived outside the boundaries of Hungary for centuries, they received constant cultural reinforcement from the transplanted Seklers of eastern Transylvania. At the same time, they retained for far longer the ballads that spread from Seklerland that the more rapidly urbanizing Transylvanian Hungarian communities. Up to the middle of the 20th century, island-like communities remained in Moldova in which the ballad form of folk poetry retained a great deal of its ancient elements. Only in Moldova and Transylvania have examples turned up of the oldest, most artistic and arch-typical creations of classic Hungarian ballad poems: *A szívtelen anya, A mennybe vitt lány, A két kápolnavirág, A hajdúkkal útnak induló lány, A megölt havasi pásztor, A huség próbája, A párjavesztett gerlice, Az ügyes házasságtöro asszony, Este guzsalyasban.*[468]

József (Joseph) Faragó has contended, supported with countless examples that the most typical of the Hungarian ballad poetry creations of the 16th-17th century were able to exist to this day in Moldova was because there the continuity of the rural Hungarian communities for the past 500 hundred years was assured. The new style ballads and lyrical songs only gained ground in their communities after the regime change of 1920, when they served in the armies of the Kingdom of Romania alongside the Transylvanian Hungarian recruits.[469]

Gradually, numerous Romanian elements became entrenched in the Hungarian-language ballad and song lyrics of the Moldovan Csángó, such as the appearance of Romanian stanzas at the end of Hungarian-language songs, or the transposition of the lyrics of an old-style Hungarian song to the tune of

---

466 Vargyas: A magyar ... op. cit. p. 171.

467 Faragó: Balladák ... op. cit. p. 26; Faragó, József – Jagamas, János: Moldvai csángó népdalok és
    népballadák [Folk songs and ballads of the Moldovan Csángó]. Bukarest, 1954, p. 39.

468 Vargyas: A magyar ... op. cit. p. 171.

469 Faragó – Jagamas: Moldvai ... op. cit. pp. 31-32.

a newer Romanian piece.[470] In his research around Klézse, János Ince Petrás recorded the Hungarian version of a famous Romanian folk ballad, *Miorita*, in 1843, titled *A hagyakozó pásztor*. Its Romanian-language variation was only published seven years later, in 1850, by Vasile Alecsandri. In the following 150 years, it gradually became an important and significant symbol for Romanians.[471] From the studies of József Faragó, we learn that the Moldovan Hungarian ballads *Györgyikérol és Ilonáról* and *Az esküvore hazatéro kedves* are not of classical French origin but rather continues to live on Csángó lips as a result of late 20th century Romanian adaptation.[472] Although the ballad *A halott testvér* embodies ancient superstitions (the story of Lenore) and archaic structures, yet similar to the previous pair, it can be seen as a creation adapted from Romanian folk poetry.[473]

In his work on Hungarian folk ballads, Lajos Vargyas stressed that, as sung by Moldovan Hungarians, the classical folk ballads are not as tight knit, their libretto more detailed, more epic than the versions sung in the Carpathian basin. After the dramatic climax of the ballad's story, a longer, lyrical passage usually follows in the Moldovan variants. In the oldest Csángó villages, the ballad texts did not become inflexible, as improvisation played a great part in their presentation, even in the decades following the second world war. In the region, a single person did not present a ballad alone, but rather two singers alternated and improvised.[474] The large-scale variation, long epic and lyrical passages suggest that the Moldovan Csángó seem to have retained the more archaic folklore values, predating the formation and stylistic changes of western European classical ballads.[475]

Béla Bartók already planned in 1914-1914 to investigate the folk music of the Hungarian- Csángó villages *in situ*. His plans were foiled by the events of the first world war, thus, in his monograph of 1924, *A magyar népdal* [The Hungarian folk song], he merely remarked that the folk music of

---

470 Almási, István: Román refrének a moldvai csángók népdalaiban [Romanian refrains in Moldovan Csángó folk songs], In: Nyelv- és Irodalomtudományi Közlemények X. évf. 1. 1966. p. 21; Faragó, József: Paralele între baladele romanesti si maghiare. Anuarul de Folclor II., Cluj-Napoca, 1981, pp.147-156; Ibid, (Faragó – Jagamas) p. 43.

471 Faragó: Balladák ... op. cit. p. 26; Fochi, Adrian: Miorita. Tipologie, geneza, texte. Bucuresti, 1964, p. 353.

472 Ibid, (Faragó) pp. 502-533.

473 Ibid, pp. 487-501.

474 Ibid, pp. 286-326; Kallós, Zoltán: Új guzsalyam mellett. (Éneklettem én özvegyasszon Miklós Gyurkáné Szályka Rózsa hetvenhat esztendos koromban Klézsén Moldvában. Lejegyezte, bevezetovel és jegyzetekkel ellátta Kallós Zoltán.) [Beside my new spinning wheel] Bukarest, 1973, pp. 9-10.

475 Vargyas: A magyar ... op. cit. p. 173.

the Hungarian communities around Bákó remained unexplored.[476] Bartók's statement gave an impetus to Pál Péter Domokos to fill this void. The researcher from Csík carried out his most significant poetic and folk song collecting in Moldova between 1929 and 1932, the brunt of which he published shortly after in several volumes.[477] As a result of his local research, he came to the realization that the Csángó retained a unique folklore and that Moldova represents a separate branch of the Hungarian folk music dialect. This opinion was later reinforced János (John) Jagamas, a musical specialist of Kolozsvár, based on the analysis of several thousand recorded tunes.[478]

After the groundbreaking work of Pál Péter Domokos, Sándor Veress, Gábor Lüko and Péter Balla did folk poetry research in Moldova. It must be specially noted that of them, Sándor Veress was a pioneer in the use of a phonograph in his folk musical recording in 1930, aided by Constantin Brailoiu (the president of the Romanian composers union), in Bogdánfalva, Forrófalva, Ketris, Klézse, Somoska, Szabófalva and Trunk.[479]

The two decades following WWII afforded new opportunities for the Transylvanian researchers to make regular trips among the Csángó villages and do field work in folk poetry. The first, and most significant, fruit of their labors was published in 1954. The volume edited by József Faragó and János Jagamas contained 30 Hungarian ballads and 125 variants of archetypal lyrical songs.[480] The ethnographers made a total of 4,145 recordings of Hungarian-language folklore compositions in Moldova between 1950 and 1977.[481]

Zoltán Kallós carried out his Moldovan collecting in the decades immediately after the second world war, while he was a teacher in the

---

476 Béla Bartók was eventually able to collect Moldovan Csángó folk songs in 1938 when two families came
to Budapest from Trunk to the World Eucharistic Congress. Their songs were recorded in the studio of the
Hungarian Radio. (Domokos, Pál Péter: Bartók Béla kapcsolata a moldvai csángómagyarokkal. Népdalok,
népmesék, népszokások, eredetmondák a magyar nyelvterület legkeletibb részérol [Béla Bartók's contact
with the Moldovan Csángó-Hungarians. Folksongs, ~tales, ~customs and myths from the easternmost
edge of the Hungarian-speaking region]. Budapest, 1981, pp. 11-12)

477 Domokos: A moldvai ... op. cit.

478 Jagamas, János: Beitrage zur Dialektfrage der ungarischen Volksmusik in Rumanien, In: Kodály, Zoltán
/ed./: Studia memoriae Bélae Bartók sacra. Budapest, 1956, pp. 469-501.

479 Veress, Sándor: Moldvai gyujtés. (Gyujtötte Veress Sándor. Szerkesztette: Berlász Melinda és Szalay
Olga) [Moldovan anthology]. Magyar Népköltési Gyujtemény XVI., Budapest, 1989.

480 Faragó-Jagamas: Moldvai ... op. cit.

481 Faragó, József: A mai romániai folklórgyujtés vázlata [An sketch from the Romanian folklore compilation
of today], In: Kós, Károly – Faragó, József /ed./: Népismereti Dolgozatok. Bukarest, 1980, pp. 17-19.

Hungarian school of Lészped, between 1956-57.[482] The major results of his fieldwork was published in 1970, under the title *Balladák könyve* (Book of Ballads), to critical acclaim.[483] Kallos was able to collect Hungarian folklore in Csángó villages that were never visited by an ethnographer. To his incontestable merit, he was able to gather a wealth of classical Hungarian-language lyrical works from the generation born at the end of the 19th century. He was able to establish such an intimate connection with his subjects as to draw out their most hidden lore. He made sure to conduct regular, wide ranging discussions with the outstanding folklore elders during his trips.

In his volume, titled *Beside My New Spinning Wheel*, Kallós presented 26 Hungarian-language ballads, 36 laments, 59 love songs, 31 humorous songs and 11 pairing songs [of young men and girls-*Ed.*] of the peasant woman from Klézse, Rózsa Szályka, married to one Gyurka Miklós. The material culled from the woman's amazing folkloric storehouse of ballads and songs, runs to 1,010 verses and 3,786 lines. This huge body of folklore reinforces the central role of individuals in the Moldovan Hungarian communities in the oral traditions of retaining, storing and passing-on of verbal poetry.[484] In the face of pressure from Romanian authorities, pressing for rapid assimilation, Zoltán Kallós continued his Moldovan research in secret in the 1970's and 1980's, finally publishing his new material in a volume in 1996, titled *This Is My Passport*.[485]

Luca Hodorog, Mrs. György Lorinc, who also lived in Klézse along the Szeret, saw her favorite folklore creations appear in an independent volume in 1994. This ordinary farming woman played an important role in maintaining the contacts between the Hungarians of Transylvania and the Moldovan Csángó during the increasingly heavy-handed anti-minority policies of Ceausescu.[486] Here, we must note that there is no other village in the Carpathian basin, or perhaps even Europe, such as Klézse, where researchers (e.g.- János Ince Petrás, Pál Péter Domokos, Zoltán Kallós, Péter Halász, István Pávai, Ferenc Pozsony, Gergely Csoma and others) were able

---

482 Diószegi, László /ed./: A moldvai csángók tanítója [The teacher of the Moldovan Csángó]. Diószegi László beszélgetése Kallós Zoltán néprajzkutatóval. Alföld 42. 6, 1991, pp. 63-71.

483 Kallós: Balladák ... op. cit.

484 Kallós: Új guzsalyam ... op. cit.

485 Kallós, Zoltán: Ez az utazólevelem. Balladák új könyve [This is my passport. Book of new ballads]. Budapest, 1996.

486 Pozsony, Ferenc: Szeret vize martján. Moldvai csángómagyar népköltészet [By the waters of the Szeret. Moldovan Csángó-Hungarian folk poetry]. A klézsei Lorinc Györgyné Hodorog Lucától gyujtötte, bevezetovel és jegyzetekkel ellátta Pozsony Ferenc. A dallamokat hangszalagról lejegyezte és sajtó alá rendezte Török Csorja Viola. Kriza János Néprajzi Társaság Könyvtára 2, Kolozsvár, 1994.

to gather such a vast amount of folkloric material, and of such significance, from the middle of the 19th century to this day.[487]

The motifs of the lyrical songs of the Csángó exhibit countless similarities with the love songs and poetry of the Renaissance troubadours. At the same time, we are able to discern a number of popular elements in their songs that were recorded on 17th century Hungarian love-poem manuscripts.[488] The laments formed one of the most popular type of songs in their communities up to the end of the second world war. These usually encapsulated the sorrow of unrequited love, the bitterness of having to leave one's homeland and the grief of prisoners carried off to foreign lands. A number of elements show a close connection with the poetry of the anti-Austrian Kuruc uprising that began in eastern Hungary at the turn of the 16th-17th century. This we don't view as accidental, as the rebels of the unsuccessful uprising, led by Ferenc (Francis) Rákóczi II, fleeing from Austrian reprisals, introduced the lyrics and motifs of the most popular Kuruc songs.

It is also interesting how frequently the names of bodies of water appear in the songs of the Csángó that are to be found in the center of the Carpathian basin and the Hungarian-speaking region (such as the Danube and Tisza rivers).[489] Research carried out in the second half of the 20th century in Moldova reveals that the Csángó adapt the more complex verse structure of the more modern Hungarian songs by truncation, that is, by [490]omitting lines or sections of the tune. As a result of Romanian influence, in countless cases, they relax the tighter verse structure, tainting their songs as to make them almost impossible to articulate into verses.[491]

The folklorists from Cluj recorded several thousand folk songs in the Csángó villages in the decades following the second world war. Subsequently, János Jagamas conducted the assessment of this vast body of music: "Moldova is an independent dialect. What clearly separates it from the musical characteristics of other regions are the retention of the oldest traditions, the number of songs unknown from other regions, the minimal

---

487 Faragó: Balladák ... op. cit. p. 28.

488 Demény, István Pál: A moldvai csángó népdalok és a népköltészet történetével kapcsolatos dilemmák [Dilemmas regarding the history of the folk songs and folk poetry of the Moldovan Csángó]. Erdélyi Múzeum LXII. évf. 3-4, 2000, pp. 246-247.

489 Küllos, Imola: Csángó dalok és balladák kvantitatív módszeru vizsgálata [Quantitative analysis of Csángó songs and ballads]. Népi Kultúra – Népi Társadalom XI-XII., Budapest, 1980, pp. 351-372.

490 Jagamas, János: Adatok a romániai magyar népzenei dialektusok kérdéséhez [Data to the question of dialects in Romanian Hungarian folk music], In: Szabó, Csaba /ed./: Zenetudományi írások. (Bukarest, 1977) p. 36.

491 Demény: A moldvai ... op. cit. p. 246.

number new style songs, the evident wealth of ornamentation and foreign influences, especially Romanian influences, which manifests itself in the adoption of tunes, lyrics, refrains and certain musical elements."[492]

The Hungarian researchers, lead by János Jagamas, carried out a monographic folk music collection between 1950-1953 in Trunk, on the right bank of the Szeret River, where they were able to record 708 variations of 302 melodies. As 31 of the melodies were transplanted by Hungarian intellectuals from Transylvania, they were only able to assign 649 variations of 271 melodies to the village's intrinsic folk music tradition.[493]

Melodic category	Number of melody types	Number of versions
Children's song	9	18
Lament	1	6
Dirge parody	1	2
Ancient folk song	81	305
New style folk song	4	10
Semi-folk song	14	40
Of foreign origin	65	94
Folk version of older composed music	5	15
Popular song	33	72
Church folk hymn	58	87
Total	271	649

The folk music collected in Trunk underscores that, in Moldova, the older style Hungarian melodies dominate, which can be explained by the centuries-old isolation of these communities. At the same time, the table clearly shows that there are a large number of folk melodies from foreign sources, mainly Romanian and Russian. Yet, the folk music researchers found very few 'new style' melodies among the Moldovan communities. Local research shed light on this. Up until the first world war, new style melodies only occasionally cropped up on the lips of the Csángó, while, elsewhere in the Carpathian basin, the song repertoire of the Hungarian communities consisted of little else (beside semi-folk and popular songs). The research of János Jagamas also pointed out that the archaic elements of the folk music of the Moldovan Hungarians bears a notable similarity to the ancient melodies and airs of the Transylvanian Mezoség [the central hilly portion-Ed.].[494]

---

492 Jagamas: Adatok ... op. cit. p. 36.

493 Jagamas, János: Szemelvények Trunk népzenéjébol [Selections from the folk music of Trunk], In: Jagamas, János: A népzene mikrokozmoszában. Tanulmányok. Bukarest, 1984, pp. 208-227.

494 Jagamas: Adatok ... op. cit. p. 36.

144

The dance music of the Csángó retained its olden characteristics up until the middle of the 20th century, i.e., the ornate four and five-note scales. Their favorite musical instrument was the six-hole recorder, the *szültü*, which they played with a hum and growl in their throat. At family or community events, they danced to the koboz [the successor of the medieval lute-*Ed.*], the doromb [trump, or Jew's harp-*Ed.*], violin and bagpipe until the early 20th century. In the decades following the second world war, the brass bands much favored by the Moldovan Romanians and the broadcast of Romanian melodies over the radio gradually displaced the traditional Csángó dance music.[495] Today, for this very reason, the most significant Romanian influence can be observed in the folk music and folk dances of the Moldovan Csángó (asymmetry, three row forms, etc).[496]

The research conducted together by György Martin and Zoltán Kallós in the 60's and 70's revealed that the dance heritage of the Moldovan Csángó differs fundamentally from Transylvanian traditions. *"Their dance repertoire is essentially the same as the Romanians of Moldova-Carpathia, yet exhibits more ancient characteristics due to their way of clinging to traditions. More characteristic of their dance heritage is the olden, almost medieval, collective form and the almost complete absence of the individual genre, hence it contains few Transylvanian or Hungarian traits."*[497]

While men's and couples' dances usually dominate in the Carpathian basin, in Moldova, the popular dances are circle dances of a communal nature and interactive, structured pairs' forms. The circle dances were, until very recently, danced in segregation by sex, as a result of the vehement objections of the Italian and Polish priests in their villages to having young girls dance together with young men. Thus, well into the second half of the 20th century, couples' dances were the exclusive domain of married adults. The young were only permitted to dance in the church-yard, to be 'under supervision', the church attempting to maintain strict control over the observance of moral norms, even at public events. Of the most popular circle dances, the *kezes* and the *öves* are, today, danced in mixed form. The slower styled *kezes* is more or less the equivalent of the Romanian *hora*, while the faster *öves* resembles the Romanian *sârba*. The couples' circle dances in favor today are the *csimpolyászka* (cimpoiasca), a *hóra-polka* (hora-polca) meg a *lugosánka* (lugosanca). Among the clearly pairs'

495 Pávai, István: Az erdélyi és a moldvai magyarság népi tánczenéje [Folk dance music of the Transylvanian and Moldovan Hungarians]. Budapest, 1993.

496 Martin, György: A keleti vagy erdélyi táncdialektus [The eastern or Transylvanian dance dialect], In: Felföldi, László - Pesovár, Erno /ed./: A magyar nép és nemzetiségeinek tánchagyománya. Budapest, 1997, p. 278.

497 Ibid, p. 276.

dances, many are of Transylvanian, Carpathian and Ukrainian origin, such as the *didoj* (de doi), *árgyeleánka* (ardeleanca), *magyaros, csárdás, ruszászka* (ruseasca), *románka* (romanca), etc.[498]

Research into the folk tales of the Moldovan Hungarians, compared to the recording of song and dance, is relatively recent, post-second world war. The earlier, sparse records, however, hinted at the fact that the Csángó have retained the archaic folk tale forms of the Hungarians living in the Carpathian basin.[499] Since a number of Csángó were resettled in Baranya County subsequent to the second world war, the material collected among them was published in 1952 by Lajos (Louis) Hegedüs in a volume of stories and 'chats'.[500] Between 1956 and 1964, Zoltán Kallós collected and catalogued the folk tale knowledge of Anna Jánó of Lészped, married to Antal Demeter. These stories of this woman with the gifts of extraordinary memory and performing ability show that the narratives of the Moldovan-Hungarians retained countless motifs of eastern, shamanistic origin. At the same time, they also contain colorful, comic, apocryphal legends about the creation of the Earth and the earthly acts of Jesus, too.[501]

József (Joseph) Faragó collected the 'tales' of one of the most talented Moldovan storytellers, András (Andrew) Baka of Gyoszén, between 1957 and 1958. His 125 stories illustrate that 20th century storytelling among the Csángó communities primarily served as entertainment for adults. It is interesting to note that the audience usually insisted on amusing stories, and that the storyteller continuously embedded into his Hungarian-language repertoire the neighboring Romanian's popular stories and elements.[502]

New research done in the last decades of the 20th century reinforced that the Moldovan Csángó played an important tradition-guarding role of works in the epic form. Narratives collected from a number of their settlements contribute to the archaic folktale material of Hungary and Europe. The recently recorded stories, however, shed light the storylines have become simpler, romantic, religious and humorous, instead of the more convoluted fairy tales and heroic stories. Although the decline of the

498 Ibid, p. 277.

499 Domokos: Bartók Béla ... op. cit. pp. 107-108.

500 Hegedüs, Lajos: Moldvai csángó népmesék és beszélgetések [Moldovan Csángó folk stories and conversations]. Budapest, 1952.

501 Kallós, Zoltán: Világszárnya. Moldvai népmesék. (Elmesélte a lészpedi Demeter Antiné Jánó Anna. Gyujtötte Kallós Zoltán 1956 és 1964 között.) [Moldovan folk tales. Related by Demeter Antiné Jánó Anna . Collected by Zoltán Kallós between 1956 and 1964.)] Stúdium Könyvkiadó, Kolozsvár, 2003.

502 Baka, András: Tréfás beszédei. Moldvai csángómagyar népmesék. (Gyujtötte, szerkesztette, bevezeto tanulmánnyal, jegyzetekkel és tájszójegyzékkel közzéteszi Faragó József.) [Amusing stories. Moldovan Csángó-Hungarian folktales]. Kriterion Könyvkiadó, Kolozsvár, 2003.

Hungarian vocabulary, and the inclusion of Romanian expressions, is minimal in their structured folk poetic works, the syntax of the collected narratives is often awkward.[503]

Up until the middle of the 20th century, the Csángó retained a body of beliefs rich in archaic elements and practices, woven through with magic. "The Moldovan-Hungarian's view of the world is an archaic view, with many-many facts, which enrich or modify our current knowledge. The many facts known about the 'speakers with the dead' shed light on shamanistic beliefs, from trances to modern, everyday practices. The tales – and the underlying beliefs behind them – validate the rich fabric of beliefs of magic grasses able to raise the dead, dragons and witches. This dualistic world view, anchored in the extended family, is richly created on many levels.[504]

Since their settlements are mainly ringed by Orthodox communities, many supernatural concepts and practices of Romanian origin took root. As the Roman Catholic priests, leaders and definers of their religious existence, did not undertake to carry out the countless "supernatural" practices (e.g.- the exorcism of the Devil from a thief or a possessed person), the Csángó often resorted to an Orthodox priest or monk for this service. As they had scant belief in institutional justice, the wronged persons attempted to uncover, and punish, the guilty by strict fasts (i.e., they ate nothing at all on an odd number of Tuesdays or Fridays) or the casting of beans [similar to the reading of tea leaves-*Ed.*].[505]

To this day, the Csángó firmly believe that, with special rites (such as the laying of a spell, burning, the capturing of a footprint, etc.), human being can be harmed. This being the case, they apply certain preventive procedures to forestall the efforts of certain evil individuals (e.g.- the use of garlic, red thread, holy water, reading of cards, casting of lead, etc.).[506] The Romanian religious historian, Mircea Eliade, attributes the appearance and spread of the rapture of sorcerers and magicians (as documented in the Bandinus codex) to the Csángó-Hungarians.[507]

---

503 Pozsony: Újesztendohöz ... op. cit. pp. 159-215; Iancu, Laura: Johófiú Jankó. Magyarfalusi csángó

népmesék és más beszédek. (Összeállította Iancu Laura, szerkesztette és bevezette Benedek Katalin.)

[Johnny, the Good Boy. Csángó folktales and other stories from Magyarfalu]. Budapest, 2002.

504 Bosnyák: A moldvai ... op. cit. p. 8.

505 Pozsony: Újesztendohöz ... op. cit. pp. 227-229.

506 Csoma, Gergely: Varázslások és gyógyítások a moldvai csángómagyaroknál [Witchcraft and healing

among the Moldovan Hungarian-Csángó]. Pomáz, 2000, pp. 15-23.

507 Eliade, Mircea: „Samanizmus" a románoknál? [Shamanism among the Romanians?] Létünk. Társadalom,

tudomány, kultúra 2, 1988, pp. 312-321; Pozsony, Ferenc: Sámánizmus és medvekultusz Moldvában?

[Shamanism and the cult of the bear in Moldova?] In: Csonka Takács, Eszter – Czövek, Judit – Takács,

147

Although the view of the world of the Csángó is fundamentally defined by the teaching of the Roman Catholic church, countless pre-Christian notions survived. In their view of the world, a close intermingling, and interplay, of pagan and Christian elements can be observed. Their vision of the lives of the saints brings to life the view of a medieval man's set of beliefs. To this day, the old still firmly believe in witches, ghosts, apparitions, giants, devils, gnomes, dragons, sirens, shamans and fairies. They firmly believe that some chosen people have special powers (to quell the rainfall or, in time of drought, to bring it on, etc.). They still assign special meaning to visions encountered in sleep, attempting to augur the outcome of their fate or future from them.[508]

In their more remote villages, medical services are sparse, or the majority are unable to buy the expensive drugs, hence numerous 'old-style' healing procedures survive in their communities. For example, bewitched children have a cross drawn on their forehead, or charcoal- water is made, a sty on the eye 'healed' with a sickle and an incantation, scared children are treaded with smoke. Although Romanian influence is significant in the folk-cures of the Csángó, in the healing process of the middle-aged or elderly, a great deal of Hungarian-language incantations, spells and prayers are said.[509] The Moldovan Csángó are familiar with a wide variety of plant lore and employ a number of herbal teas in their various healing processes.[510]

The Moldovan Csángó have an extremely archaic and dualistic view of the creation of the Earth and the universe, in view of the surviving Hungarian-language sagas of the rivalry between God and Lucifer. The Moldovan Hungarians, similar to other eastern people, imagine that, in the beginning, there was darkness and endless water; that, in the act of creation, the Devil also took a part, not solely God. Lucifer, after three dives, brought up soil under his fingernails, which gradually began to expand on the surface. Of that, God created man – and the Devil created woman.[511]

To this day, such archaic religious incantations and prayers are recited in the everyday life of Moldovan Hungarians, which have no integral place and role in official Roman Catholic liturgy. These texts usually exist without official Church sanction – the priests are usually unaware of their

András /ed./: Mir – Susné – Xum II. Tanulmányok Hoppál Mihály tiszteletére. Akadémiai Kiadó, Budapest, 2002, pp. 745-761.

508 Bosnyák: A moldvai ... op. cit. pp. 60-145.

509 Ibid, pp. 146-185.

510 Csoma: Varázslások ... op. cit. p. 22.

511 Bosnyák, Sándor: Magyar Biblia. A világ teremtése, az özönvíz, Jézus élete s a világ vége napjaink szájhagyományában [The Hungarian Bible. The creation, flood, the life of Jesus and the apocalypse in oral tradition of our time]. Budapest, 2001, pp. 5-7.

existence – and, since they are verbally transmitted, are passed from grandparents to parents to grandchildren. In most villages, they existed as morning and evening, sometimes as noon time, prayers. They were mumbled at the beginning, or in the midst, of important farming tasks (e.g.- plowing, sowing, harvesting), ills or other perils. They were more often recited on Friday's, especially during Lent or Holy Week, especially Good Friday. Usually, they were recited in the living room, in front of the bed, the table, the fire place, the crucifix on the wall or the family shrine; they were also silently recited before the roadside shrine, the Calvary or the cemetery. These forms also appeared in the customary poetry of the Moldavians, such as in the Christmas songs and greetings.[512]

The Hungarian folklorists discovered relatively late, in the second half of the 20th century, the apocryphal characteristic of the archaic folk prayer-poetry. Among the first, Zoltán Kallós recorded such texts among the Csángó of Moldova and Gyimes (Ghimes).[513] Later, during the recording movement begun by Zsuzsanna (Susanna) Erdélyi in the early 1970's, and the subsequent text-philology and cultural history research soon revealed that variations of the more archaic Moldovan texts can be found in great numbers in the medieval literature and folklore of the European nations. Parallels to the Moldovan prayers were found by the Hungarian researchers not only among the poetry of the western Christian church but also among the ancient Christian and Greek religious literature, the Byzantine apocrypha, as well as the medieval Slav and German remnants. At the same time, they are in a close relationship with the monastic prayers and hymns of the 16th century, the passion plays depicting the suffering of Jesus, the literary heritage of medieval revelations and the popular Hungarian-language laments of the Virgin.[514]

The significance of the texts of the Moldovan Hungarian prayers, containing countless medieval elements, is emphasized and supported by several factors. Their variants can be found among western European cultures mainly in written form. Since most Hungarian medieval written records were destroyed, the oral tradition of the Csángó have retained to our time this unique form of European archaic poetry. Thus, the prayers of the Csángó effectively contribute to documenting the cultural history of this important era, not merely for Hungarians but also for all of Europe. Through their texts and motifs, it is possible to reconstruct a picture of the literary and textual life of Hungarian-language religious literature that was destroyed in

---

512 Erdélyi, Zsuzsanna: Hegyet hágék, lotot lépék. Archaikus népi imádságok [I scale mountains, pace leagues. Archaic folk prayers.] Budapest, 1976, pp. 23-24.

513 Kallós: Ez az ... op. cit.

514 Erdélyi: Hegyet ... op. cit. pp. 27-28.

the subsequent turbulent centuries, the world view and religious heritage of the people of that time.[515]

Until very recently, the Csángó have retained Hungarian-language religious hymns rich in archaic elements. Since religious life in their homeland only became institutionalized and strengthened since the end of the 19th century, the foundation of religious lyrical songs in their communities can be attributed mainly to peasant cantors, often called clerks, who, in most cases, received their training in Transylvanian monasteries, arriving in Moldova with printed and handwritten copies of Hungarian-language hymnals. Copies of the third edition (1805) of the *Cantionale Catholicum*, originally published in 1676 in Csíksomlyó by János Kájoni, enjoyed a great deal of popularity in their midst.[516] However, lacking a school system and liturgy in their mother tongue, this religious poetry, so rich in medieval elements, gradually tended to the vernacular, becoming part of the popular culture. In spite of the spirited prohibition of the Moldovan Catholic clergy, their laments remained extant to the end of the 20th century, keeping alive several Gregorian chants to our time. Their communities gave continued life to many 16th-17th century religious hymns, mainly as a result of the hymnal published by János (John) Kájoni. These remnants of religious lyrical song and poetry represent an incalculable music-history value, not only for Hungary, but also for all of Europe.[517]

The folkloric customs of the Moldovan Csángó preserved a number of archaic practices and Hungarian-language rhythmic texts. Until the collectivization following the second world war, mothers in the villages rocked their children to sleep with Hungarian lullabies. Under the influence of public schooling, children's folklore of today shows significant Romanian influence. At the same time, the interaction of Moldovan young men and girls managed to retain a large number of archaic Hungarian-language folklore elements: the incantations to 'charm' a young man, love songs, humorous games, etc.[518]

515 Tánczos, Vilmos: Nyiss kaput, angyal! Moldvai csángó népi imádságok. Archetipikus szimbolizáció és élettér [Angel, open thy gate! Moldovan Csángó common prayers. Archtypical symbolism and existence]. Budapest, 2001, pp. 232-274.

516 Domokos, Pál Péter: A csíki énekeskönyvek [The hymnals of Csík]. In: Csutak, Vilmos /ed./: Emlékkönyv a Székely Nemzeti Múzeum ötvenéves jubileumára.Sepsiszentgyörgy, 1929, pp. 102-112.

517 Seres – Szabó: Csángómagyar ... op. cit. pp. 10-11.

518 Benedek H., Erika: Út az életbe. Világképelemzés csángó és székely közösségek szüléshez fuzodo hagyományai alapján [Road to life. Analysis of the view of the world of Csángó and Sekler communities, based on their traditions regarding birthing]. Kolozsvár, 1998; Bosnyák: A moldvai ... op. cit. pp. 186-195.

The traditions surrounding a wedding are, even today, among the most vibrant and alive. Even in the past decades, a girl is usually asked to be betrothed through Hungarian event-appropriate rhyming verses. The most animated facets of a Csángó wedding are the gay whoops (*ijjogtatások*) that accompany the making of the principal food of the reception (*geluska*) and the wedding procession as it winds its way along the streets. These good natured, often ribald, satirical bellows are among the most creative Hungarian-language folk creations among the Moldovan Csángó.[519]

The funeral of a youth has great similarities to a wedding among the Moldovan communities. Since, according to their ideas, a marriage represents the fulfillment of life, they attempt, through rituals, to create it for the benefit of the young deceased. They view death as a natural event of life. They do not cry aloud beside the dying, to permit easy passage of the spirit from the body. With the final bath water, they circle the house three times, to accompany the departing spirit. The body is dressed in Sunday best clothes, the casket is filled with wild flowers and home-spun scarves. The body is laid out in the 'clean room' [the rarely used front room-*Ed.*] of the house. Until recently, close relatives, neighbors and friends hold a wake on the evenings and nights before the funeral, reciting Hungarian-language prayers and religious songs. Even now, they hold that the soul of the departed leaves the room when the church bells ring during the funeral. In their opinion, the deceased's soul temporarily lingers for 40 days around the house. To prevent the soul from returning later, and not to have it turn into a harmful being, the food prepared for the wake is given away, as is the clothing of the deceased. The Roman Catholic Csángó, living among the Orthodox, have adopted a number of Romanian traditions in regard to funeral rites.[520]

Today, in the early years of the 21st century, we may still meet women in their villages, blessed with such acute perception, who are able to gain insight into the world of the departed and are able to convey messages between the living and the dead.[521]

---

519 Pozsony: Újesztendohöz ... op. cit. pp. 149-155.

520 Mohay, Tamás: Temetés a moldvai Frumószában [A funeral in the Moldovan village of Frumósza], In: Pozsony, Ferenc /ed./: Kriza János Néprajzi Társaság Évkönyve 5. Kolozsvár, 1997, pp. 96-105; Nyisztor, Tinka: "Rendes" temetések Pusztinában ["Proper" funerals in Pusztina], In: Pozsony, Ferenc (szerk.): Kriza János Néprajzi Társaság Évkönyve 5. Kolozsvár, 1997, pp. 106-112; Virt, István: Elszakasztottad a testemtol én lelkemet. A moldvai és a Baranya megyei csángók halottas szokásai és hiedelmei [You rent my soul from my body. The funereal practices and beliefs of the Csángó of Moldova and Baranya County]. Kolozsvár, 2001.

521 Kóka, Rozália: A lészpedi „szent leján" [The "holy woman" of Lészped]. Tiszatáj XXXVI. 8., 1982, pp. 29-44.

Until very recently, the Csángó saluted their neighbors, friends and family with Hungarian carols and sayings on Christmas Eve. Up to the outbreak of the second world war, Hungarian Christmas plays were staged in Lészped and Trunk. The youth and young men of the Sekler Csángó villages ritually 'caned' the girls on December 28 with limber willow twigs, while reciting Hungarian ritual sayings.[522]

Since Romania only introduced in 1924 the calendar reform introduced by Pope Gregory XIII in 1528, in Moldova, the local calendars read December 11, while the Transylvanian Hungarians were already celebrating Christmas (December 24). It is interesting to note that those Hungarians who migrated to Pusztina, Frumósza and Lészped after the 1764 revolt of Mádéfalva continued to commemorate on December 11 that, back in Csík, Christmas was being celebrated; although the priest did not announce the Feast of Christmas, they did not yoke their oxen, did not transport manure to the fields but placed twigs in water to have them bud in time for the Moldovan holiday. Even at the end of the 20th century, the women of Pusztina referred to the period between December 11 and 24 as "between the two Christmases," which they deemed suitable for making thread.[523]

The young Csángó men spent the first day of the new year going from house to house, greeting the farmers with verses wishing good harvest, luck and health. The verses fundamentally covered the growth cycle of wheat and were meant as a rite of agrarian well-wishing.[524] The ritual pulling of a plow, the *plugusor,* is still a popular, living Romanian tradition.[525] Up to the outbreak of the first world war, the groups of young men of Szabófalva said their verses of salutations in Hungarian, those of Lujzikalagor to the end of the 20th century.[526]

The masked traditional folk plays of the Csángó connected to the new year contains very many archaic and shamanistic ritual elements. The masks portraying bears and goats are extremely popular in their villages. The processions are accompanied with noisemaking and drumming, usually

---

522 Pozsony: Újesztendohöz ... op. cit. p. 244.

523 Halász: Nem lehet ... op. cit. p. 61.

524 Kallós, Zoltán: Hejgetés Moldvában [Intonations in Moldova]. Néprajzi Közlemények III. 1-2, 1958, pp. 40-50;

Kallós, Zoltán: Hejgetés Moldvában [Intonations in Moldova]. Muvelodés XXXI. 12, 1968, pp. 42-43.

525 Adascalitei, Vasile: Istoria unui obicei. Plugusorul. Editura Junimea. Iasi, 1987, p. 23.

526 Wichmann, Júlia: A moldvai csángók babonás hitébol [The superstitions of the Moldovan Csángó]. Ethnographia XVIII., 1907, pp. 213-214; Kallós: Hejgetés ... op. cit.

ending in the evening with the lighting of a fire and the rolling of burning wheels.[527]

Previously, in the traditional calendar of the Moldovan Hungarians, as opposed to the Orthodox Romanians, an important role was played by the masked revels and dances held at the end of the carnival, on the day before the beginning of Lent, on Shrove Tuesday, which were customarily held outdoors in the region. Up until the very end of the 20th century, the residents of Pusztina slaughtered hens on Shrove Tuesday and bade farewell to the merry weeks with gay abandon.[528]

In their villages, too, Easter is the most important religious event of the spring. In the northern Csángó villages, up to the end of the 20th century, young men splashed water on the village girls from wooden pots and vessels. This rite must have had an ancient magical meaning, connected with fertility and bringing forth beauty. The effect of the custom was only enhanced that the water was sprinkled on the unmarried girls using only with a handful of sweet basil. The groups of young men in the Seklerized villages (e.g.- Bohána, Diószeg, Szitás, Szolohegy, Tatrosvásár and Újfalu) kept the tradition to the middle of the 20th century of visiting houses with eligible girls on Easter Monday (vízbeveto hétfo) and saluting them with Hungarian greeting verses. There, they sprinkled them with the aid of sprigs of basil, receiving hand painted eggs, in return. Today, the tradition of sprinkling the girls on Easter Monday is no longer observed. Rather, observers report the prevalence of collective, outdoor games and dances.[529]

The Sunday following Easter, White or betrothal Sunday, is a day of heightened importance in the Csángó calendar. Up until the collectivization of 1962, young girls of close friendship swore an eternal sisterly love to each other through a well defined ritual.[530] Usually, the younger girls, more rarely boys, who had no sibling of the same sex, chose a 'sister' of similar age. The newly 'related' exchanged a plate of hand painted eggs and referred to each other as blood relations (mátka, vérje). In the Csángó inhabited villages, it was common that these pseudo-relatives became godparents to each other's children, thereby strengthening the bonds. In many places it was thought that

---

527 Pozsony: Újesztendohöz ... op. cit.

528 Ibid, p. 166; Wichmann: A moldvai ... op. cit. pp. 288-289.

529 Halász, Péter: A moldvai magyarok tavaszi ünnepkörérol [The spring holiday cycle among the Moldovan Hungarians], In: Czégényi, Dóra – Keszeg, Vilmos /ed./: Kriza János Néprajzi Társaság Évkönyve 8. Kolozsvár, 2000, pp. 233-275;

Halász, Péter: „Vízbeveto hétfo" a moldvai magyaroknál [Easter Monday traditions among the Moldovan Hungarians]. Néprajzi Látóhatár IX. 3-4, 2000, pp. 425-435.

530 Halász: A moldvai ... op. cit. pp. 271-273.

these 'relatives' became brothers and sisters after death.[531] In olden days, this pseudo-relative phenomena was to be found all over the Hungarian speaking territories. In the Trans-Danubian counties of Zala and Somogy, the girls exchanged a *bridal plate*, heaped with richly decorated eggs.[532]

The region inhabited by the Csángó usually experienced summer droughts; the communities had various customs to bring rain. As but one example, in Gajdár, in the valley of Tázló, the first farmer to head out to begin plowing had his plow and oxen liberally doused with water, a canteen of wine and loaf of bread hung on each of the oxen's horns. During times of extended drought, an odd number of young boys who have not yet had sex, hence, from a ritualistic point of view were considered pure, were covered with green branches and leaves. They, called the twelve apostles, on their return from the fields to the village, were strewn with flower petals and liberally watered. In Lészped, a pregnant woman's water mug was buried beside the well and the woman was thoroughly doused. In the villages along the Szeret River, girls, who were 'pure' from the ritual's viewpoint, were chosen and appointed to place a plank on the river on which were lit candles and ritualistic pastries. In the hopes of bringing rain, they were to follow it on the riverbank until the items sank.[533]

European cultural and societal research, by the middle of the 20th century, has already made it unequivocally clear that communities living in islands of linguistic, cultural and ethnic isolation retain their unique traditional cultures on three different levels: one, the retained of old, two, arising internally, i.e., their own, and three, the elements adopted from the surrounding majority.[534]

The smaller groups that became isolated from the larger whole (e.g.- the Transylvanian Saxons, the Balkan Romanians, the Schwabians of the Banate, etc.) retain a great deal of the ancient elements in the structures of their culture. Similar to them, the Moldovan Csángó were able to retain, until the very end of the 20th century, archaic Hungarian-language apocryphal prayers, religious hymns, sayings, classical ballads and songs rich in Renaissance motifs. The new style ballads, emerging during the 19th century,

---

531 Ibid, pp. 268-273.

532 Tárkány Szücs, Erno: Magyar jogi népszokások [Hungarian legal folk customs]. Budapest, 1981, p. 496.

533 Pozsony, Ferenc: „Adok néktek három vesszot..." ["I give thee three twigs..."] Dolgozatok erdélyi és moldvai népszokásokról. Pro-Print Könyvkiadó, Csíkszereda, 2000, pp. 19-36.

534 Weber-Kellermann, Ingeborg: Zur Frage der interethnischen Beziehungen in der „Sprachinselvolkskunde". Österreichische Zeitschrift für Volkskunde 62., 1959, pp. 19-47; Weber-Kellermann, Ingeborg: A „nyelvsziget-néprajz"-ban jelentkezo interetnikus viszonyok kérdéséhez [Addenda to the questions of inter-ethnic relations arising in the ethnography of linguistic islands]. Néprajzi Látóhatár IX, 2000, pp. 11-25.

only reached Moldova erratically. Their lyrical song librettos were, primarily, rooted in the love songs of the 16th-17th century Renaissance, as well as the early 18th century Kuruc era's written and oral singing traditions, whose most characteristic traits they managed to preserve. The motifs of the newer styles are only present in their songs sporadically, introduced by Transylvanian Hungarian soldiers and teachers in the periods after the two world wars.

"Moldova is as much a separated part to Hungarians, as Carinthian Gottschee is to the Germans, the Asia-Minor Ak-Dag are to the Greeks and, to a degree, the French-Canadians of Canada are to the French, where, beside the many foreign influences and local, often pale, traditions many important ancient values may be found. New trends always reach the geographically isolated areas, at some distance from the main linguistic bloc, after some delay but are retained longer. We can trace this from the spread of the new-style ballads, which started from the Hungarian lowlands, along the river valleys into Transylvania, first to Kalotaszeg, then up the Szamos valley to the Mezoség [the low, undulating central part of Transylvania-*Ed.*] and finally to distant Moldova."[535]

The isolated communities are only able to create new cultural works from their existing elements. This was the process in the Csángó villages where countless ballads were created, based on existing motifs. Many new concepts were called by familiar words already within their vocabulary, e.g.- big brawl for world war, etc. Linguistic traditions, based on oral transmission of the mother tongue, effectively aided the continued strengthening and representation of their Hungarian identity up to the time the establishment of the Romanian nation state.

The isolated linguistic group's traditional popular culture is continually enriched by elements adopted from the majority's differing language, religious and cultural traditions. The Hungarian mother-tongued Moldavians' culture was continually enriched and augmented by components and layers adapted from the surrounding Romanians. A strong Romanian influence can be found in the culinary culture, dances, music, medicines and beliefs of the Csángó who migrated from Transylvania to Moldova. Here, we must stress that it was the Moldovan, and not the Transylvanian (nor, within that, the Seklerland) Orthodox Romanians whose culture enriched the Csángó traditions. If the Moldovan Csángó were semi-Hungarianized Romanians of Transylvanian origin, then we should find countless examples of Transylvanian-Romanian elements in their traditional culture.

The adoption of Romanian cultural elements, integration into the majority society and culture were promoted by the mass migrations following the 1962 collectivization, the opportunity for local and societal mobility, and

---

535 Vargyas: A magyar ... op. cit. p. 172.

155

the government policy of assimilation, served by the educational and religious organizations. In the decade following the 1989 regime change, Romania, and to a degree the Csángó region, has seen an increased modernization and globalization, whose combined impact has lead to a sudden weakening of position and importance that traditional folklore works of art had previously filled. In the end, this contributes to a diminishing of the earlier ethnic identity. A distancing from traditional culture has taken place in the Carpathian basin. But there its place was taken by a Hungarian-language popular culture, while in Moldova, the Csángó communities have adopted the fashionable Romanian-language popular culture. Closely entwined with, and gradually emerging from, this shift of language is their most effective assimilation into the Romanian majority nation.

V. THE HUNGARIAN DIALECT OF THE MOLDAVIAN CSÁNGÓ

The systematic linguistic research carried out in the Moldovan villages unanimously proves that the Csángó communities still harbor an archaic Hungarian dialect, rich in medieval elements. Their isolation, fringe location and great distance from the centers of renewing Hungarian culture has lead to their language and culture being continually enriched and expanded by new elements and words absorbed from the surrounding Romanians.[536] National homogenization, raised to the status of state policy since the end of the 19th century, accelerated the loss of Hungarian-speaking territory in Moldova. Not to be overlooked, the Roman Catholic Church activities in the region, as well as the educational establishments, were deeply committed to serve this assimilative policy.

In the decades after the second world war (especially 1949-1962), linguists from Cluj regularly visited those Moldovan settlements where they still spoke Hungarian,[537] where they collected the dialectical material, later published,[538] clearly mapping the internal dialectical distribution of this region. This systematic research revealed that the Moldovan Hungarian communities can be divided into three main dialect groups (Northern, Southern and Transylvanian).

1. The Northern Csángó dialect is spoken around Románvásár (e.g.- in Balusest, Bargován, Jugán, Kelgyeste, Szabófalva and Újfalu). The Northern block is of medieval origin, a fact supported by linguistic and historical documents. The central location of this language group also points to this, as the original Hungarian settlers would certainly occupy the most fertile locations, where they would be able to proliferate over the centuries under advantageous conditions.

The Hungarian settlements in Moldova led a relatively isolated existence until the end of the 19th century. This isolation favored not only the retention of an archaic culture, both physical and psychological, but also the survival of a local Hungarian dialect rich in bygone elements. In these Northern villages, linguistic traces can still be found that harkens back to the

---

536 Szabó: A moldvai ... op. cit.

537 In total, they found 94 settlements inhabited by Hungarian-speakers. (See Murádin, László – Péntek, János (ed.): A moldvai csángó nyelvjárás atlasza I-II [The map of Moldovan Csángó dialect]. A Magyar Nyelvtudományi Társaság Kiadványai, 193. sz., Budapest, 1991, pp. 6-8.)

538 Ibid.

Middle Ages, such as pronouncing the letter /s/ in a lisping manner[539] and still retain the phonic for /ly/, which has long dropped out of everyday Hungarian. After the creation of the Kingdom of Romania, the area underwent rapid social and economic changes. The industrializing market towns began to attract the working-age males, especially after the building of railroads. Although their womenfolk hardly ventured past their village boundaries, the breadwinners began to do so, more and more often, and this change in lifestyle soon began to be mirrored in their use of language. Ferenc Kovács already noticed during his Moldovan travels in 1868 that the Romanian influence can primarily be noted among the men, while the phenomenon can not yet be heard among the women and children.[540] The region's industrialization continued between the two wars but accelerated after the second world war. Between 1949 and 1962, agriculture was collectivized here too, which began the mass migration of the younger generations to the cities. After completing elementary school, they enrolled in schools at various distances from home. There, after completing their studies or learning a trade, they usually had a job assigned and started families in the tenements.

Those family members who settled in the Romanian towns soon became unilingual – Romanian – which also had repercussions on the families left behind. Grandparents could no longer communicate in Hungarian with grandchildren vacationing in the village. In Szabófalva and Kelgyeste, Hungarian is spoken today mainly by those older than 40. In these settlements, parents intentionally did not teach their children born after 1965 their own mother tongue to assist their integration in school, profession or place of work. As a result, a strange situation arose: the emotionally charged mother tongue vanished, meaning that the language of mother and child, in these villages, is different. Today, they still speak Hungarian in Bargován, Jugán and Újfalu, as well as Balusest and Ploszkucény,[541] populated by those moving away from Szabófalva. The Hungarian population of the settlements of Acélfalva, Barticsfalva, Bírófalva, Burjánfalva, Butea, Dávid, Domafalva, Dzsidafalva, Farkasfalva, Halasfalva, Korhán, Nisziporest, Tamásfalva and Teckán have gradually became linguistically completely assimilated in with the Romanians.

2. The Southern Csángó dialect is spoken in the villages South of Bákó (Bogdánfalva, Gyoszény, Nagypatak, Trunk, Szeketura and Újfalu.

---

539 This archaic linguistic anomaly was also noted by Péter Zöld who, in his report after spending four years among the Moldovan Csángó, wrote that: " … they speak Hungarian clearly but pronounce it with a lisp." (See Szabó: A moldvai … op. cit. p. 483.)

540 Ibid, p. 489.

541 This last settlement can be found along the Szeret River, in the vicinity of Egyedhalma.

Hungarians also settled this region in the Middle Ages. Based on their archaic 'lisping' dialect, they also can not be taken as being of Transylvanian origin. The population of Újfalu migrated from Bogdánfalva after the first world war. In Szeketura today, only the elderly understand Hungarian; the dialect spoken in Gyoszény contains many Sekler elements. At the same time, in the villages belonging to the Sekler-Csángó group, Forrófalva, Klézse and Lujzikalagor, many older, southern-Csángó characteristics occasionally surface, leading one to deduce that the later arriving groups from Transylvania gradually Seklerized the language of the previously settled Hungarian communities they found there.

In both the Northern and Southern dialects, a characteristic of the Transylvanian Mezoség region can often be found, whereby the *o* in the second, unaccented, syllable is pronounced as *a*. Even today, villages of both dialects retain the antiquated phonic of *ly* (pronouncing *lány* [girl] as *lyán*).[542] We have already noted the most prominent and characteristic phonic trait of both Northern and Southern Csángó, speaking with a lisping *s*. Similar to it is their habit of using *c* in place of *cs* [In Hungarian phonics, the diphthong *cs* is used to represent the sound of *ch*, as in church-*Ed.*]. It is a further characteristic of both that in common usage, instead of the phonic of *ty* and *gy*, their postalveolar pair of *cs* or *zs* is spoken. In the Csángó dialect spoken to this day, the bilabial phonic *v*, documented as part of medieval Hungarian, proves the archaic characteristics retained by it. Their system of vowels was enriched, through Romanian assimilated words, by the velaric sounds of *î* and *a* (*gîszka* 'goose', *katîr* 'mule', *karuca* 'wagon', *padurar* 'forester'). The closed sound *ë* can occasionally be found in the southern group, while rare and inconsistent among the northerners.[543] In the northern Csángó villages around Románvásár, often times a medium strength use of *í* can be heard.[544] Loránd Benko has illustrated with language historical and dialect data that the previously noted characteristics consistently and widely appear only among the Hungarian settlements of central Trasylvania, more narrowly, along the middle Maros and lower Aranyos rivers. In his opinion, the ancestors of the northern and southern Csángó could only have come from this area, where these phonetic peculiarities can be consistently noted over a wide area. Since the vernacular of the Csángó and the central Transylvanian Hungarians shows such close relationship, Benko holds that the ancestors of the northern and southern Csángó originally came from from

---

542 In those Moldovan communities that were settled by Transylvanians, were regularly note the widespread

use of *j* instead of the usual *ly* (Miháj, instead of Mihály).

543 The guttural *ë* regularly appears in the Moldovan Sekler communities and plays an important meaning-

differentiator role.

544 Kiss, Jeno (ed.): Magyar dialektológia. Budapest, 2001, pp. 307-310.

there, over the Radna and Borgó passes, the valleys of the Beszterce and Moldova Rivers, to settle in Moldova at the end of the 13th and beginning of the 14th centuries, where they retained for centuries the unaltered basic vocabulary and traits of their central Mezoség language.[545]

Apart from the already noted lisping pronunciation, another characteristic is the existence of the *dzs* phonic. This sound appears widely old Hungarian, changing gradually into *gy* by the turn of the 15 [th]-16 [th] century.[546] This seems to lead to the conclusion that the ancestors of the Csángó left the Carpathian basin at the time when this usage change had not yet taken place. This archaic usage has also remained in the western Hungarian dialects (in Orvidék, today Burgenland) due, in all likelyhood, to their peripheral location.[547]

3. The Sekler Csángó dialect is today spoken in more than 70 villages, or is familiar to about two-thirds of the Moldovan Hungarians. The most significant settlements can be found in the basin drained by the Aranyos-Beszterce, Tatros and Tázló Rivers.[548] Research in the fields of language distribution and settlement patterns has conclusively proven that the ancestors of those speaking the Seklerized Csángó dialect came from the eastern parts of Seklerland, the wholly Catholic counties of Csík, Kászon and Gyergyó, as well as from the mixed, Protestant and Roman Catholic, Háromszék.[549] The majority of the Sekler Csángó villages were established in the decades after the Mádéfalva revolt, during the second half of the 18th century. But, migration continued into neighboring Moldova well into the 19th century from a Seklerland unsuited for intensive farming and gradually being overpopulated. These settlers arrived with a more advanced version of Hungarian and components of an awakening civil national awareness. Since the Seklerland they left already possessed a network of higher level Hungarian-language schools and an intensive religious practice in the mother tongue, the Sekler families and communities settling in Moldova were in possession of a more articulated ethnic and linguistic awareness. They were more emphatic and insistent in voicing their need for a liturgy in their mother tongue, often inviting their cantors from the Seklerland to Moldova, keeping Hungarian hymnals and prayer books in their homes, and maintaining close contact with the Franciscan center in Csíksomlyó.

Researchers hold it to be quite likely that the older, medieval founding population of some South Csángó settlements (e.g.- Forrófalva,

---

545 Benko: A csángók ... op. cit.

546 Benko: A Magyar nyelv ... op. cit. pp. 517-518.

547 Benko: A csángók ... op. cit. p. 36.

548 Tánczos: Hol vannak ... op. cit. pp. 374-375.

549 Murádin – Péntek: A moldvai ... op.cit.; Szabó: A moldvai ... op. cit. p. 521.

Gorzafalva, Gyoszény, Klézse, Lujzikalagor, Onest, Szászkút and Tatros) could well have been Hungarian whose dialect and culture were gradually diluted by the large numbers of Sekler settlers arriving after 1764.[550] At the same time, language distribution mapping reveals that the Seklers never mixed with the Hungarians living in the northern areas. János (John) Ince Petrás recorded the same observation in 1841 when he wrote: *"It is worthy of careful note that, although they live amicably with the noted Sekler newcomers, they always refer to them as Seklers, their women as Seklerfolk, but make family ties with them through marriage only rarely, if ever. Let it serve as an example that Csángó girls will not marry Sekler men, preferring instead to stay by the family hearth. In like manner, it is even rarer for a Csángó man to take a Sekler wife, preferring far more to see his grey mustache than his Sekler wife."*[551] Family structure research carried out in the last decade reflects that, until the beginning of the mass migration to cities following collectivization in 1962, there was no intermarriage between Roman Catholic youths in the North and South blocs. The northern Csángó settlements, possessing excellent and extensive agricultural lands, gradually became overpopulated, resorting to exporting their surplus population, and were unable to absorb the new Sekler arrivals.

The various sized groups of Seklers, arriving through the 18th-19th century, settled in and around existing Romanian settlements. We feel it quite possible that several villages, created by clearing the forest, were founded concurrently by the Seklers and the Romanians. Since their communities were dispersed over a large area – and in many places they live in close proximity with Orthodox Romanians - , today their linguistic and cultural assimilation is well advanced. Among the group of Sekler settlements, the loss of Hungarian-speaking territory is the greatest along the Tatros River, where a large number of industrial concerns were built during the 20th century. The establishment of large factories, and the accompanying artificial urbanization, exerted a strong influence on the population of the surrounding villages, accelerating their social, cultural and linguistic assimilation.

The mother tongue of the Hungarian communities of Moldova, living for centuries as they were for centuries in a minority position, received significant Romanian influence, which was manifested primarily by the inclusion of borrowed words. Research done by Gyula (Julius) Márton disclosed that the Csángó dialects contain about 2,730 borrowed words. These can be grouped according to the following general topics: 380 relate to human life and living, 70 with family relations, 190 with modes of clothing, 120 with eating and food, 360 with the house and its surroundings, 19 with the village, 175 with agriculture, 180 with animal husbandry, 115 with

550 Ibid, p. 518.

551 Domokos: Édes hazámnak ... op. cit. p. 1329.

activities around the house, 345 with nature, 260 with handicrafts and commerce, 150 with customs, traditions, beliefs and cultural life, 220 with public administrative functions, and 150 of various others.[552] It is interesting to note the large number of Romanian borrowed words relating to the house (furnishings, the yard, gardening, fruits and orchards), to the person (body parts, sicknesses, means of healing, activities and social interaction), to modes and means of clothing, to nature and to the production of everyday needs. Also interesting to note that 80% of the Romanian-origin borrowed words are nouns, with verbs making up a mere 9% and adjectives only a further 7.7%. This illuminates a fundamental rule of borrowing: in the Csángó tongue, those words dealing with aspects of material and intellectual concepts were accepted the easiest and fastest, with which the members of the Hungarian communities could only come into contact in their new environment. In spite of the centuries long close Romanian-Hungarian contact, the store of borrowed verbs and adverbs dealing with abstract ideas shows significantly less Romanian influence.[553]

The proportion of borrowed words is significantly different in the three dialect groups. They are considerably more in the northern dialect zone than in the Sekler villages, as they are in the southern dialect zone, than the neighboring Sekler communities. As but one example, the borrowed Romanian vocabulary dealing with agriculture and forage gathering in the northern bloc village of Szabófalva is 54, in the southern bloc village of Bogdánfalva it is 50, while the Sekler village of Lészped contains only 32.[554]

Secondly, the Moldovan Csángó dialect contains many borrowed Romanian words pertaining to modern technology, social, administrative, political and military expressions. These entered the literary language of the Carpathian-basin Hungarians relatively late, appearing after the language reforms of the late 18th century, others are more recent international expressions. The words expressing this latter group of concepts entered into the usage of the Csángó communities through the transmission of the local Romanian dialects. Research carried out by László (Leslie) Murádin in Külsorekecsin proves that the words originating from the Hungarian language reforms carried out at the turn of the 18th-19th century did not become part of the Csángó dialects. Instead, they usually resorted to borrowed Romanian words, occasionally using internally developed expressions. This process was promoted by the fact that, in the subsequent centuries, the Csángó maintained relatively few contacts with communities in

552 Márton, Gyula: A moldvai csángó nyelvjárás román kölcsönszavai [The Romanian borrowed-word
vocabulary of the Moldovan Csángó dialect]. Bukarest, 1972, pp. 26-27.

553 Ibid, p. 28.

554 Ibid, p. 29.

the Carpathian basin; secondly, because of a lack of education and liturgy in their native tongue, newer expressions of modern life failed to reach them. Their vocabulary retained countless ancient Hungarian words: *filesz* 'nyúl' [rabbit], *lér* 'sógor' [brother-in-law], *mony* 'tojás' [egg], *nép* 'asszony or feleség' [woman or wife], *szaru* 'csizma' [boot], *szültü* 'furulya' [recorder], *üno* 'tehén' [cow], *vasvero* 'kovács' [smith], etc.[555] In a few cases, words formed during and after the language reform only have a Hungarian equivalent because they were created from existing elements (*first great fight,* meaning the first world war).[556]

Borrowed words aside, the most important and fundamental concepts are still expressed with Hungarian words, such as the basic parts of the body. For body parts, only the following Romanian words were adopted: *bárba* (beard), *musztáca* (mustache), *burik* (belly button), *fáca* (face), *sztomák* (stomach).[557] All over Moldova, the house is called by its Hungarian name but newly introduced elements (vestibule, kitchen, bedroom) are expressed using words of Romanian origin (*ántrét, buketeria, odáj*).[558] It is an interesting fact that in rhyming verse folk literature (ballads, lyrical songs, etc) there are significantly less borrowed words than in works of prose or everyday communication. Also interesting to note that, in countless folksongs, such Hungarian words may appear (*biro* [judge], *gozkocsi* [steam engine], *kaszárnya* [barracks]) for which Romanian words are used exclusively in everyday usage.[559] Furthermore, it is intriguing that from a phonetic perspective, the words borrowed from Romanian conform to the phonetic characteristics of the Hungarian dialect spoken in Moldova. In the northern villages, instead of the Romanian *s*, they sound their usual *sz* in the adopted words also (e.g.- *gejinusza* (gainusa 'little hen'), *szervét* (servet 'smaller scarf'), *maszina* (masina 'machine') stb.)[560] The borrowed words of Romanian origin are not marginal in their vocabulary, since they have become a central and essential parts of everyday interaction.

The influence of the Romanian language has not been limited to the vocabulary, since their phonetic structure was also significantly modified. Two sounds characteristic of Romanian, *a* and *î,* have taken root; among the diphthongs *oa, ua, au, eu* have spread, while a number of consonants, typical of Moldovan-Romanian dialects, have also made inroads. Romanian

555 Lüko: A moldvai ... op. cit. pp. 72-79.

556 Murádin, László: A nyelvújítási szók csángó megfeleléseihez [Csángó equivalents to language reform words]. (Studia Univ. „Babes-Bolyai." Tom. III. nr. 6. Series IV. Fasc. 1., 1958) pp. 197-199.

557 Márton: A moldvai ... op. cit. p. 30.

558 Ibid, p. 31.

559 Ibid, p. 37.

560 Ibid, p. 81.

influences can also be detected in inflections and expressions of the Csángó dialects, as well as shifts in the emphasis, cadence, intonation and more rapid pace of speech.[561]

Missionaries visiting Moldova continually reported, beginning in the 17th century, that the Roman Catholic Hungarians were already gradually losing their mother tongue but that, in their religion and traditional folk culture and identity, they determinedly differentiated themselves from the Romanians. Travelers from the Carpathian basin also reported during the 19th century that the Hungarian language was losing ground in many villages. However, we must stress that the majority of the Seklers, who arrived in the late 18th century, have managed to preserve their native language.

The numeric and proportional change among the Moldovan Roman Catholics, who hold their mother tongue to be Hungarian, is also reflected in the official Romanian census data.

	Number of Roman Catholics	Mother tongue: Hungarian
1859	52,811	37,823 (71.6%)
1930	109,953	23,886 (21.7%)
1992	239,938	1,800 (0.7%)

The official census carried out in 1859 enumerated a total of 37,823 registered persons who declared their mother tongue to be Hungarian, who comprised a significant proportion (71.6%) of the region's Roman Catholics. At the same time, in Bákó County, where the majority of the southern and Sekler Csángó lived, 25,896 Roman Catholics were counted, of whom 22,426 (86.6%) declared themselves still to be Hungarian. In Román County, inhabited by the northern group, the census showed 15,588 Roman Catholics, of whom 14,736 (94.6%) declared themselves as Hungarian. "Thus, in the middle of the 19th century, the ethnic proportion of the two large Csángó groups still closely resemble that of the Seklerland of today, since, at the time, the majority of the Catholic population professed themselves to be Hungarian (even according to the data of the Romanian census)."[562]

During the second half of the 19th century, the growth of a civil nation state in Romania accelerated, which rapidly resulted in the linguistic and ethnic assimilation of the Moldovan Hungarians. This process is also

---

561 Kiss: Magyar ... op. cit. p. 312.

562 Tánczos: Hungarians in ... op. cit. p.10.

clearly reflected in the population figures gathered in the 31 settlements of
Bákó and Román Counties.[563]

County	Number of settlements	Proportion of ethnic Hungarians (in 1859)	Percentage whose mother tongue is Hungarian (in 1895)
Bákó	19	86.60%	78.30%
Román	12	94.60%	61.10%
Total	31	89.60%	71.10%

The table above graphically shows that, in the 40 years between
1859 and 1895, in the two counties where the majority of the Csángó lived,
the proportion of Hungarians within the Roman Catholic category declined
by almost 20%. This drop was especially stunning in Román County, where
it plummeted from 94.6% to 61.1%, meaning that, during this time, a third of
the ethnic Hungarians became Romanian. This assimilative process was later
accelerated by the events of the first world war, as Romania attacked the
Austro-Hungarian Empire in 1916. The data of the official census of 1930 (in
spite of all its distortion) clearly reflects the intensity and attainment of the
assimilation process.[564]

County	Number of Roman Catholics	Number of ethnic Hungarians	Number whose mother tongue is Hungarian	% whose mother tongue is Hungarian
Bákó	47,139	8,497	13,999	29.69%
Román	32,462	2,050	462	1.42%
Total	79,601	10,547	14,461	18.16%

If we compare the figures of the 1930 census in the table above with
the numbers from the end of the 19th century, we can see that in Bákó County
the number who declared their mother tongue to be Hungarian declined from
78.3% to 29.69% between 1895 and 1930. In Román County the decline,
over the same period, was a dramatic drop from 61.1% to 1.42%. According
to the data of the same 1930 census, the proportion of Roman Catholics and
Hungarians of the Moldovan region, now part of a Greater Romania, altered
in the following manner:[565]

---

563 Szabados, Mihály: A moldvai magyarok a román népszámlálások tükrében 1859-1977 között [The

Moldovan Hungarians, as reflected in the Romanian census between 1859-1977], In: Kiss, Gy. Csaba

/ed./: Magyarságkutatás. A Magyarságkutató Intézet Évkönyve. Budapest, 1989, p. 94.

564 Ibid, p. 95.

565 Ibid, p. 95.

Total population	Roman Catholic	Mother tongue Hungarian	Ethnic Hungarian
2,433,596	109,953 (4.51%)	23,802 (0.98%)	20,964 (0.86%)

Thus, the 1930 census shows significantly fewer Hungarians, a total of 23,802, who made up 21.7% of the Roman Catholics of Moldova. At the time, Roman Catholics of various denominations lived in 875 settlements, of which ethnic Hungarians lived in 433 but only 352 of those were inhabited by those of Hungarian mother tongue. In the period between the two wars, a significant proportion of Moldovan Hungarians were already living sparsely dispersed.[566]

In the totalitarian decades following the second world war, according to the extremely manipulated official census figures, the number of Hungarians living in Moldova continued to diminish. The census of 1956 figures showed a total of 12,952 ethnic Hungarians and 18,817 who held their mother tongue to be Hungarian. The same figures in the 1966 statistics showed 7,167 and 9,516 in the Moldovan counties, where their numbers shrank to one-third since the 1930 count.[567]

The official Romanian census conducted in 1992 registered a total of 4,749 Roman Catholic Hungarians in Moldova. If we deduct the Hungarians of Gyimesbükk who, in the meantime, were transferred administratively from Csík to Bákó County, then we can realistically only count about 1,800 Csángó Hungarians, representing a mere 0.75% of the region's Catholics.[568]

The data of the 2002 census particular to Bákó County clearly show that, in the recent decades, the total population of Moldova has continuously shrunk, as well as the number of Roman Catholics and Reformed Protestants.[569]

	1992	2002
Population of Bákó County	737,512	708,751
Roman Catholics	125,805	120,579
Reformed Protestants	207	143

At the same time, the last population count also reports the decline of urban Hungarians in Moldova.[570]

---

566 Ibid, p. 96.

567 Ibid, pp. 98-99.

568 Tánczos: Hungarians in … op. cit. p. 376.

569 Hegyeli : Nott a … op. cit. p. 8.

570 Ibid, p. 9.

City	Roman Catholics		Ethic Hungarians		Ethnic Csángó		Hungarian mother tongue
	1992	2002	1992	2002	1992		2002
Bákó	24,566	21,045	214	198	164	108	191
Ónfalva	5,884	5,823	311	214	11	15	178
Mojnest	1,365	1,331	47	28	4	7	25
Buhus	367	281	26	15	11	0	15
Kománfalva	1,577	1,318	63	72	9	0	58
Aknavásár	1,445	1,260	178	20	43	5	18

The Bákó County census data from 1992 and 2002 also indicates that, in the previous 10 years, the number of people who earlier declared themselves to be Csángó has declined, while the number who declared themselves Hungarian has risen modestly (from 4,365 to 4,523).[571]

Census data from the last century and a half unambiguously show that, within the Roman Catholic population of Moldova, the proportion of Hungarians fell from the 1859 count of 71.5% to 21.7% in 1930 and 0.75% in 1992. Since there were no significant episodes of migration during this period to diminish the number of Roman Catholics, in fact, their numbers grew as part of the total population of the region, the dramatic decline of the number of Moldovan Hungarians can best be explained firstly by systematic, institutionalized assimilation; secondly, by the effects of coercion and threats brought into play during the official census enumeration process.[572]

Although the cited official census figures clearly reflect the ethic and linguistic assimilation under way in Moldova, yet they present a distorted and false picture.[573] During the 1930 census, for example, in the 2,249-strong Roman Catholic community of Klézse, they registered only one person as Hungarian. In 1992, of the 4,235 registered Catholics, the local investigation of Vilmos (William) Tánczos disclosed that approximately 3,000 (90%) still spoke the language of their ancestors.[574]

The 1992 census disclosed that a total of 239,938 Roman Catholics were to be found in Moldova. Of those 43%, or 103,543 persons, were distributed among 85 settlements where, in the closing decade of the 20th century, Hungarian was still spoken to some degree.[575] In the middle of the

571 Ibid, p. 8.

572 Stan – Weber: The moldvaian ... op. cit. p. 13.

573 Szabados: A moldvai ... op. cit. p. 98.

574 Tánczos: Hungarians in ... op. cit. p. 378.

575 In the 1950's, linguists from Cluj found a total of 92 villages where at least a few people still spoke
Hungarian. (See Murádin – Péntek: A moldvai ... op. cit. p. 6.)

'90s, Vilmos Tánczos methodically visited these 85 villages, counting the number of Hungarian speaking residents and determining their proportion of the local Roman Catholics. His findings are presented in the table below, summarized by the dialect regions.

	Total	Northern Csángó	Southern Csángó	Sekler-Csángó		
				Szeret valley	Tázló valley	Tatros valley
Number of villages examined	85	7	6	24	19	29
Number who spoke Hungarian	62,225	8,180	9,520	23,260	6,095	15,170
Hungarian-speaking Roman Catholics as a % of total Roman Catholics.	60.09%	38.77%	73.34%	81.91%	68.14%	47.21%

The table above clearly shows that linguistic assimilation in Moldova is most advanced in the northern dialect zone, around the town of Román, where, today, only the generation born before 1965 are conversant with Hungarian. Vilmos Tánczos recorded more wide spread knowledge of Hungarian in the southern zone, the villages around Bákó, where three-quarters of the Roman Catholics still speak and are familiar with the Hungarian language. Interestingly, the table also shows that the groups of villages settled by the Seklers shows a wide-ranging discrepancy. It must be noted that, of the three, the region around the Tatros valley is the most industrialized.

In 1993, we conducted a survey of the Sekler-dialect village of Csík, where we were able to poll over 75% of the families. The table below shows the generational distribution of what each person holds as their mother tongue:

Generations	Number of registered persons	Declared mother tongue		
		Hungarian	Romanian	Csángó
First	300	83%	2%	15%
Second	150	80%	3.33%	16.66%
Third	318	74.21%	11.94%	13.83%
Fourth	99	26.26%	24.24%	49.49%
Total	867	72.77%	8.41%	18.80%

The overwhelming percentage of old people in the village, 83%, still regarded Hungarian as their mother tongue, while a significant number designated it as Csángó. Two of the women among them confessed that they can not speak proper Romanian, at all. One sixth of the working-age group also declared Csángó as their native language but the language of their children is more diverse: of the school age children, 13.83% declared Csángó and 11.94% as Romanian. This is not surprising as a significant portion live in an urban environment. The grandchildren of the polled breadwinners were divided as 49.49% as Csángó and 24.24% as Romanian, illustrating the acceleration of assimilation. It was also noted that among the adults there was one, among the children 22 and

As we have noted, according to the surveys of Vilmos Tánczos, a significant portion of the Roman Catholic population of Moldova has become Romanianized by the end of the 20th century. In his estimate, a total of 62,225 people speak Hungarian in Moldova, which, according to the data of the 1992 census, only represents a quarter (25.8%) of the region's total registered Catholic population of 239,938.[576]

There are a great number of internal and external causes for linguistic assimilation in Moldova. Everyday life has continuously and dynamically altered in the region over the last 150 years. The rapid change of economic and social reality introduced a great number of new factual or abstract concepts, which the biblical Hungarian language, so rich in ancient and archaic elements, was unable to express. Inside the Csángó families and communities, the more complex emotions and thoughts could not be expressed by the ancient language, hence it gradually accumulated linguistic innovations adopted from Romanian, specific Romanian expressions and phrases.

The increasing local and social mobility of the Csángó resulted first in a balanced bilingualism, followed by a heterogeneous status whereby events outside the immediate family and the village (e.g.- work, health and central administrative related) were voiced solely in Romanian. The assimilation process tends more and more toward a Romanian dominated bilingualism, which is merely a temporary, intermediate station towards

---

576 Tánczos: Hungarians in … op. cit. p. 380.

linguistic unification, the total integration into the Moldovan Romanian structure. Thus, in the early stage, the native tongue is found to be restrictive on the functional level, then, its worth on a social interactive plane sees a spectacular loss of value, and finally, it closes with the complete substitution of Romanian for Hungarian.

The linguistic assimilation under way in the Csángó villages was effectively aided by the Romanian-language educational and religious institutions, which continuously and consciously - in many places using brutal means – demolished the esteem of the Hungarian language. The Romanian-born Catholic priests and Orthodox teachers visiting their villages from nearby towns mocked and stigmatized the dialect spoken by the Csángó, referring to it as a deficient, bird-like twittering language – something of which to be ashamed.

In the early 20th century, the Hungarian language was gradually, sometimes rapidly, supplanted from the village churches: initially, only the native language sermons were omitted, then the priests, who resolutely accepted a Romanian identity, banned Hungarian liturgy, prayers and hymns from the house of God. The native language texts lived on temporarily in the private sphere, in family events organized by the elderly, such as wakes, etc. In the meantime, the members of the younger generations only learned the Roman Catholic prayers and church hymns in Romanian. Thus, they only understand the Mass celebrated in church in Romanian. This gradual process resulted in Romanian becoming the language of devotion for all persons born after the second world war, through which it became an integral part of the cognitive system of the rural Csángó communities.[577] It is indicative of the close emotional and mental bond with the language of ritual that the majority of Csángó youth, who have resettled in Transylvanian towns, even those with a Hungarian majority, continue to attend Romanian-language Masses. Parallel to it, the elderly who remain in the vicinity of their ancestral village can only perform the very intimate act of confession, in spite of the direct and firm prohibition of the liturgy in Hungarian.

Today, a significant portion of the Csángó still relate to their native tongue, free of ideology, not attributing any special, symbolic, community uniting significance to it. Lacking adequate contact and information, most are not aware that their language is the same as the vernacular spoken in the Carpathian basin, the language of the Hungarian nation. Since they consider the communicative functions of the language as paramount, they hold the

577 Boross, Balázs: „Majd egyszer lészen, de nem most". Adalékok a moldvai csángók identitásának komplex valóságához egy kulturális antropológiai esettanulmány tükrében ["Maybe someday, but not now." Addenda to the complex reality of the Moldovan Csángó identity, as reflected in a cultural anthropology case study]. Pro Minoritate, Budapest, 2002, pp. 59-60.

language transformation a natural phenomenon, not comprehending it as a tragic loss of value.[578] It is not possible to speak of a unified linguistic picture covering the Csángó communities today. There are villages where even the youngest is taught the language of their ancestors; others where it is not. We can still find families where the Hungarian language is a natural and intrinsic part of everyday communication. In other families, the parents consciously strive to raise their children as Romanians, to shield them from later discrimination in school, the workplace and society at large.

The complexity of the present situation is illustrated by the fact that, during our field surveys, we met countless families where the older children possessed a well defined sense of Hungarian language pride and identity, while their younger siblings were only willing to communicate in Romanian. This heterogeneous situation is, of course, only a temporary, intermediate state, since the language usage in the Csángó villages is rapidly tending towards a linguistic amalgamation. When enough personal and family decisions are suddenly taken, the end result will be that, in a generation or two, entire village communities (e.g.- the Roman Catholic settlements around Románvásár) will have exchanged their former native language. As it stands today, in most of the northern Csángó villages, the Hungarian language has reached the last stage. Only on rare occasion does a Hungarian devotional text (prayer, hymn) surface or, perhaps, a fragment of one in the silent dialogue an old woman might conduct with God.[579]

---

578 Tánczos: Hungarians in ... op. cit. p. 383.

579 Tánczos: Gyöngyökkel ... op. cit. pp. 51-68.

VI. IDENTITY AND MODERNIZATION

An awareness of their ethnic connection is at the basis of the Moldovan Csángó's identity. Since we primarily consider a sense of identity as a cultural and social phenomenon, we feel that the Csángó's view of their own identity can only be examined and understood in connection with their own culture and societal structures. A national culture and identity is such a construct, we feel, which may carry different meaning to local or social groups. The conscious alteration of identity in our modern era has been, primarily and typically, the work of a cultural and political elite, which usually defined as one of the most important values the *nation*. The intelligentsia represents and strengthens, through unique institutions, the cohesion of this imaginary community, assigning decisive role to national culture, national language and national history. In the modern age, the creation of a sense of national identity has also been closely linked with nationalism. The end result of a successful nation building effort results individuals who make the core values of an imagined national group their own. Those who have a sense of belonging to the group thus created can be successfully mobilized at any time in defense of national goals – as defined by the elite groups.[580]

The nation building efforts of the Hungarian and Romanian political elite have, over the past century and a half, usually paralleled each other, occasionally diametrically opposed with the attendant conflicts flaring up. This fact resulted in the members of these two national communities to define themselves in terms of dissimilarity from each other. The differences in points of view between the rival Romanian and Hungarian elites is also weighed down by the fact that both consider the Csángó of Moldova as their own target group, ready to be conquered or converted.[581]

In this chapter, we shall firstly examine how the self-view of identity of the Moldovan Csángó differs from the national identity of the Hungarians of the Carpathian basin. Secondly, we shall attempt to seek an explanation as to why they cannot be considered an integral part of the Romanian nation, in spite of having lived for centuries in the midst of a Romanian majority.

The Moldovan Hungarians lived, until the end of the 19th century, in rural agricultural communities, possessing a sense of ethnic identity unique in structure, with medieval elements. It was a fundamental part of this identity consciousness that contributed to the Csángó speaking Hungarian in a sea of Romanian, that they hold affiliation to the Roman Catholic Church,

---

580 Anderson, Benedict: Imagined Communities: Reflections on the Origin and Spread of Nationalism.

London, 1983.

581 Kántor, Zoltán: Az identitás kapcsán [Through the link of identity]. Provincia II. évf. 11. sz., 2001, p. 15.

surrounded as they are by Orthodox communities, and that they still possess uniquely individual folk traditions. Since they inhabited an area East of the Eastern-Carpathian Hungarian border during the age of nation building, they did not, thus, take part in the principal events at the core of the creation of a civil Hungarian nation. But, at the same time, for a long time they were outside the significant processes of the Romanian nation building, too.[582] Zoltán Kántor states his point of view, in regard to the Csángó of Moldova and the Romanians living in the Balkans South of Romania: "Where nation building did not take place, we cannot speak of a national identity."[583]

In their rural, agricultural communities, an archaic concept of identity lingered on, which did not attribute any symbolic function or significance either to folklore traditions in the native tongue or, indeed, to the native tongue itself. To them, belonging to a national group does not represent the most important or significant aspect of their lives. Indeed, they seem unconcerned with which national group they may be affiliated. In their value system, the most important aspect is not national identification but health and the ability to work, so necessary to their survival.

In their identity structure, beside close ties to the Roman Catholic religion, the strongest element is a sense of local identity.[584] Ties to the village of one's birth were formerly embodied by countless physical elements: unique local costume, building and decorative methods, dialect, folk customs, etc. This affection and loyalty manifests itself in the past few decades by having those who moved to distant places make regular visits *back home* (occasionally at great cost) and take part in a community event of some significance for the village (e.g.- a christening, wedding, funeral or church festival). The regular visit of family members who settled in nearby, or distant, cities unambiguously represents close ties to the village of origin.

Since the Csángó have been separated for centuries from the Hungarians of the Carpathian basin, from an economic, social, cultural and identity perspective, they became aligned with, and integrated into, their Moldovan environment. Until very recently, this region represented for them the only well-known, comprehendible territory - the safe and comfortable homeland.[585] The groups that arrived from Transylvania at various dates are

---

582 Tánczos: Hungarians in ... op. cit. pp. 1-2.

583 Kántor: Az identitás ... op. cit.

584 Boross: "Majd egyszer ... op.cit. p. 53.

585 In the past few decades, the young who went to school far away from their village, then worked abroad for extended periods, have not had an opportunity to become acquainted with the culture of the village of their birth. Since they were omitted from all the rites and ceremonies that most strongly displayed and bound the village community, their emotional ties gradually weakened towards the village. During returning visits they no longer feel comfortable or 'at home'. (Ibid, p. 56)

still well separated, segregated from each other. This differentiation is expressed by the mocking texts of one village against another, based on dialect differences, and by their system of maintaining inter-group communications, whether marriage, economic or ceremonial.[586]

The various mocking, pejorative ethnic expressions alive to this day express the unanimous differentiation that the Roman Catholic Moldovan Hungarians feel for the Orthodox Romanians who live in their proximity, whom the called *Vlahs* until the middle of the 20th century. The group name *Romanian* has only in the past few decades come to replace the former, non-pejorative use of the earlier group name. The Orthodox Romanians, in their turn, usually called the Csángó as *gypsy* or *Ungur* [Hungarian]. The budding nationalism of the late 19th century spawned in their vocabulary the collective ethnic titles of *bozgor* and *bangyin,* intentionally meant to demean and irritate.[587] A number of stereotypes in use by the Csángó further expresses their distancing and differentiation from the Romanians: according to them, the Hungarians are more industrious and hard working, are better farmers, are cleaner, while the Romanians are lazy, slackers and thieves, etc.[588]

The intellectual strata has played an important role, Europe wide, in the last three centuries in the process civil nation building. A good number of Hungarian artisans and businessmen lived in Moldovan towns during the Middle Ages, who played an important role during the 16th century in the Reformation and the achievement of religion in the vernacular.[589] The maelstrom of history destroyed this Hungarian-speaking and cultured civic stratum. Hence, when the civic-character national movements emerged, the Moldovan Hungarians did not have the corresponding stratum, which could have effectively ensured the identity formation of the rural population and protected their interests.

The Romanian nation state was born of the union of Moldova and Muntenia in 1859, followed by the war of independence in 1877, at the end of which the country was freed after centuries of Turkish occupation. The peace treaties following the first world war suddenly enlarged Romanian territory with Transylvania and Bessarabia. In short order, the creation of a civil Romanian nation and culture was begun in the young Romanian state. During this period, the Romanian political elite – quite openly – strove for the rapid assimilation of other-tongued groups, using every means to prevent the emergence of an intellectual stratum or network of institutions among the Moldovan Hungarians. The governments of the day consistently appointed

---

586 Halász: A moldvai ... op. cit. pp. 7-26.

587 Szilágyi, N. Sándor: Bozgor, In: by same author: Mi egy más. Közéleti írások. Bukarest, 2003, p. 717.

588 Halász : A moldvai ... op. cit. pp. 12-13; Boross: "Majd egyszer ... op.cit. p. 54.

589 Binder: Közös ... op. cit. pp. 106-126.

Orthodox Romanian administrators and priests to the Csángó settlements, who often used drastic means to banish the use of the Hungarian language.

In 1884, the Romanian authorities consented to the setting up of a Roman Catholic bishopric and theological institute based in Jászvásár which, in exchange for the undisturbed operation of the Church's institutions, promised to rapidly Romanianize the Csángó. As a result, the peculiar situation arose in the eastern regions of Romania, whereby the priests coming from among the Hungarian community and (re)trained in Jászvásár, consciously served the Romanian assimilation attempts – now on a national policy level -, brusquely turning aside the basic request of the faithful the hear Mass and partake of confession in their native language. The majority of those priests, raised in the intolerant nationalistic attitude, besides undermining the prestige of the Hungarian language, deliberately disseminated the official point of view among the faithful, that "the Csángó are merely Hungarianized Romanians, the *Roman* Catholics are, basically, *Romanian* Catholics, the *bird-like* language of the Csángó is something to be ashamed of, etc."[590]

The elite Romanian ruling class in power has always vehemently rejected all the modest, local initiatives, which aimed at bringing about Hungarian-language education in Moldova. Thus, the public schools organized in Csángó villages soon became the important establishment for the dissemination of the Romanian language and Romanian national pride, consciously and continually denigrating the stature of the national tongue. Since children were never taught, in a consistent and organized manner, to read and write in Hungarian, they were never exposed to the European-level values of Hungarian literature. They do not consider their mother tongue to be an integral part of the vernacular of the Carpathian basin or, at the very least, a regional dialect.

In the years following the second world war, the education organized in Moldovan schools by the Hungarian People's Alliance of Romania /HPAR/ persisted for a short time - and on a fairly low level. Since the educators ordered to Moldova from Transylvania were expected to propagate anti-Church and class-struggle ideology, the Roman Catholic priests were able to marshall the extremely religious local population in opposition to the teachers. In many places, they were able to induce the community to force the Hungarian teachers, spouting atheist ideology, to depart from the school and the village.[591] This short-lived, over ideologized and poor quality Hungarian-languaged education did not contribute in a major way to the reinforcement of a Hungarian identity but, as a result, a

---

590 Tánczos: Hányan vannak ... op. cit. p. 384.

591 Vincze: Csángósors ... op. cit. pp. 203-250.

generation grew up in Moldova that, more or less, learned to read and write in Hungarian.[592]

Since Hungarian-language schools and religious organizations were never able to function in their villages, the collective historical memory of the Moldovan Csángó differs radically from that of the Hungarians in the Carpathian basin. Lacking Hungarian-language written literacy, their knowledge of the common Hungarian past was, primarily, passed orally from generation to generation. The Moldovan Csángó have managed to retain the lore of the outstanding medieval rulers of Hungary (for example, kings Saint Stephen, Saint Ladislaus and Mathias) in oral form, in folktales, ballads and songs.[593] It is interesting to note that, in this vast material of folk poesy, such geographic place names occur regularly (e.g.- Tisza and Danube Rivers), which can be found in the center of the Hungarian-speaking territory.[594]

As they were living in another country during the Hungarian Age of Enlightenment and Reformation of the 18th and 19th centuries, their collective memory does not have any knowledge of any of the decisive events of the period (e.g.- the 1848 revolution), which fundamentally defined the formation of a Hungarian civil consciousness in the Carpathian basin. At the same time, the Romanian educational and religious organizations active in their communities circulated those notable people and events of Romanian history, which presented Hungarians as the barbarian ancestral enemy, something of which to be ashamed. It can still be noted in their communities that the episodes of Hungarian past, passed on in an oral tradition, are often at odds with the symbols and topics of Romanian history spread by the schools and the Church. One such example is linkage they make between King Saint Stephen (the first king of Hungary) and the person of Stefan Nagy (a Moldovan voivod). As oral tradition is losing its effectiveness today, they know of no certain episodes pertaining to the Hungarian past, which they could use to buttress their unique culture, protect or legitimize their minority rights.[595]

---

592 The more dedicated Transylvanian teachers paid particular attention that their more talented students carry on their education. As a result of their efforts, a few Csángó youths obtained diplomas at the Bolyai University of Cluj. The authorities so intimidated them that they were unable to turn their talents to the service of their communities.

593 Magyar: Szent László ... op. cit. & Szent István ... op. cit. & A liliomos ... op. cit.; Vargyas: A magyar ... op. cit. pp. 528-531.

594 Faragó, József: A moldvai csángómagyar verses népköltészet vízrajza [Survey of the Moldovan Csángó-Hungarian folk poetry], In: Pozsony, Ferenc /ed./: Csángósors. Moldvai csángók a változó idokben. Budapest, 1999, pp. 145-154.

595 Pozsony, Ferenc: A moldvai csángók történeti tudata. Néprajzi Látóhatár XI. 1-4., 2002, pp. 341-362.

The Romanian nationalistic and assimilative propaganda that emerged at the end of the 19th century was stated, aims and means targeting the Csángó, in an article in a family newspaper of Szamosújvár in 1880. The gist of the article formulated it thusly: *"In two of the biggest and most scenic counties of Moldova, in Bákó and Roman, the primarily agricultural population consists of small-holding farmers who only speak Hungarian. When you enter their villages, you are greeted with a situation worse than in Hungary; you must go with an interpreter; their women and children are unable to say 'Good morning' in Romanian. This situation is the inexcusable error of our leaders, who never devoted time to their Romanianization, leaving in the heart of Moldova a community of two hundred thousand who are alien from us in language and religion. Minister of Culture and Education, Mr. Nicolae Cretiulescu, it seems as if the Seklers entrusted you with a solution to this problem. Achieve that this rural population, among whom land was distributed on May 2, be one in their language and in their heart, since the future of the country depends on this solution; hence, Romanianize these Csángó; free them of that ugly handle, which even they are loath to wear, and you will earn our eternal gratitude. Toward this end, you must implement the following measures: a school must be established, even in the most remote valley; the children must be made to attend school, summer and winter, by bailiff if necessary, especially the girls, who will become mothers and teach their children in Romanian; secondly, priests must be brought to their churches from the Romanian communities of Transylvania, who will speak, read and preach to them in Romanian. When the priest gives his benediction in Romanian, when the cantor sings to them in Romanian, when the mothers sing their lullabies in Romanian, only then will we reach our goal."*[596]

---

596 „În Moldova în doue din cele mai mari si mai frumose judetie, mai cu sema Bacaulu si Romanulu, locuitorii tierani, cari suntu mai toti razasi, mosneni si proprietari mici, vorbesc numai unguresce. Cându intri în satele loru, e mai reu decâtu în mijloculu Ungariei; trebue se mergi cu talmaci: femeile si copii nu sciu se dea nici „buna demanetia" românesce. Culpa neiertata este a omeniloru nostri de statu ca n-au ingrigitu nici odata de romanisarea acestui elementu si a lasatu în inima Moldovei o populatiune de preste doue sute de mii, streina si de limba si de religiune. Domnule Nicolae Cretiulescu, Ministru culteloru si instructiunei publice, se vede ca seculii ti-a pastratu d-tale resolvarea acestei cestiuni nationale. Fa ca poporulu ruralu, caruia i-au datu pamântu la 2 maiu, se fie unulu si acelasi si în limbâ si în animâ, caci în elu sta vietia tierei; romaniseza pre acesti Ciangai, scapa-i de uritulu nume, ce nu voru nici ei se-lu porte, si vei ave eterna recunoscintia. Mesurile ce ar trebui sa se ia suntu: mai antâiu indesuirea scoleloru prin tote satele, catunele si fundaturile unguresci; copii luati cu vatasielulu si dusi la scola erna si vera, mai cu sema fetele, care devenindu mame si voru invetia copii românesce; si alu doilea, pe la tote bisericile loru, adusi preoti dintre Românii din Transilvania, ca sa le vorbesca si se le cetesca romanesce. Cându preotulu le va da

177

The quotation cited above reflects the views of an intolerant and hot-tempered Eastern Rite Catholic Romanian intellectual, who can not be accused of skewing his description in favor of the Hungarians of Moldova. He considered it an indefensible situation that large, contiguous Hungarian-language areas lie in the heart of Moldova. In a distilled form, he laid out the most important aims and tools for the assimilation of the Hungarian-language Csángó communities: one, the forcible education of children in Romanian; two, the introduction into their churches of Romanian-language priests from Transylvania; three, the creation of an ethically homogeneous Romanian nation state through linguistic and cultural assimilation. The suggestions made by the writer of the Szamosújvár article were soon followed by appropriate measures.

The fledgling Romanian state rapidly established its most important institution in Moldova during the second half of the 19th century. The local and county administration, mandatory military service, unified system of education, as well as the Roman Catholic Church, all toiled toward the creation and strengthening of Romanian national culture, history and self-esteem. In reality, their actions effectively aided and served the rapid assimilation of communities of other languages and cultures (e.g.- Hungarians, Armenians, Jews, Ukrainians, etc.). The assimilation practices, raised to official state policy at the end of the 19th century, as well as the intolerant anti-Hungarian propaganda during the first world war, finally achieved its aim. In the 1930 census, of the 109,953 Moldovan Roman Catholics, only 23,886 (21.7%) dared to declare their origin as Hungarian.[597]

In the 15 years following the second world war, when Hungarian-language schools were permitted to operate in the Csángó villages, the prestige of the Hungarian language temporarily bolstered, in spite of the prejudiced language policies of the Church. The Romanian Communist propaganda apparatus suddenly terminate this modestly evolving process in the years following the unsuccessful 1956 revolution in Hungary. The rabidly nationalistic Romanian leadership quickly grasped the opportunity presented. While Russia and its allied ruthlessly put down the restless and rebellious Hungarians, it quickly moved to eradicate, by any means possible, the Moldovan educational system that was beginning to show some promise. The efforts to assimilate the Csángó took off after 1965, when Nicolae Ceausescu took power, because the dictator decided on a rapid assimilation of the Csángó.

---

binecuventarea în limba româna, cându dascalu le va cânta romanesce, si cându mama va legana copilulu

sî-i va dîce: haidi, nani, puiulu mamei, resultatulu va fi dobânditu!" (See Polescu, Ioanu: Limba

ungureasca în Moldova. Amicul Familiei IV. 2., 1880, p. 27.)

597 Tánczos: Hányan vannak ... op. cit. p. 376.

He had a book published, thoroughly re-worked by extremist nationalistic intellectuals, which was the amateurish, dilettante work of a teacher (from a northern Catholic village that has lost its identity and became completely Romanianized) in which he advocated the origin of the Csángó as Transylvanian Romanians. This imposing-looking volume, printed in large numbers, basically attempted to manipulate the common historical awareness of the Csángó. The Romanian nationalistic propaganda apparatus quickly turned the basic premises of the work into indisputable dogma, making it the only officially acceptable, printable point of view in Romania.[598] It is a sad fact that, in the decade after the events of 1989, an amended version of the book was published in large numbers (in English and Italian) and younger historians accept its theses without critically questioning the source.[599]

The propaganda apparatus, attempting to accelerate assimilation, officially forbade the use of Hungarian in the public areas of the Csángó villages: children playing in schoolyards were threatened for speaking Hungarian, in many places, their parents were fined. Church officials, going out of their way to curry favor with the nationalistic authorities, went so far as to ban the use of Hungarian at wakes held in private houses. They threatened their deeply religious followers with, "Hungarian is the language of the Devil," implying that those who use it will go to Hell. During the 1980s, the political police persecuted the Hungarian-language religious leaders with frequent searches of their dwellings, constant convictions and fines. Researchers from Transylvania and Hungary, expressing an interest in the culture of the Csángó were harassed with subpoenas and arrests, locals welcoming them into their homes were arrested, intimidated and fined. The authorities used every means they could to frustrate any meeting or contact between the Csángó and larger communities of Hungarians. Gradually, the Csángó were afraid to openly declare Hungarian identity, their linguistic, cultural and ethnic uniqueness.[600]

Immediately after the 1989 collapse of the nationalistic Romanian regime, the 'democratic' census of 1992, registered a total of 239,938 Catholics in Moldova, of whom a mere 1,800 (0.7%) stated their ethnicity as Hungarian. In this large territory, the number of Catholics grew from 109,953 to 239,938 between 1930 and 1992, all the while there was a significant

598 The Martinas work was published in 1985, one of the most difficult years of Ceausescu's reign. The editors of the publication craftily exploited the deep religiosity of the Csángó, illustrating the work with countless Moldovan Roman Catholic churches, a colored picture of Ceausescu and the Pope. (See Martinas: Originea ... op. cit.; Martinas, Dumitru: The origins of the changos. Iasi, 1999)

599 Martinas: The origins ... op. cit.; Stan – Weber: The moldvaian ... op. cit.

600 Demse, Márton: Csángó küzdelem [Csángó struggle]. Hargita Kiadóhivatal, Csíkszereda, 2005, pp. 7-14.

exodus from the rural communities, not only the Csángó.[601] Thus, in the 20th century, while the number of Moldovan Catholics doubled in a mere 60 years, official statistical data professes to show a spectacular drop in the numbers and proportion of Hungarians within this group.[602] These numbers are a result, on the one hand, of the rapid assimilation following the second world war and, on the other hand, to the intolerant propaganda and countless other methods of intimidation employed during the 1992 census.[603]

As noted previously, the linguistic assimilation process of the younger Csángó who moved to the smaller Seklerland towns came to completion in the eastern Transylvanian region, in towns inhabited by a majority of Hungarians. The newcomers were offered countless advantages – if they declared themselves to be Romanian. The continual persecution of the political police ensured their rapid integration, since they systematically intimidated those Csángó youth in Transylvania whose families instilled a strong sense of Hungarian identity in them, back in Moldova, and who began to attend Hungarian-language Masses in Seklerland.[604]

We have already pointed out several times that, before the emergence of modernizing processes, in the ethnic consciousness of the Csángó, not much changed from medieval times, fundamental and defining aspects were the Hungarian-language customs and traditions. In 19th century Eastern Europe, where the advent of a civil society and nation states was greatly delayed and lacking outstanding 'traditions', folklore had an significant and esteemed role in the creation of national cultures.[605] Since a native language lay or religious intellectual strata was unable to emerge in the Moldovan villages, folklore in their mother tongue did not acquire any symbolic functions during the 19th-20th centuries, did not particularly cement their sense of belonging to the Hungarian national community.

---

601 In the same period, the decade after the second world war, approximately 50,000 Roman Catholics modev from overpopulated Moldova to the cities of Transylvania and, according the the estimate of Vilmos Tánczos, another 15,000 left for Muntenia and Dobrudja. (Tánczos: Hányan vannak ... op. cit. p. 376.) The distribution of these Moldovan Catholics in other counties was: Temes, 14,436; Brassó, 9,835; Hunyad, 9,119; Krassó-Szörény, 6,269; Arad, 5,743 and Szeben, 2,000. The situation in the three Sekler counties was as follows: Hargita 3,357, Kovászna 2,829, Maros 2,091, mostly a mix of Roman Catholics of Moldovan and Csángó origin. (Tánczos: Hányan vannak ... op. cit. p. 387 & Hungarians in ... op. cit. p. 9.)

602 Ibid, (Hányan vannak ...), p. 376.

603 See Romániai Magyar Szó [Hungarian Word of Romania] 1992. évi, 635. számát.

604 Tánczos: „Én román ... op. cit. pp. 174-189.

605 Hofer, Tamás: A „népi kultúra" örökségének megszerkesztése és használata [The compilation and use of a 'folk culture' legacy], In: Hofer, Tamás /ed./: Népi kultúra és nemzettudat. Budapest, 1991, pp. 7-14.

The Moldovan villages are today undergoing a rapid cultural change, during which the traditional agrarian culture is replaced by a newer widespread culture under the pressure of modernization. The process results in the Hungarian-language folklore elements, expressing their cultural uniqueness, disassociated from the new value system construct, hence losing its power of building and creating a Hungarian identity. The members of the younger generation no longer amuse themselves with ancient circle dances, no longer sing classical ballads or laments in an ancient tongue, no longer don shirts or blouses embroidered with ancient folk patterns. This process has played out everywhere among the Hungarian communities of the Carpathian basin but the events of post-acculturalization built a new popular culture based on their own mother tongue. Among the Moldovan Csángó, this cultural turnover ended in the conquest of Romanian-language popular culture. First through radio, then television, since the middle of the 20th century, Romanian language folklore and pop music spread among their communities, as in the whole region. In the long run, the success of popular culture will effectively advancement the integration of the Csángó into the Romanian culture and community.

The dynamic economic, social, cultural, linguistic and ethnic processes being played out in the Moldovan Csángó villages reminds us that, regarding Csángó identity, we can not speak about a common model, since different villages, parts of villages, families and family members have a different concept of ethnic identity. It follows from this fact that, at different stages and situations of life, an individual's sense of identity will differ, uniquely reacting to the local community or the wider social strata. A person's sense of ethnic and national identity is fundamentally defined in the Moldovan villages by close family ties, the network of friend made early in life, the connections to different institutions (e.g.- school, church, its leaders, the local administration, Hungarian or Romanian Csángó associations, etc.), the social or cultural impressions gathered while working in the 'West', whether in Transylvania, Hungary or further afield. The uniquely individual opinions, attitudes, interests and motivations gathered are clearly dissecting the identity, value system and adaptive strategy of a Csángó villager along visibly clearer lines.[606] The difficulty of today's situation is increased by the complexity where an element or layer of a Csángó person's identity may surface in different ways in different situations, in effect, making their sense of identity of a situational nature.[607]

The relationship between their language use and sense of identity effectively highlights the complex picture we gather within their communities and inside their families. Up until the beginning of the 20th century,

---

606 Boross: "Majd egyszer … op. cit. p. 49.

607 Ibid, p. 54.

Hungarian was their language of communication, and the family played a decisive role in its learning and transmission. Up until the very end of the second world war, children learned Romanian in school. Among women, it was very widespread, and not at all unusual, to be unilingual to the middle of the century; men usually learned it at a more mature age, usually outside their village, while serving in the army, or later, at some industrial workplace. The relatively rapid political, economic and social changes following the second world war ended the relative isolation of the Csángó villages, fostering bilingualism. In the final three decades of the 20th century, after the transitional bilingualism of their communities, the domination of the Romanian language grew among them, as a result of which, many today define themselves as having Romanian as their mother tongue.

The young often feel the weight of an ethical imperative, whereby they feel that to truly honor their parents, they must learn their language and carry on the traditions of their ancestors. But in this post-modern life, the problems attendant with their imprecise and imperfect expressions in an archaic Hungarian dialect (precisely lacking native language education and religion) creates to many communication problems. The gradual turnover of their language does not lead to a full-blown ethnic identity crisis, since the temporarily bilingual reality creates an attendant, new 'Csángó' identity. In this phase, both languages are impaired; in time, the Hungarian dies out by degrees, then disappears.

Since the Csángó relate to their language, in their villages and inside their families, in a manner free from ideology, its loss and replacement with Romanian is, most often, not seen as a tragic event. After the exchange of their language, they still feel themselves to be the same Moldovan Roman Catholic farmers that they were previously.[608]

While the intellectual strata of the Carpathian basin deem the loss of language and assimilation of the Csángó into the Romanian nation an erosion of values, the Csángó themselves see it quite differently. "An exchange of identity, as a social accommodation, even if it stresses a person and damages him, is usually not dramatic. Instead, if you will, it is a sort of conflict resolution, the creation of a new equilibrium, a sort of advancement. The individual certainly sees it that way."[609] At the same time, the exchange of

---

[608] We are confronted with similar situations among the scattered Transylvanian Hungarian communities, where the farmers usually leave to the intellectuals (e.g.- the minister or teacher) the acceptance of, and representation towards, the bolder declarations of national identity. (Feischmidt, Margit: Etnicitás és helyi intézmények.Jegyzetek egy mezőségi faluról [Ethnicity and local institutions. Notes of a Mezőség village]. Regio, V. 3, 1994, pp. 119-128)

[609] Komoróczy, Géza: Meddig él egy nemzet? [What is the lifespan of a nation?] In: Bezárkózás a nemzeti hagyományokba. Budapest, 1995, p. 288.

language is not immediately followed by an immediate change in ethnic identity, since countless elements of their culture may, for a long time to come, express their 'otherness' (e.g.- different religion, costume, traditions and customs, etc.). We can meet with numerous people, especially in the northern bloc who, although of Romanian mother tongue, declare themselves to be Hungarian. At the same time, especially in the Sekler Csángó villages, we can often meet the opposite of the above situation: young people who speak their Hungarian native tongue well, and use it exclusively within their families, yet declare themselves to be of Romanian nationality.

This same complex picture emerges when we try to map the name they use for themselves, or given to them. Among themselves, they call themselves Hungarian, Csángó-Hungarian, Csángó, Catholic or Romanian. In 1993, we visited 75 families in the village of Csík. The members of the various generations defined their national affiliation in the following manner:

	First generation	Second generation	Third generation	Fourth generation	Total
Hungarian	50.0%	53.4%	36.5%	17.2%	41.8%
Romanian	5.3%	8.0%	9.5%	27.3%	9.8%
Csángó	24.7%	22.0%	26.8%	14.1%	23.8%
Catholic	13.7%	13.3%	13.8%	11.1%	13.4%
Hungarian-Csángó	5.0%	2.0%	6.2%	8.1%	5.3%
Romanian-Csángó	1.3%	1.3%	7.2%	22.2%	5.9%
Total	300	150	318	99	867

In this relatively isolated village South of Bákó, the distribution of how the populace defined themselves is: 41.8% Hungarian, 23.8% Csángó, 5.3% Hungarian-Csángó, 13.4% Catholic and 9.8% Romanian. Of the 'commute' (second) generation that defines current village life, over half (53.4%) still hold themselves to be Hungarian, almost a quarter as Csángó, and a few (2%) as Hungarian-Csángó. Those who were socialized outside the village boundaries (see the 3rd and 4th generations) seem to lack a singular sense of identity. The table above shows that their identity categories are more dispersed, compared to their parents or grandparents. It is interesting to note that of the members of the youngest generation of the village (the 4th), 27.3% declared themselves Romanian and 22.2% as Romanian-Csángó, which signifies the escalation and materialization of the assimilative process in Csík.

Those who declare themselves to be Hungarian usually justify it by saying that, within the family and in the village, they speak Hungarian, hence, they are of Hungarian origin; even the Moldovan majority Romanians and the Gypsy musician refer to them as *maghiar* and *ungur*, or mock them as

183

bozgor or *bangyin.* In some of the villages, one comes across some elders who still hold themselves to be Seklers.[610]

The ethnonym *Csángó* is usually used by the Orthodox Romanians and Gypsies who live in their close proximity, in most cases as a teasing or derogatory nickname, although, at the same time, the Hungarians of Hungary and Transylvania, the media and the scientific literature also refers to them by that name. In the Catholic villages of Moldova, we can discern that this title is gaining ground and they define themselves as *Csángó*. It is primarily among the Hungarian mother-tongued that we meet the *Hungarian-Csángó* expression, while the *Romanian-Csángó* ethnonym is mainly used by those with a more fluent knowledge of Romanian and an increasing sense of Romanian national identity. Far fewer choose the category *Catholic*, when asked by a visitor. This category most often reflects a transitory state between the Hungarian and Romania communities and identities, or is done at the suggestion of the local priests. The ethnonym *Romanian* has also been gaining ground in the past few decades, mainly among the young. This reflects the fact that a significant portion of the Moldovan Csángó have made close economic, social and cultural ties with the majority Orthodox Romanians. Today, not only their value system and mentality but their sense of identity is articulated based on their relationship with the Romanians. The everyday life of a Csángó village is influenced to a great degree by its interaction with the majority (e.g.- education, health, local and county administration, police, banking, etc.), thus, the dynamics of life accelerate the process towards a rapid shift in linguistic and cultural balance and equilibrium.

After the events of 1989, the region inhabited by the Csángó began to undergo fundamental political, economic, social and cultural changes. To some extent, the political oppression eased, which, in any case, was unable to completely eliminate or control the contacts and meetings of the Csángó with the Hungarians of the Carpathian basin. Since the mega-industries built under Ceausescu all went bankrupt, the cities no longer represented the magnets they once were. Today, there is a quiet trend of return to the villages where families have had lands returned that were confiscated during the collectivization of 1962. At the same time, this re-settlement results in they having to adapt themselves to the language, culture and society of the village of their birth, its daily life and value system. At the instigation of the Csángó intellectuals who were educated in Transylvania, they began such lobby groups after 1990 whose primary goals were the introduction of Hungarian language education and liturgy, the retention of their unique traditions, as well as the strengthening of their distinctive ethnic identity, as tied to their linguistic culture.

---

610 Pávai: A moldvai ... op. cit.

In the decade subsequent to the 1989 regime change, many factors decelerate the rapid assimilation of the Csángó. As but one example, the wide ranging freedom of mobility affords opportunity for contact with Transylvanian and Hungarian communities. Every year, more and more Csángó attend religious gatherings in Transylvania and Hungary where they can attend services in their ancient mother tongue. Hundreds of Moldovan children spend summer vacations in Hungarian villages where they become familiar with the European-level values of Hungarian culture and, in many cases, they rapidly broaden their modest or latent knowledge of their native tongue. Many work temporarily in Transylvania or Hungary where they come into contact, on an everyday level, with the hopes, aspirations and values of the Hungarians of the Carpathian basin.

Although the above mentioned tendencies may curb, in the short term, the linguistic, cultural and ethnic assimilation of the Moldovan Csángó, in the long term, the sense of ethic and national identity held by their communities will be decided by the pace of the ethno-cultural processes under way in their region, as well as the successful establishment of European-style democracy in Romania.

VII. ECONOMIC REALITY, THEN AND NOW

The new attitudes to geography, natural history and private property, life-style models, social, cultural and political traditions, as well as the unique thought and mental processes decidedly defined the economic options and strategies of Hungarian families settling in Moldova. The Hungarian settlers from Transylvania found themselves in a new environment, where they gradually had to adapt to a new ecological structure, leading to continuous identification and adaptation to new plants, animals and techniques. During the centuries, close relations were formed with the neighboring Orthodox settlements, which led to a close interrelation of the economic life of the Moldovan Csángó with their farming Romanian neighbors.

Up to the middle of the 19th century, a significant portion of the land in Moldova was the property of the ruler, the Orthodox monasteries and the boyars; a lesser amount was held by freehold farmers.[611] The continually changing fortunes of the principality, languishing under Turkish overlordship, are exemplified by its ever-changing property owners.[612] The frequent change of owner created innumerable conflicts in the Csángó villages. To cite but one example, the Hungarians of Forrófalva, who worked the land belonging to the distant Orthodox monastery of Solca, revolted in 1744 when their former rights and obligations were changed. They kept up their legal plaint into the 19th century in an attempt to reclaim their former rights.[613]

A significant portion of the landed properties in this region continued to be owned by the rich boyars and Orthodox monasteries, beginning with the creation of the Romanian nation state (1859) up to the beginning of the second world war. Some villages still exist from the golden age of the principality, which were primarily inhabited by small-holding, freed-men (razesi, or sharecroppers). At the end of the 18th century, 32% of the Moldovan villages were still composed of such free status settlements.[614] According to oral tradition, Klézse, Lujzikalagor, Somoska and Terebes were such proud, self-respecting 'cropper villages. The memory of the locals recounts that they received their land grants in the time of Stefan cel Mare for their brave services. Similar to the tradition of the Sekler villages, they

---

611 Mihordea, V.: Relatiile agrare din secolul al XVIII-lea în Moldova. Bucuresti, 1968, pp. 54-80.

612 Ibid, p. 62.

613 Ibid, pp. 174-175.

614 Ibid, p. 79.

communally owned the fields, pastures and hay-fields, annually apportioning them among the families.[615]

During the 16th-17th centuries, the Mongol and Turkish raids caused great devastation in the region.[616] The boyars gladly accepted Sekler settlers in the depopulated villages. While the settlers who arrived from Transylvania in the 14th-15th centuries were able to own their lands relatively unrestricted, the latter settlers were able to acquire only modest building plots, agricultural lands or vineyards, for the use of which they were required to toil on the estates of the major landowners or boyars.[617] By the middle and late 19th century, the majority of the Hungarian families in the overpopulated villages were close to poverty.

The authorities made artificial revisions to this system of property ownership on several occasions. Prince Alexandru Ioan Cuza, ruler of united Moldova and Muntenia, initiated land reforms after ascending the throne in 1859. Since, at the time, 25% of the arable land of Moldova was in the possession of the Orthodox Church, mainly the monasteries, the land was first nationalized on December 25, 1863, then, according to a new law enacted on August 26, 1864, the land was divided among the peasants – in proportion to their existing holdings.[618] In the years following the land grants, agricultural production temporarily declined in Moldova, since most of the farmers did not have the required capital or organizational skills to establish independent farms. Conservative forces compelled Prince Cuza to abdicate on February 11, 1866 and into exile. In 1889, the Romanian government, in an attempt to curb increasing poverty and shortages, gave newlyweds small plots of land from state landholdings.[619]

King Ferdinand I of Romania announce another land reform after the first world war. He signed a law on December 15, 1918, which confiscated a total of 2 million hectares from the largest estates, which were distributed among the peasants on the basis of a law enacted in 1921. The King's edicts placed most of the Catholic Moldovan Csángó in a disadvantageous position. In most of their villages, they received no land

---

615 Kós, Károly: Csángó néprajzi vázlat [Csángó ethnographic sketches], In: Tájak, falvak, hagyományok.

Bukarest, 1976, pp. 105-106.

616 Mihordea: Relatiile ... op. cit. pp. 28.

617 The later Hungarian settlers from Transylvania became part of the social strata called "vecini" (neighbour).

(Observation made by Liviu Pilat.)

618 In Pusztina, in 1864, a quarter of the boyar's lands were doled out among about 80 farmers, while those

who possessed teams of oxen received larger parcels. (See Bartha, András: Pusztina – Pustiana.

Gondolatok egy csángó falu múltjáról, jelenérol [Thoughts on the past and present of a Csángó village].

Balatonboglár, 1998, pp. 20-21.)

619 Kós: Csángó ... op. cit. pp. 106-107.

because, among their settlements, there were quite a number of free-hold villages. In these settlements of freed-men, there were few, if any, boyar estates, which could be divided among the families sinking into poverty. Secondly, in the vicinity of these overpopulated settlements, there were simply no pieces of land which could be divided. This resulted in the surplus population of the Csángó villages receiving land only in distant regions. The situation was made more complex because the central and local Orthodox Romanian administrations used every means to bring the Catholic Csángó-Hungarians into unfavorable circumstances, consciously striving to bring about their dispersal, scattering them in remote areas. These facts resulted in the poorer families from the Csángó villages moving to distant parts, where land for distribution was more freely available. The successor settlements of many villages were a result of this migration (from Szabófalva to Balusest, Ploszkucén, Traján; the Hungarian communities around Jászvásár, e.g.- Jázu Porkuluj; the new villages of Dózsa and Ferdinánd, South of Bákó; the Csángó settlements of Ojtoz and Kogâlniceanu close to the Black Sea).

In the years after the second world war, Romania was one of Eastern Europe's most backward countries, 76.9% of whose population was rural and made its living from agriculture. The Left-wing government of Peter Groza announced a new land reform law on March 22, 1945, which set a maximum of 50 hectares that a family could own. As part of the land reforms, a total of 1,057,674 arable hectares were distributed among 769,129 poorer Romanian farming families. Even earlier, the number of small- and micro-landowners was significant in Romania but the land reform of 1945 further contributed to the subdivision of lands into ever smaller parcels. In 1949, 53.2% of Romanian farms were less than 3 hectares [approx. 7 acres-*Ed.*]. The land reform act of 1945 was shortly followed by new, radical economic and social measures. At the end of the 1940's, large estates were liquidated; in the following decade, the well-to-do farmers, the kulaks, were also "removed". Finally, in 1962, the agricultural land that gives meaning to a rural community was confiscated from every farmer; the vineyards, so important in the life of farming families, were destroyed in Moldova, in the 1970s.[620]

After the forcible collectivization of all agriculture by the Communist authorities, it degraded the farmers into poorly paid laborers in the collectives or national agri-businesses. However, since a number of the Moldovan Csángó villages have, for centuries, worked the lands belonging to the boyars or the monasteries, a sense of farming pride, typical of

---

620 Oláh, Sándor: Csendes csatatér. Kollektivizálás és túlélési stratégiák a két Homoród mentén (1949-1962) [Quiet battleground. Collectivization and survival strategies along the two Homoród Rivers]. Csíkszereda, 2001, PP. 12-13; Catanus, Dan – Roske, Octavian: Colectivizarea agriculturii in România. Dimensiunea politica 1949-1953. Bucuresti, 2000.

independent farmers, did not take hold in these settlements. To them, collectivization did not represent a fundamental shift in their lives, merely a change in the governing elite who dominated their settlements and sources of strength.[621]

As the totalitarian Communist regime purposely neglected the agrarian sector, agricultural production declined drastically between 1965 and 1989. Beginning in the mid-1970s, Romania was faced with serious problems of food production, hence the role of the elderly, rural relatives gained importance as a survival tactic among the Csángó families. In the gardens around the village houses, they grew the basic fruits and vegetables, while raising poultry and pigs for their children, grandchildren in the city. In spite of the situation, after 1962, farm work was disparaged by the young people who moved to the cities; the mocked and made fun of those who stayed behind in their ancestral villages to work the land.

After the regime change of 1989, the new government in Bucharest began yet another land distribution scheme under which a family could regain a maximum of 10 hectares [app. 25 acres-*Ed.*]of their family's previous holdings. These days, privatization in Romania is most advanced in agriculture, although from a legal perspective, it can not be held to be completed. The privatization of land, begun in 1990, has again resulted in the breaking of holdings into smaller pieces. In Moldova, the tiny family plots that resulted from the process can not offer a decent living for the populace of the villages. In the village of Csík, South of Bákó, for example, a medium sized farm rarely exceeds 3-4 hectares, from which the farmer is expected to support his 5-6 married children and 20-25 grandchildren. Similar is the situation in neighboring Klézse, which had a total population in 1992 of 7,600 and possessed 2,400 hectares of pasture and hay fields, 1,000 hectares of arable land and 100 hectares of vineyards.[622]

Other factors also influenced the creation of today's landholding situation in Moldova. In the decades after the second world war, a significant demographic growth – overpopulation – took place. Shortly after the events of 1989, the vast industrial conglomerates went bankrupt, one after the other, and a portion of the workers families, suddenly unemployed, gradually drifted back to their native villages. Thus, a direct result of the current gradual reorganization of the Romanian economy is the rural repatriation of

---

621 Benedek H., János: Csángó falvak gazdasági problémái [The economic problems of Csángó villages], In: Pozsony, Ferenc /ed./: Dolgozatok a moldvai csángók népi kultúrájáról. Kriza János Néprajzi Társaság Évkönyve 5., Kolozsvár, 1997, pp. 196-197.

622 Benedek H., János: Egy moldvai magyar parasztcsalád gazdálkodása [The farming practices of a Moldovan Hungarian peasant family], In: Pozsony, Ferenc /ed./: Dolgozatok a moldvai csángók népi kultúrájáról. Kriza János Néprajzi Társaság Évkönyve 5., Kolozsvár, 1997, pp. 212-213.

the Csángó youth who earlier left for the cities. This returning flood of migrants must face up to the ruralization of their lives, the resurgence of informal methods based on village, community or family ties (e.g.- barter, working bees), while watching the withering of previous urban existential strategies. The reality of today is that it is the older generation who own the lands recently returned to the large families, it is usually they who make the decisions regarding organizing the farm labor, the crop planting and the apportioning of the crops. In this farming economy based on extended, large families, totally lacking modern machinery and adequate numbers of draught animals, manual labor continues to play a crucial role. Without capital, they cannot rent farm equipment, which means that at crucial periods (preparing the soil, tending the crops, harvesting) the members of the extended family must be mobilized for manual labor.

In the Csángó villages, everyone, from the youngest to the oldest, has a well defined set of chores within the annual farm cycle. Young children spend spring and summer tending the smaller animals, such as sheep and goats, the older ones look after the cows and horses. While these children were out in the nearby pastures with the family's animals, they also had to look after their younger siblings. As soon as a child was old enough, stern tasks were assigned. In the Moldovan villages, it was within the family circle that a growing child received socialization; within its confines, children learned imperceptibly the necessary farming skills. The shared family toil not only ensured their subsistence but also contained an important measure of ritual: it symbolized the unity and strength of the family towards outside groups.

Among the Moldovan Hungarian communities, ancient agricultural implements and methods can still be found today. Until recently, every major task was started on the first day of the week. Forests were freely cleared until the second world war, to make way for fields. In the northern villages, Béla Gunda came across a two-handled plow, whose form is unknown in the Seklerland but is widely found in the northern part of Transylvania, along the Szamos River, as well as the valleys of the Tisza and Szeret rivers. The plows found in the villages along the Ojtoz, Tatros, Tázló and Szeret rivers resemble those in the Seklerland. Dr. Károly (Charles) Kós also hold that the hand sickle, the harvest wreath [various shaped ornaments (crown, wreath, helix of a snail) woven on the first or last day of the harvest from grain stalks-*Ed.*], threshing by hand and the use of barns were brought from Seklerland and preserved. The Sekler elements connected with agriculture, bee keeping and fishing were continually expanded with concepts and techniques adopted from the neighboring Romanians. Since the harsh weather conditions in Csík and Háromszék make their growing impossible,

190

their knowledge of the cultivation of corn and grapes must have been acquired in Moldova.[623]

Corn-based foods represent a significant portion of the Csángó diet, which is why a sizeable portion of their arable lands are used to grow corn. Close to their settlements, on scattered smaller plots, they grow grapes, while around their houses we find fruit trees, vegetable plots and herb gardens to fill their families' needs.

Even today, in a great number of their villages, they use a harrow made of thorn branches to break up the clods left behind the plow, and employ an archaic method of planting grape vines with the aid of a pointed stick. Grains are still sown by hand in many places, worked into the soil with a wooden harrow made of branches. In the summer, they harvest the grains using a serrated hand sickle, to be threshed by hand with a wooden flail or by horses' hooves in a threshing yard.[624] The ripe grapes are picked in the fall, placed in large barrels, where they are crushed, the must is decanted but not strained. The remainder is placed in a tub, covered, and distilled into brandy after Christmas. Up until the second world war, they made cooking oil of from the seeds of hemp, sunflowers and pumpkins. After collectivization, the oil necessary for cooking was bought in stores. Their villages are located along creeks and rivers that originate in the eastern Carpathians, which, in olden days, held plentiful fish. The adults used old-style dip nets or weirs, the children caught fish with their bare hands.[625] Wax and honey has always played an important role in the life of the Moldavians and since the region inhabited by the Csángó is full of flowering valleys and hillsides, beekeeping has, for centuries, been an important occupation and economic facet. Up to the beginning of the 20th century, there were still a great number of wild hives in the forests. In the villages along the Szeret, honey was collected on the day of St. Elias (July 20) - in the area of Tatros, on Mary's name-day (August 15) - to be used primarily in home remedies, eaten and the wax used in candles.[626] In recent decades, more advanced, modern forms of beekeeping have gradually taken hold in the Csángó region.

Every village farmstead has at least one cow. Historical sources reveal that the Moldovan Hungarians kept significant numbers of oxen during the Middle Ages, with which they carried out significant trade during

623 Kós: Csángó ... op. cit. pp. 118-122.

624 Gunda: A moldvai magyar ... op. cit. pp. 39-45.

625 Ibid, pp. 47-48.

626 Kós: Csángó ... op. cit. pp. 128-132.

the 16th-17th centuries.[627] In his record made at the beginning of the 18th century, Dimitrie Cantemir drew attention to the importance of oxen in the export of the Moldavians aimed toward Poland.[628] In that period, the Saxons of Brassov and the Armenians organized the cattle trade towards Northern and Western-Europe.[629] The Saxons alone dispatched 26,000 cattle annually from Moldova to Vienna in the second half of the 18th century.[630] The research conducted by Péter (Peter) Halász reveals that, during the mentioned period, the preferred occupation of the Hungarians of Moldova was raising cattle, while, in the Romanian communities, the majority bred horses. In those settlements that were close to important market places or along commercial roads (Bahána, Gorzafalva, Gyoszén, Lujzikalagor, etc.), there was a higher than normal proportion of horse breeding, mainly to be used in cartage. In mid-19th century, oxen still played an important role in the economy of the region. Their importance is reflected by the fact that, during the land reform of 1864, Moldovan farmers received new lands based on the number of oxen they owned. An interesting sidelight, in many places, they paid for the lands with cartage service: their ox-drawn wagons hauling government salt from Aknavásár to Galac. In the Moldovan Csángó villages, cattle still played a more important role than horses, even in the 20th century, while their economic importance gradually waned among the Hungarians in the Carpathian basin. Although the number of horses has significantly increased in their villages in the decade after 1989, in many places, farmers still plow behind a team of cattle.[631]

On their farms, we find relatively few goats; they prefer to breed sheep. Although the Transylvanian Seklers, with their extensive mountain pastures, kept large numbers of sheep, the Moldovan Hungarians received their knowledge of sheep raising primarily from the Moldavians.[632] They herd their sheep to fields in the vicinity of their villages at the end of March and move them to the mountain pastures on St. George's Day (April 24). From St. Demeter's Day (October 26) onward, they again pasture the flocks on the fields close to the villages. The division of the produce, the cheese, is apportioned in a manner similar to the Seklers: each farmer receives a

---

627 Halász, Péter: A ló és a szarvasmarha gazdasági jelentősége a moldvai magyaroknál [The economic significance of horses and cattle among the Moldavian Hungarians], In: Novák, László /ed./: Néprajzi Tanulmányok Ikvai Nándor emlékére II. (Szentendre, 1994) p. 28.

628 Cantemir, Dimitrie: Moldva leírása [Description of Moldova]. Bukarest, 1973, pp. 59-60; Mihordea: Relatiile ... op. cit. pp. 32-33.

629 Ibid (Mihordea), pp. 48-49.

630 Ibid, p. 49.

631 Halász: A ló ... op. cit. pp. 28-32.

632 Kós: Csángó ... op. cit. pp. 108-109.

previously agreed amount after each ewe. They usually buy their hogs from the Romanian farmers.[633]

These days, Hungarian potters are active in Gorzafalva, on the banks of the Ojtoz, while Romanian Orthodox ones are working in Fruszmósza, along the Tázló River. These centers remained in existence to the end of the 20th century because the Moldovan women prepared the majority of the food on traditional cooking hearths, in pottery vessels. Several pottery centers are active in Moldova today, where they mainly make everyday functional pots, because ornamental pots are not a part of their decorative needs. At the end of the 19th century, a more modern cooking manner took root among the Seklerland settlements, so that the population no longer had a need for the traditional pot styles. Most of the Sekler potters gradually began to produce them for use among the Moldavians and their older cooking style. When a levy war broke out between Austria-Hungary and Romania at the end of the 19th century, many potters from Bereck, in Háromszék, relocated to Gorzafalva, those from of Csíkmadaras settled in Palánka, in the Gyimes valley, where they continued their trade.[634] The master potters of Korond, in Udvarhelyszék, still produce a vessel type, which the Moldavians only use in rituals connected with death, i.e., to be used only on occasions celebrating the memory of a deceased relative.[635]

One of today's best known pottery centers in Moldova is Gorzafalva, where, before collectivization, 400 Hungarian craftsmen worked. Although their products retained many Transylvanian characteristics and elements, gradually they adapted to Moldovan requirements and local traditions. In light of increasing foreign and Transylvanian tourism, they could sell a great deal more of their products but their traditionally seasonal view of the work inhibits continuous output to satisfy market demand. Over the centuries, the Moldovan potters became completely entrenched into the life-rhythm of the farming villages, until they, too, became farmers, only turning out pots during the major breaks in farming activity – winter, or summer rainy spells. They provided their family's food through their own labors, while the (pottery)wheel provided the cash for monetary expenses. In a given year, they only fired up their kilns three or four times, the rest of their time being taken up with the crops or animals.[636] Until collectivization brought an end in 1962, they visited the villages of Moldova and Háromszék on their wagons, bartering their handmade ceramics for barley, wheat, rye,

---

633 Gunda: A moldvai magyar ... op. cit. pp. 60-66.

634 Kós: Csángó ... op. cit. p. 154.

635 Tófalvi, Zoltán: A sóvidéki népi fazekasság [Folk pottery in the Só region]. Marosvásárhely, 1996, pp. 85-86.

636 Benedek: Csángó falvak ... op. cit. p. 208.

oats, hemp, corn, beans and potatoes. This lifestyle engendered a specific division of labors within the family: a part primarily concerned with the preparation of the raw materials, the throwing on the wheel, the firing, while others ranging far and wide hawking their wares from their wagons in distant villages. A similar life was followed by the inhabitants of Pusztina, who also ranged great distances, to Foksány and Bucharest, selling their woven willow baskets. As their settlements were usually located on the bank of a river, the willows growing alongside provided the material for the various baskets they produced.

The Hungarian settlers in Moldova gradually grew to know the sheep rearing means of the Romanians, with it the furrier's trade. Usually, the larger villages had one or two furriers, who made various articles of clothing out of sheepskin (e.g.,- fur caps, coats and vests). Every village had a cooper, or two, a shingle cutter, a carpenter and a blacksmith. Similar to the potters, they too only turned to their specialties during breaks in the farming calendar. These rural artisans primarily satisfied only the local demand, rarely sending their goods afield to other villages or cities.

Péter (Peter) Halász identified three means of trade exchange by the Moldovan Hungarians: 1. some sell cheaper to traders, who come from other locations to buy locally; 2. many go from village to village, selling from the back of their wagons; and 3. others set up at the various markets, where they usually sell their wares for cash.[637] Most of their output goes to satisfy the needs of their communities, thus very little of it is converted to cash. The Moldovan Csángó have established and maintained economic ties with communities that have, for geographic or other reasons, specialized in the production of other goods – complementary trade. In 1844, János (John) Jerney noted that the northern Csángó's main agricultural export to the market held in Jászvásár were potatoes and vegetables, meaning that in the middle of the 19th century, the Moldovan Hungarians played an important role in the feeding of Moldova's capital.[638] On the same topic, Gábor (Gabriel) Lüko noted in the first half of the 20th century that the wagons of the farmers of a Jugán, Kelgyeste and Szabófala continue to carry potatoes to the markets of Jászvásár, Karácsonyko and the other larger markets. The farmers of Domafalva, Dzsidafalva and Tamásfalva grow large quantities of cabbages and onions for sale on market days.[639] In 1949, Károly (Charles) Kós wrote that the traders from Gorzafalva brought to the markets of Onyest,

637 Halász, Péter: Áruértékesítés és árucsere a moldvai magyaroknál. In: Halász, Péter /ed./: „Megfog vala apóm szokcor kezemtül…" Tanulmányok Domokos Pál Péter emlékére. Budapest, 1993, p. 92.

638 Jerney: Keleti ... op. cit. p. 30.

639 Lüko: A moldvai ... op. cit. p. 14.

beside their ceramic pots, also sawn planks, wagons, yokes, homespun bedspreads, millstones and animals for sale.[640]

In the years following the first world war, the Csángó farmers usually headed their wagons in the fall towards Transylvania, where they transported grapes and wine, to exchange for potatoes, sawn planks, wooden vessels or tools. Since the colder climate of Csík and Háromszék was not suitable for the cultivation of corn, the Csángó farmers took their own corn to Seklerland villages or towns, where it was bartered for potatoes, painted wooden (hope)chests, more ornately styled and decorated articles of clothing. The Seklerland Hungarians also regularly visited the Moldovan Csángó villages on their wagons, bringing potatoes and all manner of wooden and ceramic goods, returning with grains, grapes or wine.[641] The Armenian or Jewish traders from other towns visited Lészped, Pusztina and Klézse to buy locally the animals offered for sale by the Hungarians. The Jewish merchants of Bákó and Ónfalva bought beans in Pusztina, while those from Románvásár bought potatoes in Szabófalva. The merchants from the colder climate of Bukovina mostly came to Klézse to buy wine and spirits, while, in the 1930s, the farmers of Magyarfalu shipped wine, with the assistance of Bucharest merchants, to Budapest.[642]

For centuries, the Hungarian communities of Moldova produced and marketed significantly more material goods than their ethnic proportion in the region.[643] During the time of the Moldovan Principality, the urban Hungarian population played an important role in the manufacture and marketing of handicrafts and cottage industry output. The 1646 record left by Bandinus notes that there was a populous weekly Thursday market organized in Husz, while the one held in Románvásár was well supplied with wine, wheat, legumes, game, fowl, fish, horses and handicrafts.[644] In the region inhabited by the Csángó, farmer's markets were organized in several locations. The one held three times a year in Onyest (starting on Palm Sunday /before Easter/, the Feast of the Holy Cross /September 14/, Saint Demeter's day /October 26/) ran for a week each time. Goods came from all over: pottery from Gorzafalva and Csíkmadaras, fur clothing from the Romanian villages, woolen homespun textiles from Bereck, homespun bedspreads from Gorzafalva and Bereck, petroleum from Mojnest, wooden vessels [buckets and pails-*Ed.*] from Haraly, woven osier baskets from Pusztina, rush carpets from Foksány, straw hats from Mezofele and Bözöd in

---

640 Kós: Csángó ... op. cit. pp. 169-175.

641 Gunda: A moldvai magyar ... op. cit. pp. 66-67.

642 Halász: Áruértékesítés ... op. cit. p. 93.

643 Ibid, p. 91.

644 Ibid, p. 91.

Transylvania, wooden shingles from Csík, sawn boards from Ozsdola and Gelence, in Transylvania, and painted furniture from Kézdivásárhely, also in Transylvania.[645]

The markets, organized in conjunction with church fairs, accurately reflect the natural agricultural and societal interaction of the Moldovan Csángó: furniture, wooden implements and tools, pottery and articles of clothing were primarily bought from Transylvanian makers. Petroleum products, salt, honey, vegetables, grains, pork and cattle were usually bought from Moldovan Hungarians or Romanians. To this day, the Moldovan Csángó have preserved their economic contacts with the Hungarians of Transylvania. In the decades after the second world war, when intensive potato cultivation was the order of the day in Seklerland, in many Csángó villages, organized groups set off in the fall, heading for one or another village in Háromszék or Csík County to lend a hand digging potatoes (pityókaszedés). For their labor, they received room and board, potatoes and some pay. These work contacts created opportunities for the Transylvanian youths to meet Moldovan Hungarian girls, whom they considered more modest and hard working than the Transylvanians. In the past decades, almost every Transylvanian village 'imported' Csángó brides, who were willing to bear far more children than the more urbanized Transylvanians.[646] The family ties between the Moldovan and Transylvanian Hungarians effectively contribute to the continued natural economic relations between the two regions.

Károly (Charles) Polányi identifies two fundamental socio-economic divisions: a) in an archaic structure, the economy serves to satisfy the internal needs, hence, reciprocation and redistribution play a large role; b) in more developed societies, the marketplace has a decisive role in the integration of social and economic classes.[647]

Until very recently, the methods of farming (archaic in some aspects) carried on in the Moldovan villages were largely untouched by industrialization. Since their socio-economic reality was not rigidly segmented – there were no exclusive groups or classes based on occupation – division of labor or exchange failed to emerge. The economic approach of the Csángó harkens back to the pre-modern, pre-industrial age: their villages are , to this day, organized to provide self-sufficient agricultural food production; the small industries are neither planned nor organized in a rational way, rather, their primary goal is the preservation of the family. In

---

645 Kós: Csángó ... op. cit. pp. 168-170.

646 Balázs: "Száz lejes ... " op. cit.

647 Polányi, Károly: Az archaikus társadalom és a gazdasági szemlélet [Archaic societies and economic attitudes]. Budapest, 1976.

this traditional economic order, the marketplace does not play a significant role. Rather, the informal aspects are more integral and significant functions, as their reality is usually built on exchange of labor, on the return of donated labor and the exchange of information at a personal level.[648]

A significant portion of Moldovan families today are striving to produce the basic food necessities for their own use. In this situation, little affected by market influences, local community traditions and acquired experiences dictate the strategy and order of production. True, the small, cottage industries occasionally generate some surplus, which is then informally exchanged for goods, which the constraints of their natural environment make impossible to produce locally. Although the Moldovan Csángó farmers have been going to markets for a long time, and practice the various forms of natural trade, the marketplace does not particularly affect their stratagem, does not play and integrating role; they do not create rational calculations of their expenditures and incomes – their economic order has not yet become profit oriented.[649]

The fundamental problems today with the family-based micro farms in Moldova are the serious lack of capital, outdated equipment and technology, low productivity, as well as the fragmentation of holdings into tiny, dispersed tracts. These days, a Moldovan family's holdings average between 0.5 and 5 hectares, very rare is a family farm of 8-10 hectares. Based on the terms of the last land reform, everyone who received land did so where they previously had holdings, meaning that after 1990 there was no consolidation of scattered small parcels. The already small farms are made up of 5-8 distant tracts, which intrinsically hampers the mechanization of farming. There are other, both legal and administrative, obstacles preventing land consolidation in Moldova: the new owners have not yet received clear title to the returned properties, the different parcels are not accurately surveyed and registered, hence, they are not saleable, since they cannot be reliably transferred to a new owner.

A significant proportion of the younger generation is attempting to make a living in areas other than farming. Land ownership is, by default, mainly in the hands of the older generations who do not possess a great deal of education, as well as being risk averse. The land redistribution post-1989 caught most of the Moldovan families unprepared. In the early 1990s, there was a general significant technological decline, in Moldova too. When the

---

648 Benedek: Egy moldvai ... op. cit. pp. 218-221.

649 Földes, László: Árucsere és piac a hagyományos társadalmakban [The exchange of goods and the market in traditional societies]. Világosság, 1976, pp. 348-349; Kotics, József: Gazdálkodói mentalitás és paraszti polgárosodás. Egy régióvizsgálat tanulságai [Farming mentality and peasant urbanization. The lessons of a regional review], In: Mások tekintetében. Miskolc, 2001, pp. 124-125.

collectives and state farms ceased to exist, the families were unable to afford the purchase of modern farming implements. Of necessity, they were forced to work the land using outmoded pre-WWII machinery. Adding to the seriousness of the situation, on the one hand, the traditional farming knowledge disappeared, while, on the other hand, there was no technical training or source of advice to learn and apply the more modern knowledge.[650]

Their farming is dependent on the humble, yet useful for draught, local breed of mountain cattle, which requires little in the way of special fodder. If they were to switch to modern western European breeds, they would suddenly be faced with countless problems. They would require larger and more protected barns, which, in the already tight barnyards, would be totally impracticable. Also, these dairy types cannot be used for draught, meaning that they would have to be replaced by horses or machinery. Finally, these breeds need more selective fodder, which would necessitate the growing of new types of fodder, leading to a fundamental restructuring of crop allocation in the current tight land availability.

Horses in some numbers have only recently appeared in their villages, although their ownership is generally seen by the community as the advancement of the family's standing.[651] The research done by Péter Halász bears out that formerly, the possession of a pair of showy horses used to raise the social and economic status, not to mention adding to the prestige, of a Moldovan Hungarian farmer.[652] At the same time, this process of exchanging cattle for horses, for a European point of view, is synonymous with the lagging modernization and urbanization of the Moldovan population. We feel that it is quite probable that the usual tendency in their farming practice will be to directly replace the cattle with a tractor.

The deep and fundamental socio-economic changes that took place in the Moldovan region bring into question the long term viability of the self-supporting family farm model. This agricultural model, drifting toward the crisis point, is facing a myriad of problems: the lack of large farms, the lack of continuous soil enrichment and fertilization, etc. Up to the second world war, Moldovan family farming practices were in harmony with the local ecological environments. This equilibrium – ecological, social and economical – was radically upset by the explosive demographic growth after the war. The limited, and already tight, resources were unable to adequately

---

650 Vincze, Mária: Régió- és vidékfejlesztés. Elmélet és gyakorlat [Regional and rural development. Theory and practice]. Kolozsvár, 2000.

651 Farkas, Tibor: Moldvai magyarok - Csángó magyarok. Társadalom, gazdaság, kultúra [Moldovan Hungarians - Csángó Hungarians. Society, agriculture, culture]. Gödöllo, 2000, p. 29.

652 Halász: A ló ... op. cit. p. 32.

accommodate the needs of the suddenly expanded population. The situation was exacerbated with the building of large chemical factories in the region during the Ceausescu era, which inflicted serious, long-term ecological damage, leading to the rapid degradation and ruin of the environment.[653]

Land use was strictly prescribed before WWII: the use, non-use (fallow) and improvement of tilled lands, hay fields, pastures, forests, rivers and lakes. In the forcible nationalization of private property, this system ceased to operate: common pastures and roads were no longer tended, forests were mindlessly stripped, and, lacking money, many arable fields were left unplowed. The previously well-operating agricultural model, although static, today cannot sustain the overpopulated numbers in the villages. Most families try to temporarily counter its effects by drastically cutting consumption, hoping to avoid more profound changes. Since they are unable to effect change either through intensive (e.g.- land consolidation, mechanization, crop rotation) or extensive (e.g.- the increase of arable lands at the expense of forests) methods, there is a serious imbalance between most settlements and their environments.[654]

The agricultural effort, drowning in its own inertia, is slowly eroding the little reserves the Csángó families possess, gradually yielding the result that the excess workforce is quietly leaving this sector, the young are almost exclusively looking for better paying work abroad. The processes noted above would require that the Moldovan families, in the interest of their survival, quickly and flexibly alter their lifestyles and strategies.[655] Rapid modernization has created an environment in their midst where the acceptance of individual economic and lifestyle choices has taken root. The Romanian media continues to bombard them with such consumer goods, the possession of which, for them, symbolizes the embodiment of Heaven on Earth. Since they are unable to obtain these goods within the constraints of the traditional economic system, often times they must look for new, unique solutions. However, the attendant symptoms of modernization (e.g.- individualism, large degree of mobility) are starting to appear in Moldova, bringing with them the rapid dissolution of the Moldovan communities and the integration into a larger (global) socio-economic structure. If the Hungarian communities of the Carpathian basin were fortunate to experience gradually the gentrification and modernization of their economic systems, here in Moldova, these processes often proceed at the same time, to be aggravated by the relentless march of globalism. The greatest problem facing Moldova today is that the rural population is totally unprepared for the growing role of globalization, modernization and the market economy.

---

653 Farkas: Moldvai ... op. cit. p. 31.

654 Ibid, p. 31.

655 Ibid, pp. 29-31.

Agriculture, privatized since 1990, was unable to accommodate, and offer appropriate employment to, the workforce of the younger generation. Since travel restriction were somewhat eased since the 1989 events, the work force of the Csángó villages deemed to be excess now regularly stream toward Hungary, Italy, Germany and Israel. It is an interesting phenomenon that initially only the younger men took part in this practice. In recent years, women with small children are now going abroad to try and earn money as domestic help. Although these itinerant practices radically rearranged the internal and external ties within the Csángó families, it has not resulted in a great deal of change in their short term thinking or lifestyle. The hard earned money they make abroad does not become income producing capital; it is not rationally invested. Most is spent on prestige goods and luxury items (e.g.- color TV, VCR, parabolic satellite dish, western cars, etc.).[656] Yet, within their families, there still exist the old values, which dictates, for example, that a son must build himself a house before marrying.

Recently, we have come across a few members of the younger generation who, having earned money abroad, have not only acquired luxury goods or a house but have also bought more modern agricultural machines or land. Some have invested by starting small companies (e.g.- auto repair shop, pub, mill, bakery, etc.), others have tried their hand at retail commerce but in these villages specialized to be self-sufficient, there is no money. Any cash they have is usually earned outside the village, not from agriculture, which greatly influences their consumption. The invisible 'underground economy' is beginning to appear in their communities, in most cases to exploit the legal or economic gray areas left undefined or unwatched by the authorities. In actual practice, these manifest themselves in the uninhibited plunder of the environment (lumber from the forests, fish from the lakes, etc.) or the illegal acquisition of oil and petroleum products.

Due to the unviable nature of the economic model detailed above, archaic in countless of its elements, fundamental change in Moldova is more and more urgent. Since extensive methods are no longer appropriate here either, in our opinion, the solution lies primarily in the intensive use of the land. With adequate technical knowledge, their medium quality soil could be used to start intensive vegetable growing operations to be sold in city markets near and far. Secondly, it would be beneficial to restart and cultivate such handicraft trades, which already existed in their villages before collectivization, to effectively contribute to the future growth of rural tourism. These, however, have a large number of preconditions: the introduction of 'new' knowledge into the Csángó villages, the raising of the

---

656 Hegyeli, Attila: „Mint a gomba, ide benottek..." Moldvai csángók vendégmunkája Magyarországon

["They spread like mushrooms here ..." Moldovan Csángó's guest-work in Hungary.], In: Pozsony,

Ferenc /ed./: Csángósors. Moldvai csángók a változó idokben. Budapest, 1999, pp. 169-170.

level of education, the introduction of more 'marketable' trades, regional co-operation, the creation of a rational development plan, etc.

VIII. VILLAGE SOCIAL STRUCTURE

Hungarian ethnographers and linguists have, in the last 150 years, revealed the Hungarian-language literary and physical folk culture, so rich in archaic elements, of the Csángó, being slowly assimilated in their language and culture. Alongside these extensive studies, the examination of the social structure of the Moldovan villages was long overdue. Researchers only began to pay attention to the relationships between individuals and their groups beginning in the middle of the 20th century with the new developments in sociology.[657] The socio-ethnic interpretation, under the influence of social anthropology, brings us closer to understanding and analyzing why the Csángó gave such typical responses to the lesser or greater events and challenges of the 20th century.

In this chapter, I primarily seek to uncover the prospects and pitfalls of an emerging civil society among the Moldovan Hungarian communities, a topic already gently broached at the end of the 18th century by the poet Mihály (Michael) Csokonai Vitéz.[658] [The poet speculates on the extent of the territories of the Hungarian Crown and whether the Csángó might be considered fellow citizens-*Ed.*]

Hypothetical framework

The starting point for the analysis of Moldovan Csángó society is the 1983 work by Ferdinand Tönnies *Közösség és társadalom* [Community and Society] in which he sets down the hypothetical and conceptual frameworks.[659] The German scientist isolates two fundamental forms of interpersonal relationships in his work, which is still valid today. He defined as Gemeinschaft (community) that group of people who are bound by tight, personal and natural bonds, which were established through internal, organic means.[660] Beside the traditional terminology of community, typically applied to groups and villages, Tönnies introduces the concept of Gesellschaft (society), which primarily he applied to town dwellers and more modern

---

657 Szent-Iványi, István: A magyar kultúra egysége [The extent of Hungarian culture], In: Balázs, Géza /ed./:

Magyar néphagyomány – európai néphagyomány. Budapest – Debrecen, 1991, p. 83.

658 „Vajha Moldvának is kies parlagjai,

A' Meddig terjednek a' Pontus habjai,

Magyar Koronánknak árnyékába menne,

S a' Tsángó Magyar is Polgártársunk lenne!!!"

(Csokonai Vitéz Mihály: Marosvásárhelyi Gondolatok, 1798)

659 Tönnies, Ferdinand: Közösség és társadalom [Community and society]. Gondolat, Budapest, 1983.

660 Ibid, pp. 15-56.

societies. Society is formed by the free association of legally unencumbered persons, whose members have a contractual relationship dominated by independent trade ties, whose institutions are man-made and organized in nature.[661] In his book, Tönnies defined modernization as that process during which the social ties that depend on reciprocity are gradually suppressed, to be more and more replaced on an interpersonal level by individualism and a personal career. In the society that emerges as a result of modernization, market forces - formalized barter - are dominant, which is interlinked with the gradually emerging process of role differentiation and segmentation.[662]

According to Hungarian sociologists, there is an intermediate stage between the beginning of the disintegration of traditional society and its radical modernization, the period of an emerging civil society.[663] The fundamental and rapid transformation of human relationships was already noted in the era between the wars, as unavoidable results of urbanization and industrialization. It became evident at the time that as a result of the emergence of a civil society, the micro-environment of the rural population will also gradually change; the process will inexorably lead to a member of a community becoming an individual, a citizen. Thus, he quickly becomes distanced from the value system of the previous community, one based on local and family ties, his life work no longer measured against strict norms but planned as an independent person, decided by his own decisions. His place in society is no longer decided by his inherited family status but defined and denoted by his personal accomplishment.

The theory used by sociologists in the second half of the 20th century, not based on institutions but human centric, revealed the invisible bonds and nodes between people. Based on these, Mark Granovetter identified strong and weak bonds.[664] While in the traditional rural setting, strong bonds dominate, in modern societies, the role of casual bonds are more significant.[665]

According to the most recent social anthropological research, modernization is seen to be a process, which is closely intertwined with globalization and Americanization. As a result of the large scale social and local mobility, the dissolution of rural communities is hastened, the micro-

---

661 Ibid, pp. 57-116.

662 Ibid, pp. 76-79.

663 Benda, Gyula: A polgárosodás fogalmának történeti értelmezhetősége [The concept of civil society in a historical context], In: Századvég 2-3, 1991, pp. 169-176.

664 Granovetter, Mark: A gyenge kötések ereje [The strength of casual ties]. In: Angelusz, Róbert – Tardos, Róbert /ed./: Társadalmak rejtett hálózata. Új Mandátum Könyvkiadó, Budapest, 1995, pp. 371-340.

665 Csata, Zsombor – Kiss, Dénes – Sólyom, Andrea: Vallás és modernizáció a Mezőségen [Religion and modernization in the Mezőség]. WEB. Szociológiai Folyóirat, Kolozsvár, p. 38.

environment undergoes rapid change, families disintegrate and the roles and relationships of the sexes and the generations fundamentally change. At the same time, due to the rapid change in lifestyle and culture, individual and group alienation and uncertainty grows.[666]

Internal partitions and institutions of a village

Due to unique historical, economic and political circumstances, Moldovan villages retained relatively archaic, pre-industrial social structures all the way to the middle of the 20th century.[667] While the more concentrated urban Hungarian communities gradually disappeared, the rural Roman Catholic population was able to continuously regenerate itself, in spite of all difficulties. Hence, today, the rural community represents the most significant strata of Csángó-Hungarian society at the local level.

In the past, a significant portion of Moldova's Hungarians lived in *free* villages, the later settlers moving to lands and villages owned by the boyars. Although there are few written records in existence, researchers believe that the order of the free (*razesi / részes*) villages (e.g.- Klézse, Somoska, Forrófalva, Lujzikalagor, etc.) emerged because of the practice of common landholding and communal values. The people of a village usually held in common the settlement's grazing lands and untilled fields. New fields, gained through the clearing of forests, were commonly distributed by the drawing of random lots. The self-government of the Moldovan Hungarian villages was never formalized in writing as it was primarily left to the care of the community's common memory, traditions and judicial practice.[668]

The village council was the most important institution in a Csángó community, right up to the end of the second world war. These were usually convened in early spring, before the beginning of the agricultural cycle. Usually, only married men took part but widows who lead a household or a farm were also invited. The gathering assembled in the yard of the parish hall and they elected, first the community's cowherd, then the guards (*jitari*) for each of the gates leading into the community, and finally, the shepherds (*gardieri*). Then, they settled on each of their annual pay. While all the families usually paid the cowherd with money, corn and food stuff, the gatekeepers and shepherds were, by custom, entitled to the crop on the 3 - 3.5 meter strip at the bottom of the fields, or were given a tithe-like donation

---

666 Fejos, Zoltán: Modernizáció és néprajz [Modernization and ethnography], In: Szucs, Alexandra /ed./:

Hagyomány, modernizáció a kultúrában és a néprajzban. Budapest, 1998, pp. 7-20.

667 Halász: A moldvai ... op. cit. pp.. 423-433.

668 Kós – Szentimrei – Nagy: Moldvai ... op. cit. pp. 21-22.

from the harvest of corn, potatoes, hemp, etc.[669] Any conflicts that arose between the shepherds were usually settled by the oldest.

The village elders, wearing their hair long in the back and a beard, played a prominent position in the Moldovan settlements until the introduction of civil law. They were usually treated with great deference and respect in the village, advising the elected village justice between council meetings, as well as the gendarme captain, appointed by the central administration, and the parish priest, sent by the Roman Catholic bishop.[670]

These days, the Roman Catholic Csángó only form compact communities in rural villages. The rural Csángó settlements were little affected by industrialization until the collectivization of 1962. The social makeup of their communities was homogeneous, since the relatively isolated village society was extremely careful that no significant division could take place, material or financial, taking definite steps to prevent an individual from amassing a greater amount of goods than his neighbors. The strict – but unwritten – rules of their communities also paid careful attention that the Csángó settlements would not become too focused towards any of the various occupations or social groups.

Interestingly, the size of a landholding did not significantly differentiate – internally – the population of a Csángó village. The holdings of more modest families usually ran around 1-3 hectares and, since they could not make a living off that, they rented land from others, worked as laborers on the boyar's lands, or took on sharecropping. Those with farms of 3-5 hectares could support their immediate families but, during the winter, they took jobs in the boyar's forests. Usually, every Csángó rural community had 3-4 families who possessed over 10 hectares of land (plowed, hay fields and forest). On the flatlands around Románvásár, farmers usually had about 3-4 hectares until 1962. In the decades following forced urbanization, they used intensive methods to produce and ship vegetables to the markets of nearby towns.[671] It is interesting to note that a greater number of children of vegetable growing families were educated to a higher level.

These days, the Csángó do not have their own urban middle class, intelligentsia, trade and craft class, to unite them. During the golden age of the Hungarian kingdom of the Middle Ages, the Moldovan towns developed significant civil communities, which played an important role in the emergence of crafts and trade, the spread of Protestantism in Moldova, the court events of the Moldovan principality, the administration of the

669 Imreh, István – Szeszka Erdos, Péter: A szabófalvi jogszokásokról [Legal customs in Szabófalva].

Népismereti Dolgozatok. Bukarest, 1978, p. 199.

670 Ibid, p. 199.

671 Halász: A moldvai ... op. cit. pp. 426-427.

voivodine, diplomatic relations and defense. The series of Mongol and Turkish incursions during the 16th-17th centuries destroyed these urban communities. Thus, by the 18th-19th centuries, the Moldovan Hungarians no longer had meaningful numbers of town dwellers. Although members of the younger generation sought a better life in the nearby towns (e.g.- Bákó, Onest, Románvásár, etc.) or farther afield (e.g.- Brassó, Csíkszereda, Fogaras, Sepsiszentgyörgy, Temesvár, etc.) during the artificial industrialization or collectivization after the second world war, nowhere did they form an independent social entity. Everywhere they integrated into the urban lifestyle dominated by Orthodox family values.

The social structure of the Moldovan Hungarian communities is weak because of the scarcity of the intellectual stratum. In most of their villages, education was of a poor quality. Lacking their own educated stratum, no one drew the young's attention to the fact that education was the fastest and most effective method of rising in society. With the establishment of the bishopric of Jászvásár at the end of the 19th century, higher theological instruction was begun in Moldova. First, the various Catholic seminaries, then the Jászvásár theological institute, trained such 'blessed' priests from the children of the Csángó-Hungarian families who consciously turned against their own native language and, except for a small minority, did not serve the communities consigned to their care but lorded over them, in a feudal manner.

The Church remains the most fundamental, significant institution of rural Csángó society. Every family in a Catholic Moldovan village is able to experience its everyday and holidays only as part of the Church. In these settlements, the Church has retained its community character. The young and old of a village are intrinsically part of its life. Those who are unable to become a part of the local structure soon become so alienated that, in most cases, sooner or later leave the village.

The parish priest is not only the local representative of the Roman Catholic Church, not only looks after the spiritual care of the flock, but plays an important role in the community's family, educational and moral life. The clergy has consciously and unequivocally taken on the propagation and dissemination of Romanian national identity in the Csángó populated region since the end of the 19th century. Similar to the Orthodox churches active in the region, most have directed the villages relegated to their care with feudal methods. Usually, there is an asymmetrical relationship between parishioner and priest who, as God's earthly embodiment and representative, is due unquestioning respect. They stand on an unattainable level above the congregation, able to pry into the intimate details of everyone's life, yet no one is entitled to find any human failings in their lives, much less to point it out. The priest is still within his rights to appraise the moral fiber of his parishioners, punish the sinners and, similar to the Orthodox ministers, able to carry out some arcane, paranormal tasks. Those individuals who hold opinions that differ in any way from the priest – and give voice to them – are, in many villages, most often shamed and intimidated by brutal means (e.g.- sermonized from the pulpit, threatened with excommunication, etc.). As a matter of course, these medieval means are employed against those persons or families who openly dare to ask for liturgy and education in their native tongue.[672]

Beginning in the 17th-18th centuries, when the Roman Catholic Church was gradually reorganized, a system of defined fees came into being. The parishioners were obligated to pay a pre-set amount for a christening, wedding, funeral or a memorial Mass for the deceased.[673] These 'donations' grew to such an extent by the end of the 19th century that the Catholics around Románvásár threatened their church leaders with mass conversion to the Orthodox rite.[674] It is not unknown today that a widow will pay an amount to the parish priest that sorely tries her annual income – and existence – to have a Mass said for the memory, and salvation, of her deceased husband.

To the very end of the 19th century, few priests were active in their villages, and those all represented the unification and assimilation aspirations of the majority in the nation during the period of the creation of the Romanian nation state. Alongside these priests, the role of *cantors* (or deacons), whom the Csángó called *clerk* (deák in Hung.), assumed greater prominence in their villages in the early 20th century.[675] In the centuries before the current civil era, these cantors guided them - in their native language - in their religious affairs, as opposed to the missionaries who spoke Italian, Polish, Bosnian and later, only Romanian. Although they did not have the bishop's authorization, especially during the serious priest shortage at the end of the 19th century, they performed such rites (e.g.- confession, communion, baptism, marriage, funeral, etc.) for which they had no dispensation. Over the centuries, virtual dynasties of cantors sprang up in the Moldovan Hungarian villages. Most completed their studies in the Carpathian basin and were familiar with several languages. They had important roles in the organization, preparation and guidance of groups visiting the religious fairs. Under their tutelage, the Moldovan Hungarians most often went to the fair held during the Feast of the Pentecost in

---

672 Benedek H: Út az ... op. cit. p. 12.

673 See Almanahul ... op. cit. pp. 24-72.

674 Pilat: Aspecte ... op. cit. pp. 98.

675 Tóth, István György: Diákok (licenciátusok) a moldvai csángómagyar muvelodésben a XVII. században
[Students (licentiates) in 17th century Moldovan Csángó-Hungarian education], In: Zombori, István /ed./:
Az értelmiség Magyarországon a XVI-XVII. században. Szeged, 1988, pp. 139-147.

Csíksomlyó. There, they first visited the shrine-church, completed the Stations of the Cross on Calvary Hill, usually spending the night in the nunnery church. On Saturday, they attended the main Mass of the festivity; at dawn, on Sunday, they waited on the mountainside – facing East – to await the Holy Spirit in the guise of a dove. In the sacred grove at the top of Calvary Hill, they tore alder branches to touch the icon of the Virgin with those and kerchiefs brought from home. Attendance at the festivities in Csíksomlyó, organized by the cantors, first of all represented a spiritual rejuvenation for the Moldovan Hungarian communities. Secondly, they were able to come into contact with other Hungarian-language groups from Transylvania, learn the popular songs and prayers of the Seklerland, and purchase Hungarian-language religious publications.[676]

Until the very end of the 19th century, the Roman Catholic population of a settlement chose and invited a deacon to lead the community. After the emergence of nation states, the borders became harder to cross. These deacon families were now unable to send their young men to attend Hungarian religious institutions. In spite of this constraint, they continued to keep their Hungarian-language prayer and song books; their knowledge was passed verbally from father to son. To about the middle of the 20th century, some indulgent priests turned a blind eye to the parishioners singing and praying in the church in Hungarian, lead by the cantor, until the beginning of the Mass. Later, it was only in the private sphere, in a private dwelling, where they could sing and pray in their native language, mainly at vigils beside the deceased and wakes. In the closing three decades of the 20th century, the men of the Securitate searched the houses of the deacons in many settlements, mainly at the instigation of the Roman Catholic Church of Moldova, confiscating their Hungarian books. They were also forbidden to lead the singing of religious hymns or prayers in private dwellings.[677] During the most difficult years of the Ceausescu dictatorship, the place of the peasant cantors was gradually filled by 'lead singers,' even less educated than the cantors, but with an excellent repertoire of Hungarian-language religious hymns and prayers. During the 1980s, Luca Hodorog in Klézse doggedly and determinedly filled such a role.[678]

676 Tánczos, Vilmos: A moldvai csángók pünkösd hajnali keresztútjárása a Kis-Somlyó hegyen [The dawn ritual of the Stations of the Cross by the Moldovan Csángó during Pentecost on Little Somlyó], In: Asztalos, Ildikó /ed./: Hazajöttünk ... Pünkösd Csíksomlyón. Kolozsvár, 1992, pp. 40-48.

677 Csoma: Elveszett ... op. cit. pp.36-90.

678 Tánczos: „Deákok" ... op. cit. pp. 82-98.

Local social restratification after 1944

Similar to Stalinist authorities in the two decades after the second world war, Romania also strove for the rapid homogenization of its society, suddenly dispensing with the social structures that emerged naturally over the centuries.

The basic social changes only took place after the collectivization of 1962, when the totalitarian regime stripped the farming families of their lands, farm implements and animals. However, it soon became evident that the poorly operating collective farms were unable to support the continually growing rural population, leading to an exodus by the younger and middle aged generation toward the massively oversized industrial centers. The Csángó families intentionally strove, especially after 1965, to have their children educated in one of the larger towns, however distant, for them to be able to obtain a job there and start a family. This exercise in mass departure shortly resulted in the children and the younger generation not being socialized within the confines of their native village, surrounded by their family but in a Romanian-language artificial urban setting established by the Communist authorities.[679]

This also brought about a gradual loosening of the formerly close family and kinship ties and this process began the gradual fracture and disintegration of rural Csángó society. More and more, every family had to deal with members who left for greener pastures, until, in a space of about three decades, such deep rooted changes took place in the social make-up of rural society that it exerted considerable stress on all concerned. For example, only about a quarter (26.66%) of the men born after the second world war in Csík (Ciucani) remained in their village, as most of them commute daily, or return only on weekends, while earning their living. Until 1989, the majority of their wives (94.66%) remained behind, contributing to the family's income with modest incomes from the collective or state farms.

	Grand fathers	Grand mother	Husbands	Wives	Children	Grand childrn	Total
Number	150	150	75	75	318	99	867
Farmer	107	140	20	71	94	-	432
Worker	12	2	24	2	61	1	102
Commuter	15	-	13	-	9	-	37
Unemployed	1	-	12	1	13	-	27
Office worker	1	-	1	-	-	-	2
Dometics	-	8	-	1	2	-	11
In school	-	-	-	-	138	98	236
Other	14	-	5	-	1	-	20

---

679 This became especially evident when, beginning in 1990, the young began to be unemployed and were forced to move back 'home'. The difference of their socialization made their reintegration difficult.

In the survey made in 1993, the makeup of the village of Csík was predominantly of farmers up to the 1962 collectivization. Two-thirds of the men born between 1900 and 1920 supported their large families from agriculture and animal husbandry. After the collectivization of agriculture, a few of this generation also departed for industrial centers near and far – others adopting the commuter lifestyle – while their wives stayed at home to run the household and raise the children.

The male generation born after the second world war shows a more diverse picture: of 75 in the village, 20 farm in and around the village, 24 work in industrial concerns, and 13 commute to some industrial jobs in nearby towns. In the years after the regime change of 1989, this generation was hard hit by the rapid and radical change in Romania's economic reality. The vast industrial works went bankrupt, one after the other, making many of them unemployed. The majority of their wives stayed behind, carrying on what farming they could in lieu of their absent husbands, raising the children who now see no future whatsoever within the confines of their native village.

In the ten years after 1989, a significant portion of those commuting from village to town were let go from their places of work, returning to their village bitter and disappointed. The current occupational model remains to be for Csángó families to orient their children towards industrial jobs in urban centers but the mass unemployment following 1989 continues to effectively frustrate them. This excess workforce is now drifting farther afield (Italy, Spain, Germany, Hungary and Israel) in search of work. In 1992, for instance, 10% of the population of Tázló, out of a total of 931 people, worked in the intensively cultivated greenhouses around Szeged, Hungary.[680] The acceptance of temporary work abroad has completely reorganized life in Magyarfalu, lying between the Szeret and Prut rivers, where close to 10% of the working-age males work out of the country. Out of this relatively isolated villages, in 2001, 21 breadwinners (men) were temporarily in Israel, five in Hungary. From among their children, 38 were working in Israel, 30 in Hungary, 5 in Italy and 1 in Greece. In Klézse, close to a quarter or approximately 1,000 people, have only accepted work abroad in the past few years.[681]

It is interesting to note that working in foreign lands has not yet reorganized their value system, tradition and modernization existing peacefully side by side. They see nothing strange in the sight of a middle

---

680 Ozsváth, Gábor Dániel: Székelyek és csángók a csólyospálosi homoki gazdaságokban [Seklers and Csángó on the sandy farmlands of Csólyospálos], In: Juhász Antal /ed./: Migráció és anyagi kultúra. Szeged, 1999, p. 164.

681 The population of Klézse consisted of 4,331 people in 1992. (See Tánczos: Hányan vannak ... op. cit. p. 378.)

aged woman – in traditional voluminous skirt (katrinca) – talking on a cell phone, in the middle of a plowed field, with her husband who is working in Italy. Or, to go into an Internet café in Bákó to send an email to his grandchild living in Spain. Although the work in distant lands brings them into contact with countless elements and values of modern life, when they return to the village, they slip into the traditional lifestyle seamlessly.[682]

Although there were active artisans in the Moldovan Csángó settlements (furriers, tanners, carpenters, potters, smiths, etc.), they mostly produced their wares and services to satisfy the local demand. The lifestyle and value system of the rural artisans, due to the peculiar dynamic of Moldovan social and economic life, was not significantly different from the way of life of the farmers. The potters of Gorzafalva did not increase their output to satisfy the demand represented by tourism after 1989. They continue work at their craft during breaks from farm tasks, whirling their wheels on rainy days and, true to ancient tradition, only firing up their kilns two or three times a year. For most of the year, they plow, plant corn, hoe by hand, cut firewood and cut hay, etc. in days gone by, very few of the young would be sent to a nearby town to apprentice in a workshop, where they could have come into contact with the elements and values of an emerging middle class. A particular craft, and its lore, was usually passed from father to son.

Relations between generations and sexes

The Moldovan Csángó villages, seemingly homogeneous from the outside, are partitioned internally by well defined family, kin, generational and sexual boundaries. In their communities, the only acceptable social position was within the state of marriage. Elderly bachelors or unmarried girls were, in most of the settlements, held in contempt, marginalized and continually scorned. Up to the very beginning of the 20th century, boys usually married at 17-18, girls at 16-17. Among the surrounding Orthodox, they married even younger.[683] In the decades following the second world war, this practice adjusted: women married at 20-26, men at 24-30. After the wedding, the young couple usually moved in with the groom's parents but soon built a house of their own with the combined support of the extended families. In the Csángó villages we find not only nuclear families but also extended, three-generational ones as well. The immediate family unit formed by the ceremony is in continuous contact not only with their immediate parents but also the wider kinship. As a rule, they tended their meager lands

682 Hegyeli: "Mint a … op. cit.

683 Pilat: Aspecte … op. cit. pp. 94.

as a family unit and also celebrated the various church feasts together.[684] The extremely tight-knit network, based as it was on mutual assistance of family and kin, until very recently still provided a measure of safety and protection for an individual.

The relatively tight-knit family relationships is still evident in the Csángó settlements, which is reflected in the richly detailed family terminology. This diversity partly stems from the fact that the ancestors of some communities settled in Moldova from the Carpathian basin at different times and from different regions. As contact with the Romanians increased during industrialization, the terminology for relatives also expanded with Romanian expressions: *bunika* for grandmother, *tátám* for father, *nyepót* for grandchild, etc. We must, however, stress that, in many cases, even in those northern Csángó villages where they no longer speak the language of their ancestors on a daily basis, they still use the Hungarian terminology. Secondly, we must point out that in their kinship terminology, they retain many archaic nouns to this day, e.g.- *lér* for 'husband of older sister'. They have special pseudo-relative names (*vérem, vésár, mátkám*) for those with whom they formed a ritual kinship during ceremonies enacted on *White Sunday* [a week after Easter-*Ed.*].[685]

Today, Moldova is the most populous region of Romania, where the most significant demographic reserve came into being after WWII. In this area, between 1930 and 1992, the total population has essentially doubled, within which the 118% increase of Roman Catholics was even more spectacular.[686] As but one example, the village of Gajdár, on the banks of the Tázló River, had a total population of 411 in 1930, and rose to 931 in 1992. although the rapid industrialization of the area affected the village through migration to the city, in a relatively short 62 years, the settlement doubled in size.[687]

An in-depth analysis of the family structure shows that, at the end of the 20th century in Moldova, a pre-industrial family model existed, devoid of family planning.[688] In the village of Csík, hidden among the hills South of Bákó, the large family model is still the most common in our time. In this settlement, 20% of the families still raised three children in the 1990s, while many had 4-5-6-7 children. Up until the regime change of 1989, the inhabitants of Magyarfalu, some distance away, large families were in vogue.

---

684 Benedek H.: Út az ... op. cit. pp. 11-14.

685 Halász: A moldvai ... op. cit. pp. 428-429.

686 Tánczos: Hányan ... op. cit. pp. 375-376.

687 Ibid, p. 378.

688 Benedek H.: Út az ... op. cit. pp. 15-18.

At the end of 2001, the distribution of the number of children per family was as follows:

# of children	# of families (281)
0	8.9%
1	14.6%
2	21.7%
3	13.2%
4	9.6%
5	8.5%
6	9.2%
7	6.4%
8	4.7%
9	1.5%
10	0.7%
>10	1.0%

It is only in the past two decades that the young consciously put off having children for a few years after marriage. As a response to urbanization and working abroad, 14.6% of the families in this relatively isolated village are now uniparous and 21.7% have two children. Hence, the two-child family is becoming more and more the model, although the earlier large family model still remains in parts of Moldova.

The resolute and unequivocal anti-abortion stand of the Roman Catholic Church, as well as the cultural and family models that influence Moldova, result in that, in spite of the mass migration of the young, the Moldovan villages are neither being depopulated or aging. The age and sex distribution of the population of Csík is as follows:

Age groups	Male	Female	Total
1-7	44 (11.13%)	16 (4.05%)	60 (15.18%)
8-16	29 (7.34%)	28 (7.08%)	57 (14.43%)
17-25	34 (8.60%)	36 (9.11%)	70 (17.72%)
26-40	48 (12.15%)	49 (12.40%)	97 (24.55%)
41-60	37 (9.36%)	39 (9.87%)	76 (19.24%)
Over 61	19 (4.81%)	16 (4.05%)	35 (8.86%)
Total	211 (53.41%)	184 (46.58%)	395 (100%)

The population distribution of these relatively isolated villages is still comparatively balanced today: children up through school age make up a third of the village; young, married earners make up a quarter; and the 41-60 middle-aged group forms 20%.

It is noteworthy how few elderly live in the village. In Csík, the number of 61 or over do not even reach 10%. As a result of the Romanian and Moldovan demographic explosion after 1968, the village social structure is primarily dominated by the younger generation. This situation we can attribute to the major political, economic and social events of the 20th century, which have substantially thinned the ranks of the elderly still alive. Their formative years were greatly impacted by the second world war and the serious droughts in the following years. At an early age, they lived through the forcible nationalization, anti-kulak hysteria, and collectivization imposed by the Communist regime; the Ceausescu dictatorship with its serious food distribution problems that tried the personal integrity of all; and the re-privatization following 1989. During our research, we noted with surprise the extent that the younger generation has distanced itself in the last few decades from their elderly family members.

The Moldovan Csángó families living in this isolated existence devoted little care to the education of their children up until the end of the second world war. To take Csík as an example, 50% of the older generation, today's grandparents, had no formal education at all and a further 47.3% only completed grade 4. Of the 75 heads of households, four were without any schooling whatever, 38.7% finished grade 4 and 24% completed all eight elementary grades. Although the majority of them received their socialization post-WWII, only 13.3% finished middle school and 18.7% went to trade school. Among their wives, 15 received no formal schooling. While a shade more attended elementary school than their husbands, substantially less completed the compulsory eight years. It is only thanks to the social and local mobility following collectivization that a number of them were able to finish middle school. It is a sad fact that, in the half century after the war, of all the youths of Csík only one was able to gain acceptance to university. A similar pattern was found in Magyarfalu at the end of 2001:

	Husbands	Wives	Total
No education	4	9	13
Grades I-IV	89	92	181
Grades V-VIII	88	91	179
Grades IX-X	62	67	129
Trade school	10	-	10
College	12	6	18
University	-	-	-
Total	265	265	530

It is primarily among the elderly, male and female, that we find some who were unable to complete even four grades of elementary school.

Of the men and women of the older generation, 35% finished only grades 1 to 4. The majority those who grew up post-WWII successfully completed their elementary 8 grades. During the 1970s and '80s, the 8 grades of elementary school were compulsory. It is notable how few went on to middle and trade school from this village. After 1989, a number of local children enrolled in Transylvanian and Hungarian middle schools, a few in university.

The educational levels attained by the Csángó were defined by several fundamental factors. For one, up to collectivization, education had no real value or particular significance in the life stratagem of the family. As noted before, the more middle-class families of the Csángó villages have only realized in the last decades that education is one the surest and quickest paths to social advancement. The Hungarian-speaking Csángó were always treated by the appointed administration of the day with disdain and condescension; the level of education was intentionally not raised. There has always been a grave shortage of trained teachers in the villages of Moldova (in the Orthodox settlements, too), Romania's most backward region. The school board of Bákó County most often appointed untrained teachers to these villages labeled as second-rate. These Orthodox 'teachers', of Romanian origin and mother tongue and commuting from nearby towns, were astounded even in the 1970s to note how badly the Csángó children spoke Romanian. Hence, in most of the Roman Catholic villages, they deliberately neglected their spiritual instruction and education.

It is an interesting phenomenon that the socialization of young children in Moldova does not come from their parents of grandparents, rather their older siblings play a more defining role. In the Moldovan settlements, the younger children and youths play an important role – within the family framework – in the raising of animals and crops. Boys, on approaching their teens, take part in rituals important to the whole of local village society. In times gone by, the Csángó youths became part of a group (ceata), whose most important task was the organization and running of the local festivities. On Shrove Tuesday, the boys of Szabófalva, for instance, would dress up resembling scarecrows (matahala) and greet the parish priest in front of his house, who would present them with gifts of boots and articles of clothing. At the open air festivities, they created a merry atmosphere with their comic outfits.[689] The flock of boys had an important role during the local church fairs, too. They greeted the Roman Catholic bishop of Moldova at the outskirts of the village, usually on horseback and in their Sunday best, and escorted him to the church in the center of the village amid singing and music. After the official memorial Mass, they organized an outdoor entertainment, complete with dancing, on the village square. For these

---

689 Wichmann: A moldvai ... op. cit.

events, they usually obtained the church and state permissions, hired the musicians and looked after order.

The girls of the Moldovan Roman Catholic villages were able to meet the young men at these public dances and lay the basis for pair-bonding. If, as a result of one of these events, a girl eloped with an Orthodox lad to get married, the local parish priest would firmly intervene and, with the assistance of the local authorities, prevent the marriage from taking place – even if the Romanian boy gladly expressed an interest in converting to the girl's religion.[690] The Roman Catholic Church and the Csángó families vehemently banned planned marriages with Orthodox youths, and this strict religious segregation led to many unfortunate suicides by love struck couples.

The winter spinning gatherings [communal preparation of wool for homespun linens-*Ed.*] of the past represented important meeting opportunities not only for the girls but also for the boys. Up until the 1962 collectivization, wool, flax and hemp played an important part in the making of clothing and textiles for home use. The spinning houses represented important meeting places where the boys could gauge a girl's work ethic, dexterity and artistic ability, where they could get to know each other and have a good time together. In the Moldovan villages, in the two weeks before a wedding, the young people would gather at the bride's house and hold a sewing bee, together producing the bride's linen dowry.[691] Since the 1970s, mate selection among the young has largely been based on emotional attraction. Of late, the majority of girls meet their future partners at the city school, place of work or a disco.

The role of local contacts

Until the outbreak of the first world war, the Csángó villages led a relatively closed lifestyle. The settlements were surrounded by fence, berm and rampart, the access points from them protected by gates and guards. The inhabitants fixed the surrounding fence every spring, which not only prevented their animals from straying but also provided significant protection from external attack.

The settlements were subdivided into smaller, internal group of structures (cot) and external farmsteads (catun). The inhabitants of these smaller units were usually linked by close family or friendship ties, which usually provided security against outside groups.[692] There was an unwritten law in the Moldovan villages that governed neighborly relations of mutual respect and assistance. The families living next to each other helped one

690 Pilat: Aspecte ... op. cit. pp. 95.

691 Imreh – Szeszka: A szabófalvi ... op. cit. p. 204.

692 Ibid, p. 200.

another not only during major family events (e.g.- christening, wedding, funeral) but during the course of everyday events. In Szabófalva, it is still the living tradition that, after the slaughter of a hog, it is not only the relatives but also the closer neighbors who receive a portion of meat, bacon or sausage.[693] During recent times, if someone wanted to sell his land, it was an unwritten law that it be first offered to the relatives to purchase, then to the neighbors.[694]

Péter (Peter) Halász examined the relationship between the Moldovan Csángó villages.[695] According to his findings, the northern Catholic bloc, living around Román, is precisely divided from the southern and Sekler Csángó settlements. Up until the very end of the 20th century, the Catholic communities of the northern and southern blocs were characterized by strict rules of endogamy. Interestingly, the young Csángó living in the larger – and more distant – cities of Brassov, Timisoara, Fogaras soon overcame the cultural and territorial boundaries separating them. In the Transylvanian towns, a Csángó searching for a mate gave precedence to a Catholic young person more familiar with Moldovan traditions than a better situated or socially higher ranked Transylvanian Hungarian.

The settlements northwest of Bákó, in the valleys of the Tázló and Beszterce Rivers (e.g.- Pusztina, Frumósza, Lészped) are, to this day, in close religious and family connection with each other. These ties may also become evident in the choosing of a mate; at the very least, they visit each other's churches during the fairs. The group of Csángó villages South of Bákó are separated by the Szeret River. The villages lying on its left bank (Gyoszény, Ketris, Magyarfalu, Lábnik) form a small sub-group, in spite of their settlement history and dialect differences. The similar state of their language, the relatives who moved to Hungary and the migration of workers towards Hungary strengthened their mutual sense of identity.[696] Similarly, good relations are evident in the villages on the right bank of the river (Lujzikalagor, Nagypatak, Bogdánfalva, Forrófalva, Klézse, Somoska, Csík, Rekecsin), although they can not be considered homogeneous from a historical or linguistic perspective. The neighboring, lisping dialect, Csángó and Sekler villages have deeper family and economic ties with each other than with the left bank villages of the Szeret or with those living in the Tázló

---

693 Imreh – Szeszka: A szabófalvi ... op. cit. p. 205.

694 Ibid, p. 202.

695 Halász, Péter: Új szempontok a moldvai magyarsok táji-etnikai tagozódásának vizsgálatához [New perspectives to the regional and ethnic partition of the Moldovan Hungarians], In: Pozsony Ferenc /ed./: Dolgozatok a moldvai csángók népi kultúrájáról. Kriza János Néprajzi Társaság Évkönyve 5. Kolozsvár, 1997.

696 Ibid, p. 22.

valley.[697] The people of the Hungarian villages found between the Ojtoz, Tatros and Tázló rivers (Bohána, Diószeg, Gorzafalva, Onyest, Szitás, Szolohegy) also differ markedly from the previously described groups in their familial, economic, social and religious relationships.[698]

The Moldovan Csángó villages were characterized by relative isolation up to the 1962 collectivization. This was evident in their selection of mates when, even after their migration to the cities, the younger generation consistently married partners from their own, or a neighboring, village.

Since we were able to successfully examine the structure of 75% of the family units in the village of Csík in 1993, we shall illustrate the shift in local mobility with an example from there. Of the 75 husbands, 21 (16%) is from some other village, some from neighboring villages and a few from as far away as Transylvania. In the case of the wives, 25 (33%) were imported, mostly from the vicinity.

The moral and legal value system

The moral value system and the view of the world are closely intertwined in the Moldovan villages. Not only in their holidays but also in their everydays, it is a medieval-like view that allows them to decipher the world around them, a view that is largely unaffected by the Rationalism of the Enlightenment or the Materialism of our own day. Every action and expression of theirs is given a deeper meaning by their profound faith in God and in a life hereafter. "The world view is rendered solid and static by the certainty of a God, and earthly events only have any real value within the context of this hereafter. Life here has not yet lost its Catholic metaphysical perspectives."[699] Every individual in every Moldovan Csángó village essentially strives all his life to ensure divine redemption after death. Their ethical and legal value system, inseparable from a deep sense of religion, is fundamentally based on the ten commandments. In their communities, until very recently, murder, robbery and abortion,[700] theft, agnosticism and not attending church were held to be among the most serious sins. Second to a faith in God, their moral outlook was defined by their work ethic. They held a man to be an honest person if he supported his family by honest labor. They

---

697 Ibid, p. 23.

698 Ibid, p. 25.

699 Tánczos, Vilmos: A nyelvváltás jelensége a moldvai csángók egyéni imarepertoárjában [The phenomenon of language adjustment in the personal prayer repertoire of the Moldovan Csángó]. *Kétnyelvüség* III. évf. 2. sz., 1995, p. 290.

700 In Klézse, they still hold that a woman who has an abortion will have to consume 40 tons of rotten child-flesh in the afterlife.

deeply despised those unwilling to work, irresponsible drunkards and thieves.[701]

It sheds some light on the Moldovan Csángó mentality on how they respond to crimes against property. Most wronged individuals would visit an Orthodox priest or monk and have a Mass said, in the hopes of inflicting stern punishment on the transgressor. Often they would resort to fasting (not even taking water on odd-day Fridays) in an attempt to bring punishment on the thief through ritualistic means. Others would resort to reading beans or cards to identify the thief. Most often they would relate these magical and ritualistic acts to relatives and neighbours and the guilty one, under psychological stress, would either return the stolen goods or publicly admit to the deed.

The village community dealt with local crime according to ancient traditional and codified means. If someone killed a neighbour's cow, the village council would convene and, if the accused admitted to the act, he would be obliged to purchase a similar animal or pay an equivalent amount.[702] They were more lenient in lesser matters, such as the stealing of fruits. The thief would usually be forced to beg for forgiveness and have to return the purloined items. If a second occurrence happened, the punishment meted out consisted of having the stolen items displayed around his neck, paraded up and down the village streets, while shouting: "Whoever does what I did, will get what I did!" After this shaming ritual, the offender would most often disappear immediately from the village, where he would not dare to return, even after long decades.[703]

In the past, the village communities consistently and sternly punished murderers. If anyone was undeniably proven to be a killer, the assembled 20-25 men – relying on the right of self-judgment – would kill the criminal without a second thought. In one instance in Szabófalva in 1947, a gang of thieves killed the saloon-keeper. When the gang was captured and taken to the scene of the crime, the men of Szabófalva were stunned to find two of their own among the criminals. The enraged crowd lynched them on the spot for having committed an unpardonable sin and for bringing shame on their village.[704] Since the village council dealt with all manner of serious wrongs and conflicts in the Csángó settlements, it has only been since the

---

701 Kotics, József: Erkölcsi értékrend és társadalmi kontroll néhány moldvai csángó faluban [Moral value systems and societal control in some Moldovan Csángó villages], In: Mások tekintetében. Miskolc, 2001, p. 32.

702 Imreh – Szeszka: A szabófalvi ... op. cit. p. 201.

703 Ibid, p. 201.

704 Ibid, p. 202.

middle of the 20th century that they have begun to turn to the government courts.

Up until the 1962 collectivization, everyone in their villages had to relate the same way to the model of moral norms and behaviours held to be the correct and exemplary. Every local community continually evaluated every detail of an individual's life and reserved the right to intervene at any time. The people in a Csángó village were able always to gain insight into the lives of their neighbours, thus having very detailed information about each others' lifestyle. By day, every action and saying of an individual was observed by neighbours; by night, God did the observing. Thus, with the power of public opinion, the village communities punished transgressors with the severity of social rule. Those persons who deviated, the villages most often resorted to such 'handling', which primarily shamed the guilty person and family. Secondly, the aim was to replace the equilibrium of local social order. The process against the sinners usually took place in public before the village community. Until the mass migration at the end of the 20th century, individuals accepted without reservation the verdict of the local community and related to their actions in a manner expected by the community: they admitted to stepping outside the community's accepted standards and felt *shame* at the public punishment meted out. They thus internalized the community's judgemental opinion.[705]

In most villages, persons found guilty of deviation were severely marginalized and mocked but were reaccepted back into the community after having concluded their punishment. Only in the most serious cases were persons expelled from the community. A most effective means of punishment for one who overstepped the societal rules was – gossip. A man or woman carrying on a sexual relationship outside of marriage soon became the talk of the village. Since everybody was on guard to uphold their good name and reputation, they went to great lengths to avoid being the general topic of conversation. A husband or wife having an affair was usually castigated by the priest from the pulpit during Sunday Mass. The Roman Catholic church was poorly organized in Moldova to the end of the 17th century, hence many Catholics adopted the looser lifestyles prevalent among the Orthodox families (e.g.- men could simply leave their families and take another wife). With the gradual establishment of the Church during the 18th-19th centuries, replacing the institutionalized lax morals, the leadership of the church and its representatives took a more serious leadership position in the eyes of the parishes. The priests strictly condemned the age old practise of the abduction of girls [elopement, really-*Ed.*], the young men who indulged in it were excommunicated.[706]

---

705 Heller, Ágnes: A szégyen hatalma. Két tanulmány [The power of shame. Two studies]. Budapest, 1996.

706 Pilat: Aspecte ... op. cit. pp. 94.

The Roman Catholic families placed great value and attention to have their daughters retain their purity until their marriage. If a girl hid from her fiancée the fact that she was no longer a virgin and it became apparent on their wedding night, the husband was entitled to send her packing back to her parents, similar to the Orthodox practise. This was also ritualized with an intent to shame: the girl, in a torn shift, was tied atop a harrow made of thorns – drawn by a donkey – and transported back to her parents' house. A great shame to fall on a family – in the eyes of the village. The duped husband usually demanded an increased dowry from his father-in-law, normally in the form of money and livestock. Later, at home, he would thoroughly chastise his wife – whom he would also mistreat later on – and attempt to wring from her the name of the man. In most cases, his vengeance was more focused on the other man, who was seen as a rival, than on his wife. The young man, so deeply injured in his self respect, could, at times, physically destroy his perceived competitor.[707] In Klézse, an Orthodox man only found out on his wedding night that his Csángó bride was no longer a virgin, sending her packing back to her parents, only taking her back when she converted to the Orthodox faith.[708] These days, the usual practice in Moldova is that those who reject the mores of the Roman Catholic communities normally leave and become Orthodox.

If it became known in a village that a young man and girl were having a sexual relationship, until recently, they could expect to be humiliated publicly. In Szabófalva, a girl found to be in a sexual liaison was taken to the church steps, had a yoke put around her neck and caned by the priest,[709] as an example for the other girls. If a girl became pregnant, she and the boy had to stand in front of the altar during Sunday Mass, each holding a black candle. In other communities, they had to hold a black cross in their hands during Mass. These public measures were deemed to be a great shame and humiliation. The affected young people had to accept it, else the priest would not sanction their betrothal and subsequent official wedding. The young men refused to accept this humiliating ritual after the middle of the 20th century – it usually fell to the girls to endure it – instead paying a substantial amount to the Church.

In the years after the regime change of 1989, in the following power, ideological and ethical vacuum, the position of the Church in Moldova again solidified. Without naming names, priests continue to reprimand from the pulpit pregnant girls, marginalizing unwed mothers. They

707 Ibid, p. 95.

708 Kotics: Erkölcsi … op. cit. p. 33.

709 Imreh – Szeszka: A szabófalvi … op. cit. p. 206.

become involved in the family life of husbands and wives who quarrel and fight; suicides are not buried with full Church rites.[710]

As a result of modernization, the moral and legal value system has undergone rapid transformation in Moldova. One of the most obvious change is the treatment of women who step over the line. Until 1962, public opinion punished them more seriously than men for any transgression. Earlier, any woman who was seen to frequent a pub was dealt with most sternly. In recent decades, married women are also taking part in the work-migration, leaving children and homes to work as domestics in Italy, Spain, Germany or Israel. This increased frequency of leaving the village confines has lead to the situation where, if girl or woman becomes the topic of conversation for her looser morals, she simply leaves her village – head held high and without any sense of remorse – and pointedly takes up residence with an Orthodox male.

The result of the large scale local mobility is that, not only the younger generation but increasingly other groups as well pointedly reject the overview of local village society. As a consequence of rapid individualization, countless aspects of moral and sexual activity no longer fall within the sphere of public opinion, becoming a private matter in the Moldovan Csángó villages, too. The masses of foreign job opportunities undertaken has exposed the Csángó to a multitude of other cultures, resulting in a fundamental shift of opinion of communities and individuals who think and act differently. This increasingly rapid process, a part of globalization, effectively influence the pluralisation of moral and ethical standards, fundamentally altering the inter-relationship of the various generations and their relationship to the Church. Increasingly, they question in their villages the validity of a faith based value system.[711]

Conclusions

As we stated in the preface, Moldovan social structures to this day retain elements and facets of a pre-industrial society. Family and relatives continue to play a large role in their lives. Even those working abroad are expected to take part in significant family or village events (e.g.- church fairs). The hard earned money, made in distant cities or foreign lands, is most often spent on symbolic goods, hence the rituals demonstrating family unity often quietly consume it.

Due to unique historical, social and economic reasons, the emergence of a civil society has lagged in the region to the very end of the 20th century, which contributed to the prolonged existence of influential structures, effectively hindering the freedom of personal choice and

710 Kotics: Erkölcsi ... op. cit. pp. 44-45.

711 Kotics: Erkölcsi ... op. cit. p. 42.

individual career options. Although governmental and administrative influence waned in their villages after 1989, the role and position of the Roman Catholic Church has strengthened, leading to a one-sided reformation.

Increasingly during the 19th-20th centuries, many such institutions came into being in the Carpathian basin settlements where people with a common interest or point of view could meet (e.g.- musical groups, choirs, women's groups, farmer co-operatives). In Moldova, the governments of the day and church authorities stifled every attempt of organization from the bottom up, essentially impeding and delaying an individual from becoming a free citizen, the emergence of a civil society. A few associations came into being in their villages in the past decades – primarily as a result of outside pressures – but they are not the free gatherings of individuals with similar interests or views, being operated for the interest, and by the contact network, of individual families.

For centuries, the Csángó were used to having their lives dictated by an external authority or power. They accept, with biblical stoicism, their difficult situation and fate, casting a resigned look toward an uncertain future. In their value system, the fundamental goal was the precisely reliable social, economic and political position, which is why they still have a horror of fundamental changes and do not rebel against their lot in life. They live and evaluate their lives, in biblical acceptance, based primarily on the Christian values of the Roman Catholic Church.

In the decade of local and social mobility following the 1989 'revolution', in a relatively short time – and at the same time – such significant forces are operating as the mass migrations due to forced urbanization, rapid class changes, modernization, globalization, cultural and identity shifts. While the traditional folk culture of settlements inside the Carpathian basin was replaced with a new, but Hungarian-language, popular culture, the Csángó who drift away from the traditional Hungarian-language folklore have only the option of living in the Romanian-language mass culture of Moldova. The assimilation espoused by governments and Church powers has been accelerated by the cultural assimilation present with modernization.

The impact of the listed processes has resulted the break-up of many village communities, as individualism spreads, replacing the certainty of traditional lifestyles and values with uncertainty and dread. We can clearly state that the rapid changes that come with globalization and modernization have caught the citizens of Moldova unprepared, that the road to Europe – and its ideal of *fellow citizen* – will be a long and arduous one for the Hungarian Csángó settlements. In our opinion, this fact alone will essentially define, in the decades to come, the results of the modest advocacy and integration attempts of the Moldovan Hungarians.

IX. ADVOCACY EFFORTS OF THE CSÁNGÓ AFTER 1989

Background

The intellectuals living in the Carpathian basin discovered at the end of the 18th century the Moldovan Hungarian communities living outside their borders. This awareness intensified during the 19th century, the time of the creation of a Hungarian nation and culture of civil characteristics, and modest advocacy efforts were drafted with respect to the Csángó. Hungarian lay and clerical intellectuals founded the Society of Szent László in 1861, whose main aim was the religious, cultural and educational care of Hungarian communities outside the national borders. This institution established the Standing Csángó Committee in 1867 and sent special representatives to Moldova.[712]

Since 1920, the Moldovan Csángó and the Transylvanian Hungarians were part of the same country, living within Greater Romania. Since there were desperate battles during the first world war between Romanian and Austro-Hungarian troops in the region inhabited by the Csángó Hungarians, the Romanian government and local administration introduced an intolerant and conscious assimilative policy between the two wars. Their impatience towards the Hungarian communities, and increasing loss of legal rights, escalated after 1940, when northern Transylvania was returned to Hungarian control. In the era between the two wars, it was primarily the ethnographers who brought news of the fate of the Moldovan Csángó.

In the years following the second world war, the Romanian Communist regime temporarily tolerated that the Hungarian People's Alliance of Romanian /HPAR/ (Magyar Népi Szövetség) built and operated a network of Hungarian schools in Moldova. During these years, Hungarian linguists and folklorists from Cluj carried out research among the Hungarian communities in dialects, folk poetry and ethnography. After the 1956 Hungarian Revolution, the now openly nationalistic Romanian Communist leadership nipped in the bud every effort at advocacy: they quickly ended all education in the mother tongue and openly supported the banishment of Hungarian in Church and religious matters. In the final decade of the Ceausescu dictatorship, it was forbidden to print the word 'Csángó' in a Hungarian newspaper or publication. At the same time, the ultra-nationalistic and totalitarian regime used every means at its disposal to prevent meetings

---

712 Hajdú, Demeter Dénes: A Szent László Társulatról [The Society of Saint László], In: Halász, Péter /ed./:

"Megfog vala apóm szokcor kezemtül…" Tanulmányok Domokos Pál Péter emlékére. Budapest, 1993, p.

157.

and connections between the Csángó and the Transylvanian Hungarians; the ethnographers on collecting trips to the Csángó villages were threatened with serious consequences, the houses of local hosts offering them a bed were continually searched.

The unaddressed educational, cultural and advocacy problems of the Moldovan Hungarian communities once again rose to the surface in the years following the 1989 regime change, when the solution to these advocacy efforts became an indicator of the democratization and modernization of the Hungarian political environment. In the past 14 years, the Csángó problem is no longer a topic for Hungarian or Romanian elites, as in the meantime, the European institutions for the protection of minorities have taken note of this isolated Moldovan community, unique in its ethnicity, language, culture and religion.

Institution building

The political and social democratization of Romania still progressed relatively slowly after 1990, presenting difficulties and roadblocks for the lobbying efforts on behalf of the Moldovan Csángó-Hungarians, too. The intolerance and anti-minority attitudes raised to the level of national and party policy during the years of the Ceausescu dictatorship (1965-1989) continued, after 1989, to obstruct and deter the effective lobbying in the interests of the various Romanian national and ethnic minorities. The rapid organization of national minorities caught the majority off-guard and Moldova also saw the emergence of lobby groups taking up the cause for the more important Csángó-Hungarian demands: Hungarian-language education in their villages, the introduction of liturgy and cultural expression tied to folk traditions in their mother tongue.

As it was impossible for an intellectual class to emerge in the Moldovan Roman Catholic villages, the protection of the Csángó-Hungarian culture and dialect - the need for its long term viability and European significance - was primarily advocated by those who had settled in Transylvania. Those Csángó who possessed a more defined Hungarian identity decided on March 25, 1990 to form an organization to protect and advance their interests. The committee appointed by the founders prepared the group's charter and the delegates met on October 20, 1990 in the Kovászna County Library in Sepsiszentgyörgy to form the Asociatia Maghiarilor Ceangai din Moldova (Association of Csángó-Hungarians of Moldova / Moldvai Csángómagyarok Szövetsége /MCsMSz/), which was duly registered in 1991 in Kovászna County. The association's fundamental goal was the protection and representation of the interests of the Csángó-Hungarians of Moldova, the safeguarding and handing down to future generation their traditional culture based on their mother tongue. The lobby became an associated member of the Democratic Alliance of Hungarians in Romania (RMDSz) in 1995. Since 1997, except for a short period when its central offices were in Gyimesbükk (Ghimes Faget), it has operated an information center in the city of Bákó (Bacau).

The lobby group has consistently urged since the early 1990s that, under the terms of the Romanian education laws in effect, the teaching of Hungarian language, literature and culture be made available in the Csángó villages to children whose parents request it in writing. They requested masses in the vernacular for those who proudly bear their Hungarian identity. The group organizes numerous events, which enable the meeting of Moldovan-Hungarians with those from the Carpathian basin, making cultural contacts possible.

A committee of the RMDSz arranged for the publishers of the Sepsiszentgyörgy *Háromszék* daily newspaper to begin the monthly *Csángó Újság* (Csángó Gazette / Gazeta Ceangailor din Moldova). The periodical was begun in March of 1990, in Hungarian and Romanian languages. From the same press, the MCsMSz has been publishing between 1992 and 1998, with minor interruptions, the *Moldvai Magyarság* (Moldovan Hungarians), also in two languages. There was a short, involuntary hiatus beginning in 1998, then monthly publication resumed in January 2000 from the Hargita publishing house in Csíkszereda, with support from the Seklerland Foundation (Székelyföld Alapítvány).

In the years following the events of 1989, several institutions were engaged in providing education to the small children of the Csángó villages in their mother tongue. The Pál Péter Domokos Foundation was officially registered in Csíkszereda on December 4, 1992. Its president, teacher Erzsébet (Elizabeth) Borbáth has, for over a decade, looked after the education, boarding and bursaries for the Hungarian-language education of Csángó students in Csíkszereda and other Transylvanian towns. The Pál Péter Domokos Students Union (Budapest) looks after the interests of high school and university students studying in Hungary. The Charitable Organization of the Hungarian Knights of Malta began a Csángó Information Office and library in 2002. With the support of the Ministry of Education (Budapest), more than ten deserving Csángó students can pursue studies at various Hungarian universities or higher educational institutions.

In the decade since the government change, not only the civil sphere of Hungary but the Hungarian government has also undertaken to remedy the problems and represent the interests of this Hungarian language minority group. Since 1990, an annual Csángó folklore festival and camp is organized in Jászberény, Hungary, which has, in recent years, gradually become the meeting place of the endangered minorities of Europe. Also, an annual Csángó Ball and exhibition has been organized since 1997 in Budapest during the carnival season. The Demeter Lakatos Association has also been active in Hungary since 1990, which, like the 19th century Society of Szent László, coordinates fundamental research into the history, culture and education of the Csángó people. It has undertaken the showcasing of the treasures of the Csángó culture through conferences, publications and exhibitions. The Ince János Petrás Cultural Society of Eger organizes an annual summer camp in Hungary for Csángó children. On November 8, 2003, they affixed a plaque on the wall of the Roman Catholic Religious Institute of Eger, commemorating the birth, 190 years before, of Ince János Petrás, the noted Moldovan priest and folk poetry researcher. The memorial was made by Gergely (Gregory) Csoma, a sculptor and photographic artist.

András (Andrew) Duma, the head of the Klézse local of the Association of Csángó-Hungarians of Moldova, who for a decade after 1989 worked and petitioned for education in the local schools in Hungarian, began a magazine in 1997, *Mi magunkról* (We about Us / Noi despre Noi), which became the publication of the *Szeret Klézse Foundation* after 1999. This institution's first goal is the nurturing of the Hungarian identity of the village children and the passing on of their native culture. The foundation acquired in 1999, and later enlarged and furnished, a property in which effective mother tongue and culture nurturing programs could be organized for young and old, similar to houses operating in the Carpathian basin.

In 1996, the Csángó youth organized the *Via Spei Csángó Ifjúsági Szervezetet* (Csángó Youth Organization of Via Spei), which was officially registered in 1999. Its stated aim was the organization of Hungarian-language education for the young Moldovan Csángó (of Klézse, Forrófalva, Pusztina and Újfalu) and the reinforcement of their Hungarian identity. They have organized countless camps, seminars, technical outings to parts of Moldova and Transylvania where the young people become acquainted with the world-class aspects of Csángó and Hungarian culture. The *Szent István Egyesület* (Saint Stephen Society), started by Tinka Nyisztor, started its activities in Pusztina in the past three years, staking out as its goal the introduction of Hungarian-language liturgy, as well as organizing instruction based on native language folklore and tradition.

Over the past few years, those Moldovan Csángó who, in the years after 1989, have been studying abroad in Transylvanian or Hungarian institutions have been gradually returning. These young people suggested and organized groups and associations aimed primarily at keeping local customs alive and well, independent of the weight of the majority's opinion. In Külsorekecsin and Somoska, they organized camps and festivals for those young people of Romania, Hungary - and the world beyond - who wish to become acquainted *in situ* with the archaic aspects of Csángó folklore: classical folk ballads, lyrical songs, folk music and dance, textile arts, etc. In Pusztina, they organized village festivals where the locals could become better acquainted with not only their own traditions but also that of the Hungarians of the Carpathian basin.

A notable event occurred in the life of the Moldovan Hungarian-Csángó in November of 2003, when modest steps were taken toward the creation of a political organization. Although the RMDSZ has grass roots membership in 42 Moldovan settlements, a majority of those present during the November 8 general assembly, called together in Bákó, decided to form a Bákó County arm of the RMDSZ. The vice-presidents of the RMDSZ for Education and Youth Affairs, Gyula (Julius) Szép and Bálint (Valentin) Porcshalmi, were present at the meeting. The 24th regional organization of the RMDSZ proposed that the Moldovan Csángó-Hungarians take part in Romanian public administration in proportion to their success in the 2004 local elections.

On November 21, 2004 and in front of a large assemblage, a statue of King Saint Stephen, created by Gergely Csoma, was dedicated in the center of the village of Pusztina, in the church square. The 10 ft. carved wooden statue carried the following inscription: SZENT ISTVÁN REX HUNGARORUM 975-1038, SFINTE STEFAN ROAGA-TE PENTRU NOI – SZENT ISTVÁN KÖNYÖRÖGJ ÉRETTÜNK [Saint Stephen, King of Hungary 975-1038, Pray for Us]. The creation of the statue was the collective work of Marcel Bartos, *Szent István Egyesület*, Kallós Zoltán, *Lakatos Demeter Egyesület*, *Magyar Kollégium* and local farmer, József (Joseph) Eross. As the parish priest of the village, Eugen Deac, ultimately did not make an appearance at the event, the village chaplain blessed the statue after the morning Mass. After his departure, the women of Pusztina sang Hungarian-language religious songs about King Saint Stephen, were addressed by the president of the Association of Csángó-Hungarians of Moldova, Szilvia Róka, the leader of the Saint Stephen Society, Tinka Nyisztor and the secretary of the Demeter Lakatos Foundation, who dwelled on the significance and importance of the event. Finally, it was drawn to a close with the singing of the Hungarian national anthem.

Initiatives towards the introduction of native language education

Countless Csángó living in Moldova after the events of 1989 felt that, as part of the emergence of democratic institutions, once more a possibility arose for the introduction of education in their native tongue (similar to the period between 1945 and 1958). In many of the Csángó villages (e.g.- Szabófalva, Lészped, Pusztina, Klézse, Gyoszén), some people who possessed a stronger sense of Hungarian identity organized weekend classes in their own homes for the children. In short order, the authorities ruthlessly swooped down on these modest initiatives outside the educational system. In Szabófalva, for example, the language classes organized by history teacher Mihály (Michael) Perka were deemed to be illegal and unconstitutional, banned and its participants were continually pestered and intimidated by the authorities. Another case in point, in Lészped, the local farmers and workers organized the Hungarian-language instruction for the village children. Their activities were continuously interrupted by the local and county police forces; their work made impossible by various means, such as: a campaign in the local press to discredit them, numerous summons to appear before the police, the use of verbal aggression, etc. The organizers and parents were sufficiently intimidated that these initiatives quietly disappeared.

Consequently, the political elite of the majority, striving for the rapid and compulsory assimilation of the Csángó, was unwilling to accept - even after 1989 - that an ethno-cultural and religious minority existed in Moldova, which had a fundamental, communal right to use its native language in church and school. Since the authorities made it impossible for any grass roots initiative to succeed, the MCsMSz called for a meeting in Klézse on April 25, 1995, to discuss the institutionalized establishment of native language education and cultural activities. The organizers invited the executive president of the RMDSZ, along with the vice president of cultural and religious affairs. The extremist political parties in Bákó County and the local leaders of the Roman Catholic Church decided to use every means possible to prevent the discussions from taking place. The priests, for example, spread a rumor that the activists of the RMDSZ will try to convert the Roman Catholic Csángó to Protestantism. To prevent Hungarian-language instruction, the school principal mobilized a flock of children. The misled – and in many cases drunk – people stopped the cars of the delegates and invited guests at the outskirts of the village, employed physical and verbal abuse against them, damaged video equipment and burned Hungarian-language school texts found in the cars.

Subsequent to the 1996 Romanian elections, an alliance of the former democratic opposition and the RMDSZ formed the new government. Shortly, the dean of the Babes-Bolyai University of the Sciences in Cluj, Andrei Marga, became Minister of Education. In this new environment, the MCsMSz tried to attain that, at the request of parents, Hungarian language and literature be taught as regular subjects in the state schools of the Csángó villages, as essentially permitted and regulated by decree 3113/2000 of the Romanian Educational Ministry, enacted into law. The law of January 31, 2000, drafted by Undersecretary of State József (Joseph) Köto, went so far as to state that not only parents but organizations representing the rights of a minority may request the inclusion of native language classes into the curriculum of the state schools.

In September of 2000, the parents of seven children petitioned in writing in Lészped, 25 in Klézse, for the introduction of Hungarian-language education. Since the principal of the school in Pusztina refused to accept the petition, the parents also repeated their request individually and in person. The chief school superintendent of Bákó County considered the previously cited ministerial directive a grave mistake, which would open the way for the teaching of Hungarian in Moldova, and he firmly stated that he would never carry out its terms.

A state close to civil war erupted on September 14, 2000 in Klézse when a committee made up of the Hungarian counselor of the Educational Ministry (Attila Sántha), the assistant chief school superintendent of Bákó County, the representatives of the county prefecture and the Ministry of Minorities carried out a local appraisal among those requesting Hungarian-language courses in the school. While the parents continued to hold their former position, the local mayor, the Roman Catholic parish priest and heads of the extremist political parties bought drinks for, and encouraged, a 20-25 group of locals who then resorted to verbal and actual physical aggression in an attempt to intimidate the parents and thus prevent the start of Hungarian-language teaching. In spite of the tense situation, of the 30 former petitioners in Klézse, 13 parents repeated their request to the committee, in Pusztina, nine out of 17, while in Lészped only one out of the original nine maintained their original demand. The committee then concluded that there exists a realistic demand in Moldova for education in Hungarian; the minutes of the meetings were signed by the school superintendent and the prefecture.

Gabriel Andreescu, Romanian president of the Helsinki Committee announced in a press conference on September 22, 2000, that a comprehensive report will be made of the events regarding the situation of the Csángó, after which the Council of Europe will begin its local investigation. The local representative of the human rights committee felt that the event was significant because it allowed the Romanian Educational Ministry and the Minorities Ministry to present to public scrutiny the situation that has developed in Moldova. Romanian Minister of Education, Andrei Marga, made a statement on September 24, 2000 that every condition existed for the ministry to sanction Hungarian-language education in Bákó County. The Romanian press swung into violent counterattack, accusing the Minister of irresponsibly surrendering to Hungarian propaganda through decree 3113, which made native language education possible for all Romanian minorities. The prefecture of Bákó County warned the Prime Minister in writing that the introduction of Hungarian into the schools would create needless ethnic conflicts in the region. On the next day, the Education Minister now stated that the requests of the parents will have to be verified by the county school board.

The officials of the Bákó County board of education re-examined the petition signed earlier by the parents of Klézse so that their children could take Hungarian classes in the village school. The reeve of the county tried to convince the parents to permanently withdraw their earlier petition. Finally, a significant number of the parents withdrew their signatures but not before being threatened with more serious intimidation. In short order, a counter-petition was obtained from 598 persons from Klézse, which stated that it was without foundation to request the introduction of Hungarian language in the local school since all the Csángó, without exception, hold themselves to be Romanian. The document was sent to Emil Constantinescu, asking the President to see to it that in the Moldovan churches and schools the language of the state, i.e., Romanian, would continue to be used. Zsolt Szilágyi, RMDSZ member of the Romanian Parliament, posed a question to the head of the government, expecting an answer regarding the events, according to the standing legal custom, both at home and in Europe generally. The President did not deign to reply to the representative, asking the Ministries of Education and Public Administration to examine the situation.

Faced with the fiasco, the leaders of the MCsMSz decided at a meeting convened in Gyimesfelsolok that they will organize native language educational curriculum, to be held outside the state schools, in private or community buildings, on weekends or afternoons. In the fall of 2000, Attila Hegyeli, a teacher of Hungarian and ethnography, began instructing the local children in the premises of the Szeret-Klézse Foundation. Since there was a relatively large amount of interest in these afternoon classes of Hungarian language, culture and computers, in short order, the parents also began to sign up for these alternative educational courses. This program, organized by the MCsMSz, was directed, professionally and administratively, by the Association of Hungarian Teachers in Romania, and supported financially by the National Cultural Heritage Ministry [Nemzeti Kulturális Örökség Minisztériuma /NKÖM/ (Budapest)]. This form of instruction was continued in Klézse in the fall of 2001, while making it also available in Somoska, Pusztina, Trunk, Külsorekecsin and Gyoszén.

On November 14, 2001, when the Ministerial Commission of the Council of Europe drafted its position paper regarding the Csángó, the authorities of Bákó County took harsh steps against the native language instruction organized in the Csángó villages. The assistant of the chief school superintendent, several department heads, the mayor and deputy mayor of Klézse, the local chief of police and the principals of the local schools took part in this action of intimidation. The Klézse families were all 'invited' to appear at the police station where they were threatened with searches of their premises and fines if they made their premises available for these extracurricular classes or provided room and board for the teachers who came from Transylvania. The chief school superintendent swore that if the local curriculum was not acceptable, they could all move to Hungary. The following day, the school board visited Pusztina where they inspected the room in the home of Jeno (Eugene) Bilibók where the Hungarian class was held. Although the young teacher was not at home, the visitors took away several of his Hungarian-language books. Interestingly, the Transylvanian parents of those teachers taking part in organizing shortly received visits from the Seklerland police.

While the Romanian Foreign Ministry announced that, at the November 14 session in Strasbourg, the Ministerial Commission of the Council of Europe accepted EU Parliamentary recommendation 1521 regarding the protection of Romanian Csángó culture, the head of the Bákó County prefecture also made a visit on November 16 to Klézse. There, he visited all the private dwellings which provided rooms for the extracurricular classes, being mainly interested in the textbooks used by the Transylvanian teachers. Though asking for health certificates and operating permissions, he also took from the private houses several history books published in Hungary. At the written request of the prefecture, the officials of the Bákó County Public Health Office appeared in Klézse on November 19, 2001, where they inspected all the sites of the extracurricular classes. They concluded that neither the community hall nor the private residences met the legal requirements for public health, hence they were temporarily closed for any educational activity. While they were engaged in doing that, in Bákó County there operated 223 public schools totally without any health certificates. Not one of them has been closed since, either. At the same time, heavy fines were promised if Hungarian classes were resumed without the necessary renovations and permissions. On November 21, the Romanian press announced that the examination requested by the school principals of Klézse was completed. It thus became evident that the lack of health certificates was merely an excuse for the authorities to put a stop to the extracurricular native language afternoon and weekend classes. The head of the program and the vice president of the MCsMSz were officially cited to appear before the Bákó County school board on November 29. There, they tabled an application, signed by 37 parents, for permission to use a school room in one of the public schools for the afternoon classes. The committee, headed by the chief school superintendent, eventually came to the conclusion that the organizers of the program were only negligent in obtaining all the necessary permits.

On December 7, 2001, at the written request of the Bákó County school board, the police in Klézse again cited the Hungarian teachers, as well as their hosts and landlords. During the aggressive interrogation, the police focused on finding out if the teachers were staying legally in the village. The extracurricular language classes and activities continued quietly after the intimidating acts until finally the leaders of the MCsMSz decided to obtain all the necessary official permits to legally continue the classes. While this was going on, the county school board brought a suit in Bákó against the

Szeret-Klézse Foundation to permanently cease its operations as a result of the 'illegal' native language educational activities. The county school board also brought a similar suit in Kovászna County against the Association of Csángó-Hungarians of Moldova /MCsMSz/ on the grounds that the advocacy group illegally organized native language instruction for Csángó children.

The Social-Democratic Party of Romania, the currently governing party since 2000, are intent in integrating Romania into Western European defense and political institutions. However, to achieve the desired, spectacular foreign policy results, the expectations of Western European bodies regarding the solution of the minority problem must be carried out unequivocally, precisely and consistently. To this end, the governing party came to an agreement in 2002 with the RMDSZ (an organization created as a political advocacy group for the Hungarians of Romania), in which they agreed to set up a committee of experts from both sides to search for solutions toward ensuring native language education for the Moldovan Csángó. The leaders of the MCsMSz decided in a March 1, 2002 meeting in their Bákó offices to henceforth have parental requests, for including Hungarian in the curriculum of the public schools, officially notarized.

In the first week of May 2002, Béla Markó, the president of RMDSZ, leading an official, high-level RMDSZ delegation, visited the Csángó inhabited villages to compile an inventory of the concerns of the Csángó-Hungarian communities, and to search for solutions. At an open forum organized in the Szeret-Klézse Foundation headquarters, many Csángó came from neighboring villages, with many posing the question how to energize the economic plane of the region. On May 2, the delegation carried on talks in the Bákó prefecture regarding the native language education. The parties intended to honor the principles and spirit of the cooperative agreement between the governing Social-Democratic Party and the RMDSZ. The Prefect of Bákó County, the chief school superintendent and his deputy, the executive officer of the Educational Ministry and the vice-president of the Social-Democrats were present at the discussions. The RMDSZ representatives requested from the county officials to severely punish those teachers who intimidate those children wishing to learn Hungarian. They further, asked that county officials cease their harassment of Hungarian organizations and foundations. The two sides agreed that in Klézse and Pusztina, there were adequate number of signed, and notarized, requests for the school board to ask the Education Ministry for permission to include Hungarian in the curriculum. On June 13, the Education Ministry consented to the notarized request of the Klézse and Pusztina parents and instructed the Bákó County school board to take the necessary steps to begin native language classes in the Fall. In September, 2002, Attila Hegyeli started native-language classes with a class of 17 in Klézse, Jeno Bilibók with a class of 24 in Pusztina - in a classroom in the local public school. In both of the villages, Hungarian classes could only be held outside of regular school hours, i.e., between 7-8AM, twice a week for combined classes for the school year of 2002-2003.

In June of 2002, the courts in Bákó rejected the suit brought by the county school board against the Szeret-Klézse Foundation. In November, the school board settled out of court with the Foundation in the face of mounting pressure from the Council of Europe. Several months later, in March of 2003, the Court of Appeals in Brassov rendered a final decision, on the third appeal after more than a year of wrangling, denying the school board's request to ban the activities of the MCsMSz.

Beginning in the Spring of 2003, Csángó-Hungarian parents from other communities forwarded notarized requests for Hungarian-language instruction, notifying the county and local educational entities in ample time of the number of requests. A local parish priest became so frightened by the large number of requests that he preached a sermon in Külsorekecsin, in which he called the Hungarian-language instruction a mortal sin. His intolerant speech was undeniably aimed against the inclusion of Hungarian into the school curriculum.

Since the Bákó County school board opted for a passive resistance of inactivity, RMDSZ President Béla Markó made a visit to Bákó at the beginning of July, 2003. he was accompanied by Gyula (Julius) Szép, vice president of education, Árpád Márton, parliamentary representative, and László (Leslie) Szepessy, the head of the organization's executive offices in Marosvásárhely (Tirgu Mures). The RMDSZ delegation and heads of the MCsMSz were met at the county prefecture by Viorel Hrebenciuc, the vice president for Bucharest of the governing Social-Democrats, the county Prefect and the chief school superintendent. Agreement was reached in a rapid and problem free half-hour meeting, whereby, on the basis of requests received, in September of 2003, native language classes can also begin in Frumósza, Külsorekecsin, Magyarfalu, Lészped and Somoska. In early September of 2004, the school board of Bákó County notified the MCsMSz in writing, that Hungarian-language classes can also be started in Diószén and Lábnik.

The Franciscan friar Csaba Böjte, president of the Saint Francis Foundation (Déva), proposed in early 2005 the building of a Hungarian educational center in the outskirts of Rekecsin. On May 15, 2005, the *Regina Pacis School Center* had cornerstone officially laid, immediately after the Pentecostal fair of Csíksomlyó. Pál (Paul) Benke and Szilvia (Sylvia) Róka greeted, on behalf of the Association of Moldavian Hungarian Csángó, the huge crows assembled from Moldova and the Carpathian Basin. Speeches were said by Dalma Mádl, wife of the President of the Hungarian Republic, Gabriel Berca, the prefect of Bákó County, Vasile Ichim, mayor of Rekecsin, Csaba Takács, executive president of the RMDSZ and Csaba Böjte, the moving force behind the school. The assembled throng was then treated to a folklore presentation put on by Csángó Hungarians.

Since the Hungarian teacher, appointed after an official competency examination, was unable to begin her work at the beginning of the 2005-2006 school year, Mihály (Michael) Matekovics, executive director of minority affairs in the Romanian Ministry of Education, visited Bákó County on October 13, 2005. He met with the county school superintendants and visited the public schools of Klézse, Diószén and Magyarfalu where, with the superintendents, he examined the situation and problems facing the teaching of Hungarian as a native language. At the end of the visit, the chief school superintendent stated that, for the next school year, the positions for teachers of the Hungarian language will be officially open for competition, Hungarian language texts will be ordered from the Ministry and continuing education group for Hungarian-language teachers in the county will be organized.

Ultimately, in the 12 settlements of Bákó County, 725 students began to study Hungarian as a native language during the 2005-2006 school year. At the same time, 369 children in 13 villages took part in extracurricular activities; 93 Moldovan Csángó students are enrolled in high schools in Csíkszereda, Bucharest and Székelyudvarhely. A further 10 have begun university studies in Budapest, with the help of bursaries. The Hungarian teachers in the Csángó villages organize annual Hungarian-language events featuring poetry recital, folk songs and storytelling. An anthology, aimed at the small children learning Hungarian, was published by Éva (Eva) Ferencz and Gyöngyi (Pearl) Borsi. Reflecting the success of, and the need for, Hungarian-language education in Moldova is the publication *Reverinda*, published and edited by the Csángó Hungarian-language students.

Steps towards native-language religious practices

The Hungarian oriented Csángó of Moldova began to demand native-language Masses more and more firmly after 1989. Their requests for Hungarian-language liturgy were usually not acknowledged - certainly not answered - but the requesters were intimidated through various means until they withdrew their demands. In August of 1991, a petition signed by 200 people requested the introduction of Hungarian liturgy in their churches. The then auxiliary-bishop, Grigore Duma, quickly put a stop to the initiative. The congregation of Pusztina signed yet another petition in 1998 in which they clearly stated some facts: they are aware of their unclear affiliation, they would like not to become a political or Church problem but they wish to remind that, in light of the more recent European laws and educational traditions, it would seem only right if they too could partake in native-language religious rites. They reminded the Church authorities that, although we are at the end of the 20th century, in the land of the Csángó it is only in secret, and in private residences, that they can participate in Masses celebrated in Hungarian. They felt that their demand is not only just but easy to carry out as the Roman Catholic Poles of Bukovina have always had Masses in their mother tongue. They closed their letter with the words that, until His Holiness approves the beginning of Hungarian-language Masses in their churches, they have no recourse but to continue to pray to God.

The Roman Catholic auxiliary-bishop of Iasi, Gabor Dumitru, and Dean Stefan Erdes met on February 23, 1998 in Bákó with the representatives of the MCsMSz, who wished to present to the prelates a petition signed by 160 people from the parish of Pusztina, asking for Hungarian-language liturgy in their village. The prelate, behaving and speaking in a manner unfitting his position, rudely refused to accept the petition on the implausible ground that each petitioner has to request it individually. At the same time, he questioned the authenticity of the signatures and staunchly maintained that Masses will continue to be celebrated in Romanian in all the churches in his diocese. Two weeks later, two Church counselors and the parish priest of Pusztina visited all the signatories, followed a few days later by Eugen Diac, a local priest. A number withdrew, or denied making, the request. Finally, on April 18, 1998, 80 persons signed a new request (signatures were verified at the signing), which was eventually forwarded to the Papal Nuncio in Bucharest, as well as to the Romanian association for the protection of human rights (APADORCH).

In a letter dated June 20, 1998, István (Stephen) Gergely, Roman Catholic priest of Csíksomlyó, Transylvania, asked the Roman Catholic bishop of Iasi, Gerghel Petru, to allow him to celebrate one Hungarian-Language Mass in the church of Pusztina. Three days later, auxiliary-bishop Gabor Dumitru replied that only they look after the pastoral issues of their diocese and that, since there has never been a complaint from the local population of Pusztina, only external *provocateurs* and agitators have made trouble in the past. „În urma cercetarilor si studiilor facute s-a hotarât ca limba lituurgica în Moldova este limba româna, afara de câteva cazuri izolate."[713] Although the bishop of Iasi did not grant his approval for the Hungarian-language Mass, the priest from Csíksomlyó still held it - in the local pub, on an altar made of planks. The Moldovan bishops found the event to be scandalous and objected strenuously to the archbishop of Alba Iulia, that the Hungarian-language Mass, by a priest from the Transylvanian diocese, rudely infringed on Roman Catholic church law.

The Hungarian-feeling parishioners of Klézse wrote another letter in 1997 to the Moldovan bishop, in which they requested Masses in Hungarian.

---

713 "The local surveys and studies have shown that the language of the liturgy in Moldova is Romanian, with the exception of a few isolated instances."

In their petition, they refer to the Romanian constitution, specifically to article 6, paragraph 1, which guarantees the right of national minorities to protect, cultivate and express their ethnic, cultural, linguistic, religious identity and traditions. As law abiding citizens of Romania, they asked the bishop to authorized one Hungarian-language Mass each week. The prelate did not even deign to reply.

Petru Gherghel took part in a conference of Romanian Roman Catholics bishops held in Cluj in October of 2000, where he deemed the signature collection among the Csángó to be a fraud since, in his opinion, some took advantage of the naïve members of his flock. "These attempts a preposterous, not based on facts. The Moldovan people have never asked for the introduction of Masses in other languages."[714] At the same event, he called the native language of the Csángó a mere jargon (meaning a shameful patois). He stated that he consulted with Pope John Paul II several times in this matter and that the Holy Father has left the liturgy decision completely up to him. He also felt it unfortunate that an organization such as the MCsMSz became involved in the internal affairs of the bishopric since, in his opinion, they do not at all represent the Catholic followers.

Although the Papal Nuncio, Jean-Claude Perisset, had earlier rejected the native-language religion attempts of the Hungarian-Csángó, at his May 2001 visit to Cluj, to the Greek Catholic bishop, he said that he has made local enquiries in Moldova on this topic. At the same time, the Vatican's ambassador to Bucharest did not wish to comment on the recommendations of the Council of Europe regarding the Csángó as, according to him, the position on native-language liturgy is primarily the responsibility of the European body.

Ferenc (Frank) Mádl, President of the Hungarian Republic, made an official visit to the Vatican on October 9, 2001, where he raised the question of the introduction of native-language religious rites for the Moldovan Csángó-Hungarians. After a private audience with Pope John Paul II, the Holy See signaled a willingness, for the first time, to take concrete steps for Hungarian-language religious observance among the Csángó. Commenting on the visit to the editor of the *Krónika,* bishop Gerghel Petru stated: "No one will force us. It is imperative that they consult us in this matter. We will analyze the situation and decide what is to be done."

In the Fall of 2001, over 300 people from Pusztina signed a petition for Hungarian-language liturgy. In response, the bishop's chancery sent a delegation to the scene to realistically gauge the need. Their finding was that the petitioners are drunkards, whose signatures need not be taken seriously. The Pusztina Csángó finally had enough of not receiving a meaningful answer to their request, in fact, to be regarded as unreliable and of loose

---

714 Krónika II. (2000). 253. sz.

morals, on April 12, 2002, about 40 of them journeyed by bus to Iasi. There, auxiliary bishop Aurel Perca was only willing to receive four people from the delegation, questioning the need for the meeting. He also stated that they will publish in writing the diocese's position when bishop Petru will return from his visit to Rome. He also conveyed to those present that, in any decision regarding the Csángó, the Vatican will always consult the position of the Moldovan Roman Catholic bishopric.

In the Roman Catholic Theological Institution of Iasi, a scientific research department was created (Departamentul Cercetarii Stiintifice al Episcopiei Romano-Catolice din Iasi) with the aim of proving scientifically the Transylvanian Romanian origins of the Csángó. As one of the first results, Ion H. Ciubataru, director of the Iasi folklore institute of the Romanian Scientific Academy, published in 1998 the publication titled *Catolicii din Moldova. Universul culturii populare.* The impressively illustrated and expensively published picture book tried to support, making use of one-sided ethnographic data, the Transylvanian Romanian origins of the Moldovan Catholics. The Iasi publishing house of Presa Buna published Volume II in 2002, in which the folk traditions and rites attached to the Moldovan Catholic feast days were examined with similar methods.

In the power vacuum following the December 1989 events, the power, social role and prestige of the Church grew significantly, especially in Moldova. The altered role of the Church was evident in the priests intervening in everyday and private affairs, over-representing itself at significant nationa, political and military programs. After the regime change, Romania craftily arranged its relationship with the Vatican so that the seat of the archbishop became the capital, Bucharest, and not the traditional millenial seat of the Transylvanian Roman Catholics, Alba Iulia. Although close to a million Roman Catholics live in Transylvania and the Partium (outside the Carpathians they are less than 300,000), in 1999 the Pope only visited the Orthodox-majority Bucharest, since the nationalistic Orthodox Church (acting as if it was the state religion) made every effort to make it impossible for the Holy Father to visit His Moldovan or Transylvanian followers. The Ecumenical Mass held in front of the gigantic palace, planned by Ceausescu at the expense of countless innocent lives, was attended by over 500,000 on May 9, 1999. A significant number of them were Moldovan Catholics. The local and international media interpreted this visit as a symbolic rapprochement between the Catholic and Orthodox churches. Hence, we should not be surprised that the request personally handed to the Pope during His 1991 visit to Hungary (requesting Hungarian-language Masses in Moldova) has not been addressed to this day. The diplomats of the Vatican value far more the existence of several hundred thousand Romanian speaking and oriented Roman Catholics, this well after the collapse of

Communism in Eastern Europe, than the reversal of the inexorable assimilation of the Moldovan Csángó.

In recent decades, mass migration from the Moldovan Roman Catholic villages has become the standard, especially to Hungary, Italy and Spain. The changes brought about by the migrant workers and the expectations of the European institutions with respect to Romania's treatment of its minorities has brought about very modest and sporadic results in the region.

Newly ordained priest József (Joseph) Ababei Tampo, born in Lujzikalagor, celebrated his first Mass on June 15, 2002 in Budapest, at which eight Moldovan priests were co-celebrants. The organizers naturally assumed that the guest priests will use Romanian for the liturgy. A month later, the priest was able to say a few words in his mother tongue at the Sunday 'primicila' [first Mass-*Ed.*] organized in the village of his birth. The following day, a Hungarian-language Mass was organized in Lujzikalagor for 150 of the faithful. The Mass was said by József Ababei Tampo, the sermon was preached by Imre (Emeric) Kozma, Apostolic Protonotary and President of the Knights of Malta Caritative Service of Hungary – much to the delight of those present.

In June of 2003, the parishioners of Lujzikalagor could again take part in a Hungarian-language Mass, this time celebrated by Ágoston (Augustine) Palkó, who finished his studies in Alba Iulia. The church, filled to overflowing, was crowded with the relatives of the newly ordained priest, and regulars of the pilgrimages to Csíksomlyó. The sermon was delivered by József (Joseph) Salamon, parish priest of Gyergyóhodos. A week later, it was the turn of Róbert (Robert) Pogár, who graduated from Kaposvár in Hungary, to offer a Hungarian Mass in the village of his birth, Magyarfalu. Although the Mass was not announced by the ringing of the bells, nor accompanied by the sound of the organ inside, close to 200 people listened with rapt attention and teary eyes to the sermon in their mother tongue and the religious hymns taught to the young people by Gergely (Gregory) Csoma. The day was capped by the program of the folk dancers and musicians from Somoska. There was not a hint of trouble at any of the Hungarian-language Masses listed above.

Béla Markó, president of the RMDSZ, sent a letter to the Holy Father in November of 2003, to inform Him that the Council of Europe, in its regulation 1521/2001, specifically mentions the right of the Moldovan Csángó to be able to freely use their mother tongue in religious and educational practice. In his letter, he stressed that the Romanian state has admitted the right of the Csángó to use their native language by permitting the teaching of Hungarian in the public schools of seven villages beginning in September of 2003. with the mediation of Jaques Santer, past president of the European Commission, Pope John Paul II granted a private audience on

November 12, 2003 to Tibor Szatmári, foreign affairs expert of the RMDSZ, at which he delivered Markó's letter. Szatmári brought the Pope's attention to the letter of the King Saint Stephen Association of Pusztina, the petition signed by the 200 villagers of Pusztina, the earlier correspondence between the MCsMSz and the bishop of Iasi, which unequivocally rejects any dialogue with the Hungarian-speaking parishioners of Moldova. Since the Romanian-Hungarian politician was unable to meet with the Vatican's Foreign Minister at the time of his Papal audience, Stephen Biller, representative of the European People's Party, representing the European Christian-Conservative parties, personally handed a copy of Markó's letter and other documentation to Cardinal Jean Luis Tavran.

Tinka Nyisztor, president of the King Saint Stephen Association, requested an audience in November of 2003 with Jean-Claude Parisset, the Bucharest representative of the Vatican, repeating emphatically the desire of the Moldovan Csángó-Hungarians to religious rites in their native language. Attached to the request were copies of previous requests and correspondence. Shortly, and much to everyone's surprise, an affirmative answer came from Nuncio. On November 25, an open and sincere meeting took place at which the Vatican's Bucharest representative thanked them for the 10 years of struggle for the establishment of native language Masses. At the audience, Jean-Claude Perisset expounded that, wherever there are more than 50 expressing the need, they can not be denied native language liturgy. The Nuncio promised the five person delegation that his recommendations will be sent shortly to bishop Petru, and also a copy to the Vatican.

A synod of the Roman Catholic bishops of Moldova was first convened in 2004. Tinka Nyisztor kept requesting for the three years since the synod was announced to have representatives of the King Saint Stephen Association be able to take part. After continual refusal, immediately before the beginning of the synod, they were notified that one person, named by the local parish priest, may address the gathering. Finally, a group of nine left for Iasi, where five were admitted to the affair. Demeter Szocs, a member of the Association, read out the request of the Pusztina populace on November 25, 2004, to the body comprised of more than 300 priests as part of the synod's cultural section. On behalf of the Association, the people of Pusztina earnestly asked for permission for Hungarian-language masses and other rites (e.g.- confessions, marriages, baptisms, funerals) in their parish. In his speech, he stressed that the teaching of Hungarian has already been accomplished in the local state funded public school, which undeniably shows that the locals want native language education and liturgy, that they consistently cling to their Hungarian culture.

As recently as July 13, 2005, Irinel Iosif Iosub, Roman Catholic priest in Pusztina, at the funeral of Katalin László, noted storyteller and balladeer, rebuked and slandered the deceased for her final wish to have the villagers attending her wake listen to her performing Hungarian-language funereal songs from a cassette. The King Saint Stephen Association, seeing the shock of the family and the villagers, reported the events to the Romanian National Anti-Discrimination Council. The organization, at their October 27 meeting, reprimanded the Roman Catholic bishopric of Iasi for denying the native language liturgy requested by the Csángó. As the bishopric rejected the Council's decision, at its next sitting in December, the Council again declared that the Moldovan bishopric discriminated against the Moldovan Csángó, when it denied them Hungarian-language liturgy.

Moldovan Csángó on the European and Romanian political stage

Antal (Anthony) Csicsó, president of the MCsMSz, received an invitation to Brussels in 19976 to a meeting of the Open Assembly of the Cultures of Europe, where he was able to address the body along with the representatives of the European gypsies. It came as something of a shock in the center of united Europe to learn that the Moldovan Csángó are unable to use their native language in either church liturgy or education, although Romania was first to sign the 1995 agreement in Strasbourg on the protection of minority rights. During the introductions, Nicola Girasoli, a Vatican diplomat who established the Brussel foundation for studying minority rights, 'Promoting Studies and Knowledge of Minority Rights', immediately took note of the turbulent past and cruel present of the Moldovan Csángó community.

At the urging of Father Girasoli, a Bucharest historian, Valentin Stan, and Renate Weber, a human rights expert and a member of the Helsinki committee of Romania, prepared a study on the origins, the past and the present of the Moldovan Csángó. The superficial and biased booklet was presented in 1998 in Budapest, in the presence of the President of the Hungarian Republic, the Papal Nuncion and a number of diplomats and politicians. At the event, Vilmos (William) Tánczos, a professor at the university in Cluj, drew attention to the inconsistencies and superficiality of portions of the publication written by the Romanian authors.

In January of 1999, the Regional Committee of the European Union, with the assistance of the Yehudi Menuhin Foundation, invited the president and vice-president of the MCsMSz to the series of programs whose topic was the endangered minorities, where Lord Menuhin said: "The smaller cultures must be protected, be they sovereign states or European minority cultures such as the Moldovan Csángó, the Bulgarian pomaks [Muslim Bulgarians- Ed.] or the gypsies, whose home can be found in many European countries." During the event organized in Brussels, there were exhibits, publications, videos and presentations of the traditional Moldovan Csángó culture.

242

Madame Tytti Isohookana-Asunmaa, parliamentary member of the Council of Europe, formerly the Finnish Minister of Education, visited the larger Moldovan Csángó settlements in July of 1999. She wrote her experiences and conclusions in an eight point report. She thought it important to state which fundamental human rights are due to the Csángó. She encouraged the introduction of native-language in the schools and the church liturgy. The commentary of the Finnish reporter was vehemently rejected in the cultural and educational committee of the Council of Europe by the Romanian representative and the Roman Catholic archbishop of Bucharest. Both were of the opinion that the report formed a fundamental part in the subversive campaign to Hungarianize the region inhabited by the Csángó.

On February 15, 2000, Zsolt Németh, political Under-secretary of the Foreign Ministry of Hungary, accompanied by József (Joseph) Köto, Romanian RMDSZ Under-secretary of the Ministry of Education, made a visit to Csángóland where they visited, in Klézse, the community center provided by the Szeret-Klézse Foundation. During his visit, the politician confirmed that the Hungarian state is paying particular attention to, and will continue to support, the self-preservation efforts of the Moldovan Hungarian-Csángó community. On August 19, 2000, US ambassador to Romania, James Rosapepe, visited the Csángó villages. The authorities of Bákó County did their utmost to prevent the representatives of the MCsMSz from getting close to the ambassador. The leaders of the Csángó association were surrounded by a ring of aggressive and contrived people, until finally, it took police intervention to free them from the hostile crowd. In September of 2000, the Portugese Secretary-General of the Educational and Cultural Committee of the Council of Europe, Joao Ary, visited Moldova, accompanied by József (Joseph) Komlósy, vice-president of the Federative Union of European Nationalities (FUEN). During their trip, they met with the leaders of the MCsMSz, ordinary farmers of Pusztina and Klézse, as well as the heads of Bákó County's administrative, political, educational and cultural life. During his visit, the politician was deeply astounded that the local authorities in no way fulfill the laws already accepted and ratified by Romania; in many places intimidating the parents – along with their children – petitioning for native-language education and liturgy. The Portugese expert made a report of the data gathered during his visit, which he later presented to the Educational and Cultural Committee of the Council of Europe.

In the presence of local, county and state political, administrative, educational and religious representatives, the Dumitru Martinas Federation was established on March 17, 2001 in Bákó. The organizers exhorted those present in the most aggressive terms to prevent by every means, or at the very least restrict, the right of organization of the Csángó-Hungarians, the open acknowledgement and organized manifestation of their identity. The organizers were actually attempting to send a message to the European institutions that there is no place in Moldova for petitions for native-language education or liturgy, since the Csángó are basically of Romanian origin. The Federation has, in the meantime, published numerous propaganda publications of dubious value and quality, all attempting to prove the Romanian origins of the Csángó.

On April 26, 2001, the Committee on Culture, Science and Education of the Council of Europe accepted the draft report in Strasboug of Madame Tytti Isohookana-Asunmaa regarding the protection of the Csángó culture. The report accepted by the committee contained a 10-point practical proposal for the protection of Csángó culture (see appendix A, paragraph 35). The report to the Council of Europe opened the possibility for the 'Csángó question' to be tabled in front of the permanent committee. The Romanian representative present at the session, well known for intolerance and anti-minority sentiments, attempted to categorically deny the mere existence of the Csángó, then tried to prevent the report from becoming an agenda item through heated, aggressive arguments. The Romanian Parliamentary representative, Gheorghe Prisacaru, shortly tabled another report, which purported to state that the Csángó are not really demanding native-language education but that the Transylvanian and Hungarian politicians are creating an artificial, so called-, Csángó question. The Permanent Committee of the Parliamentary General Assembly of the Council of Europe accepted Madame Isohookana-Asunmaa's report in Istambul on May 23, 2001. The body set out its recommendations to Romania in nine points (see Appendix A, paragraph 9). The Romanian representative to the permanent committee eventually voted to accept the report. According to him, the report is beneficial because it refutes all those who attempt to make it seem as if the Csángó are a wholly Hungarian-originated group. The Romanian representative also warned that the document recommends native-language, i.e., Csángó, and not Hungarian-language education. He announced that the Roman Catholics bishopric of Iasi has created a scientific working group, which will draw up a written version of the Csángó language (!!).

On November 14, 2001, the Ministerial Committee of the Council of Europe issued a position paper regarding the protection of the cultural traditions of the Csángó living in Moldova. In it, the body urged support for native-language education and liturgy, as well as welcoming the Holy See's attempts to supply the Csángó settlements with parish priests who spoke the language, ultimately an attempt to ensure Csángó-language liturgy. According to the document, the parents living in the Csángó hamlets must receive all necessary information regarding the education of their children. An adequate number of government paid teachers must be ensured who will instruct in the native language, as well as the necessary number of school rooms. The executive committee of the Strasbourg body reinforced the June recommendations of the Parliamentary General Assembly of the Council of Europe.

The members of the Romanian Human Rights Committee and representatives of the Pro-Europe League made a visit to Bákó County in December of 2001 to check on the incidents of ill-treatment reported earlier by the MCsMSz. In the report written after their visit to the affected locales, they emphatically stated that there is a consciously directed, well thought out, assimilative influence being exerted on the Moldovan Csángó-Hungarians. Active in this pressure are not only the local administration and the Interior Ministry but also the Roman Catholic Church and the media. They clearly stated in their report: their national minority status must be acknowledged, they must have representation in the Romanian Parliament and they must be free to determine their identity in the 2002 census.

At the December 10-11, 2001 session of the Committee on Culture, Science and Education in Paris, the Romanian parliamentarian, Gheorghe Prisacaru, although greeting the November recommendations of the committee in diplomatic terms, rejected in no uncertain terms the incorporation of the Moldovan Csángó with the Hungarians. He encapsulated the Romanian point of view in a separate text.

The Pro Minoritate Foundation and the Foundation for the Protection of National and Ethnic Minorities of Central Europe organized an international conference in Budapest on February 15, 2002, dealing with the endangered situation of European minorities. As part of the conference, Madame Isohookana-Asunmaa, Finnish representative of the Council of Europe, made a presentation on the preservation of Moldovan Csángó culture. She reported that the Council of Europe is paying particular attention to the European Gypsy and Yiddish communities, as well as the efforts made on behalf of the Aroman, the smaller Ural peoples and the Moldovan Csángó. She stressed that the archaic quality of the Csángó culture represents a unique treasure, which makes its preservation and passing on such an important duty.

As part of the Sixth Csángó Festival, organized on February 16, 2002 in Budapest, various tradition preserving groups took to the stage. At the closing speech of the festival, Ferenc (Frank) Mádl, President of the Hungarian Republic, handed a young and older Pusztina couple the symbolic Hungarian Identity Card.

The Ministerial Committee of the Council of Europe accepted, in March 2002, Resolution CMN (2002) 5 of the implementation of the Framework Convention for the Protection of National Minorities by Romania, which, although it praised the efforts made by Romania in the area of minority rights, firmly and unequivocally stated that the authorities in Bucharest must make further steps in coming up with a solution to the

Csángó question, as the members of this community are not able to enjoy those rights, ensured by law, as are available to other minorities.

A census was held in Romania beginning on March 18, 2002. On the questionnaire, the ethnicity of *Csángó* was one of the choices available. Preceding this important event, Bishop Petru circulated a carefully worded letter in an attempt to influence the freedom of choice among his flock in answering the identity question. The letter contained veiled references and allusions. "Crestinii catolici nu trebuie sa uite nicicând ca limba pe care o vorbesc nu este un monopol al numanui, este un instrument daruit de Dumnezeu, asa încât ei o vor folosi pe aceea care le este proprie, care le da satisfactia participarii la celebrarile comunitare si care îi uneste cu cei din jur si îi face utili societatii."[715] The prelate was essentially urging the people to declare themselves as Romanians in the upcoming census. The national president of the RMDSZ protested at a press conference that in Pusztina the census enumerators refused to accurately record the answers of people who declared themselves to be of Hungarian ethnicity and having Hungarian as their mother tongue.

Thus, the events of 2002 were a repeat of those of 1992 when the representatives of the bishop of Iasi and the local parish priests emphatically directed the population of Szabófalva to be enumerated as Roman Catholic Romanians. A few days later, the congregations were threatened that, if they declared themselves as Hungarians, a situation similar to 1940 could emerge, when it was proposed to strip Hungarians of their civil rights and deport them from Moldova. Heated verbal exchanges took place during March, 2002 in Pusztina between the enumerators and the registrants because the officials refused to record – there and then – the registrants' Hungarian ethnicity and mother tongue.

The Romanian Academy organized a seminar on April 29, 2002 under the title *The cultural identity of the Moldovan Roman Catholics* in the capital's Parliament building. Collaborating organizations, at very high levels, were the Romanian Educational and Research Ministry (Ministerul Educatiei si Cercetarii), the Dumitru Martinas Association (Asociatia Romano-Catolicilor „Dumitru Martinas"), the Romanian Research Institute of Covasna-Hargita counties (Centrul European de Studii Covasna-Hargita) and the Roman Catholic bishopric of Iasi (Episcopia Romano-Catolica Iasi). The funds for the event came from the government's Information Ministry (Ministerul Informatiilor Publice). The organizers of the conference

---

715 "The Roman Catholic christians must never forget that the language spoken by them is not the exclusive monopoly of anyone but is an instrument granted by God, hence they will use that which is theirs, with the aid of which they are able to take part in the Masses celebrated for the community, which binds them with their neighbours and makes them productive in society." (See Lumina Crestinului XIII. (2002). 3 (147).)

attempted to send an unmistakable message to Strasbourg: the current Romanian historians and ethnographers are trying to prove the Romanian origins of the Moldovan Csángó, thus, they wish to sway the Council of Europe from its previously taken position. At the same event, they released the figures gathered in Moldova by the Bucharest University of Sciences and the CURS public opinion survey company, which purported to show that the majority of the Csángó felt themselves to be Romanians. The conference was by invitation-only. Not one researcher was invited to the event who saw the origins of the Csángó in a different light from the organizers. It was only after the resolute actions of the RMDSZ parliamentary representatives that the representatives of the MCsMSz were allowed into the site. Lajos (Louis) Demény, an associate member of the Hungarian Scientific Academy and a historian, living in the Romanian capital, was only permitted the opportunity of a short address.

As a result of the pressure applied by the stern tone of the Council of Europe's recommendations, the Romanian Academy and the lower house of the Parliament organized another 'scientific' conference on July 4-5, 200, in the Europe Hotel in Iasi, dealing with the origin, language and culture of the Moldovan Csángó. Madame Tytti Isohookana-Asunmaa, the Council of Europe's Csángó expert, and Joao Ary, Secretary-general of the EC's Scientific and Educational Committee, were present. The conference was moderated by Mihai Baciu, Romania's representative to the Council of Europe. Ion Iliescu, President of Romania, and Nicolae Vacaroiu, president of the upper house of the Parliament, greeted those present. Valer Dorneanu, president of the lower house of the Parliament, and Gerghel Petru, Roman Catholic bishop of Iasi, made their views known to the assembly in person on the topic of the conference.

The organizers provided time for more than 15 Romanian participants but only three Hungarians (Vilmos (William) Táczos, professor at the University of Cluj, Lajos (Louis) Demény, historian from Bucharest and András (Andrew) Bartha, president of the MCsMSz). In the extremely belligerent debates, András (Andrew) Duma, Tinka Nyisztor, Ferenc (Francis) Pozsony, Csaba Sógor and Sándor (Alexander) Szilágyi were permitted short remarks. Certain of the Romanian presenters attempted to prove – using historical, ethnographical, linguistic, sociological and physical anthropological means that echoed Fascist methods – the origin-myth attributed to Dumitru Martinas and his amateurish book, namely that the ancestors of the Moldovan Csángó were essentially more or less Hungarianized Romanians from Transylvania.

The president of the Dumitru Martinas Association, Gheorghe Bejan, having no political affiliations to constrain him, frankly and bluntly summed up the opinion that the Council of Europe fell victim to Hungarian propaganda when it wrote and approved the recommendations regarding the

Csángó, whereas the Roman Catholics of Moldova are Romanians – and have always been so – and actually take offense if they are taken for a Csángó.

As the organizers held the Hungarian participants to be the greater source of possible conflict, their presence, opinions and influence were intentionally channeled between predetermined boundaries. At the end of the conference that produced no narrowing of the differences, the organizers took the participants to two northern Csángó villages where the Romanian language and identity are a palpable reality, the result of the assimilative pressures of the 20th century. In Szabófalva, anti-terrorist units of the armed forces kept the locals, dressed in their colorful folk costumes, far away from the visitors. Then, the western European and Hungarian visitors were treated to a massed performance in the overfilled Roman Catholic church hall, reminiscent of the megalomaniac Ceausescu era and its cast of thousands. While the crowd and the placards on the wall declaimed, "We are Romanian!", the school children chanted mocking ditties, reminiscent of Fascist practice, that there was something wrong with the Csángó chromosomes. The organizers of the tightly scripted event were, in essence, sending a message to the Council of Europe: if the Csángó are all Romanians already, then education and liturgy in their mother tongue is already being provided. Ergo, the offer is pointless.

On October 3, 2005, Pál (Paul) Benke, vice-president of the Moldavian Csángó-Hungarian Association /MCSMSZ/ met in the Information Office of the EU with members of the European Center for Minority Issues. During the meeting, among positive achievements, he listed the introduction of Hungarian as a native language in the public schools. At the same time, he stressed that effective cooperation was not able to be established with the principals and teachers of several schools and that an aggressive media anti-campaign in the local papers was having a detrimental effect. The vice-president also raised an objection against the continued deflection of the request for the introduction of Hungarian-language liturgy in their churches. He noted that the local representatives of the Roman Catholic Church most often react with hostility toward any events organized for the cultivation of the Hungarian language or traditions. In the same EU Information Office, Gheorghe Bejan and Anton Cosa, representing the Dumitru Martinas Association of Bákó, expressed their view that the linguistic assimilation of the Csángó was a normal process, since they were Romanians, anyway, and that at the last census, very few people in Bákó County declared themselves to be ethnic Hungarians.

Conclusions

248

The attempts outlined above to protect minority civil rights clearly show that the Romanian authorities, at the turn of the 20th-21st century, have not the least intention of coming to a long term accommodation with its minorities. Instead of a precisely written and codified 'social contract', forming a workable and verifiable base, it tends to lean towards empty agreements, which can be renegotiated from time to time, or used for coercion, or simply overridden.

At he same time, any advocacy initiative must be cognizant of the fact that, over the course of the centuries, the Csángó-Hungarians have become an essential part of the Romanian economic, social and cultural landscape. "The aim – to preserve the Moldovan Csángó community – can not be assured by external initiatives. Any change will only have a positive outcome if the impetus comes from within."[716]

As all the local civil institutions underwent a critical change in the years after the 1989 regime change, only the Church was able to retain its wider social support in Moldova, as elsewhere. In my opinion, it is only a fundamental reassessment of the Roman Catholic Church's policy toward the Csángó that can ensure fundamental change toward the retention of the Hungarian language in Moldova. The protection of the traditional Csángó culture, based as it is on an archaic version of Hungarian, is not, however, the duty of only the Transylvanian and Hungarian intellectuals. The ancient language variant spoken by the Csángó communities and their traditional culture represents a cultural value befitting, and enriching, all of Europe.

When broad social coalitions worldwide unite to provide protection for endangered plant and animal species, and celebrated Parisian actresses lobby on behalf of the stray dogs of Bucharest, then surely it must be the mission of every intelligent European and Romanian person to protect and ensure the survival of the traditional Csángó culture.

---

716 Kapalo, James: Közelebb a csángókhoz [Closer to the Csángó]. Muvelodés XLVI. 3., 1994, p. 31.

APPENDIX

Csango minority culture in Romania

Doc. 9078
4 May 2001

Report
Committee on Culture, Science and Education
Rapporteur: Mrs Tytti Isohookana-Asunmaa, Finland, Liberal, Democratic and Reformers' Group

For debate in the Standing Committee see Rule 15 of the Rules of Procedure
Pour débat à la Commission permanente – Voir article 15 du Règlement

Summary

The Csangos are a non-homogeneous group of Roman Catholic people of Hungarian origin. This ethnic group is a relic from the Middle Ages that has survived in Moldavia, in the eastern part of the Romanian Carpathians. Csangos are associated with distinct linguistic peculiarities, ancient traditions, and a great diversity of folk art and culture. For centuries, the self-identity of the Csangos was based on the Roman Catholic religion and their own language, a Hungarian dialect, spoken in the family and the village community.

Today only 60,000 – 70,000 persons speak the Csango language. To try to preserve this example of Europe's cultural diversity the Assembly recommends that the Committee of Ministers encourage Romania to support the Csangos through concrete measures in particular in the field of education.

I.   Draft recommendation *[link to adopted text]*

1.   Further to its report on the endangered Uralic minority cultures in Russia and the adoption of Resolution 1171 (1998) the Assembly is concerned about the situation of the Csango minority culture, which has existed in Romania for centuries.

2.   The Csangos (Ceangai in Romanian) are a non-homogeneous group of Roman Catholic people. This ethnic group is a relic from the Middle Ages that has survived in Moldavia, in the eastern part of the Romanian Carpathians. Csangos speak an early form of Hungarian and are associated with ancient traditions, and a great diversity of folk art and culture, which is of exceptional value for Europe.

3.   For centuries, the self-identity of the Csangos was based on the Roman Catholic religion and their own language spoken in the family and the village community. This, as well as their archaic life-style and world-view, may explain their very strong ties to the Catholic religion and the survival of their dialect.

4.   Those who still speak Csango or consider it their mother tongue have been declining as a proportion of the population. Although not everybody agrees on this number it is thought that between 60,000 and 70,000 persons speak the csango language.

5.   Today in Moldavia, the language of the school and the church is Romanian. There is local teaching in Ukrainian and the study of Polish, Roma and Russian as mother tongues. Despite the provisions of the Romanian law on education and the repeated requests from parents there is no teaching of Csango language in the Csango villages. As a consequence, very few Csangos know how to write their mother tongue.

6.   The Csangos make no political demands, but merely want to be recognised as a distinct culture. They ask for assistance in safeguarding it and, first and foremost they demand that their children be taught the Csango language and their church services be held in their mother tongue.

7.   The Assembly recalls the texts which it has adopted on related matters, notably Recommendation 928 (1981) on the educational and cultural problems of minority languages and dialects in Europe, Recommendation 1203 (1993) on Gypsies in Europe, Recommendation 1283 (1996) on history and the learning of history in Europe, Recommendation 1291 (1996) on Yiddish culture and Recommendation 1333 (1997) on the Aromanian culture and language.

8.   Diversity of cultures and languages should be seen as a precious resource that enriches our European heritage and also reinforces the identity of each nation and individual. Assistance on the European level, and in particular from the Council of Europe, is justified to save any particular culture and is needed in the case of the Csangos.

9.   The Assembly therefore recommends that the Committee of Ministers encourage Romania to ratify and implement the European Charter of Regional or Minority Languages and to support the Csangos, particularly in the following fields:

     i.   the possibility of education in the mother tongue should be ensured in accordance with the Romanian Constitution and the legislation on education. In the meantime classrooms should be made available in local schools and teachers working in the villages teaching Csango language should be paid;

ii   Csango parents should be informed of the Romanian legislation on education and instructions should be issued on how to apply for its provisions concerning languages;

iii   there should be an option for Roman Catholic services in the Csango language in the churches in the Csango villages and the possibility for the Csangos to sing the hymns in their own mother tongue;

iv.   all Csango associations should be officially recognised and supported. Particular attention should be paid to the correct registration of the Csango minority at the next official census;

v.   access to modern mass-media facilities should be promoted. Financial support should be given to Csango associations in accordance with the availability of funds, in order to help them to express actively their own identity (in particular through the issuing of a monthly publication and the functioning of a local radio station);

vi.   specific programmes should be set up for the promotion of Csango culture in the context of raising awareness of and respect for minorities. International discussions and seminars of experts should be organised to study the Csangos;

vii.   an information campaign should be launched in Romania concerning the Csango culture and the advantages of co-operation between the majority and the minorities;

viii.   the unique linguistic and ethnographical features of the Csangos should be appropriately recorded;

ix.   the economic revival of the area should be encouraged for example through the establishment of small and medium enterprises in Csango villages.

II.   Explanatory Memorandum by Mrs Tytti Isohookana-Asunmaa

Contents:

Introduction

Who are the Csangos?

Historical background

The language of the Csangos

Folklore and popular ornamental art

The religious aspect

Education

Practical proposals for the preservation of the Csango culture

Appendices :

INTRODUCTION

1.   The term "Csango" (Ceangai in Romanian) is used to identify a non-homogeneous group of Roman Catholic people of Hungarian origin living in Romania. This ethnic group is a relic from the Middle Ages that has survived in the melting potof Moldavia, in the eastern part of Romania. The Csango is archaic Hungarian, in some respects centuries behind our times, with a distinct ethnicity, linguistic peculiarities, ancient traditions, and a great diversity of folk art and culture.

2.   In our rapidly changing world the Csangos are helplessly exposed to the very strong influences of their environment and in particular the village priests and the Romanian local authorities. By now they have reached a late stage of assimilation. What can be done to save this unique Central European heritage, to strengthen this ethnic group and its individuals in their identity?

WHO ARE THE CSANGOS?

3.   The Csangos are one of the most enigmatic minorities in Europe. There is no consensus on who were their ancestors, where they came from, when they settled in Moldavia or how many they are today. Even the origin of the word "csango" is controversial. The only undisputed feature about the Csangos is their strong Roman Catholic faith. They live in western Moldavia (Romania), near the eastern slopes of the Carpathians, in villages around the cities of Bacau (southern group) and Roman (northern group), along the rivers Siret, Bistrita, Trotus and Tuzlau, where they preserve traditional European methods of agriculture, body of beliefs, and mythology, as well as the most archaic dialect of the Hungarian language.

4.   Their number ranges, depending on the definition, from as many as 260,000 (which corresponds roughly to the Catholic population in the area), even if more than two thirds of them cannot speak the language, to as few as a couple of tens of thousands (based on the fact that in the last official census only less than 3,000 persons declared themselves as Csangos).

5.   The Csangos are one of the best examples of the beneficial effects of European cultural diversity. The group has for centuries been living more or less isolated from other areas where Hungarian is spoken, in an area with a Romanian majority. This resulted in the development of a pocket with an individual, most specific culture, interacting with elements of Romanian culture. This is perhaps best illustrated by the folk songs and ballads, which

253

are living and developing even today. They show mainly Hungarian but also Romanian elements. It is well known that many of the European ballads cross the political and ethnic frontiers. One of the last fortresses of this common European ballad-culture is that of the Csangos the study, fostering and conservation of which is therefore a very important task both for Hungary and Romania, as well as for Europe.

6.   The lifestyle of this ethnic group still shows in many respects the marks of the middle Ages. Its folklore and ornamental art flourish even today, achieving new products. The same is true for the folk-tradition, the body of beliefs and mythology.

7.   This culture is today on the verge of extinction. Out of the maximum figure of 260,000 Csangos only 60,000 – 70,000 speak the Csango dialect. Assistance on the European level is needed to save their culture.

8.   For centuries, the self-identity of the Csangos was based on the Roman Catholic religion and the Hungarian language spoken in the family. This, as well as their archaic life-style and world-view, may explain their very strong ties to the Catholic religion. It is not unusual that the Csango, to the question "What nationality are you?" wouldanswer: "I am a Catholic". In spite of this, there appear to be influences from the surrounding Romanians even in the practice of religion. Thus, for example, the Catholics of Moldavia followtheir dead in an open coffin to the grave – an Orthodox tradition.

9.   Their religious life has preserved many elements of the middle Ages. Even elements of pagan rites may be discerned, such as traces of the sun-cult. Their body of beliefs is extremely rich, with many archaic features.

10.   The ethnic conscience of the Csangos is much weaker than that of other Hungarian-speaking ethnic groups. This may have several causes. It may reflect the weakly developed concept of nation among the settlers of the Middle Ages or the fact that their settlements are geographically dispersed, but an important factor has been the self-conscious, policy of assimilation practised over the centuries by the surrounding society and in particular the Catholic Church.

11.   To my knowledge the Csangos or their associations do not express any claim for political autonomy or for the status of an ethnic minority. On the contrary they consider themselves Romanian citizens and are loyal to their country. The fact that many speak a Hungarian dialect does not mean that they feel they are "Hungarians". Those who leave Moldavia and settle on

the other side of the Carpathians or in Hungary do so more for economic than for nationalistic reasons.

HISTORICAL BACKGROUND

12.	Historical, linguistic, as well as ethnographical research and the study of place names have resulted in different interpretations as to the origin of the Csangos. Some researchers believe that they descend from a group of Hungarians who split from the main group before it arrived in the Carpathian basin around the year 900 and others suggest that they descend directly from the Cumans, the Pechenegs or other tribes that settled in Moldavia at the turn of the Century. All these theories are improbable as it is unlikely that any people living there survived the 1241-42 Mongol invasion led by Batu Khan, which swept the whole region.

13.	Some Romanian authors claim that the Csangos are in fact "magyarised" (or "szeklerised") Romanians from Transylvania. This theory has also to be dismissed: it is not conceivable that these "Romanians" could persist in using a "foreign" language after centuries of living in Romania surrounded by Romanian speaking Romanians.

14.	It is therefore generally accepted by serious scholars (Hungarian but also Romanian) that the Csangos have a Hungarian origin and that they arrived in Moldavia from the west. The first groups may have settled there as early as the 13th century, when the Hungarian king Béla IV christianised the people of Cumania and founded a bishopric in Milko but, as we have seen, these are unlikely to have survived the Mongols. It is not before the mid-fourteenth century that evidence is found again of Magyar, Romanian and Saxon settlements in Moldavia.

15.	It is also generally accepted that the first waves of the Csangos were settled east of the Carpathian Mountains, along the strategically important mountain passes, in order to control and defend Hungary from eastern intruders and this could only have been done when the Mongols had lost much of their power. These settlers were later joined by other groups of Hungarians from across the Carpathians, the Szeklers, who either mixed with them or settled in different villages.

16.	Some of the forebears of the Csangos held important posts in the state apparatus of the Moldavian voivodship. The relative freedom of the Moldavian Principality and the fertility of its soil attracted Hungarians seeking their fortunes beyond the borders of the Kingdom of Hungary. For many reasons the connections between the Hungarians of Moldavia and their original homeland were weak. Over time the intelligentsia died out and their status as privileged free peasants was abolished. After the Hungarian Franciscan Order ceased being active all institutionalised forms of Hungarian culture came to an end in Moldavia. Contacts with the Szeklers in Transylvania continued, however sporadic, and some families, for several reasons, continued to cross the Carpathian Mountains to settle in Moldavia until the 19th century. A significant number of settlers came after the massacre of Szeklers in Madefalva in 1764 (the so-called "siculucidium").

THE LANGUAGE OF THE CSANGOS

17.   Whatever can be argued about the language of the Csangos there is no doubt that this is a form of Hungarian which belongs to the Finno-Ugrian family. This ethnic group has been isolated from the Hungarian cultural development. The Hungarian language went through a renewal in the 18th-19th centuries, but this did not affect the language of the Csangos. Their oldest sub-dialect, northern Csango, preserves numerous elements of the Hungarian language of the late middle Ages. It also contains new elements, specific to this language area. The geographical dispersion of the Csango settlements and their relative isolation contributed for a non-homogeneous language although experience shows that the different dialects are mutually intelligible and that those Csangos that still speak their language understand modern Hungarian. The wide proliferation of television aerials for TV Duna, a Hungarian language channel, in Csango villages is an indication that they understand Hungarian.

18.   The Csango dialects offer unusual possibilities for linguistic research regarding the conserving effects of isolation and at the same time, the development of innovations under such circumstances. They also provide a series of informative examples of mutual influence between two languages, belonging to entirely different language families. This Moldavian dialect of the Finno-Ugrian language was enriched by numerous lexical elements of the Indo-European Romanian language. Similarly, there are many Hungarian loanwords in the Romanian dialect of Moldavia, often pertaining to agriculture, handicraft and state administration.

19.   Today in Moldavia, the language of the school and the Church is Romanian. Our former colleague, Senator Dumitrescu, informed me that the Minister of Education also organises teaching in Ukrainian and the study of the mother tongue for Polish, Roma and Russian children in Moldavia. There is however no teaching of Hungarian in the Csango villages. As a consequence, almost all Csangos are illiterate as regards the writing of their mother tongue. The Hungarian language survived for centuries as the language of the family and the village community. The epic culture – of tales

and legends – still rich among the aged people and spread by oral tradition, contributed significantly to the preservation of the language.

20. At present, however, the Csango dialects face extinction and may be wiped out within one or two generations. The disruption of the village community, which in the countries of Central and Eastern Europe has occurred through the 19th and 20th centuries, unsurprisingly affects the villages of the Csangos. The authority of the Romanian language, learned in school, is much higher among young people than that of the impoverished Hungarian, used in the family. Romanian is in a monopoly situation ensured by the official culture and mass media so that young people use the family language less and less in communicating with each other.

21. Without powerful, official support for the Csango mother tongue, a European legacy will doubtlessly disappear, a legacy, which has preserved the cultural development, the elements of the reciprocal influence and of the ethnic symbiosis between Hungarians and Romanians. It should be noted that in the North Csango communities, which are the most interesting from a linguistic and ethnographic point of view, no one under the age of 40 speaks Csango.

FOLKLORE AND POPULAR ORNAMENTAL ART

22. The majority of Csangos are peasants. This fact, along with the strong persistence in the tradition of isolated cultures explains the highly traditional forms of their national costume (embroidery and weaving) and of their ceramics. In recent years, however, the replacement of traditional costumes by factory products is proceeding on a large scale.

23. The folk songs and ballads of the Csangos comprise a rich source of the most archaic strata of Hungarian folk music. Their instrumental music as well as their rich system of dance show many elements shared with those of the neighbouring Romanian villages. The couple's dance and the individual male dance that spread during the Renaissance from Western Europe towards the East did not cross the East Carpathian Mountains. At the same time as the most developed and sophisticated forms of folk dance were created in the Romanian and Hungarian villages of Transylvania east and south of the Carpathians the medieval ring dance and circle dance reached perfection. The Csangos preserve the special varieties of the folk dance of the neighbouring Romanians. There are villages in which one may find more than thirty different folk dances.

24. Among their musical instruments there are such ancient pieces as the bagpipe, lute, trump and the peasant flute with six holes, but they also use the

violin, piano accordion and drum. In some villages Balkan-type bagpipes are used, in other villages an ancient type of Hungarian bagpipes to be found only in Moldavia.

25.   The use of Hungarian vocal folk music, as the tradition of the folk costumes, is associated with poverty. Until recent times, folk songs and ballads of the Moldavian Csangos was the most living dialect of Hungarian folk music. It also preserved some archaic elements of the Romanian folk songs and ballads. The folklore was alive and flourishing, it was developing. There existed a specific repertoire of folk songs for weddings and other significant events, which were not performed on other occasions. New ballads were created to commemorate great events. At present, however, folklore is also on the decline.

THE RELIGIOUS ASPECT

26.   The strong Roman Catholic faith of the Csangos has already been mentioned. It is not by chance that the Roman Catholic Archbishop of Bucharest, the Inspector for religious education and representative of the Bishop of Iasi (the capital of Moldavia) and the great majority of the catholic priests in Moldavia are all of Csango origin.

27.   Until the end of the 16th century there were two Hungarian episcopates in Moldavia. Their function was gradually taken over by a new episcopate in Bacau, while a Franciscan monastery was founded there as an affiliate of the Franciscan province of Transylvania. Due to wars and poverty in the 16th and 17th centuries many Catholic communities in Moldavia lost their priests, some of who were replaced by Italian and Polish monks and priests. In 1884 the episcopate of Bacau was dissolved and an archbishopric was created in Bucharest and a bishopric in Iasi. In 1895 a law prohibited the use of bilingual catechism.

28.   Today the Csangos seek the possibility to sing their ancient religious hymns (in their Hungarian dialect) in the church, as they used to until the 1950s, as well as for mass in Hungarian, which they have never enjoyed. The representatives of the Catholic Church, both in Iasi and in Bucharest, while agreeing on the need to preserve the Csango language, dismiss these requests as having been "invented" by "non religious people" under the influence of Hungarian nationalistic propaganda. We are told by the Bishop of Iasi that those who so wish have the possibility of saying confession in their mother tongue.

29.   The main argument for the use of Romanian in church services is the fact that all the 260,000 Catholics of Moldavia understand it and not all

understand the Csango dialect or Hungarian. Or the other hand the bishopric of Iasi set up a committee, chaired by Professor Despinescu, to study the possibility of making the Csango dialect into a written language and to organise a referendum among the catholic population to find out where there is a demand for religious services in Csango.

30.   There seems to be no justification however for the fact that last year the Bishopric of Iasi forbade a Hungarian-speaking priest (from Miercurea Ciuc) to hold a mass in Hungarian in the church of a Moldavian village inhabited by Csangos, at their request. The mass in question was held in a sort of pub and was followed by almost the entire population of the village.

EDUCATION

31.   Romanian education legislation provides that parents can choose the language of education for their children (art 180 of the 1995 Education law). There are three possibilities: education in Romanian; education in the mother tongue with history and geography in Romanian; and education in Romanian with the mother tongue as an optional subject (the latter is the one chosen by most Csango parents). The Csangos (and their Associations) ask for their right to education in their mother tongue to be respected. It should be noted that this is much less than what Hungarians get in Romania, be it in the departments of Hargita and Covasna, where they are the majority, or in other regions of Transylvania.

32.   The local authorities in Bacau state that they are willing to observe European standards and to implement their own law. They claim however that the Csango dialect (which does not exist in written form anymore) is not a language. They claim also that it is not by introducing "literary Hungarian" that they will help the Csangos who, so they say, do not even understand it. They also claim that they do not have the financial means to provide Hungarian and that anyway the children whose parents had asked for Hungarian were among the lowest performers and would not be able to take up another subject. All these arguments however should not be accepted as excuses for not implementing the legislation.

33.   Some Csango parents have been asking for Hungarian classes for their children since 1977 and it is beyond any doubt that there is a demand for Hungarian as a subject in some villages inhabited by the Csangos. The fact that some families send their children to Hungarian speaking schools in Transylvania illustrates this. I visited one of such schools in the village of Guimes and observed that roughly one third of the (around 100) pupils were from Moldavia. Despite a clear provision in the Romanian law and the requests from parents in the last four or five years, there is no such subject in

any of the schools concerned. Some parents who had asked for Hungarian classes for their children complained of pressure from the School Director and/or the priest.

34.   It would appear that there is a lack of will (at local level) and incapacity (at central level) from the Romanian authorities to implement their own education law.

PRACTICAL PROPOSALS FOR THE PRESERVATION OF THE CSANGO CULTURE

35.   In order to encourage the Csangos to want actively to preserve those singular and, even on European terms, important cultural values, which they possess, the present situation must be changed. These values should not be associated with poverty or isolation and they should not be despised. This can only be achieved by strengthening this population culturally and economically.

> i.   Parents living in Csango settlements should be informed of the Romanian legislation on education and instructions should be issued on how to apply for its provisions concerning languages;
>
> ii.   The possibility of education in the mother tongue should be ensured in accordance with the Romanian Constitution and the legislation on education. In the meantime classrooms should be made available in local schools and teachers working in the villages teaching Csango language should be paid;
>
> iii.   There should be an option for Roman Catholic services in Hungarian in the churches in the Csango villages and the possibility for the Csangos to sing the hymns in their own mother tongue;
>
> iv.   Csango associations, such as the Association of Csango-Hungarians in Moldavia (ACHM), should be officially recognised and included in the list of the Council for National Minorities. Particular attention should be paid to the correct registration of the Csango minority at the next official census;
>
> v.   Access to modern mass-media facilities should be promoted. Financial support should be given to Csango associations to enable the issuing of a monthly publication and the functioning of a local radio station;
>
> vi.   A local institute should be set up for the promotion of Csango culture with in the context of raising awareness of and respect for minorities;
>
> vii.   An information campaign should be launched in Romania concerning the Csango culture and the advantages of peaceful co-operation between the majority and the minorities;

viii.   An international committee of experts should be established

ix.   to study the Csangos;

ix.   The unique linguistic and ethnographical features of the Csangos should be appropriately recorded;

x.   The economic revival of the area should be encouraged for the example through the establishment of small and medium enterprises in Csango villages.

Appendix 1

Bibliography

On the Origin of the Moldavian Csángós, Robin Baker, in the Slavonic and East European Review 75 (1997)

Les "Tchangos" de Moldavie, rapport de Jean Nouzille (1999)

Hungarians in Moldavia, Vilmos Tánczos, Institute for Central European Studies, Budapest (1998)

The Origins of the Changos, Dimitru Martinas, The Center for Romanian Studies (1999)

Précisions en ce qui concerne la situation religieuse des catholiques de Moldavie, lettre de Mgr Petru Gherghel, Evêque de Iasi, du 20.i.2000

Lettre de l'Archevêque de Bucarest, Mgr Ioan Robu, du 21.i.2000

Contempt for Linguistic Human Rights in the Service of the Catholic Church : The case of the Csángós, Klára Sándor in Language: a right and a resource, Central European University Press (1999)

Letter from Senator Cristian Dumitrescu of 20.i.2000

Magyars, Mongols, Romanians and Saxons: Population Mix and Density in Moldavia, from 1230 to 1365, Robin Baker, Balkan Studies, Thessalonica, 1996

Les Hongrois de Moldavie (Les Tchangos) aux XVIe et XVIIe siècles, Kálmán Benda, in Ethnicity and Society in Hungary, Budapest, 1990

The Moldavian Csango, Valentin Stan and Renate Weber, International Foundation for Promoting Studies and Knowledge of Minority Rights.

Appendix 2

Dissenting opinion presented by Mr Prisacaru on behalf of the Romanian delegation

1.   The protection of national minorities in Romania

?   The question of the Csango people ("ceangai" in Romanian) is dealt with by the Romanian authorities in the wider context of the promotion and protection of national minorities.

?   Romania's policies now accord the highest priority to the promotion and protection of human rights, including those of people belonging to national minorities.

Romania has acceded to most of the international instruments for the protection of human rights in the United Nations system, as well as a large number of Council of Europe conventions - the European Convention on Human Rights, the Framework Convention for the Protection of National Minorities, the European Charter of Local Self-Government, and the European Social Charter (revised) - and is in the process of ratifying the European Charter for Regional or Minority Languages.

The incorporation of these international standards into domestic law is facilitated by the provisions of Article 20 of the Romanian constitution, which stipulates that, in human rights matters, international treaties shall be incorporated into and take precedence over domestic law.

The significant progress made in recent years in consolidating the legislative and institutional framework protecting national minorities has played a part in the preservation, development and expression of the ethnic, cultural, linguistic and religious identities of Romania's minorities, and in the creation of a climate of tolerance and multiculturalism.

?   Romania attaches equal importance to the protection of all the ethnic, cultural, linguistic and religious minorities living on its territory, and believes that their cultures and civilisations are an important part of its national heritage.

Unfortunately, little research on the Csangos has been carried out in Romania. Specialist international publications are rather unclear, and give contradictory information about their numbers, origins, traditions, customs, language, and so on.

2.   General observations about the Csangos

?   The name "Csango" appeared relatively recently. It was Petru Zold who used it for the first time, in 1780.

?   The name Csango is used to describe two different ethnic groups:

- those concentrated in the county of Bacau (the southern group) and in the area surrounding the city of Roman (the northern group). We know for certain that these people are not Szeklers. They are Romanian in appearance, and the majority of them speak a Transylvanian dialect of Romanian and live according to Romanian traditions and customs. These characteristics suggest that they are Romanians from Transylvania who have joined the Romanian Catholic population of Moldavia.

- those of Szekler origin, most of whom settled in the valleys of the Trotus and the Tazlau and, to a lesser extent, of the Siret. Their mother tongue is the same as that spoken by the Siculs, and they live side by side with Romanians.

? As regards numbers, at the most recent census (7 January 1992) 2,062 people described themselves as Csangos (1,352 in Moldavia, 81 in Walachia, 100 in Dobrogea, 7 in Oltenia, 472 in Transylvania, and 50 in Banat, Crisana and Maramures).

The total population recorded for the historical province of Moldavia was 3,751,783, of whom 3,691,420 were Romanian, 5,895 Magyar, 5,940 German and Polish, 1,352 Csango and 47,194 other nationalities.

It should be noted that the census recognised the right of every individual freely to declare his or her ethnic, linguistic and religious origins.

Romania guarantees its citizens the right freely to express their ethnic, cultural, linguistic or religious identity in keeping with international standards. Article 3 of the Framework Convention for the Protection of National Minorities stipulates that "every person belonging to a national minority shall have the right freely to choose to be treated or not to be treated as such", and Article 32 of the Document of the Meeting of the Conference on the Human Dimension of the CSCE states that "to belong to a national minority is a matter of a person's individual choice".

? As regards the language spoken by the Csangos, there are no reliable figures for the number of Csangos who speak the so-called "archaic Hungarian" referred to in the report. At the 1992 census, of the 2,062 individuals who described themselves as Csangos, 1,489 spoke Romanian as their mother tongue, 403 Hungarian, 20 the languages of other minorities, and 150 "another language". It is believed that the 150 individuals who described themselves as having "another mother tongue" speak the Csango dialect. Data from the same census shows that of the 5,895 individuals of Hungarian nationality in Moldavia, 5,270 said that their mother tongue was Hungarian, 621 Romanian, and 4 another language.

3. Education in the Csango language

? The new Education Law (Law No.151/1999) guarantees the right of minorities to study and to receive instruction in their mother tongue at all levels and in all forms of education, and provides for the establishment of multicultural higher education institutions.

? The Romanian authorities are concerned to provide education in the Csango language, but real difficulties exist due to the fact that:

- the Csango language is not a written language, but it is handed down orally from one generation to the next;

The diocese of Iasi has set up a study board, under the leadership of Professor Anton Despinescu, to look into the possibility of transcribing the Csango language.

- consequently, there are no textbooks in the Csango language;
- there are no suitable teaching staff;

-       the small number of pupils would considerably increase the costs of teaching in Csango, costs which it would be difficult for Romania to meet in the economic conditions facing the country.

?   The Ministry of Education and Research (MER) has received several requests for study of the Hungarian language in a few localities in the department of Bacau. These requests came not from parents, but from the Association of Hungarian Csangos of Moldavia (in accordance with Order No.3113 issued by the Minister for Education on 31 January 2000, organisations of members of national minorities are allowed to put such requests on behalf of the persons they represent).

As a result of the challenges which have come from parents of pupils whose names appear on the lists of the Association of Hungarian Csangos of Moldavia (ACHM), the MER has set up a joint board (with representatives of the MER, local authorities, the Department for the Protection of National Minorities – currently the Department for Inter-Ethnic Relations – and the AHCM) to verify the situation in respect of these requests for study of the Hungarian language.

Following discussions with the parents on 14 and 15 September 2000, it was noted that major differences existed between the numbers and names of pupils included on the ACHM lists and the parents' actual requests. Ultimately, only 25 requests were filed for study of the Hungarian language (13 in the village of Cleja, two in Lespezi and 10 in Pustiana).

On 4 February 2001, another request was filed, again by the ACHM, on behalf of 77 parents, with a view to obtaining a classroom in the Pustiana school for the study of the Hungarian language outside the school curriculum. The board found that the list of names of children had been drawn up and signed by the ACHM without consulting the parents.

In practice, the board found that most of the parents did not wish their children to study the Hungarian language, and the few who did so wish only requested one hour of optional study per week. The legislation provides for the mother tongue to be studied for three to four hours a week, as well as one hour of study of the history and traditions of national minorities.

The parents have shown that study of the Hungarian language represents an act of individual will, and they do not agree with the submission of their requests, where these exist, by the organisations of national minorities.

It has also been found that most of the requests were put forward by parents under pressure from members of the ACHM (threats to remove children studying without payment of fees from the schools in the departments of Harghita and Covasna, promises of financial assistance for the treatment of children who are ill, gifts, incorrect information about study arrangements relating to the mother tongue, rather than as an optional subject, as the parents had understood, and so on).

?   We are concerned to preserve the Csango language, which represents a real asset for the European cultural heritage. We cannot, however, agree with the idea in the report that teaching in the Hungarian language will be the answer.

A similar initiative existed after World War II, when teaching in Hungarian – and not in Csango – was introduced in a few villages of Moldavia. This initiative was rapidly dropped, because a large number of people did not know Hungarian or even Csango.

4.   Religious identity

?   Most Csangos are Roman Catholics and are members of the diocese of Iasi.

According to the 1992 census, 1,306 of the 1,352 Csangos in Moldavia are Roman Catholics.

In Moldavia, 245,137 individuals described themselves as Roman Catholics. 233,632 (95.3%) of these are of Romanian nationality.

?   There are sufficient documents attesting that, from the very beginning of the process by which the inhabitants of Moldavia became Catholics, most of the believers were Romanian, although some people have nevertheless tried to identify the Catholic population of Moldavia as a whole with the population of Hungarian origin.

?   In Romania, religious groups are independent of the state. They are governed by and carry out their work according to their own statutes. Religious denominations are allowed to use their followers' mother tongues in their ceremonies.

The same difficulties as for teaching in Csango, arising from the fact that there is no written form, apply to the religious lives of Csango-speaking Csangos.

?   It should be noted that most Csangos say that they belong to a religious rather than an ethnic minority, and describe themselves as "Catholics" or "Romanian Catholics". The Romanian scholar prince Dimitri Cantemir said that Catholics in Moldavia described themselves "as Catholics as much because of their parents as their religion". Many of them regard the name Csango, given to them by Hungarian scholars at the beginning of the 18th century, as pejorative.

?   As we have shown, most Catholics in Moldavia are of Romanian nationality.

Catholics are known to have lived in Moldavia since the Middle Ages. At the beginning of the 13th century the diocese of Comania, in Milcov, was directly answerable to the Holy See, but was destroyed by the Tatars. The influence of Dominican and Franciscan monks led to the foundation in 1371, during the reign of Latcu Voda, of the Catholic diocese of Siret.

265

The catholicisation of the Romanians in Moldavia has continued, with varying intensity, down the centuries. Romanian Catholics have always lived peacefully alongside Saxons and Siculs who have settled in Moldavia and Romanians from Transylvania.

5.   Comments on the proposals made in the report for the protection of the Csango culture

?   We welcome many of the practical proposals made at the end of the report: the preservation of the Csango language, the creation of small and medium-sized businesses in these areas, co-operation between the majority and the minorities, job creation, and so on.

?   When Csango also exists as a written language, it will be possible to achieve other aims relating to its use in teaching, religious worship and the media, if the demand exists among those who speak Csango.

The law on the organisation of public administration and the general rules on local autonomy, recently adopted by the Romanian Parliament, guarantees that the Csango language may be used in public administration and that bilingual signs may be sited at the entrances to places where more than 20% of the total population speak Csango.

The Education Law provides for elementary-level teaching in minority languages, so that Romanian history and geography are taught in pupils' mother tongues at this level. At secondary level, history and geography are taught in Romanian.

It should be noted that these provisions were adopted after lengthy debate in parliament, and were approved in this form by the representatives of the national minorities.

The new Education Law meets the relevant European standards. The OSCE High Commissioner on National Minorities considers it to be one of the most progressive education laws in Europe as regards respect for the rights of individuals belonging to national minorities.

?   Some proposals have already been implemented. A Csango association has been founded in Sfantu Gheorghe (in the Department of Covasna) and transferred to Bacau, and has been officially recognised by the Romanian authorities. This is the Association of Hungarian Csangos of Moldavia.

This, however, does not fulfil the conditions for membership of the Council for the National Minorities, since, in keeping with the regulations governing its foundation and running, the Council is made up of the organisations of the national minorities represented in parliament or organisations which, though not represented in parliament, were founded before 27 September 1992.

It should be noted that Romanian law (Article 59 of the constitution and Law 68/1992 on the election of the Chamber of Deputies and the Senate)

provides for the allocation of a seat in the Romanian parliament to each national minority organisation obtaining 5% of the votes needed to elect a deputy.

? There are a number of prestigious national institutes in Romania studying the different aspects of the ethnic, linguistic, cultural and religious characteristics of the minorities which live on Romanian territory. These include, among many others, the Romanian Academy, the Romanian Institute of Human Rights, the Institute for Ethnic Studies, the Institute of Ethnography and Folklore, the Tirgu Mures Institute for Socio-Human Studies, etc. Attention also needs to be drawn to the foundation, in the near future, of the Institute for National Minorities. Some of these institutes have studied the Csango culture, but we agree that this research must be continued and must go into greater depth.

? With a view to the forthcoming census, scheduled for 2002, an inter-ministerial committee has been set up to find ways of ensuring that the ethnic, linguistic and religious structure of the population of Romania is reflected as faithfully as possible, in pursuance of every person's right freely to declare his or her membership of an ethnic, linguistic and religious group.

? The practical aspects of asserting, developing and promoting the ethnic, cultural, linguistic and religious identities of the national minorities are being dealt with by several ministries and departments, notably the Department for the Protection of National Minorities, headed by a representative of the Hungarian minority. The large number of members of national minorities who work for and hold positions of authority within these institutions is a demonstration of Romania's concern to protect its national minorities. We are convinced that this can make an important contribution to the study of the Csango culture, and above all of the archaic Hungarian dialect spoken by some Csangos, which is seen as playing an important part, from a linguistic point of view, in the history of Hungarian culture.

? We are pleased to note that concern to study the Csangos has grown in recent years, both nationally and internationally.

One example is the study of the Csangos carried out by Prof. Jean Nouzille, objectively presenting the information that exists about the ethnic origin of the Csango language and its use in religious services and in education.

The situation of the Csangos has been studied by international organisations, such as the UN and, in particular, the Council of Europe. Representatives of the Committee on Culture and Education of the Parliamentary Assembly of the Council of Europe have made several visits to Romania.

Also noteworthy is the interest expressed by several personalities and politicians from Hungary, who have, during their visits to the communities of

Catholic Romanians and of Csangos, have offered gifts of books in Hungarian, assistance, scholarships at Hungarian schools, and so on.

We take the view that the main aim of all our activity must be the preservation and development of this community's cultural, linguistic and religious identity, and that this issue must be addressed without any political connotations.

Reporting committee: Commission on Culture, Science and Education
Reference to committee: Doc. 8713 and Reference N° 2501 of 16 May 2000
Draft recommendation adopted by the committee on 26 April 2001 with 3 votes against

Members of the committee: MM. Rakhansky (Chairman), de Puig, Risari, Billing (Vice-Chairmen), Akhvlediani, Arzilli, Asciak (Alternate : Debono Grech), Bartumeu Cassany, Berceanu, Berzinš, Birraux (Alternate: Bockel), Mrs Castro, MM. Cherribi, Cubreacov, Mrs Damanaki, MM. Dias, Dolazza, Duka-Zólyomi, Fayot, Mrs Fernández-Capel (Alternate : Mrs Agudo), MM. Galoyan, Goris, Hadjidemetriou, Haraldsson, Hegyi, Henry, Higgins, Irmer, Mrs Isohookana-Asunmaa, Mr Ivanov (Alternate: Mrs Poptodorova), MM. Jakic, Kalkan, Mrs Katselli, MM. Kofod-Svendsen, Kramaric, Mrs Kutraité Giedraitiené (Alternate : Mrs Mikutiene), Mr Lachat, Mrs Laternser, MM. Lekberg, Lemoine, Lengagne, Libicki, Liiv, Mrs Lucyga, MM. Maass, Marmazov, Mateju, McNamara, Melnikov (Alternate: Gostev), Mignon, Minarolli, Nagy, Mrs Nemcova, MM. Nigmatulin, O'Hara (Alternate: Mrs Cryer), MM. Pavlov, Pinggera, Plattner (Alternate : Mrs Nabholz Haidegger), Prisacaru, Rapson (Alternate : Hancock), Roseta, Mrs Saele, Mr Saglam, Mrs Schicker, MM. Schweitzer, Seyidov, Shaklein (Alternate: Ustiugov), Sudarenkov, Symonenko (Alternate : Khunov), Tanik, Tudor, Turini (Alternate : Martelli), Urbanczyk, Vakilov, Valk, Wilshire (Alternate : Jackson), Wittbrodt, Wodarg, Xhaferi.

N.B.: The names of members present at the meeting are printed in italics
Secretariat of the committee : Mr Grayson, Mr Ary, Mrs Theophilova-Permaul, Mr Torcatoriu

BIBLIOGRAPHY

Adascalitei, Vasile: *Istoria unui obicei.* Plugusorul. (Editura Junimea, Iasi, 1987)

Albert, Erno: *Zabolai és szörcsei jobbágyok és cselédek zendülése 1802-ben.* Acta 1997. I. (Sepsiszentgyörgy, 1998)

Almanahul: *Almanahul Presa Buna.* (Iasi, 2000)

Almási, István: *Román refrének a moldvai csángók népdalaiban,* In: *Nyelv- és Irodalomtudományi Közlemények,* X. 1. 1966.

Alzati, Cesare: *„ Riforma" e Riforma cattolica di fronte all ortodossia nel secondo cinquecento romeno,* In: *Studia Borromaica 5.* (Milano, 1982)

Alzati, Cesare: *Terra Romena tra Oriente e Occidente, chiese ed etnie nel tardo 1500.* (Milano, 1991)

Anderson, Benedict: *Imagined Communities: Reflections on the Origin and Spread of Nationalism.* (London, 1983)

Andreescu, Gabriel: *Extremismul de dreapta în România.* (Cluj-Napoca, 2003)

Andreescu, Gabriel - Enache, Smaranda: *Raport asupra situatiei ceangailor din Moldova. Problema ceangailor maghiari.* (*Altera,* VIII. 17-18., 2002)

Auner, Károly: *A romániai magyar telepek történeti vázlata.* (Temesvár, 1908)

Auner, Carol: *Episcopia Milkoviei,* In: *Revista Catolica* (Bucuresti, 1912)

Baka, András: *Tréfás beszédei.* Moldvai csángómagyar népmesék. [Gyujtötte, szerkesztette, bevezeto tanulmánnyal, jegyzetekkel és tájszójegyzékkel közzéteszi Faragó József.] (Kriterion Könyvkiadó, Kolozsvár, 2003)

Baker, Robin: *On the origin of the Moldavian Csángos.* (The Slavonic and the East European Review 75, 1997)

Balassa, József: *A szlovéniai nyelvjárás,* In: *Magyar Nyelvor,* XXIII. 1894.

Balázs, Lajos: *„Száz lejes feleség."* Az exogámia különös esete Csíkszentdomokoson, In: Pozsony, Ferenc /szerk./ *Csángósors.* Moldvai csángók a változó idokben. (Budapest, 1999)

Balázs, Péter: *Egy csángófalu harca anyanyelvéért a jasi püspökség elfajzott ügynökei ellen,* In: *Igazság,* IV. február 2, 1948.

Balázs, Péter: *Kik akadályozták a népszámlálást a moldvai csángók között?* In: *Igazság,* IV. február 4, 1948.

Balázs, Péter: *„Megszámláltatott és híjával találtatott" - mert a román és magyar reakció érdeke így kívánta.* Induljon eljárás a népszámlálást meghamisító tisztviselok ellen, In: *Igazság,* IV. február 5, 1948.

Balázs, Péter: *Papi kíngyóntatás - csendori segédlettel.* Nem rossz üzlet háromnegyed millióért Klézsában papnak lenni, In: *Igazság,* IV. február 6, 1948.

Balázs, Péter: *Megjelent a sújtó Igazság Külsorekecsinben is.* Repül állásából Kotyor Gergely adóhiéna, In: *Igazság,* IV. február 8, 1948.

Balázs, Péter: *Hol késett Hojdin páter amerikai mikulása?* In: *Igazság,* IV. február 11, 1948.

Balázs, Péter: *Dózsa György nevét adták az egyik bákói csángó falunak.* Gyökeret vernek és erosödnek a MNSZ-szervezetek, In: *Igazság,* IV. február 13, 1948.

Balázs, Péter: *Dobos Ferkó és Kató Mihály ,"hazajártak".* További nyolc csángó fiút küldenek a krasznai „Fazekas Mihály" Népi Kollégiumba, In: *Igazság,* IV. február 14, 1948.

Balázs, Péter: *Egyházi átok, középkori töviskoszorúzás, vesszofuttatás Ferdinándon,* In: *Igazság,* IV. február 19, 1948.

Balázs, Péter: *Az eretnekégetések középkori szellemét idézi Gergucz páter, "valláserkölcsi" nevelése Ferdinándon,* In: *Igazság,* IV. február 20, 1948.

Balázs, Péter: *Pokoli kegyetlenkedés, csendorszuronyos inkvizíció, papi parancsra templomrombolás Pokolpatakon,* In: *Igazság,* IV. február 26, 1948.

Balázs, Péter: *Csúfos kudarcba fulladt Gergucz páter zsírosainak "világfelforgatása"* In: *Igazság,* IV. március 4, 1948.

Balázs, Péter: *Vatikáni janicsárok rabságában,* In: *Utunk,* IV. évf., 5. sz., 1949.

Balázs, Péter: *Csángók válasza,* In: *Utunk,* IV. 19. sz., 1949.

Balázs, Péter: *Moldvai csángók vallomása az 1907-es felkelésrol,* In: *Korunk,* XVI. 1-2., 1957.

Barbulescu, Mihai - Deletant, Dennis - Hitchins, Keith - Papacostea, Serban - Teodor, Pompiliu: *Istoria României.* (Bucuresti, 1998)

Barbu, Violeta: *Contrareforma catolica în Moldova la jumatatea secolului al XVII-lea,* In: Barbu, Violeta-Tüdos, S. Kinga /szerk./: *Historia manet.* Volum omagial, Demény Lajos emlékkönyv. (Editura Kriterion, Bucuresti-Cluj, 2001)

Bárdi, Nándor - Hermann, Gusztáv Mihály: *A többség kisebbsége.* Tanulmányok a székelyföldi románság történetérõl. (Csíkszereda, 1999)

Barna, Gábor: *Moldvai magyarok a csíksomlyói búcsún,* In: Halász, Péter /szerk./: „ *Megfog vala apóm szokcor kezemtül... "* Tanulmányok Domokos Pál Péter emlékére. (Budapest, 1993)

Bartha, András: *Pusztina – Pustiana.* Gondolatok egy csángó falu múltjáról, jelenérol. (Balatonboglár, 1998)

Baumgartner, Sándor: *Moldva, a magyarság nagy temetoje.* (Budapest, 1940)

Benda, Gyula: *A polgárosodás fogalmának történeti értelmezhetosége,* In: *Századvég,* 2-3. 1991.

Benda, Kálmán: *Csöbörcsök. Egy tatárországi magyar falu története a 16-18. században,* In: *Századok,* 4. 1985.

Benda, Kálmán: *Moldvai Csángó-Magyar Okmánytár (1467-1706).* I-II. (Budapest, 1989)

Benda, Kálmán: *The Hungarians of Moldavia (Csángós) in the 16th-17th Centuries,* In: Diószegi, László /ed./: *Hungarian Csángós in Moldavia. Essays on the Past and Present of the Hungarian Csángó in Moldavia.* (Budapest, 2002)

Benedek H., Erika: *Út az életbe.* Világképelemzés csángó és székely közösségek szüléshez fuzodo hagyományai alapján. (Kolozsvár, 1998)

Benedek H., János: *Csángó falvak gazdasági problémái,* In: Pozsony, Ferenc /szerk./: *Dolgozatok a moldvai csángók népi kultúrájáról.* (Kriza János Néprajzi Társaság Évkönyve 5., Kolozsvár, 1997)

Benedek H., János: *Egy moldvai magyar parasztcsalád gazdálkodása,* In: Pozsony, Ferenc /szerk./: *Dolgozatok a moldvai csángók népi kultúrájáról.* (Kriza János Néprajzi Társaság Évkönyve 5., Kolozsvár, 1997)

Benedek H., János: *Gorzafalvi fazekasság napjainkban,* In: Romsics, Imre /szerk./: *A másik ember.* (Kalocsa, 1997)

Benko, Loránd: *A csángók eredete és települése a nyelvtudomány szemszögébol.* (A Magyar Nyelvtudományi Társaság Kiadványai, 188. sz., Budapest, 1990)

Benko, Loránd /szerk./: *A magyar nyelv története.* (Budapest, 1978)

Benko, Samu - Demény, Lajos - Vekov, Károly: *Székely felkelés 1595-1596. Elozményei, lefolyása, következményei.* (Bukarest, 1979)

Beno, Attila - Murádin, László: *Csángó Dialect - Csángó Origins,* In: Diószegi, László /ed./: *Hungarian Csángós in Moldavia.* (Budapest, 2002)

Berrár, Jolán - Károly, Sándor: *Régi magyar glosszárium.* (Budapest, 1984)

Binder, Pál: *Közös múltunk.* Románok, magyarok, németek és délszlávok feudalizmus-kori falusi és városi együttélésérol. (Bukarest, 1982)

Bitay, Árpád: *Viola József a moldvai fejedelem udvari orvosa, mint a moldvai magyar népköltés gyujtoje,* In: *Erdélyi Szemle,* 1924.

Bitay, Árpád: *Moldvai csángók legrégibb írott nyelvemléke.* (*Erdélyi Irodalmi Szemle,* I. évf. 1924)

Bodnár, Erika /szerk./: *Szentmise a Szentatyával Budapesten a Hosök terén.* 1991. augusztus 20. (Budapest, 1991)

Bogdan, Ioan: *Documentele lui Stefan cel Mare II.* (Bucuresti, 1913)

Borcila, Mircea: *Un fenomen fonetic dialectal: rostirea lui s ca s si j ca z în graiurile dacoromâne. Vechimea si originea fenomenului,* In: *Studia Universitatis Babes-Bolyai.* (Series Philologia. Fasciculus 2. Anul X., 1965)

271

Boros, Fortunát: *A szalánci búcsú*, In: *Erdélyi Tudósító*, VII. 29. augusztus 15, 1924.

Boros, Fortunát: *Csíksomlyó, a kegyhely.* (Kolozsvár, 1943)

Boross, Balázs: *"Majd egyszer lészen, de nem most".* Adalékok a moldvai csángók identitásának komplex valóságához egy kulturális antropológiai esettanulmány tükrében. (*Pro Minoritate*, Budapest, 2002)

Bosnyák, Sándor: *A moldvai magyarok hitvilága.* (*Folklór Archívum*, XII. Budapest, 1980)

Bosnyák, Sándor: *Magyar Biblia.* A világ teremtése, az özönvíz, Jézus élete s a világ vége napjaink szájhagyományában. (Budapest, 2001)

Bozgan, Ovidiu : *Cronica unui esec previzibil.* România si Sfântul Scaun în epoca pontificatului lui Paul al VI-lea (1963-1978). (Bucuresti, 2004)

Bârsanescu, Stefan: *Schola Latina de la Cotnari, biblioteca de curte si proiectul de academie al lui Despot Voda.* (Bucuresti, 1957)

Brancovici, Gheorghe: *Cronica Româneasca.* (Editat de Damaschin Mioc si Marieta Adam-Chiper, Bucuresti, 1987)

Bratianu, G. I.: *Origines et formation de l' unite roumaine.* (Bucharest, 1943)

Breban, Vasile: *Dictionar al limbii române contemporane.* (Bucuresti, 1980)

Bucur, Maria: *Eugenics and Modernization in Interwar Romania.* (University of Pittsburgh Press, 2002)

Calinescu, George: *Diplomatarium Italicum.* Documenti raccolti negli archivi italiani.(Roma, 1930-40)

Calatori straini despre Tarile Române I-VIII. [Red. Maria Holban, Maria Matilda Alexandrescu, Paul Cernovodeanu, Ion Totoiu.] (Bucuresti, 1968-1983)

Canarache, Ana - Breban, Vasile: *Mic dictionar enciclopedic.* (Bucuresti, 1972)

Cantemir, Dimitrie: *Descrierea Moldovei.* (Bucuresti, 1909)

Cantemir, Dimitrie: *Descrierea Moldovei.* (Editura Minerva, Bucuresti, 1973)

Cantemir, Dimitrie: *Moldva leírása.* (Kriterion Könyvkiadó, Bukarest, 1973)

Carp, Matatias: *Cartea neagra.* Suferintele evreilor din Romania 1940 -1944. (Bucuresti, 1948)

Catanus, Dan - Roske, Octavian: *Colectivizarea agriculturii în România.* Dimensiunea politica 1949 - 1953. (Bucuresti, 2000)

Chelaru, Rafael: *Documente privind activitatea episcopului Paolo Sardi si catolicismul în Moldova (1843-1848).* (Arhiva Istorica a României, Serie noua, Vol. I. nr.1., Bucuresti, 2004)

Cihodaru, C. - Caprosu, I. - Simanschi, L.: *Documenta Romaniae Historica, A. I.* (Bucuresti, 1975)

Ciocan I., N.: *Monografia crestinilor catolici din judetul Roman.* Dupa datele culese în 1903. (Roman, 1924)

Cosa, Anton: *Cleja.* Monografie etnografica. (Editura Semne, Bacau, 2001)

Costin, Miron: *Opere.* (Editat de P. P. Panaitescu, Bucuresti, 1958)

Craciun, Maria: *Protestantism si ortodoxie în Moldova secolului al XVI-lea.* (Cluj-Napoca, 1996)

Cuceu, Ion: *Recenzie - Dumitru, Martina: Originea ceangailor din Moldova,* In: *Anuarul de folclor* V-VII. (Cluj-Napoca, 1987)

Cândea, Romul: *Catolicismul în Moldova în secolul al XVII-lea.* (Sibiu, 1917)

Czelder, Márton: *Missziói levelek Ballagi Mórhoz.* (*Protestáns Egyházi és Iskolai Lapok,* 13. 1861).

Csáki, Árpád: *Ferences plébánosok és udvari káplánok Háromszéken a 17-18. században. Acta 1998. II.* (Sepsiszentgyörgy, 1999)

Csata, Zsombor - Kiss, Dénes - Sólyom, Andrea: *Vallás és modernizáció a Mezoségen.* (*WEB.* Szociológiai Folyóirat, Kolozsvár, 2001)

Csokonai Vitéz, Mihály: *Költemények (1797-1799).* (Szerk. Szilágyi, Ferenc, Budapest, 1994)

Csoma, Gergely: *Moldvai csángó magyarok.* (Budapest, 1988)

Csoma, Gergely: *Varázslások és gyógyítások a moldvai csángómagyaroknál.* (Pomáz, 2000)

Csoma, Gergely: *Elveszett szavak.* A moldvai magyarság írott nyelvemlékei. (Budapest, 2004)

Csutak, Vilmos: *Bujdosó kurucok Moldvában és Havasalföldön 1707-1711-ben,* In: Csutak, Vilmos /szerk./: *Emlékkönyv a Székely Nemzeti Múzeum 50 éves jubileumára.* (Sepsiszentgyörgy, 1929)

Deletant, Dennis: *România sub regimul comunist (decembrie 1947 - decembrie 1989),* In: Barbulescu, Mihai - Deletant, Dennis - Hitchins, Keith - Papacostea, Serban - Teodor, Pompiliu: *Istoria României.* (Bucuresti, 1998)

Demény, István Pál: *A hejgetés meg a sámánének.* (*Néprajzi Látóhatár* III. 1-2. 1994)

Demény, István Pál: *A moldvai csángó népdalok és a népköltészet történetével kapcsolatos dilemmák.* (*Erdélyi Múzeum,* LXII. 3-4., 2000)

Demény, István Pál: *Széles vízen keskeny palló.* Magyar és összehasonlító folklórtanulmányok. (Csíkszereda, 2002)

Demény, Lajos: *A csángó-magyarok kérdése Moldva Ideiglenes Országgyulésén 1857-ben,* In: Pozsgai, Péter /szerk./: *Tuzcsiholó.* Írások a 90 éves Lüko Gábor tiszteletére. (Budapest, 1999)

Demse Márton: *Csángó küzdelem* (Hargita Kiadóhivatal, Csíkszereda, 2005)

Diaconescu, Marius: *Péter Zöld si „descoperirea" ceangailor din Moldova în a doua jumatate a secolului XVIII.* (Anuarul Institutului de Istorie „A. D. Xenopol" XXXIX-XL. (2002-2003), Iasi, 2003)

Diaconescu, Marius: *A moldvai katolikusok identitáskrízise a politika és a historiográfiai mítoszok között,* In : Kinda, István – Pozsony, Ferenc /szerk../ *Adaptáció és modernizáció a moldvai csángó falvakban.* (Kriza János Néprajzi Társaság, Kolozsvár, 2005)

Diószegi, László /szerk./: A *moldvai csángók tanítója.* Diószegi László beszélgetése Kallós Zoltán néprajzkutatóval. (*Alföld,* XLII. 6. sz., 1991)

Diószegi, László /ed./: *Hungarian Csángós in Moldavia.* Essays on the Past and Present of the Hungarian Csángós in Moldavia. (Budapest, 2002)

Damoc, Mihai: *Episcopia de Siret. Mesagerul.* (Revista de spiritualitate a franciscanilor minori conventuali. X. nr. 61, 2003)

Dobos, Danut: *Biserica si scoala.* Din istroia operelor sociale catolice în România I. (Editura Presa Buna, Iasi, 2002)

Dobrincu, Dorin: *Informatorii Securitatii în comunitatile religioase din centrul Moldovei (1950).* (Arhiva Istorica a României, Serie noua. Vol. I. nr. 1. Bucuresti, 2004)

Domokos, Mária: *The Character of the Csángó Folk Song and the History of Its Research,* In: Diószegi, László /ed./: *Hungarian Csángós in Moldavia.* Essays on the Past and Present of the Hungarian Csángós in Moldavia. (Budapest, 2002)

Domokos, Péter Pál: *A csíki énekeskönyvek.* In: Csutak, Vilmos /szerk./: *Emlékkönyv a Székely Nemzeti Múzeum ötvenéves jubileumára.* (Sepsiszentgyörgy, 1929)

Domokos, Pál Péter: *A moldvai magyarság.* (Csíksomlyó, 1931. elso kiadás.)

Domokos, Pál Péter: *Édes hazámnak akartam szolgálni.* (Budapest, 1979)

Domokos, Pál Péter: *Bartók Béla kapcsolata a moldvai csángómagyarokkal.* Népdalok, népmesék, népszokások, eredetmondák a magyar nyelvterület legkeletibb részérol. (Budapest, 1981)

Domokos, Pál Péter: *A moldvai magyarság történeti számadatai.* (*Honismeret,* XIV. 3. 1986)

Domokos, Pál Péter: *A moldvai magyarság.* (Budapest, 1987. Ötödik átdolgozott kiadás.)

Drimba, Vladimir: *Materiale pentru stadiul raporturilor lingvistice românomaghiare.* (Cercetari de Lingvistica, Cluj XIV. 1960)

Eliade, Mircea: *,,Samanizmus" a románoknál?* (*Létünk.* Társadalom, tudomány, kultúra, 2. évf. 1988)

Erdélyi, Lajos: *Magyar zsidók Romániában, Erdélyben.* (*Múlt és Jövo.* Zsidó Kulturális Folyóirat XI. 1. sz., 2000)

Erdélyi, Zsuzsanna: *Hegyet hágék, lotot lépék.* Archaikus népi imádságok. (Budapest, 1976)

Faragó, József: *Balladák földjén.* Válogatott tanulmányok, cikkek. (Bukarest, 1977)

Faragó, József: *A mai romániai folklórgyujtés vázlata,* In: Kós, Károly -
Faragó, József /szerk./: *Népismereti Dolgozatok.* (Bukarest, 1980)
Faragó, József: *Paralele între baladele romanesti si maghiare.* (*Anuarul de Folclor* II. Cluj-Napoca, 1981)
Faragó, József: *A hejgetéstol az urálásig.* Egy archaikus moldvai csángó-magyar népszokás elrománosodása és eltunése. (*Honismeret,* 1996, XXIV. 6. 53-64.)
Faragó, József: A szabófalvi hejgetés emlékei. (*Erdélyi Múzeum,* 1996, LVIII. 1.2.)
Faragó, József: *A moldvai csángómagyar verses népköltészet vízrajza,* In: Pozsony, Ferenc /szerk./: *Csángósors.* Moldvai csángók a változó idokben. (Budapest, 1999)
Faragó, József - Jagamas, János: *Moldvai csángó népdalok és népballadák.* (Bukarest, 1954)
Farkas, Tibor: *Moldvai magyarok - Csángó magyarok.* (*Társadalom, gazdaság, kultúra.* Gödöllo, 2000)
Feischmidt, Margit: *Etnicitás és helyi intézmények.*Jegyzetek egy mezoségi faluról. (*Regio,* V. 3. 1994)
Fejos, Zoltán: *Modernizáció és néprajz,* In: Szucs, Alexandra /szerk./: *Hagyomány, modernizáció a kultúrában és a néprajzban.* (Budapest, 1998)
Ferenczes, István: *Ordasok tépte tájon.* Riport-novellák. (Csíkszereda, 1997)
Ferenczi, Géza: *Újabb adalékok a moldvai csángók kérdéséhez.* (*Korunk,* III. évf., 1990)
Ferent, Ioan: *A kunok és püspökségük.* (Budapest, 1981)
Ferent, Iacob: *S-a facut dreptate.* (*Lumina Crestinului,* XXX. 1943, februarie)
Ferro, Teresa: *Ungherese e romeno nella Moldvaia dei secoli XVII-XVIII sulla base dei documenti della „ Propaganda Fide",* In: Graciotti, Sante /szerk./: *Italia eRomania. Due popoli e due storie a confronto (secc. XIV-XVIII).* (Firenze, 1998)
Ferro, Teresa: *I missionari catolici italiani in Moldavia nei secc. XVII-XVIII.* (Annuario dell Instituto Romeno di Cultura e Ricerca Umanistica di Venezia. Venezia, 1999)
Fochi, Adrian: *Miorita.* Tipologie, geneza, texte. (Bucuresti, 1964)
Fodor, István: *Magyar jellegu régészeti leletek Moldvában,* In: Halász, Péter /szerk./: „ *Megfog vala apóm szokcor kezemtül..." *Tanulmányok Domokos Pál Péter emlékére. (Budapest, 1993)
Földes, László: *Árucsere és piac a hagyományos társadalmakban.* (*Világosság,* 1976)
Földi, István: *Madéfalvától a Dunántúlig.* (Szekszárd, 1987)
Gabor, Iosif: *Dictionarul comunitatilor catolice din Moldova.* (Bacau, 1996)

Gálffy, Mózes - Márton, Gyula - Szabó T., Attila: *A moldvai csángó nyelvjárás atlasza.* (*Magyar Nyelvtudományi Társaság Kiadványai,* 193. sz., Budapest, 1991)

Gálos, Rezso: *Legrégibb bibliafordításunk.* (*Irodalomtörténeti Füzetek,* 9. sz., Budapest, 1928)

Gazda, István: *Szászkúti múlt és jelen.* (*Felebarát.* Gyülekezeti lap a szórványban élo magyar református családok számára, III. 1-2. 1992)

Gazda, István: *Karácsony Moldvában.* (*Felebarát,* III. 1-2. 1992)

Gazda, József: *Hát én hogyne siratnám.* Csángók a sodró idoben. (Budapest, 1993)

Gego, Elek: *A moldvai magyar telepekrol.* (Buda, 1838)

Gelencsér, József: *Szent István a csángóknál.* (*Fejér Megyei Hírlap,* augusztus 18, 1990)

Giurescu, C. C.: *Cauzele refugerii husitilor în Moldova si centrele lor în aceasta tara.* (*Studii si articole de istorie,* VIII., 1966)

Giurescu, C. C.: *Târguri sau orase si cetati moldovene din secolul al X-lea pâna la mijlocul secolului al XVI-lea.* (*Biblioteca Historica Romaniae* 2, Bucuresti, 1967)

Giurescu, G. Constantin: *Cauzele refugierii husitilor în Moldova si centrele lor în aceasta tara.*(*Studii si articole de istorie,* VIII. 1966)

Giurescu, C. Dinu: *Sasii si ungurii din Tara Româneasca sec. XIV-XV.* (Bucuresti, 1973)

Giurescu, C. Constantin - Giurescu, C. Dinu: *Istoria Românilor II.* (Bucuresti, 1976)

Gorovei, Stefan S.: *Musatinii.* (Bucuresti, 1976)

Gorovei, Stefan S.: *Moldova si lumea catolica.* (*Anuarul Institutului A. D. Xenopol* XXIX, Iasi, 1992)

Granovetter, Mark: *A gyenge kötések ereje.* In: Angelusz, Róbert - Tardos, Róbert /szerk./: *Társadalmak rejtett hálózata.* (Új Mandátum Könyvkiadó, Budapest, 1995)

Graur, Alexandru: *Întroducere în lingvistica.* (Bucuresti, 1958)

Grossu, Sergiu: *Calvarul României crestine.* (h.n., 1992)

Gunda, Béla: *A moldvai magyarok néprajzi kutatása,* In: Máténé Szabó, Mária /szerk./: *A határainkon kívüli magyar néprajzi kutatások.* (Budapest, 1984)

Gunda, Béla: *Mi a magyar?* (*Virrasztók.* Vígilia - antológia, Budapest, 1985)

Gunda, Béla: *A moldvai magyarok eredete.* (*Magyar Nyelv,* 84. 1. 1988)

Gunda, Béla: *A moldvai magyar népi muveltség jellegéhez: néprajzi gyujtoúton a moldvai magyaroknál.* (*Népi Kultúra–Népi Társadalom,* XV. évf., Budapest, 1990)

Gârniteanu, M.: *Catolici din Moldova sunt Daci.* (*Lumina Crestinului,* XXX. 2, 1944)

Györffy, György: *A magyarországi kun társadalom a XIII-XIV. Században,* In: Székely, György /szerk./: *Tanulmányok a parasztság történetéhez Magyarországon a 14. században.* (Budapest, 1953)

Györffy, István: *Néphagyomány a Székelyföld délmoldvai határáról (1923),* In: *Magyar nép - magyar föld.* (Budapest, 1942)

Hajdú, Demeter Dénes: *A Szent László Társulatról,* In: Halász, Péter /szerk./: *"Megfog vala apóm szokcor kezemtül..."* Tanulmányok Domokos Pál Péter emlékére. (Budapest, 1993)

Hajdú-Moharos, József: *Moldva - Csángóföld - csángó sors.* (Vörösberény, 1995)

Halász, Péter: *Egyházi jövedelmek a Román környéki csángó falvakban a századfordulón,* In: Halász, Péter /szerk./: *A Duna menti népek hagyományos muveltsége.* (Budapest, 1991)

Halász, Péter: *Adatok a moldvai magyarok kecskemaszkos játékához.* In: Viga, Gyula /szerk./: *Kultúra és tradíció I.* Tanulmányok Ujváry Zoltán tiszteletére. (Miskolc, 1992)

Halász, Péter: *A moldvai csángók magyarságtudatáról.* (*Muvelodés,* XLI. 2. 1992.)

Halász, Péter: *Áruértékesítés és árucsere a moldvai magyaroknál.* In: Halász, Péter /szerk./: *,, Megfog vala apóm szokcor kezemtül..."* Tanulmányok Domokos Pál Péter emlékére. (Budapest, 1993)

Halász, Péter: *A ló és a szarvasmarha gazdasági jelentosége a moldvai magyaroknál,* In: Novák, László /szerk./: *Néprajzi Tanulmányok.* Ikvai Nándor emlékére II. (Szentendre, 1994)

Halász, Péter: *Új szempontok a moldvai magyarsok táji-etnikai tagozódásának vizsgálatához,* In: Pozsony Ferenc /szerk./: *Dolgozatok a moldvai csángók népi kultúrájáról.* (Kriza János Néprajzi Társaság Évkönyve 5. Kolozsvár, 1997)

Halász, Péter: *A kickófalvi szent István szobor.* (*Honismeret,* XXV. 4. 1997.)

Halász, Péter: *A moldvai csángó falvak társadalmának néhány sajátossága,* In: Novák, László /szerk./: *Az Alföld társadalma.* (Nagykorös, 1998)

Halász, Péter: *A protestáns vallások szerepe a moldvai magyarok életében,* In: *A Ráday Gyujtemény Évkönyve* IX. (Budapest, 1999)

Halász, Péter: *A csángók.* A moldvai magyarság évszázadai. (*Rubicon,* X.c9-10. sz., 1999)

Halász, Péter: *A moldvai csángómagyar falvak helyneveinek néhány településtörténeti tanulsága.* (Kazinczy Ferenc Társaság 10. Évkönyve. Széphalom, 1999)

Halász, Péter: *A moldvai magyarok tavaszi ünnepkörérol,* In: Czégényi, Dóra - Keszeg, Vilmos /szerk./: *Kriza János Néprajzi Társaság Évkönyve 8.* (Kolozsvár, 2000)

Halász, Péter: *"Vízbeveto hétfo" a moldvai magyaroknál.* (*Néprajzi Látóhatár,* IX. 3-4 sz., 2000)

Halász, Péter: *Bokrétába kötögetem vala.* A moldvai magyarok néprajzához. (Európai Folklór Intézet, Budapest, 2002)

Halász, Péter: *A csíki karácsony.* (*Ethnica,* VI. 2 . 2004)

Halász, Péter: *Nem lehet nyugtunk.* Esszék, gondolatok, útirajzok a moldvai magyarokról. (Budapest, 2004)

Halász, Péter: *A moldvai csángó magyarok hiedelmei.* General Press Kiadó, Budapest, 2005

Harangozó, Imre: *„ Anyám, anyám, szép Szuz Márjám ... ”* Régi imádságok a moldvai magyaroktól. [Lüko Gábor eloszavával.] (Újkígyós, 1992)

Harangozó, Imre: *Krisztusz háze arangyosz...* Archaikus imák, ráolvasások, kántálók a gyimesi és moldvai magyarok hagyományából. (Újkígyós, 1998)

Harangozó, Imre: *Adalékok a moldvai magyarok eredetének, kultúrájának és népi emlékezetének kutatásához.* (Turán, 1999)

Harangozó, Imre: *„ Ott hul éltek vala a magyarok ... ”* Válogatás az észak-moldvai magyarság népi emlékezetének kincsestárából. (Újkígyós, 2001)

Harangozó, Imre : *Sokat gondolkoztam a régi atyákról.* Vázlat a magyar nép osi hitvilágáról és világképérol. (Budapest, 2003)

Hasdeu, B. P.: *Documente inedite din Biblioteca Doria-Panfiliana din Roma, relative la istoria catolicismului in Romania. 1601-1606.* (*Columna lui Traian,* VII. 1876-1922)

Hegedüs, Lajos: *Moldvai csángó népmesék és beszélgetések.* (Budapest, 1952)

Hegyeli, Attila: *„ Mint a gomba, ide benottek... ”* Moldvai csángók vendégmunkája Magyarországon, In: Pozsony, Ferenc /szerk./: *Csángósors.* Moldvai csángók a változó idokben. (Budapest, 1999)

Hegyeli, Attila: *Nott a Bákó megyei magyarok száma.* A 2002. évi népszámlálás elozetes eredményeirol. (*Moldvai Magyarság - Gazeta Ceangailor din Moldova,* XIII. 3. 2003)

Hegyeli, Attila: *Din Arini la Sabaoani.* (Magyarfalutól Szabófalváig). (Roman, 2004)

Heller, Ágnes: *A szégyen hatalma.* Két tanulmány. (Budapest, 1996)

Hermán, M. János: *A moldvai reformáció lengyelországi támogatása.* In: U.o.: *Johannes a Lasco élete és munkássága (1499-1560).* (Nagyvárad, 2003)

Hitchins, Keith: *Desavârsirea natiunii române,* In: Barbulescu, Mihai - Deletant, Dennis - Hitchins, Keith - Papacostea, Serban - Teodor, Pompiliu: *Istoria României.* (Bucuresti, 1998)

Hofer, Tamás: *A „ népi kultúra” örökségének megszerkesztése és használata,* In: Hofer, Tamás /szerk./: *Népi kultúra és nemzettudat.* (Budapest, 1991)

Holban, Maria /szerk./: *Calatori straini despre tarile Române I-VIII.* (Bucuresti, 1968-1983)

Horger, Antal: *A csángó nép és a csángó név eredete.* (*Erdélyi Múzeum,* XXII. évf., 1905)

Horváth, Antal: *Stramosii catolicilor din Moldova. Documente istorice 1227-1702.* (Sfântu Gheorghe, 1994)

Horváth, Lajos: *A csodaszarvas monda kései hajtása, avagy Moldva bölényfejes címere.* (*Székelyföld,* IV. 5. 2000)

Hurmuzaki, Eudoxiu: *Documente privitoare la istoria românilor I-XIX.* (Bucuresti, 1876-1922)

Iancu, Laura: *Johófiú Jankó.* Magyarfalusi csángó népmesék és más beszédek. [Összeállította Iancu Laura, szerkesztette és bevezette Benedek Katalin.] (Budapest, 2002)

Imreh, István: *Látom az életem nem igen gyönyöru.* A mádéfalvi veszedelem tanúkihallgatási jegyzokönyve. (Bukarest, 1994)

Imreh, István – Szeszka Erdos, Péter: *A szabófalvi jogszokásokról.* (*Népismereti Dolgozatok.* Bukarest, 1978)

Iorga, Nicolae: *Studii si documente cu privire la istoria românilor I-II-III.* (Bucuresti, 1901)

Iorga, Nicolae: *Privilegiile sangailor de la Târgu-Ocna.* (Bucuresti, 1915)

Iorga, Nicolae: *Oameni care au fost II.* (Bucuresti, 1935)

Iorga, Nicolae: *România mama a unitatii noastre nationale cum era pîna la 1918.* (Bucuresti, 1972)

Iorga, Nicolae: *Istoria românilor prin calatori.* (Ed. Anghelescu, A., Bucuresti, 1981)

Iorga, Nicolae: *Istoria românilor III.* (Bucuresti, 1993)

Jagamas, János: *Beitrage zur Dialektfrage der ungarischen Volksmusik in Rumanien,* In: Kodály, Zoltán /szerk./: *Studia memoriae Bélae Bartók sacra.* (Budapest, 1956)

Jagamas, János: *Adatok a romániai magyar népzenei dialektusok kérdéséhez,* In: Szabó, Csaba /szerk./: *Zenetudományi írások.* (Bukarest, 1977)

Jagamas, János: *Szemelvények Trunk népzenéjébol,* In: U.o.: *A népzene mikrokozmoszában.* Tanulmányok. (Bukarest, 1984)

Jerney, János: *Keleti utazás a Magyarok oshelyeinek kinyomozása végett 1844-1845. I-II.* (Pest, 1851)

Jénáki, Ferenc: *Egy vasárnap a moldvai magyarok között.* (*Erdélyi Tudósító,* VII. 25. június 22, 1924)

Kallós, Zoltán: *Hejgetés Moldvában.* (*Néprajzi Közlemények,* III. 1-2. sz., 1958)

Kallós, Zoltán: *Ismeretlen balladák Moldvából.* (*Néprajzi Közlemények,* III. 1-2. sz., 1958)

Kallós, Zoltán: *Ráolvasás a moldvai és a gyimesi csángóknál.* (*Muveltség és Néphagyomány* 8, Debrecen, 1966)

Kallós, Zoltán: *Hejgetés Moldvában.* (*Muvelodés,* XXXI. 12. sz., 1968)

Kallós, Zoltán: *Balladák könyve.* Élo népballadák. [Szabó T. Attila gondozásában.] (Bukarest, 1970)

Kallós, Zoltán: *Új guzsalyam mellett.* [Éneklettem én özvegyasszon Miklós Gyurkáné Szályka Rózsa hetvenhat esztendos koromban Klézsén Moldvában. Lejegyezte, bevezetovel és jegyzetekkel ellátta Kallós Zoltán.] (Bukarest, 1973)

Kallós, Zoltán: *Ez az utazólevelem.* Balladák új könyve. (Budapest, 1996)

Kallós, Zoltán: *Világszárnya.* Moldvai népmesék. [Elmesélte a lészpedi Demeter Antiné Jánó Anna. Gyujtötte Kallós Zoltán 1956 és 1964 között.] (Stúdium Könyvkiadó, Kolozsvár, 2003)

Kántor, Zoltán: *Az identitás kapcsán.* (*Provincia,* II. 11. sz., 2001)

Kapalo, James: *Közelebb a csángókhoz.* (*Muvelodés,* XLVI. 3. sz., 1994)

Kiss, András: *Mi sérti az önérzetet?* Stefan cel Mare oklevele Mátyás királlyal való hubéri viszonyáról. In: U.o.: *Más források – más értelmezések.* (Marosvásárhely, 2003)

Kiss, Jeno /szerk./: *Magyar dialektológia.* (Budapest, 2001)

Kogâlniceanu, Mihail: *Cronicele României.* (Bucuresti, 1872)

Kolumbán, Samu: *A hétfalusi csángók a múltban és a jelenben.* (Brassó, 1903)

Komoróczy, Géza: *Meddig él egy nemzet?* In: *Bezárkózás a nemzeti hagyományokba.* (Budapest, 1995)

Kóka, Rozália: *A lészpedi „szent leján".* (*Tiszatáj,* XXXVI. 8. sz., 1982)

Kósa, László – Filep, Antal: *A magyar nép táji-történeti tagolódása.* (Budapest, 1983)

Kós, Károly: *Csángó néprajzi vázlat,* In: *Tájak, falvak, hagyományok.* (Bukarest, 1976)

Kós, Károly - Szentimrei, Judit - Nagy, Jeno: *Moldvai csángó népmuvészet.* (Kriterion Könyvkiadó, Bukarest, 1981)

Kotics, József: *Gazdálkodói mentalitás és paraszti polgárosodás.* Egy régióvizsgálat tanulságai, In: *Mások tekintetében.* (Miskolc, 2001)

Kotics, József: *Erkölcsi értékrend és társadalmi kontroll néhány moldvai csángó faluban,* In: *Mások tekintetében.* (Miskolc, 2001)

Kríza, Ildikó: *Egy moldvai balladáról.* (*Néprajzi Látóhatár,* III. 1-2. sz., 1994)

Küllos, Imola: *Csángó dalok és balladák kvantitatív módszeru vizsgálata.* (*Népi Kultúra - Népi Társadalom,* XI-XII. Budapest, 1980)

Laczkó, Mihály: *A Magyarországon megtelepedett csángók,* In: Pozsony, Ferenc /szerk./: *Csángósors.* Moldvai csángók a változó idokben. (Budapest, 1999)

Lahovari, Ioan George: *Marele Dictionar Geografic al României.* (Bucuresti, 1898)

Lestyán, Ferenc: *Ki felelos a moldvai római katolikusok sorsáért?* (*Erdélyi Figyelo,* VI. 1. sz., 1994)

Livezeanu, Irina: *Cultura si nationalism în România Mare 1918-1930.* (Bucuresti, 1998)

Lozinca, Constantin: *Scrisoare catre Nicolae Iorga.* (*Revista Istorica,* XXI. nr. 10-12., 1935)

Lorinczi, Réka: *A magyar rokonsági elnevezések rendszerének változásai.* (Bukarest, 1980)

Lukács, László: *Domokos Pál Péter, Magyarország királya.* (*Honismeret,* XXIV. , 3. sz., 1996)

Lüko, Gábor: *A moldvai csángók I.* A csángók kapcsolatai az erdélyi magyarsággal. (Budapest, 1936)

Lüko, Gábor: *Moldva alapításának mondáihoz.* (*Ethnographia,* XLVII. 1. sz., 1936)

Magyar, Zoltán: *Szent István alakja a moldvai magyar néphagyományban.* (*Honismeret,* XXV. 4. sz., 1997)

Magyar, Zoltán: *Szent László a magyar néphagyományban.* (Budapest, 1998)

Magyar, Zoltán: *Szent István a néphagyományban.* (Budapest, 2000)

Magyar, Zoltán: *A liliomos herceg.* Szent Imre a magyar kultúrtörténetben. (Budapest, 2000)

Makkai, László: *A milkói (kun) püspökség és népei.* (Debrecen, 1936)

Martin, György: *A keleti vagy erdélyi táncdialektus,* In: Felföldi, László - Pesovár, Erno /szerk./: *A magyar nép és nemzetiségeinek tánchagyománya.* (Budapest, 1997)

Márton, Gyula: *A moldvai csángó nyelvjárás román kölcsönszavai.* (Bukarest, 1972)

Martinas, Dumitru: *Originea ceangailor din Moldova.* (Bucuresti, 1985)

Martinas, Dumitru: *The origins of the changos.* (Iasi, 1999)

Martinas, Ioan: *Cine sunt catolicii moldoveni?* (Iasi, 1942)

Metes, Stefan: *Emigrari românesti din Transilvania în secolele XIII-XX.* (Bucuresti, 1971)

Mihordea, V.: *Relatiile agrare din secolul al XVIII-lea în Moldova.* (Bucuresti, 1968)

Mikecs, László: *A csángók.* (Budapest, 1941)

Mikecs, László: *A Kárpátokon túli magyarság,* In: Deér, József - Gáldi, László /szerk./: *Magyarok és románok I.* (Budapest, 1943)

Mikecs, László: *A moldvai katolikusok 1646-47. évi összeírása.* (*Erdélyi TudományosFüzetek* 171., Kolozsvár, 1944)

Mikecs, László: *Csángók.* (Budapest, 1989)

Mohay, Tamás: *Temetés a moldvai Frumószában,* In: Pozsony, Ferenc /szerk./: *Kriza János Néprajzi Társaság Évkönyve 5.* (Kolozsvár, 1997)

Mohay, Tamás: *Egy ünnep alapjai.* A csíksomlyói pünkösdi búcsú új megvilágításban. (*Tabula*, 3. 2. sz., 2000)

Mohay, Tamás: *Csíksomlyói kolduló ferencesek Moldvában 1858-59-ben*, In: Czövek, Judit /szerk./: *Imádságos asszony.* Tanulmányok Erdélyi Zsuzsanna tiszteletére. (Gondolat-Európai Folklór Intézet, Budapest, 2003)

Munkácsi, Bernát: *A moldvai csángók eredete.* (*Ethnographia*, XIII. 1902)

Murádin, László: *A nyelvújítási szók csángó megfeleléseihez.* (Studia Univ. „Babes-Bolyai." Tom. III., nr. 6., series IV., fasc. 1., 1958)

Murádin, László - Péntek, János /szerk./: *A moldvai csángó nyelvjárás atlasza I-II.* (*A Magyar Nyelvtudományi Társaság Kiadványai*, 193. sz., Budapest, 1991)

Nagy, Ilona: *A föld teremtésének mondája.* (*Ethnographia*, XC. 3. sz., 1979)

Nastasa, Lucian /szerk./: *Minoritati etnoculturale. Marturii documentare. Maghiarii din România (1945-1955).* [Volum editat de Andreea Andreescu, Lucian Nastasa, Andrea Varga.] (Cluj, 2002)

Nastasa, Lucian /szerk./: *Monoritati etnoculturale. Marturii documentare. Maghiarii din România (1956-1968).* [Volum editat de Andreea Andreescu, Lucian Nastasa, Andrea Varga.] (Cluj, 2003)

Nastase, Gheorghe: *Unguri din Moldova la 1646 dupa Codex Bandinus.* (*Arhivele Basarabiei* VI-VII. Chisinau, 1936)

Nastase, Gheorghe: *Die Ungarn in der Moldau im Jahre 1646. Nach dem „ Codex Bandinus".* (Iasi, 1936)

Nyisztor, Tinka: *„ Rendes" temetések Pusztinában*, In: Pozsony, Ferenc /szerk./: *Kriza János Néprajzi Társaság Évkönyve 5.* (Kolozsvár, 1997)

Nyisztor, Tinka: *A gyertya használata mindenszentek és halottak napján Pusztinán*, In: Pozsony, Ferenc /szerk./: *Dolgozatok a moldvai csángók népi kultúrájáról.* (Kriza János Néprajzi Társaság Évkönyve 5., Kolozsvár, 1997)

Nyisztor, Tinka: *Kései fordulat.* Az étkezési kultúra újkori formáinak beépülése az 1960-as évektol egy moldvai faluban, In: Romsics, Imre - Kisbán, Eszter /szerk./: *A táplálkozáskultúra változatai a 18-20. században.* (Kalocsa, 1997)

Oláh, Sándor: *Csendes csatatér.* Kollektivizálás és túlélési stratégiák a két Homoród mentén (1949-1962). (Csíkszereda, 2001)

Olosz, Katalin: *XVIII-XIX. századi adatok a moldvai magyarok szokásairól és nevérol*, In: Pozsony, Ferenc /szerk./: *Dolgozatok a moldvai csángók népi kultúrájáról.* (Kriza János Néprajzi Társaság 5. Évkönyve, Kolozsvár, 1997)

Ozsváth, Gábor Dániel: *Székelyek és csángók a csólyospálosi homoki gazdaságokban*, In: Juhász, Antal /szerk./: *Migráció és anyagi kultúra.* (Szeged, 1999)

Pais, Dezso: *Rér*, In: *Szó- és szólásmagyarázatok.* (*Magyar Nyelv,* XXXIX. 4. sz.)

Pal, M. Iosif Petru: *Originea Catolicilor din Moldova.* (Tipografia Serafica, Sabaoani-Roman, 1941)

Pal, M. Iosif Petru: *Catolicii din Moldova sunt români neaosi.* (Almanahul Viata, 1940)

Pal, M. Iosif Petru: *Originea catolicilor din Moldova si Franciscanii pastorii lor de veacuri.* (Tipografia Serafica, Sabaoani-Roman, 1940)

Pal, M. Iosif Petru: *Franciscanii minori conventuali si limba româna.* (Almanahul Viata, 1942)

Panaitescu, P.P.: *Patrunderea ungureasca dincolo de Carpati.* (Bucuresti, 1969)

Papacostea, Serban: *Stiri noi cu privire la istoria husitismului în Moldova în timpul lui Alexandru cel Bun.* Studii si cercetari stiintifice.(*Istorie,* nr. 2., Iasi, 1962)

Papacostea, Serban: *De la geneza statelor românesti la natiunea româna,* In: Barbulescu, Mihai - Deletant, Dennis - Hitchins, Keith - Papacostea, Serban - Teodor, Pompiliu: *Istoria României.* (Bucuresti, 1998)

Pávai, István: *Az erdélyi és a moldvai magyarság népi tánczenéje.* (Budapest, 1993)

Pávai, István: *A moldvai magyarok megnevezései.* (*Regio,* VI. 4. sz., 1995)

Pávai, István: *Vallási és etnikai identitás konfliktusai a moldvai magyaroknál.* (*Néprajzi Értesíto,* LXXVIII. 1996)

Pávai, István: *Etnonimek a moldvai magyar anyanyelvu katolikusok megnevezésére,* In: Pozsony, Ferenc /szerk./: *Csángósors.* Moldvai csángók a változó idokben. (Budapest, 1999)

Penavin, Olga: *Szlavóniai (kórógyi) szótár I-III.* (Újvidék, 1968-1978)

Petrás, Ince János: *Döbrentei Gábor kérdései s Petrás Incze feleletei a moldvai magyarok felol.* (*Tudományi Tár,* VII. füzet, 1842)

Petrovici, Emil: *O particularitate a fonetismului maghiar oglindita în elementele maghiare limbii române.* (*Studii si Cercetari de Lingvistica* V.)

Petrovici, Emil: *Egy magyar hangtani sajátosság tükrözodése a román nyelv magyar kölcsönszavaiban.* (*Magyar Nyelv,* LII. 1952)

Pilat, Liviu: *Aspecte din viata cotidiana a unui sat din Moldova medievala.* (*Optiuni Istoriografice.* Buletinul Asociatiei Tinerilor Istorici Ieseni I/2., Iasi, 2000)

Pilat, Liviu: *Sabaoani pâna la sfârsitul secolului al XVII-lea,* In: Dobos, Fabian /szerk./: *Sabaoani – file de istorie.* (Editura Presa Buna, Iasi, 2002)

Pilat, Liviu: *Natalitatea si mortalitatea în parohia Rachiteni la sfârsitul secolului al XVIII-lea.* Optiuni istoriografice. Revista Asociatiei Tinerilor (*Istorici Ieseni,* II., 2002)

Pilat, Liviu: *Comunitati tacute. Satele din parohia Sabaoani (secolele XVII-XVIII)*. (Editura „Dumitru Martinas", Bacau, 2002)

Polányi, Károly: *Az archaikus társadalom és a gazdasági szemlélet.* (Budapest, 1976)

Polescu, Ioanu: *Limba ungureasca în Moldova.* (*Amicul Familiei,* IV., 2., 1880)

Pozsony, Ferenc: *Szeret vize martján.* Moldvai csángómagyar népköltészet.[A klézsei Lorinc Györgyné Hodorog Lucától gyujtötte, bevezetovel és jegyzetekkel ellátta Pozsony Ferenc. A dallamokat hangszalagról lejegyezte és sajtó alá rendezte Török Csorja Viola.] (Kriza János Néprajzi Társaság Könyvtára 2, Kolozsvár, 1994)

Pozsony, Ferenc: *Újesztendohöz kapcsolódó szokások a moldvai csángóknál.* (*Néprajzi Látóhatár,* III. 1-2. sz., 1994)

Pozsony, Ferenc: *Látomások a moldvai csángó falvakban,* In: Pozsony, Ferenc /szerk./: *Kriza János Néprajzi Társaság Évkönyve 5.* (Kolozsvár, 1997)

Pozsony, Ferenc: *„Adok néktek három vesszot... "* Dolgozatok erdélyi és moldvai népszokásokról. (Pro-Print Könyvkiadó, Csíkszereda, 2000)

Pozsony, Ferenc: *Church Life in Moldavian Hungarian Communities,* In: Diószegi, László /ed./: *Hungarian Csángós in Moldavia.* Essays on the past and present of the Hungarian Csángós in Moldavia. (Budapest, 2002)

Pozsony, Ferenc: *Ceangaii din Moldova.* (Asociatia Etnografica Kriza János, Cluj, 2002)

Pozsony, Ferenc: *The Historical Consciousness of the Moldavian Csángós.* (*Hungarian Heritage,* vol. 3, Budapest, 2002)

Pozsony, Ferenc: *A moldvai csángók történeti tudata.* (*Néprajzi Látóhatár,* XI. 1-4. sz., 2002)

Pozsony, Ferenc: *Hussitismus und Protestantismus in Moldavien,* In: Elek, Bartha - Veikko, Anttonen /ed./: *Ethnographica et Folkloristica 12-13.* (Debrecen - Turku, 2002)

Pozsony, Ferenc: *Samanizmus és medvekultusz Moldvában?* In: Csonka Takács, Eszter- Czövek, Judit - Takács, András /szerk./: *Mir - Susné - Xum II.* Tanulmányok Hoppál Mihály tiszteletére. (Akadémiai Kiadó, Budapest, 2002)

Pozsony, Ferenc: *A moldvai csángó-magyar falvak társadalomszerkezete.* (*Pro Minoritate,* Budapest, 2003/Nyár)

Pozsony, Ferenc /szerk./: *Dolgozatok a moldvai csángók népi kultúrájáról.* (Kriza János Néprajzi Társaság Évkönyve 5., Kolozsvár, 1997)

Pozsony, Ferenc /szerk./: *Csángósors.* Moldvai csángók a változó idokben. (A Magyarságkutatás Könyvtára XXIII. Teleki László Alapítvány, Budapest, 1999)

284

Pozsony, Ferenc: *A moldvai csángó magyarok.* (Gondolat Kiadó – Európai Folklór Intézet, Budapest, 2005)

Rosetti, Radu: *Despre ungurii si episcopiile catolice din Moldova.* (Analele Academiei Române. Seria II. Tom. XXVII. Memoriile Sectiunii Istorice nr. 10., Bucuresti)

Rubinyi, Mózes: *A moldvai csángók múltja és jelene.* (*Ethnographia,* XII. 1901)

Râmneantu, Petru: *Grupele de sânge la Ciangaii din Moldova.* (*Buletin eugenic si biopolitic* XIV. nr. 1-2., 1943)

Râmneantu, Petru: *Die Abstammung der Taschangos.* (Sibiu, 1944)

Sándor, Klára: *Contempt for Linguistic Human Rights in the Service of the Catholic Church: The case of the Csángós,* In: Kontra, Miklós - Phillipson, Robert - Skutnabb-Kangas, Tove - Várady, Tibor /ed./: *Language: A Right and a Resource. Approaching Linguistic Human Rights.* (Budapest, 1999)

Sávai, János: *A székelyföldi katolikus plébániák levéltára I-II-III.* (*Missziós Dokumentumok Magyarországról és a hódoltságról* I-III., Szeged, 1997)

Seres, András - Szabó, Csaba: *Csángómagyar Daloskönyv.* (Budapest, 1991)

Simon, Alexandru: *Moldova între Vilnius si Moscova. Anii trecerii de la Roma la Constantinopol (1386-1388).* (Studia Universitatii Babes-Bolyai. *Historia,* XLVIII., nr. 1-2., 2003)

Slapac, Mariana: *Cetati medievale din Moldova (mijlocul secolului al XIV-lea - mijlocul secolului al XVI-lea.)* (Editura Arc., Chisinau, 2004)

Sógor, Csaba: *„ Elszertült" reformátusok Szászkúton.* (*Felebarát,* III. 1-2. sz., 1992)

Spira, György: A magyar negyvennyolc és a csángók, In: Glatz, Ferenc /szerk./: *A tudomány szolgálatában.* Emlékkönyv Benda Kálmán 80. Születésnapjára. (Budapest, 1993)

Stan, Valentin - Weber, Renate: *The moldvaian csango.* (Budapest, 1998)

Stekovics, Rita: *Cacica - a magyar misés búcsú Bukovinában,* In: Lukács, János /szerk./: *Változás diákszemmel.* (Kolozsvár, 1994)

Sulzer, Franz Joseph: *Geschichte der transalpinischen Daciens, das ist? der Walachey, Moldau und Bessarabiens II.* (Wien, 1781)

Sylvester, Lajos: *A vér szaga. Egy könyv margójára.* (*Háromszék,* X. évf., 1998. október 3.).

Sylvester, Lajos: *„ Voltunk mük es ... " Gyergyina páter halálára.* (*Honismeret,* XXVII. 2. sz., 1999)

Szabados, Mihály: *A moldvai magyarok a román népszámlálások tükrében 1859-1977 között,* In: Kiss, Gy. Csaba /szerk./: *Magyarságkutatás.* (A Magyarságkutató Intézet Évkönyve. Budapest, 1989)

Szabó, Dénes: *A magyar nyelvemlékek.* (Budapest, 1952)

Szabó, Károly /szerk./: *Székely Oklevéltár II.* (Kolozsvár, 1876)

Szabó, T. Attila: *Kik és hol élnek a csángók?* In: *Nyelv és múlt.* Válogatott tanulmányok, cikkek III. (Bukarest, 1972)

Szabó, T. Attila: *Csángó,* In: *Erdélyi Magyar Szótörténet Tár* II. (Bukarest, 1978)

Szabó, T. Attila: *A moldvai csángó nyelvjárás kutatása.* In: *Nyelv és irodalom.*Válogatott tanulmányok, cikkek V. (Bukarest, 1981)

Szabó, T. Ádám /szerk./: *Müncheni Kódex (1466).* [A négy evangélium szövege és szótára. Décsy Gyula olvasata alapján a szöveget sajtó alá rendezte és a szótári részt készítette Szabó T. Ádám.] (Európa Könyvkiadó, Budapest, 1985)

Szarvas, Gábor: *A moldvai csángó nyelvrol.* (*Magyar Nyelvor,* III. 1874)

Szarvas, Gábor: *A szlavóniai tájszótár.* (*Magyar Nyelvor,* V. 1876)

Szarvas, Gábor - Simonyi, Zsigmond: *Magyar Nyelvtörténeti Szótár II.* (Budapest, 1891)

Székely, Maria Magdalena: *Boieri hicleni si înrudirile lor.* (*Arhiva genealogica* I (VI.). 1992)

Szent-Iványi, István: *A magyar kultúra egysége,* In: Balázs, Géza /szerk./: *Magyar néphagyomány - európai néphagyomány.* (Budapest - Debrecen, 1991)

Szilágyi, N. Sándor: *Amit még nem mondtunk el a csángó népnévrol.* (*A Hét,* X. 24. sz., 1979)

Szilágyi, N. Sándor: *Despre dialectele ceangaiesti din Moldova.* (*Altera,* VIII. 17-18. sz., 2002)

Szilágyi, N. Sándor: *Bozgor,* In: U.o.: *Mi egy más.* Közéleti írások. (Bukarest, 2003)

Szocs, János: *Pater Zöld.* (Csíkszereda, 2002)

Tagányi, Károly: *A hazai élo jogszokások gyujtésérol.* I. rész. A családi és öröklési jogszokások. (Budapest, 1919)

Tánczos, Vilmos: *A moldvai csángók pünkösd hajnali keresztútjárása a Kis-Somlyó hegyen,* In: Asztalos, Ildikó /szerk./: *Hazajöttünk ... Pünkösd Csíksomlyón.* (Kolozsvár, 1992)

Tánczos, Vilmos: *A nyelvváltás jelensége a moldvai csángók egyéni imarepertoárjában.* (*Kétnyelvuség,* III. 2. sz., 1995)

Tánczos, Vilmos: *„ Deákok" (parasztkántorok) a moldvai magyar falvakban.* (*Erdélyi Múzeum,* LVII. 3-4. sz., 1955)

Tánczos, Vilmos: *Gyöngyökkel gyökereztél.* Gyimesi és moldvai archaikus népi imádságok. (Csíkszereda, 1955)

Tánczos, Vilmos: *Keletnek megnyílt kapuja.* Néprajzi esszék. (Kolozsvár, 1996)

Tánczos, Vilmos: *„ Én román akarok lenni!"* Csángók Erdélyben, In: Tánczos, Vilmos: *Keletnek megnyílt kapuja.* Néprajzi esszék. (Kolozsvár, 1996)

Tánczos, Vilmos: *Hányan vannak a moldvai csángók?* (*Magyar Kisebbség,*
III. 1997)

Tánczos, Vilmos: *Hungarians in Moldavia.* (Institute for Central European
Studies No. 8, Budapest, 1997)

Tánczos, Vilmos: *Csapdosó angyal.* Moldvai archaikus imádságok és
életterük. (Csíkszereda, 1999)

Tánczos, Vilmos: *Eleven ostya, szép virág.* A moldvai csángó népi imák
képei. (Csíkszereda, 2000)

Tánczos, Vilmos: *Nyiss kaput, angyal!* Moldvai csángó népi imádságok.
Archetipikus szimbolizáció és élettér. (Budapest, 2001)

Tánczos, Vilmos: *Ceangaii din Moldova.* (*Altera,* VIII. 17-18. sz., 2002)

Tárkány Szücs, Erno: *Magyar jogi népszokások.* (Budapest, 1981)

Teleki, Domokos: *Egy néhány hazai utazások leírása.* (Bécs, 1796)

Teodor, Pompiliu: *Monarhia feudala. Secolul luminilor în tarile române,* In:
Barbulescu, Mihai - Deletant, Dennis - Hitchins, Keith - Papacostea,
Serban -Teodor, Pompiliu: *Istoria României.* (Bucuresti, 1998)

Todoran, Romulus: *Cu privire la o problema de lingvistica: limba si dialect.*
(*Cercetari de lingvistica* I, 1956)

Tófalvi, Zoltán: *A sóvidéki népi fazekasság.* (Marosvásárhely, 1996)

Tóth, István György: *Diákok (licenciátusok) a moldvai csángómagyar
muvelodésben a XVII. században,* In: Zombori, István /szerk./: *Az
értelmiség Magyarországon a XVI-XVII. században.* (Szeged, 1988)

Tönnies, Ferdinand: *Közösség és társadalom.* (Gondolat, Budapest, 1983)

Turai, Tünde: *Történeti tudat vizsgálata Klézsén,* In: Pozsony, Ferenc
/szerk./: *Csángósors.* Moldvai csángók a változó idokben. (Budapest,
1999)

Ungureanu, Razvan-Mihai: *Câteva aspecte ale regimului asimilarii
confesionale în Moldova.* Genealogii de „botezati". (*Arhiva
Genealogica* I (VI.) nr. 1-2., Iasi, 1994)

Ungureanu, Razvan-Mihai: *O harta a comunitatilor catolice din Moldova.*
(Anuarul Institutului de Istorie „A. D. Xenopol." Tom XXXIII., Iasi,
1996)

Urechia, V.A.: *Codex Bandinus.* Memorii asupra scrierii lui Bandinus de la
1646, urmatu de textu, însotitu de acte si documente. (Annale Academia
Romana. Seria II. Tom. XVI., Bucuresti, 1893-1894)

Vargyas, Lajos: *A magyar népballada és Európa* I-II. (Budapest, 1976)

Veress, Dániel: *A rodostói csillagnézo.* Kalauz Mikes leveleskönyvéhez.
Kismonográfia. (Kolozsvár, 1972)

Veress, Endre: *Scrisorile misionarului Bandini din Moldova (1664-1650).*
(Academia Româna. Memoriile sectiunii istorice. Seria III. Tom. VI.
13., Bucuresti, 1926)

Veress, Endre: *Documente privitoare la istoria Ardealului, Moldovei si Tarii
Românesti I-XI.* (Bucuresti, 1929-1939)

Veress, Endre: *A moldvai csángók származása és neve.* (*Erdélyi Múzeum,*
XXXIX. 1934)

Veress, Sándor: *Moldvai gyujtés.* [Gyujtötte Veress Sándor. Szerkesztette:
Berlász Melinda és Szalay Olga]. (*Magyar Népköltési Gyujtemény,*
XVI. Budapest, 1989)

Veszely, Károly - Imets, Fülöp Jákó - Kovács, Ferenc: *Utazás Moldva-
Oláhországban.* (Marosvásárhely, 1870)

Vincze, Gábor: *Csángósors a II. világháború után,* In: Pozsony, Ferenc
/szerk./: *Csángósors.* Moldvai csángók a változó idokben. (Budapest,
1999)

Vincze, Gábor: *An Overview of the Modern History of the Moldavian
Csángó-Hungarians,* In: Diószegi, László /ed./: *Hungarian Csángó in
Moldavia.* Essays on the Past and Present of the hungarian Csángós in
Moldavia. (Budapest, 2002)

Vincze, Gábor: *Asszimiláció vagy kivándorlás?* Források a moldvai magyar
etnikai csoport, a csángók modern kori történelmének
tanulmányozásához (1860-1989). (Budapest - Kolozsvár, 2004)

Vincze, Mária: *Régió- és vidékfejlesztés.* Elmélet és gyakorlat. (Kolozsvár,
2000)

Virt, István: *"Elszakasztottad a testemtol én lelkemet."* A moldvai és a
Baranya megyei csángók halottas szokásai és hiedelmei. (Kolozsvár,
2001)

Weber-Kellermann, Ingeborg: *Zur Frage der interethnischen Beziehungen in
der "Sprachinselvolkskunde".* (*Österreichische Zeitschrift für
Volkskunde* 62., 1959)

Weber-Kellermann, Ingeborg: *A "nyelvsziget-néprajz"-ban jelentkezo
interetnikus viszonyok kérdéséhez.* (*Néprajzi Látóhatár,* IX. 2000)

Wichmann, Yrjö: *Wörterbuch des Ungarischen Moldauer Nord-csángó und
des Hétfaluer Csángódialektes nebst grammatikalischen
Aufzeichnungen und texten aus dem Nordcsángódialekt herausgegeben
von Bálint Csury and Arturi Kannisto.* (Helsinki, 1936)

Wichmann, Júlia: *A moldvai csángók babonás hitébol.* (*Ethnographia,*
XVIII. 1907)

Wichmann, Júlia: *A moldvai csángók szokásaiból.* (*Ethnographia,* XVIII.
1907)

Wichmann, Júlia: *Moldvai csángó mennyegzo Szabófalván.* (*Ethnographia,*
XLVII. 1936)

Zsók, Béla: *A ,csángó" elnevezés és identitástudat alakulása a Hunyad
megyébe telepedett bukovinai székelyeknél.* (*Néprajzi Látóhatár,* VII. 3-
4. 1998)

Zsupos, Zoltán: *A moldvai magyarok eredete.* (*Néprajzi Látóhatár,* III. 1-4.
1994)

Xenopol, A.D.: *Istoria Romanilor din Dacia Traiana.* (Madrid, 1953)

GEOGRAPHICAL PLACE NAMES

(**sCs**: southern Csángó, **nCs**: northern Csángó; **SCs**:Sekler Csángó settlement)

Aknavásár	Târgu Ocna	SCs
Álbény	Bogdánfalva része	
Árgyevány	Ardeoani	SCs
Bahána	Bahna	SCs
Bákó	Bacau	
Balanyásza	Balaneasa	SCs
Balusest	Balusesti	nCs
Bánya	Moldvabánya	
Barát	Barati	
Barlád	Bârlad	
Belcseszku	Nicolae Balcescu	sCs
Bergyila	Berdila	SCs
Beringyest	Berindesti	SCs
Berzujok	Bârzulesti	SCs
Berzunc	Berzunti	SCs
Bogáta	Bogata	SCs
Bogdánfalva	Valea Seaca	sCs
Borgovány	Bârgauani	nCs
Borzest	Borzesti	SCs
Botosány	Botosani	
Braila	Braila	
Bruszturósza	Brusturoasa	SCs
Cserdák	Cerdac	SCs
Csík	Ciucani	SCs
Csöböröcsök	Ciuburciu/Kubjerzi	
Csügés	Ciughes	SCs
Degettes	Pacurile	SCs
Diószeg	Tuta	SCs
Diószén	Gioseni	sCs
Dnyeszterfehérvár	Cetatea Alba/Akkerman	
Doftána	Dofteana	SCs
Dókia	Dochia	nCs
Dormányfalva	Darmanesti	SCs
Dózsa	Gheorghe Doja	SCs
Dzsidafalva	Adjudeni	
Egyedhalma	Adjud	
Esztrugár	Strugari	SCs
Esztufuj	Stufu	SCs

289

Foksány	Focsani	
Forrófalva	Faraoani	SCs
Frumósza	Frumoasa	SCs
Furnikár	Furnicari	SCs
Furészfalva	Ferestrau-Oituz	SCs
Gajcsána	Magyarfalu	
Gajdár	Coman	SCs
Galac	Galati	
Gerejest	Gheraesti	nCs
Gerlény	Gârleni	SCs
Glodurile	Glodurile	SCs
Gorzafalva	Oituz	SCs
Gutinázs	Gutinas	SCs
Gyidráska	Versesti	SCs
Gyoszény	Diószén	
Halasfalva	Halaucesti	
Havasalföld	Muntenia	
Herló	Hârlau	
Husz	Husi	
Jászvásár	Iasi	
Jázuporkuluj	Iazu Porcului	nCs
Jenekest	Enachesti	SCs
Jugán	Iugani	nCs
Kalugarény	Calugareni	SCs
Kápota	Capata	SCs
Karácsonyko	Piatra Neamt	
Kelgyest	Pildesti	nCs
Ketris	Chetris	SCs
Klézse	Cleja	SCs
Kománfalva	Comanesti	SCs
Kotnár	Cotnari	
Kövesalja	Petricica	SCs
Kukujéc	Cucuieti	SCs
Külsorekecsin	Fundu Racaciuni	SCs
Lábnyik	Vladnic	SCs
Lárga	Larguta	SCs
Lészped	Lespezi	SCs
Lilijecs	Lilieci	SCs
Lökösfalva	Licuseni	
Lujzikalagor	Luizi-Calugara	SCs
Lukácsfalva	Lucacesti	
Lunkamojnest	Lunca Moinesti	SCs
Magyarfalu	Arini	SCs

Miklósfalva	Miclauseni	
Mojnest	Moinesti	SCs
Moldvabánya	Baia	
Nagypatak	Valea Mare	sCs
Nemc	Târgu Neamt	
Nisiporest	Nisiporesti	
Ojtoz	Oituz	
Onyest	Onesti	SCs
Orhely/Várhely	Orhei	
Pakura	Degettes	
Palánka	Palanca	SCs
Petricsika	Kövesalja	
Ploszkucény	Ploscuteni	nCs
Podoros	Lábnyik része	
Pojánánukuluj	Poiana Nucului	SCs
Pokolpatak	Valea Mica	SCs
Prálea	Pralea	SCs
Pusztina	Pustiana	SCs
Rácsila	Gârlenii de Sus	SCs
Radóc	Radauti	
Rekecsin	Racaciuni	SCs
Ripajepi	Bogdanesti	SCs
Románvásár	Roman	
Rosszpatak	Valea Rea	SCs
Somoska	Somusca	SCs
Szalánc	Templomfalva	
Szabófalva	Sabaoani	nCs
Szálka	Seaca	SCs
Szárazpatak	Valea Seaca	SCs
Szászkút	Sascut-Fântânele	SCs
Szeketura	Padureni	sCs
Szerbek	Floresti	SCs
Szeretvásár	Siret	
Szitás	Nicoresti	SCs
Szlánikfürdo	Slanic-Moldova	SCs
Szlániktorka	Gura Slanicului	SCs
Szoloncka	Tarâta	SCs
Szolohegy	Pârgaresti	SCs
Szucsáva	Suceava	
Tamás	Tamasi	SCs
Tatros	Târgu Trotus	SCs
Templomfalva	Ciresoaia	SCs
Terebes	Trebes	SCs

Tráján	Traian	nCs
Trunk	Galbeni	sCs
Turluján	Turluianu	SCs
Újfalu	Satu Nou	SCs
Újfalu	Belcseszku	
Újfalu	Tráján	
Váleákimpului	Valea Câmpului	SCs
Valény	Valeni	SCs
Válészáka	Szárazpatak	
Váliri	Rosszpatak	
Vaszló	Vaslui	
Vizánta	Vizantea Manastireasca	SCs
Zsoszény	Diószén	